THE AMERICAN WOMAN

2003–2004

Edited by

Cynthia B. Costello

Vanessa R. Wight

and Anne J. Stone

for the Women's Research and Education Institute

THE
AMERICAN
WOMAN

2003–2004

DAUGHTERS OF A REVOLUTION—
YOUNG WOMEN TODAY

First published 2003 by
PALGRAVE MACMILLAN™
175 Fifth Avenue, New York, N.Y. 10010 and
Houndmills, Basingstoke, Hampshire, England RG21 6XS.
Companies and representatives throughout the world.

PALGRAVE MACMILLAN is the global academic imprint of the Palgrave
Macmillan division of St. Martin's Press, LLC and of Palgrave Macmillan Ltd.
Macmillan® is a registered trademark in the United States, United Kingdom and
other countries. Palgrave is a registered trademark in the European Union and
other countries.

ISBN 0-312-29551-0 hardback
ISBN 0-312-29549-9 paperback

Library of Congress Cataloging-in-Publication Data
The American woman 2003–2004 : daughters of a revolution—young women
today / editors, Cynthia B. Costello, Vanessa R. Wight, Anne J. Stone.
   p.   cm.
   Includes index.
   ISBN 0–312–29551–0 (hardbound)—ISBN 0–312–29549–9 (pbk.)
   1. Young women—United States—Social conditions.   2. United States—Social
conditions—1980–   I. Costello, Cynthia B. (Cynthia Butler)   II. Wight, Vanessa
R.   III. Stone, Anne J.

HQ1421.A476   2002
305.242—dc21   002074841

A catalogue record for this book is available from the British Library.

Design by Letra Libre, Inc.

First edition: January, 2003
10 9 8 7 6 5 4 3 2 1
Printed in the United States of America.

*The editors dedicate this book
to their mothers and daughters*

*Virginia Lee Costello
Christine Anderson Wight
Catherine Abbot Johnson
Catherine Abbot Stone and Margaret Hilles Stone*

CONTENTS

DAUGHTERS OF A REVOLUTION—YOUNG WOMEN TODAY

AMERICAN WOMEN TODAY: A STATISTICAL PORTRAIT

WOMEN IN CONGRESS

LIST OF TABLES AND FIGURES

THE AMERICAN WOMAN 2003–2004: DAUGHTERS OF A
REVOLUTION—YOUNG WOMEN TODAY

CHAPTER ONE: YOUNG WOMEN: WHERE THEY STAND

CHAPTER TWO: YOUNG WOMEN, EDUCATION, AND EMPLOYMENT

CHAPTER THREE: BABY BOOM TO GENERATION X:
PROGRESS IN YOUNG WOMEN'S HEALTH

CHAPTER FIVE: THE ECONOMICS OF YOUNG WOMEN TODAY

AMERICAN WOMEN TODAY: A STATISTICAL PORTRAIT

SECTION 1: DEMOGRAPHICS

SECTION 2: EDUCATION

SECTION 3: HEALTH

SECTION 4: EMPLOYMENT

SECTION 5: EARNINGS AND BENEFITS

SECTION 7: WOMEN IN THE MILITARY

SECTION 8: ELECTIONS AND OFFICIALS

ACKNOWLEDGMENTS

DAUGHTERS OF A REVOLUTION: Young Women Today is the ninth edition of *The American Woman* series underwritten by the Ford Foundation with generous additional assistance from other organizations and individuals. It is my privilege to thank those who have provided financial contributions or in-kind support to the Women's Research and Education Institute (WREI) and its work.

As always, we are deeply grateful to the Ford Foundation for its substantial assistance to the *American Woman* project since the first edition was launched in 1986. Over the past 16 years, we have been inspired by the interest, ideas, and commitment of individuals at the foundation. Helen Neuborne, Janice Petrovich, and Barbara Phillips, in particular, have earned our gratitude for their help and good counsel. Alison Bernstein, too, deserves special thanks for her steadfast friendship and encouragement.

For this edition, we owe particular gratitude to Johnson & Johnson—and to JoAnn Heffernan Heisen, J & J's Vice President and Chief Information Officer—whose generous grant has enabled us to include the very comprehensive chapter on the health of young women.

We also wish to express our gratitude to the scores of other individuals, companies, labor unions, and foundations without whose generosity WREI would not have been in a position to prepare *Daughters of a Revolution*. They include Aetna; Akin, Gump, Strauss, Hauer & Feld; American Income Life Insurance; Associated Actors & Artistes of America; AT&T; Aventis; Avon Products, Inc.; The Boeing Company; Chlorine Chemistry Council; The Coca-Cola Company; the Communications Workers of America; Elisebeth Driscoll; Evy Dubrow and the 21st Century ILGWU Heritage Fund; the Ehrenfeld family (Elizabeth and Robert, Emily, and Martha); GlaxoSmithKline; IBM; the International Association of Machinists and Aerospace Workers; Lockheed Martin; Northeast Utilities Services Company; OppenheimerFunds, Inc.; Philip Morris Companies, Inc.; Pharmacia; the Bernard and Audre Rapoport

Foundation; SBC Communications Inc.; the United Auto Workers; United Technologies; and Wyeth.

WREI's board of directors has offered extensive practical help as well as continuing encouragement for *The American Woman*. Board chair Jean Stapleton has found opportunities to plug every edition in the series from platforms in cities and towns across this country. JoAnn Heffernan Heisen and Barbara Easterling have promoted *The American Woman* enthusiastically in the corporate and labor communities. WREI's staff is grateful to the entire board for its enthusiastic support of our efforts.

Thanks go as well to the members of WREI's advisory council, a group of creative and committed individuals who have generously shared their personal and professional insights about the revolution and its daughters.

There are certain stalwarts who never say "no" to a WREI request. What would we do without the once and future guidance of Sara Rix, WREI's first research director and first editor of *The American Woman?*

Many people at the Bureau of Labor Statistics, the U.S. Census Bureau, and other government agencies helped us track down key statistics. Howard Hayghe, who has assisted with every edition of *The American Woman*, along with Steven Hipple and Sharon Cohany, all at the Bureau of Labor Statistics, deserve our particular thanks for providing, or guiding us to, a wide range of useful data on women in the workforce. A. Dianne Schmidley and Reneé Spraggins of the Census Bureau were very helpful in finding data on the foreign-born population. Vance Grant and Charlene Hoffman of the National Center for Education Statistics were of great assistance in finding historical data on women and education.

Deirdre Gaquin, who prepared the custom tabulations of the Current Population Surveys for Chapter One, earned our thanks not only for her statistical skills but also for her initiative and interest in our project. Mark Calabria, now with the Senate Committee on Banking, Housing and Urban Affairs, and Darryl Getter of the U.S. Department of Housing and Urban Development deserve our gratitude for donating their time and expert knowledge to teasing out key information about young women's finances from the Federal Reserve Board's 1998 Survey of Consumer Finances.

Gilda Morales of the Center for American Women and Politics, Marjorie Connelly of the *New York Times*, Amanda Murer of the National Center for State Courts, and Joan Countryman of the Administrative Office of the United States Courts furnished invaluable information for the section on elections and officials. Sarah Orrick's and Catherine Stone's writing and editorial assistance have been indispensable, as have the encouragement and sympathetic support we have received from Deborah Gershenowitz, our editor at Palgrave.

We would also like to thank Barbara Fusco, Kirsten Lindquist, Rachel Mears, Ann Potter, and Kimala Price. As members of a focus group early in the project, they provided enthusiastic encouragement, direction, and insight into the issues that young women face today.

Every member of WREI's staff played a role in realizing WREI's latest volume. The editorial team, consisting of Cynthia Costello (formerly WREI's research director), Vanessa Wight, and Anne Stone, labored long to bring forth yet another outstanding edition. Lory Manning compiled and analyzed the statistics on military women. Monica Jacobe found the faces and lined up the lives of the 75 women in the U.S. Senate and House of Representatives. Anne Kuh crunched the numbers as we budgeted for this book. Marjorie Lightman and Rachel Mears were of unfailing good cheer and willing assistance throughout this yearlong gestation.

The previous (eighth) edition of *The American Woman* was dedicated to WREI's founder and president of 23 years, Betty Parsons Dooley. She was the guiding light of the book and of our organization. Betty died in January 2002. All of us at WREI miss this tiny Texan who cast a giant shadow.

I want to stress that our funders, board members, and advisors are not responsible for any errors or misstatements that may be contained in these pages. Nor should the opinions expressed in any part of the book be ascribed to anyone other than the person or persons who wrote them.

We acknowledge with warm regard these individuals and organizations who helped us build on past success to produce a ninth edition that makes us proud.

Susan Scanlan
President
Women's Research and Education Institute

Daughters of a Revolution—Young Women Today

DAUGHTERS OF A REVOLUTION: AN INTRODUCTION

Anne J. Stone

We're expected to do it all, all at the same time.

—Didem Nisanci, age 29

WITH A WRY SMILE, Ms. Nisanci, who handles tax and trade issues for a corporate government affairs office, captured in a sentence the dilemma of millions of her contemporaries—and the reason why WREI wanted America's young women to have center stage in this book, the first in the *American Woman* series to examine the status of women in a particular age group at a particular time in history.

In each of the six numbered chapters in this book, the spotlight is on the women who are a full generation younger than most of the women who made the feminist revolution. Specifically, the stars of this book are women who were between their twenty-fifth and thirty-fifth birthdays as the twenty-first century began.

Several special statistical analyses were done to enable not only the most comprehensive and accurate examination ever of the women in this cohort but also a solid base for comparing their situation with that of their mothers when they were young. So, although not (for a change) in the leading roles, the women of the baby-boom generation are an important part of the discussions in this book.

Today's young women are quite likely to be the daughters of baby-boomer women; even if they are not, they are without doubt heirs to the revolution that boomer women made. As this book suggests, it is an unfinished revolution. Nevertheless, over roughly the last quarter of the twentieth century, the outlook for women in this country changed so enormously that today's young women find hard to believe the stories older women tell about how things were when they were young.

Trying to pinpoint the most important element in any revolution is risky, but there is no doubt that a woman's ability to control her fertility without necessarily remaining celibate belongs close to, if not at, the top of the list. How many young women would undertake graduate studies or expect to establish themselves solidly in a career if going without sexual relations for years was the price they had to pay? The tension between sexual desire and the fear of becoming pregnant that was so central to most young single women's experience in "the old days" can hardly be imagined by today's young single women, who, unlike unmarried women of earlier generations, have ready and lawful access to a variety of contraceptives as well as to abortions. In short, women no longer need to marry to have sex without risking an unwanted pregnancy.

Possessing reproductive choice in the most inclusive sense, a woman in her late teens or early twenties can choose to invest time and money in an education that will prepare her for a career, can choose to invest most of her energies for a time in building her career, can choose to postpone marriage without forgoing intimacy, and, assuming she wants to have children, can choose to postpone childbearing—for a while.

Of course, a young woman's reproductive choices are likely to be determined by her circumstances. A good number do have children outside of marriage. Unmarried women may become mothers by choice or by accident, or because they lack the means to prevent an unwanted pregnancy. Poor women, especially those who live in rural areas, may have no access to family planning clinics or affordable abortions. Some oppose contraception and abortion for religious or cultural reasons. But whether or not they intended to become pregnant, young single mothers trying to make it on their own have a hard row to hoe.

Still, older women, remembering how limited women's options used to be, know how enormously things have changed—mostly for the better—in the last 25 or 30 years. The subjects of this book, too young to have understood the revolution that their mothers were making as it was being made, both enjoy and struggle with the results. Whether they recognize it or not, they have the women of the baby-boom generation largely to thank for the unprecedented range of options from which they can choose—and, perhaps, to reproach for the complications and stress that choosing entails.

Encouraged on one hand to seek career success or at least economic self-sufficiency, expected on the other hand to marry and bear and look after children, many of today's young women are still grappling with whether they should even try to make it all work and, if so, when and how. Young working women who don't have children are not necessarily reassured when they see how their working contemporaries with children struggle to keep all the balls in the air. (Indeed, a very substantial number of women in the 25–34 age group are already engaged in this effort.)

Sara Perez, who, with her mother Rosa Perez, talked candidly with Cynthia Costello for this book about their respective lives, is emblematic. Sara wrestles with the "when-to, how-to" question. Just 29, she works long hours on Capitol Hill as chief of staff for a first-term congresswoman. She's recently married; she and her husband want children. She can't imagine how she could possibly combine motherhood with the kind of job she has now, so she expects to leave the Hill when she has children. Yet she loves her work and has more career ambitions to realize. So Sara and her husband will not start a family for a while.

Rosa Perez, too, is emblematic—of the ambivalence felt by many women in "the mothers' generation." She is enormously proud of Sara's accomplishments—indeed, she and her husband made them possible by insisting that Sara (and Sara's four sisters) get college degrees. Yet Rosa very much hopes that Sara and her other daughters will have children and that they will give their children priority in their lives. The dilemma, of course, is how they can combine career and family in a way that does not undermine one or the other, or both.

The Perez women are representative, as well, of the growing number of Americans trying to reconcile two cultures whose values and traditions sometimes conflict, especially when it comes to the proper role of women. Today's young women are much more diverse culturally and racially than their mothers' generation was 25 years ago (and, incidentally, more diverse than the overall U.S. female population is now). A much larger percentage are of Hispanic origin; a somewhat larger percentage are black; and the percentage of Asian/Pacific Islanders, although still relatively small, is more than double what it was a quarter-century ago.

More than one in seven of the young women in our age group are foreign-born. Roughly four out of the seven foreign-born women are from Latin America, mostly Mexico and Central America; two are from Asia. Immigrants from these different corners of the world typically arrive here with very different educational backgrounds. Only about half of the incomers who were born in Latin America are even high school graduates; only 11 percent are college graduates. By contrast, a woman who came here from Asia is more likely than a U.S.-born woman to have at least a four-year degree.

Since ours is a labor market in which a worker's knowledge is her most valuable asset, the good jobs typically require at least some college, and the really good jobs require at least a four-year degree and probably a graduate degree, as well. So large differences in educational achievement translate into very different employment opportunities and economic prospects overall.

Workers lacking education are ill-equipped to compete for good jobs—jobs that pay reasonably well, provide benefits, and offer the possibility of advancement. The poorly educated, and especially poorly educated women (male brawn can sometimes pay fairly well), wind up competing with each other for jobs at the margins of our economy.

At least when it comes to education, Asian/Pacific Islander women (whether foreign- or U.S.-born) have the most to offer employers—more than half in the 25–34 age group have a bachelor's degree or more. Non-Hispanic white women are next: more than a third have a bachelor's degree or better. Both typically have more education than their male contemporaries.

And Asian/Pacific Islander women and white women are likely to have more education than their black counterparts. The great majority of black women age 25–34 are high school graduates, but less than 20 percent have a college degree. So even though, of all the women in our age group, black women have the strongest commitment to the labor force, and even if racial job discrimination were not an issue, the lower educational attainment levels of young black women would place them—like their Hispanic contemporaries—at a competitive disadvantage in the job market compared with Asian/Pacific Islander and white women.

Cynthia Costello's interview with Sara and Rosa Perez ("Two Generations: A Mother and Daughter Talk about Their Lives") is the prelude to six careful and thorough investigations of the situation in which today's generation of young women find themselves and of how their situation differs from that of American women who were young 25 years ago.

Demographer Martha Farnsworth Riche lays the groundwork in Chapter One. Basing her thought-provoking analysis on new tabulations of 1975 and 2000 Census survey data—tabulations that were done especially for this book—the author takes a close look at what "the numbers" show about the characteristics of today's population of young women compared with the characteristics typical of their mothers' generation at the same age. She reports striking differences—for example, that the years between the twenty-fifth and thirty-fifth birthdays are likely to be the years during which a contemporary young woman will marry for the first time (if she marries at all) and will have her first child. A generation ago, both these milestones typically were passed at younger ages. Ms. Riche writes that young women today "are experiencing an unprecedented density of roles that are simultaneously traditional and nontraditional." And, she points out, longer life expectancies mean that young women must "keep an eye on their future as they work to balance their very full present."

In Chapter Two, Marisa DiNatale and Stephanie Boraas, economists at the Bureau of Labor Statistics, assess the employment patterns and earnings of today's young women. In an analysis that includes comparisons with today's young men as well as with yesterday's young women, the authors give particular attention to the impact of women's educational gains over the last several decades. Concerning themselves with the employment situation of young women across the educational spectrum, Ms. DiNatale and Ms. Boraas report not only on the employment and earnings opportunities that higher education opens for women but also on the crippling effect that the lack of education has on a young woman's job options, current earnings, and earnings potential.

Underscoring just how stunning the change in women's work patterns—especially mothers' work patterns—has been since 1975, Ms. DiNatale and Ms. Boraas tell us that close to two-thirds of women with children under age three were in the workforce in 2000, a proportion almost double what it was in 1975. However, "raising children continues to have a greater impact on mothers' working lives than it does on fathers'."

Chapter Three scrutinizes the health of young women who are between 25 and 35 now and how it compares with the health of their mothers' generation at the same age. In this pioneering analysis—it is the first, WREI believes, to take such a comprehensive look at the health of this particular age group of women—Alina Salganicoff, Barbara Wentworth, and Liberty Greene of the Henry J. Kaiser Family Foundation consider a wide range of topics. They discuss the specific health conditions that affect young women, the barriers to good health care encountered by young women of different incomes and racial backgrounds, and the prevalence among them of risky conditions and behavior—obesity, smoking, and unprotected sex. The authors remind us that the explosion in sexually transmitted diseases over the last several decades—and in particular the spread of the deadly human immunodeficiency virus (HIV)—has made unprotected sex a risky business indeed.

To illustrate how closely entwined developments in health have been with social changes, Ms. Salganicoff and her colleagues have devised a time line that readers will find fascinating and invaluable. Many of the events on the time line are milestones in the sexual revolution, and the authors give careful attention to the impact on health of the change in the typical young woman's sexual history and behavior.

Can a woman have a paid job—especially a demanding job—and "have a life," as well? Jessica DeGroot and Joyce Fine, the authors of Chapter Four, believe that she can, but not if she just sits back and waits for somebody else to make it happen. As the founders of the ThirdPath Institute, the authors are helping women and men reconsider how they approach work and family and charting new directions for combining the two. They ask employers to rethink what they demand of employees and to reshape their workplaces accordingly. Ms. DeGroot and Ms. Fine point out that assumptions built into our work culture—such as the assumption that the more hours one works, the more one should be rewarded—undermine people's ability to have a life outside of work, much less care for children. They also emphasize that traditional role expectations on the home front are part of the problem, as well. Until institutional and domestic stereotypes have dissolved, young women—with or without partners, with or without children—need to be creative and proactive, and the authors discuss successful strategies for negotiating a balanced life.

Young women's finances are the subject of Chapter Five, by Lani Luciano, who has written extensively for *Money* magazine. She looks at how much young women have in the way of household income, assets, and debt; how young women spend their money; and whether—and how adequately—they are preparing financially for their future. Among the author's sources are new tabulations, prepared especially for this book, of the Federal Reserve Board's 1998 Survey of Consumer Finances. Ms. Luciano concludes with a consideration of the plight of the many young women who, because they lack skills and education—and, often, child care and transportation, as well—have a hard time getting by on their current earnings and no practical hope of saving for the future.

Measures to improve the prospects of disadvantaged young women, as well as measures to preserve the gains made by their more fortunate contemporaries, are the subjects of Chapter Six, in which Cynthia Costello and Vanessa Wight discuss large and small policy changes that would improve both the present situation and the longer-term economic prospects of young women, especially those who are making, or have made, the transition from welfare to work.

The authors of this chapter point out that a young woman coming off welfare with limited education and few skills may have difficulty meeting the "work first" requirements. To become self-sufficient, she will need a lot of help, including assistance with child care and financial support while she acquires the schooling and skills that will equip her for a decent job with health benefits. A young mother in a low-skilled job, like her better-off counterparts, must reconcile the demands of her paid job with her responsibilities as a parent, but her balancing act is more difficult: she must pull it off without financial resources and, usually, without the help of the other parent.

Chapter Six also argues for the importance of protecting—and indeed expanding—the policy achievements of the last several decades. Affirmative action, financial assistance for education and job training, reproductive rights, family and medical leave—all are issues of critical importance to young women and indeed to women of all ages.

Following Chapter Six, the spotlight that has focused on young women turns elsewhere. For the reader who may have concluded that this edition of *The American Woman* is indifferent to the status of women who are under 25 or over 34, here is reassurance: like all previous editions in the series, this book contains a comprehensive statistical portrait of women in the United States. Organized by subject matter—for example, employment, health, education—the 124 tables and figures in this part of the book contain a wealth of up-to-date, user-friendly information about women of all ages and nearly every measurable aspect of their lives. (Because of space limitations, updated versions of some of the tables and figures in the eighth edition [*The American Woman 2001–2002*] could not be included in this, ninth, edition. However, many of them can be found on WREI's website, http://www.wrei.org.)

Finally, like previous editions in the *American Woman* series, this one contains a section about the women in the U.S. Congress. It begins with a thoughtful and perceptive essay by Cynthia Hall about the collective successes (and frustrations) that the women in the Congressional Caucus for Women's Issues have had in advancing public policies to better women's lives. The author, president of Women's Policy, Inc., knows her subject well: she came to her present job after years of experience as legislative director for one of the caucus's most active members. Ms. Hall's article is followed by very brief biographies of all the women who are in the U.S. Senate and House of Representatives as we go to press.

In this ninth edition of *The American Woman* is plenty of evidence that there has been a revolution in American women's lives—and plenty of evidence that the revolution is incomplete. That today's young women have more education than their mothers had—and, with that education, opportunities and options hardly dreamed of by earlier generations of women—is certainly in large part the result of the modern women's movement. So is women's ability to decide if and when they will have children.

This book reminds us, however, that with more choices usually come more difficult decisions, and this is especially true for young women. "The ticking of the biological clock" may be a cliché, but the clock is a reality nevertheless, and one that seems unalterable except at the margins. Also real are the pressures brought to bear on women *and* men by the traditional expectations that many in society and its institutions still have about the roles and responsibilities of the sexes, personally and professionally.

However, unlike biology, expectations can be changed, and doing so seems to offer the best hope for finishing the revolution begun a generation ago. Employers can rethink the heavy time demands they impose on their employees, female and male, and recognize that a successful employee's life can and needs to be more than the sum of her (or his) hours dedicated to the job. Spouses and partners can rethink their expectations of each other and especially how they come to determine who has primary responsibility for particular chores. These private changes are not impossible. But public changes are also necessary. As the civil rights movement proved, good laws can lead the way.

Two Generations:
A Mother and Daughter
Talk about Their Lives

Cynthia B. Costello

I INTERVIEWED ROSA AND SARA PEREZ, a mother and daughter, in December 2001. Rosa, age 61, was born in Chihua, Mexico.* Her parents moved with their 10 children to El Paso, Texas, when Rosa was eight. Since El Paso is only 300 miles from Chihua, the family frequently traveled back and forth across the border to visit relatives while Rosa was growing up. Rosa married at age 21 and was 22 when she had her first child. Her five daughters are now between the ages of 27 and 39.

Sara, Rosa's fourth daughter, is 29. Sara and her sisters grew up in El Paso among an extended network of grandparents, aunts, uncles, and cousins. She left home when she was 20 to attend college. She married when she was 28 and is now chief of staff for a congresswoman.

My first interview was with Rosa Perez.

Rosa, what was it like growing up in El Paso, Texas in the 1940s and 1950s?

My father brought us to live in El Paso in 1948. My mother had 12 children including a set of twins that passed away. We traveled back and forth to Mexico quite a bit, where, along with my brothers and sisters, I spent summers with my aunt, uncle, and grandmother.

My dad read a lot; my mom did not. She was 17 when she married, and I think she had a grade school education. She did know how to read and write but she did not have time to read. She crocheted beautifully. My uncles on my

---

father's side went to a prestigious military school. One of my uncles, whom I loved, was a teacher and went into the mountains to help educate people.

My mom stayed home and took care of the family. My dad worked at a dairy farm; later on, he worked as a cab driver. In my home, we spoke Spanish. My dad tried to learn English all the time by taking correspondence courses. He made As in his classes but was not able to speak because he was not around others who spoke English. To him, education was very important. He was always trying to better himself.

I started in second grade in the school in El Paso. Neither my brother nor I spoke English, and the kids were mean to us. We learned English within a year. We adjusted well. I felt it was a good education. I don't agree with bilingual classes. When I went to school, there wasn't such a thing. I think children need to learn right away to speak English. My first two daughters speak Spanish very well. An Anglo family moved next to us and within a week my daughter was speaking English.

When you were growing up, what were your hopes and dreams for yourself?

I always saw how my parents struggled financially. My main dream was to help them with a nicer home when they were older. I was very lucky because I was able to do that. When my husband and I married—I was 21—we bought a house close to my parents. My mom wanted me to have a good, stable family. I did think I would be married and have kids, but I did not want 10 kids like my mom. I saw how challenging that was for her. There were always two or three children sleeping in one bed when I was growing up. I said I would have five children, and I did.

I started working when I was a junior in high school, and I have been working ever since. I have been blessed to be able to better myself. I first worked as a busgirl, and when I graduated from high school, I got a better clerical position. Now I work in the accounting field for a construction company that builds freeways, bridges, and dams.

I wish that I had gone on to school after high school. My husband wishes he had encouraged me to go to school. I have a girlfriend and we talk about this—about how when we were going to school, we never thought about going to college. My girlfriend says that I was good in math. We have another girlfriend who went to nursing school. I don't know if there were financial aid programs when I was young. There probably were not.

How did you manage working and caring for your children?

It was 1962 and I was 22 when I had my first child, Marta. Over the next 12 years, I had four more daughters: Teresa, Carrie, Sara, and Patricia. When I got married, I was working for a dairy and I did the books. When I got pregnant, I did not want to work. I stayed home for a little bit. Then I met a friend who worked at Western Auto and she invited me to work part time there. The job was close to my house, and I worked there for 10 years as the cashier and credit clerk.

I would go back and forth from work to home when the girls were driving me crazy. I would take about three months off when I had a child and then I would go back. I would work for six weeks full time and then be off for six to 10 weeks and then go back again.

When I worked, my mom and dad would take care of my children. I am the fourth child in my family, and my three sisters were in the area and they helped with the kids. It wasn't easy to do everything. I look back and ask, "Where did I get the strength to do all this?" When Sara and Patricia were both babies, the other children helped but I was still the responsible person. God is very wonderful and he sends us the strength and knowledge to do the right thing. If you have a basic upbringing, even if you don't have a formal education, you have the knowledge to be a mother. You know that your role in life is to take care of your children and to protect them. You try to make them as strong as they can be so they can go out there in the world.

Things are very different now from when I was growing up. With us, my mom was very strict. So when my girls started growing up, I was very strict with them when they lived at home. Sara left for college when she was 20, and Carrie left home when she was in her twenties. My two other daughters left when they were 25 and 27. We had rules. Everyone had a curfew; nobody stayed out all night. They respected my feelings. The right thing is the right thing, no matter what.

I tried to instill in them a sense of being very responsible, and as far as their home is concerned, it doesn't need to be a cluttered house. I wanted them to have a nice, clean home. We have always instilled in them the importance of being responsible for their actions.

What were your hopes and dreams for your daughters?

My husband and I have similar values, and we wanted our children to have strong values in life, too. We wanted them to better themselves. My daughters have more opportunities than I personally did. Now, if you really want to go to school, you have a lot of financial help. You have to pay it back, but at least you have an opportunity to go. There is more help today, and this is very important. My girls always thought they would go to college.

I always wanted my girls to get a college education and prepare themselves for the future. All my girls were able to better themselves with a good education. Marta has her master's and is thinking about getting her doctorate, and I want her to.

My hopes and dreams were that my daughters would be happy with themselves. A very important part of my life has always been my religious background. I have been married for 40 years. It is not an easy test to be married; it is only the presence of our Lord Jesus in our lives that has brought us through these years. I have always hoped that my children would turn to Jesus in difficult times.

How do you feel about the fact that your daughters have moved away from El Paso?

It was unexpected, and it has not been easy having my girls spread out all over the country from California to Washington, DC. It always frightened me that Sara wanted to go into politics. Since she was a little girl she was into politics; she would read the paper. I always worry about them. I raised them and I said, "Jesus, you take care of them." Especially now with September 11—that doesn't make things any easier.

But I know that it always works out for the best. I have to find the best in every occasion. When Sara was in school, I figured out that she was not going to come back to El Paso once she went to Washington, DC. When my husband and I retire, we can go and visit our daughters.

What do you think it is like for young women to combine work and family today?

My girls do not have kids yet. Sara is married and Teresa is getting married in May of this year. I think it is very challenging for young women to combine a career and raising children. Nowadays life is so different and there are so many pressures. I really admire parents who work and have children at the same time.

Life is so busy and there are so many temptations for children. Drugs are one. Some kids do drugs out of curiosity or they want to prove themselves—"I can do it, nothing is going to happen." You have to be very much on top of things as a parent—more than I had to be or my mom had to be. Life is so much faster. You fear that drugs are being sold in junior high and grade school. I don't remember seeing people smoking cigarettes, and definitely there was no drinking. Now there are grade school kids being exposed to these things.

I hope that my daughters have children. Some people say, "Why have children, given the bad world?" Children make you what you are. Having children is the most rewarding experience. I would not have had a complete life without them. I don't think it is an easy chore. It has never been easy because children take a lot of time and patience. And you have to discipline yourself to spread yourself between your home, your husband, and your children.

I do see both sides of staying home and having children versus working and having children. I think that it is an individual decision. Sara wants to wait and keep working for a while. She does not want to work once she has children. You can plan more than you used to. When I got married, I never thought I would work and have children, and it just worked out that way. I am very happy that I did work even though sometimes I think that I should have stayed home. But if I did not work, I would not have been exposed to computers and whatnot. It is a very personal decision. Sometimes it is a matter of choice and sometimes it is not. In many cases, women go to work for financial reasons.

Would you say that your daughters' lives are easier or more difficult than your life has been?

I don't think that life is easier, but it is different from when I was young. There is a lot of pressure for women to succeed. The expectations are so high, and if you are a woman, you are more in the spotlight than women were when I was young. Young women are always trying to prove themselves out in the world. I think there are such high expectations and so much pressure that the girls put on themselves. My daughters have the opportunities, but it doesn't make their lives simpler.

As you look to the future, what are your hopes and dreams for your daughters?

Maybe I am being selfish, but I want my daughters to have children. I think it would be very nice. It makes life complete. If they don't want any, that is their choice. You value life more when you have children. My girls are so picky in terms of men. My daughters don't compromise very easily.

What are your hopes and dreams for yourself?

It is late in our lives. My husband is 65 and I am almost 62. My husband is retired and I will be able to retire soon and I will get a part-time job. I don't know what I would do if I didn't work. I have worked all my life; there is no other life for me. Now I think, why don't I quit? But I am so used to having that little check coming into my account. That is nice. I would go crazy if I had to stay home. I have gone to school part time, but I don't see myself going back to school.

I have always been a practicing Catholic, and right now I am going back to it more than I have ever had time to before. I hope to give more time to it now that I don't have as many responsibilities.

My second interview was with Sara Perez.

Sara, could you please describe what it was like to grow up in El Paso in the 1970s and 1980s?

When I was young, we would go to Mexico, mostly in the summers. But as I grew older, we did not go as much. The ties to Mexico were somewhat less strong for me than they were for my older sisters and certainly for my mother and father. Primarily, English was spoken in our home. When my older sisters were growing up, they had a maid who spoke Spanish. My older sisters spoke English and they took care of us along with my aunt because my mom was working. Our parents would speak Spanish. I am not as bilingual as I would like to be. I have taken Spanish classes to improve my writing and speaking.

What were your parents' attitudes toward education?

My dad always said, "Whatever you do, get an education." He would say, "Have fun in high school because later on you have to work. Do well in school and pay attention to your mother." My mom was the disciplinarian and she was very strict with our grades. I went to community college right after high school. When I came home with a grade of 96, she asked, "Where are the other four points?" I was upset, but she communicated that she was very proud. To my dad, all of his daughters walked on clouds, but my mother was the one who pushed us. My parents supported us to do whatever we wanted. They said, "If you are going to end up in Africa, just go."

My older sister, Marta, was the reason that I went to college. She took me to her high school and she said, "When you get older, you are going to go to college." She filled out my paperwork and did all my financial aid papers. She was also the reason that my second sister went back to school and got a college degree. All my sisters have college degrees. One has a master's and my youngest sister has a year of graduate work.

All of my friends were Hispanic when I was growing up. Some of my closest friends did go to college. About 50 percent went to college, and the others are still in El Paso and did not go to college. In my family, I have cousins who had children at the age of 14. Education about contraception is needed in our community.

When you were growing up, what were your hopes and dreams for yourself?

In my senior year of high school, I had a civics teacher who was tough but who got me interested in government and politics. I would come home and watch *Nightline* with my dad. My focus was government in community college. My freshman year in community college, a professor got me interested in the state legislature. I thought I would work in the Texas state capitol.

Then I started getting more focused on foreign policy. I had a girlfriend in Washington, DC, who told me that the schools in Washington were good. I got the materials and decided to go to a university there without even having visited the campus. It was a very difficult move. When I told my parents about my plans, I started to cry. I knew they didn't want me to leave. I was drawn to the opportunities, but tied to my family.

How did you finance your college education?

I had a lot of financial pressure. I got scholarships but I also borrowed a lot. I worked as a bartender through college in Texas and Washington. I found a place where the owner was very flexible, and he made my work schedule around my school schedule so that I could take time off for exams. My sisters and mother sent me $100 a month while I was in college to help me with rent.

I graduated with a lot of debt—somewhere around $25,000. At the beginning, after college, I did not make enough money to even pay off my student loan, so I had to defer payment. I went into severe credit card debt from buying things I needed and wanted, and my mom helped me out of it. Now I can pay a little bit more than the minimum payment for my college loan and it is almost paid off.

Can you tell me about your work history?

When I was in my junior year at college, I started working for my congressman and I went to work for him full time after college. I started as an intern in his office and then I worked as a legislative correspondent when I graduated. Then I moved up to be a legislative assistant. When he retired, I worked for a congresswoman and was with her for five years—first as a legislative assistant, then as legislative director, and later as deputy chief of staff. Then I moved to this office, where I am chief of staff.

What are your thoughts about marriage, family, and children?

My mother said I was not to date until I was 21. My husband was my first serious boyfriend. He is Turkish and works in his family's business. One of the reasons that I liked my husband was how close he was to his family. He valued his family very highly and would spend every weekend with his family. It was not a big deal for me that he was from a different cultural background, in large part because I have always been interested in international affairs and different cultures. One benefit of marrying my husband is I have a more diverse group of friends. I still have my Hispanic friends at work, and with my husband I have Turkish friends.

I feel strongly that when I do have kids I would like to stay home, at least for the first two years. Then I think I would like to go back to work. I enjoy working. But with the hours that we work on Capitol Hill, it would be impossible and not good for young children. I might make a career move in the next few years so that I can combine career with kids. It is a problem because I really enjoy my job. Maybe in five years I will start having kids.

Typically, I go in at 9 A.M. and I leave around 7:30 or 8:00 in the evening. It works out to be about 11 hours a day, and I usually go in on Saturdays. Typically, I have a 60-hour week. The schedule is such that you don't adjourn until a couple of days before Christmas. Because my congresswoman is a freshman member of Congress, we have a lot of catching up to do. After the New Year, it should get better and I should be able to take art history classes and visit the Smithsonian and Harper's Ferry with my husband.

I would hope that working for Congress would become more family-friendly, but I haven't seen any change in six years.

What kinds of challenges do you think young women face today?

There is a lot of pressure, and a lot of it is the pressure we put on ourselves. I am trying to find that happy medium to balance everything. A lot of it has to do with the fact that the expectations we have of ourselves are so high. We went through the superwoman era, and society makes us want so much and that requires you to work extra hard to balance kids and family. And society says, "What do you mean, you can't do it all?"

In some ways, the challenges are equal for men and women, but usually it is the woman who takes care of the kids. Men worry a bit more about the finances. As women, we want to handle the children and contribute to the finances, as well. Even though we have come a long way, and more men do want to help with raising children, society still expects women to be the primary caretakers.

I don't think this is the way it should be, but in my culture—in the Hispanic culture—this is what is expected. Culturally, this is how we have been raised—that women will take care of the kids. My mom and sisters always serve the husbands and brothers first. In my marriage, my husband wants to share 50/50 with raising the children, but I want to stay home full time the first couple of years after our first child is born.

Do you think that you have more choices and opportunities than your mother did?

I think I have more opportunities because when my mom's family came to the United States, they had to make so many sacrifices. When my mom was growing up, they lived in a four-bedroom house with 14 people. For my parents, education was not in their background. It was more a matter of day-to-day survival when my parents were raising us. There was a huge difference in the educational opportunities that my sisters and I had. We also have a lot more opportunities workwise.

I don't think it is easier to have these opportunities because times are so different. I look back and it was really tough for my mom because she raised five girls. But we had a great childhood being raised by an extended family of grandparents, aunts, uncles, and cousins. We would go camping with our cousins, and it was awesome. I don't want to rob my kids of family life, but our kids aren't going to have the same experience. My husband feels the same regrets because he was raised in Turkey with an extended family, but he does have aunts and uncles here who could help if we have kids.

How much do you think things have changed for women?

I think there have been significant changes. We now have a list of the top 50 workplaces that are the most family-friendly. Just the fact that people are talking about day care and options for working at home is progress. I think that corporations want to keep women in the workplace.

Women have benefited from the women's movement in terms of career choices and family life. There are so many more options and opportunities for women now. The fact that we have 13 female senators and 62 women in the House is great—and there have been so many improvements for women.

I know that we still have a long way to go. Equal pay would make a big difference. Women still make 75 cents to the dollar made by men. That is the big issue. On the Hill, there are differences in the pay for men and women who have the position of chief of staff—and minorities are making less than whites.

When you look to the future, what are your hopes and dreams?

I am a lot like my mother when it comes to work—I like to work. In the future, I would like to find a job where I am not working 11 hours a day, and I would like to have enough time to raise children and have outside interests. The problem is that I want a job as fulfilling as this one. I really like my job, but there is no way that I would want to raise children in this environment. There is so much pressure for my women friends on the Hill who have kids. They miss out on school plays and kids end up suffering. My mom was able to do it. She worked all the way through my childhood, but she had all her sisters there to help. My mom knew who all my friends were, and she always knew where I was going.

I would like to be comfortable financially. I am focused on enjoying my job and making sure that I find a job where I can balance family life and my job. My husband wants us to make a certain amount of money so that we can be comfortable. We do own the house my husband lived in for 10 years before we married. He is totally supportive of my career, because he knows how happy I am at work, but he gets upset that I don't have enough time to do things, given how many hours I put in.

I want to find a more accommodating job, but I also want to stay another four or five years on the Hill. One day we will have a Hispanic senator, and I want to work for that senator.

One

YOUNG WOMEN: WHERE THEY STAND

Martha Farnsworth Riche

HIGHLIGHTS

YOUNG WOMEN AGE 25–34 differ in many ways from their mothers at the same age. They are more diverse, racially and ethnically. They are better educated, on average, and have more options for working outside as well as within the home. And they are choosing a greater variety of household and living arrangements. Moreover, these options and choices can vary according to race, ethnic origin, and income and educational levels.

Young women are "squeezed" by a number of different roles. These are the prime years for marrying and having children—and for investing in jobs and careers. At the same time, longer life expectancies mean that today's young women can anticipate a considerable work period without caregiving responsibilities prior to entering retirement. Key findings from this chapter include:

- Just under two-thirds of young women are non-Hispanic white, compared with more than four-fifths in 1975. Hispanics are the fastest-growing minority, nearly tripling their share of this age group over the quarter-century.
- Non-Hispanic white women continue to be more likely than most minority women to be wives in married-couple households. However, the proportion of young women in this living arrangement has declined among all racial and ethnic groups since 1975.

- Young women have more diverse households and living arrangements than their mothers did. Nearly three times as many young women age 25–34 had never married in 2000 as in 1975.
- Despite their less traditional marital patterns, young women today are having at least as many children as their mothers did, but at a later age. The birth rate for women age 25–34 is higher than that of any other 10-year age group.
- The trend toward later motherhood is particularly pronounced for Asian American and non-Hispanic white women, who are more likely to have the higher education associated with later childbearing. The trend is less pronounced for women of other racial and ethnic origins.
- The proportion of women who have not completed high school (or the GED) is barely half what it was in 1975, and the proportion with "some" college has nearly doubled. Moreover, three out of 10 younger women now have bachelor's degrees or higher.
- Racial and ethnic differences in educational attainment are stark among young women. Whereas only small percentages of younger white women and Asian women have less than a high school diploma, more than a third of younger Hispanic women are in this situation. For young black women, high school completion is becoming routine. Still, one in eight is a high school dropout.
- Women age 25–34 are more likely to work, no matter what their family situation, than women their age were in 1975. The most notable shift toward the work world is among women who have also chosen to marry and have children.
- Black women have the greatest connection to the workforce of all women in the 25–34 age group: although they have the same labor force participation rates as non-Hispanic white women, black women are more likely to be employed full time.
- Those young women with the lowest household incomes are unmarried householders without a high school diploma. These women's annual household income is only one-sixth that of women who are both college graduates and married.

INTRODUCTION

The demographic profile of the more than 19 million American women age 25–34 differs in many ways from that of their mothers at the same age; it is also more diverse. These differences and this diversity are driven by a broader array of life choices and the interaction between them, as well as by greater racial, social, and economic diversity within the American population as a whole.[1]

In essence, today's younger women display all the demographic trends that are transforming the American population. They are more diverse, racially and ethnically. They are better educated, on average, and have more options for working outside as well as within the home. And they are choosing a greater variety of household and living arrangements. Moreover, these options and choices can vary according to race, ethnic origin, and income and educational levels.

While young women continue to take on traditional roles, they experience them in a more concentrated period than in the past. Throughout history, women's primary role was to bear and raise children and to care for the family and home, although women have done "productive" work in fields and factories, as well. Now later childbearing combines with an ever-lengthening life expectancy to assign women's traditional roles to a relatively narrow segment of their lives, from age 25–34. These are the years in which today's young women marry, acquire homes to care for, and bear and raise small children, as well as begin their investment in the work world.

As a result, today's young women are experiencing an unprecedented density of roles that are simultaneously traditional and nontraditional. At the same time, relatively fewer women in other age groups, and fewer Americans in general, are sharing the traditional caregiving and homemaking roles with these younger women. Instead, longer life expectancies are creating new life stages for Americans in mid- and later life, requiring today's young women to keep an eye on their future as they work to balance their very full present.

CHANGES IN THE DEMOGRAPHIC CONTEXT

Women and men age 25–34 are in the vanguard of a fundamental change in the American population. Thanks to longer life expectancies and stable fertility rates, the proportion of the population that is over 35 is growing rapidly. This "aging" of the population is reflected in current figures: 2000 was the first year in which more than half of Americans were age 35 and older. As a result, the younger adults who traditionally have dominated the adult population are losing "market share," with predictable effects on their political, cultural, and economic impact.

People tend to think that this relative decline is the result of a small generation following the very large baby-boom generation. It is true that today's 25–34-year-olds are smaller in absolute numbers than they were in 1990. However, their decline in relative terms is probably a permanent change, as

longer life expectancies combine with stable birth rates to increase the population share of older generations. As this happens, policy concerns naturally
shift away from younger adults toward middle-aged and older ones.

Even though their numbers were considerably larger (up 25 percent),
women age 25–34 represented a slightly smaller share of the population
(13.8 percent) in 2000 than their mothers did in 1975 (14.3 percent). But in
a sign of changes now under way, females under 25 represented a considerably smaller share of the population in 2000 than they did in the past, while
older women represented a considerably larger one. In 2000, females under
age 25 represented a third of all females, a decline of more than eight percent over the quarter-century. And women age 35 and older accounted for
over half of the nation's female population, an increase of nearly 10 percent.
Thus, today's generation of young women is the first to live their lives under
a new demographic regime: one in which all but the oldest age groups are
of equal size instead of outnumbering the generation that preceded it (see
Figure I-1).

Another fundamental set of changes is geographic. Throughout its history, the nation has reshaped its population geography, as Americans, primarily young adults, chose to establish their lives in different parts of the
country. Today's young women are no exception: compared with their mothers, they are less likely to live in the Northeast and the Midwest and more
likely to live in the South and the West. More than 35 percent of all women
age 25–34 lived in the South in 2000, nearly twice as many as lived in the
Northeast. This shift is due in part to continuing immigration from south of
the border but primarily to the large flow of young adults to the Sun Belt in
the 1970s and 1980s—the mothers of the current young generation. Like
their mothers, as today's young women have children, they place new demands on southern and western states for schools and other services, while
providing those states with a potential resource for the future.

At the same time, today's younger women are continuing the pattern of
suburban living that their mothers' generation traced. Children of the sub-
urbs, they are even less likely to live in central cities or rural areas than their
mothers were.

Perhaps the most noticeable demographic change among these young
adults is their increasing racial and ethnic diversity. The numbers of non-
Hispanic white women age 25–34 barely changed between 1975 and 2000,
as minority groups accounted for most of the growth of this cohort. This is
due partly to immigration and partly to higher fertility rates among some
minority populations.

Just under two-thirds of young women were non-Hispanic white in 2000,
down from more than four-fifths in 1975. Hispanics were the fastest-

Figure I-1 • Total Female Population in the United States by Age, 1975 and 2000 (percent distributions)[1]

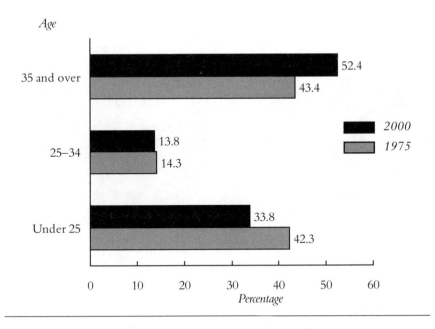

¹For the year 1975, data were population estimates. For 2000, data were from the 2000 Decennial Census.

Sources: Census Bureau, "Census 2000 Summary File 1," 2001a, Table 3, and *Preliminary Estimates of the Population of the United States, by Age, Sex, and Race: 1970 to 1981*, 1982, Table 2.

growing minority, nearly tripling their share of this age group over the quarter-century. All minority groups, however, now account for a larger share of the 25–34 age group (see Figure I-2).

LIFE CYCLE

Life cycle is a relatively new concept for most Americans because in the past most people spent virtually all of their adult lives earning a living and raising a family. But advances in health care, knowledge, and public health throughout the twentieth century continue to lengthen lives, and Americans continue to believe that two children make up the optimum family size. As a result, Americans of both sexes are spending an average of a little more than a third of the years between ages 20 and 70 in parenting, making room for new life stages (King 1999).

Figure I-2 • Women Age 25–34 by Race and Hispanic Origin, 1975 and 2000 (percent distributions)

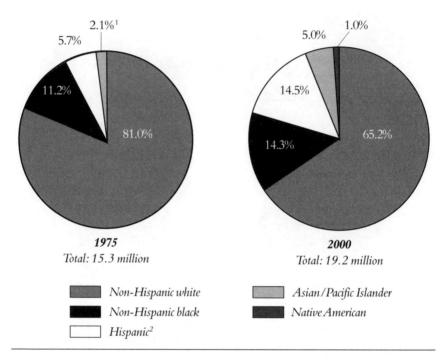

1975
Total: 15.3 million

2000
Total: 19.2 million

Non-Hispanic white

Non-Hispanic black

Hispanic[2]

Asian/Pacific Islander

Native American

[1]Includes both Asian/Pacific Islanders and Native Americans.
[2]People of Hispanic origin may be of any race.

Source: Special tabulations of the March 1975 and March 2000 Current Population Surveys, prepared by Deirdre Gaquin for the Women's Research and Education Institute (WREI), 2001.

Thus, women age 25–34 are undertaking life's major responsibilities with the understanding that they have a more complex life cycle, one that includes both retirement (for which they must save) and a considerable work period with few or no gender-role obligations to conflict with activities outside the home. On average, these women can expect to live at least five years longer than their mothers and much longer than their grandmothers—at the same time that those older generations of women are pioneering new, post-child-rearing life stages. And many demographers feel that current estimates of young people's life expectancy are too conservative, given the pace of health advances.

In this broader perspective, it is no wonder that young women are exhibiting more diverse choices in relation to living arrangements, marriage, and children; they have to take their later life stages into account. They are still marrying and having children, but they are balancing these choices with less traditional ones. And they tend to make all these decisions later than their mothers did, as preparation for adult roles, through education and early work experience, takes longer than it used to, even for people who don't continue their education. Overall, compared with earlier generations, relatively few young Americans now take on the major adult roles of financial independence, marriage, or parenthood before age 25 (Riche 2000).

MARRIAGE

Probably the most significant change, in terms of traditional expectations for women in this age group, is the pronounced decline in the proportion who are married. In 2000, slightly more than half of women age 25–34 were living in a married-couple household, compared with three-fourths in 1975 (see Figure I-3). In 2000, the median age at first marriage was 25.1 for women, up from 21.1 a quarter-century earlier, and 30 percent of women age 25–34 had not married.

In part because of the trend toward later marriage, the proportion of women who are living in married-couple households has changed much less for women age 35 and older than it has for other age groups. Meanwhile, young women age 25–34 display a variety of living arrangements (see Table I-1). As young adults postpone marriage, they tend to remain in their parents' homes longer or to live independently or with others, either as roommates or as partners.

Trends in divorce also play a role in these young women's life cycles. Although divorce rates stabilized in the early 1980s, the continued high failure rate for first marriages among young adults means that 7.8 percent of today's women age 25–34 are divorced and not yet remarried.

The change in the racial and ethnic composition of this age group also plays a part in its varied household arrangements, as non-Hispanic white women continue to be more likely than most minority women to be wives in married-couple households. However, the proportion of young women in this living arrangement has declined among all racial and ethnic groups since 1975—down 28 percent for Asians and other groups (including Native Americans), 21 percent for non-Hispanic blacks, 18 percent for non-Hispanic whites, and 12 percent for Hispanics.

In part, these racial and ethnic differences reflect cultural differences in family patterns, which can be particularly important for new immigrants. For instance, consensual unions, in which the family unit consists most often of the woman and her child, are common in African cultures, including those in the Caribbean and Central America (United Nations 2000). Extended

Figure I-3 • Marital Status of Women Age 25–34, 1975 and 2000 (percent distributions)[1]

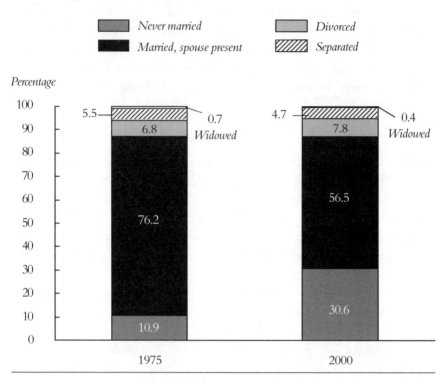

[1]Percentages may not total 100.0 due to rounding.

Source: Special tabulations of the March 1975 and March 2000 Current Population Surveys, prepared by Deirdre Gaquin for the Women's Research and Education Institute (WREI), 2001.

families, in which young couples live in a parent's household, are common in both Latin and Asian cultures, while the nuclear family has its origin in northern Europe. Consequently, the large shares of young minority women who are living with parents or other relatives probably include many who are living in unions, including marital unions.

Among non-Hispanic white women age 25–34, the proportion living with a parent or other relative increased from six to nine percent between 1975 and 2000 (and decreased for older women). Similarly, the proportion heading their own household increased from 16 to 26 percent, and the proportion living with a nonrelative increased from two to eight percent. These increases most likely represent delayed marriage, cohabitation, and single parenting, particularly after an early marriage.

Table 1-1 • Household Relationship of Women Age 25–34 by Race and Hispanic Origin, 2000 (percent distributions)[1]

	All Races	Non-Hispanic White	Non-Hispanic Black	Hispanic[2]	Asian/Pacific Islander	Native American
Wife in married-couple family	54.8	60.6	27.7	56.7	53.5	36.1
Female householder	25.9	22.5	49.3	19.7	19.4	33.9
Not living alone	17.6	13.4	39.4	17.1	(3)	(3)
Living alone	8.3	9.1	9.9	2.6	(3)	(3)
Child of householder	8.5	7.4	12.3	8.2	11.1	12.4
Other relative of householder	3.5	1.7	4.7	8.1	10.4	1.7
Nonrelative of householder	0.9	0.9	0.9	1.4	0.7	—
Unmarried partner of male	3.4	3.6	2.7	3.4	2.6	9.1
Unmarried partner of female	0.1	0.1	0.1	0.1	—	—
Roommate or boarder	3.0	3.3	2.3	2.5	2.3	6.8
Total percentage	100.0	100.0	100.0	100.0	100.0	100.0
Total number (in thousands)	18,947	12,355	2,700	2,763	933	196

[1]Percentages may not total 100.0 due to rounding.
[2]People of Hispanic origin may be of any race.
[3]Data not available.

Source: Special tabulations of the March 1975 and March 2000 Current Population Surveys, prepared by Deirdre Gaquin for the Women's Research and Education Institute (WREI), 2001.

For non-Hispanic black women in particular, patterns that prevailed when their mothers were their age have intensified over the last quarter-century, as older women in this population also have shifted away from married-couple arrangements toward all other household arrangements. In contrast, Hispanic women have experienced much less of a shift away from married-couple households, and the proportion of Hispanic women heading their own households has barely changed. Asian women show both the greatest shift away from married-couple households and the greatest shift toward living with a parent or other relative. Asians and Hispanics have the largest proportion of immigrants—and immigrants are most likely to be in their twenties and to share households with others. Overall, both Asian and Hispanic women are much more likely to immigrate on their own than they were in the past (United Nations 2000).

The rising proportion of young women with a college education may portend more marriage for this age group, not less, as they move through life. In 2000, women age 25–34 who had a bachelor's degree or higher were most likely to be wives in married-couple households, while women who were high school dropouts were least likely to be in such a living arrangement. Although less than 60 percent of these college graduates were part of a married-couple household in 2000, compared with nearly 75 percent in 1975, the married proportion of college-educated women age 35 and older stayed the same (see Table I-2).

To be sure, getting an education is associated with later first marriage, which in turn is associated with greater marital stability (National Center for Health Statistics 2001a; Bianchi 2000). Education may also be linked to cohabitation: compared with women in married-couple households, women in unmarried-partner households are more likely to be more educated than their partners. Unmarried-partner households are also more likely to be egalitarian in terms of income and work (Census Bureau 2001b). Issues of power and dependence within relationships become more complex when individuals, not family or society, determine living arrangements and life choices.

There is still no single, agreed-upon way to measure cohabitation, but it is on the rise, particularly among young adults, many of whom will eventually formalize their unions. Among people who live together "all of the time," more than three-fourths of women age 25–34 who were living with nonrelatives in 2000 (six percent of all women in that age group) said they were living with an unmarried partner (including same-sex partners) (Census Bureau 2001b). In general, the increase in cohabitation has offset the decrease in marriage (Bumpass, Sweet, and Cherlin 1991).

Table 1-2 • Household Relationship of Women Age 25–34 by Educational Attainment, 1975 and 2000 (percent distributions)[1]

	Not a High School Graduate		High School Graduate, No More		Some College[2]		Bachelor's Degree or More	
	1975	2000	1975	2000	1975	2000	1975	2000
Wife in married-couple family	69.7	47.2	78.3	54.9	73.9	54.2	74.2	57.9
Female householder	20.6	28.6	13.3	24.7	16.1	26.5	17.1	25.3
Not living alone	18.5	25.8	9.8	20.3	8.0	19.4	4.0	10.2
Living alone	2.1	2.8	3.5	4.4	8.0	7.1	13.1	15.2
Child or other relative of householder	8.0	14.9	7.1	12.7	7.9	12.3	6.1	9.7
Nonrelative of householder[3]	1.7	9.2	1.3	7.6	2.2	7.0	2.6	7.0
Total percentage	100.0	100.0	100.0	100.0	100.0	100.0	100.0	100.0
Total number (in thousands)	3,105	2,082	7,037	5,479	2,488	5,704	2,684	5,681

[1]Percentages may not total 100.0 due to rounding.
[2]Includes two-year degrees.
[3]In this table, "nonrelative of householder" would include women living with partners in the partners' households. Conversely, "female householder" would include women whose partners live in their (i.e., the women householders') households.

Source: Special tabulations of the March 1975 and March 2000 Current Population Surveys, prepared by Deirdre Gaquin for the Women's Research and Education Institute (WREI), 2001.

CHILDREN

Young American women may display less traditional marital patterns than their mothers did, but as a group they seem to be having as many if not more children. In 2000, the fertility rate (the number of children each woman age 15–44 would have in her lifetime if current rates continue) was 2.13. This was the highest rate since 1971 (National Center for Health Statistics 2001b). In 1975, the fertility rate was 1.77, and the nation was concerned about a "baby bust." The bust ended a few years later, and demographers realized that the low fertility rates had largely been an artifact of postponed, not forgone, childbearing. However, it is too soon to tell whether today's young women will have more children, on average, than their mothers did; current data suggest that they will have at least the same number.

Like their mothers, young women are having their first child later than earlier generations did. Nearly half of women who had their first child in 2000 were age 25 or older, compared with little more than a fourth of women in 1975 (see Figure I-4). In other words, more women age 25–34 who are having babies are having their first child, rather than a later child. According to preliminary data, fully two out of five women who had their first child in 2000 were age 25–34. Indeed, in 2000, birth rates for women age 30 and older were the highest in 30 years (National Center for Health Statistics 2001b).

Whether they are having a first or a later child, women age 25–34 have a higher birth rate than any other 10-year age group. (Birth rates refer to actual births; fertility rates are estimates of how many children women will have in total, including those they might have at later ages.) Today, women age 25–29 have the highest birth rate and women age 20–24 have the second highest; but women in their early thirties have a much higher birth rate than teenagers. Between 1999 and 2000, according to preliminary data, the birth rate rose three percent for women age 25–29 and five percent for women age 30–34. It rose one percent for women in their early twenties and dropped to historic lows for teenagers (National Center for Health Statistics 2001b).

The trend toward later motherhood is particularly pronounced for Asian American and non-Hispanic white women, who are more likely to have the higher education associated with later childbearing (National Center for Health Statistics 2001b). The trend is less pronounced for women of other racial and ethnic origins. In 2000, about three in four black and Native American women were under 25 when they had their first child, as were more than two in three Hispanic women (see Table I-3). Over all ages, the fertility rate is about 80 percent higher for Hispanic than for non-Hispanic white women, who have the lowest fertility rate.

Figure I-4 • Age of Mother at Birth of First Child, 1975 and 2000 (percent distributions)

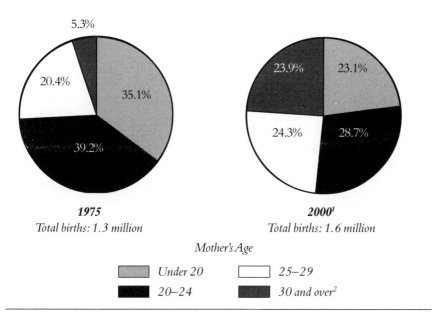

1975
Total births: 1.3 million

2000[1]
Total births: 1.6 million

Mother's Age

Under 20   25–29

20–24   30 and over[2]

[1]Data for 2000 are preliminary.
[2]No age breakdown is available for first births in 1975 to mothers 30 and over, probably because there were so few of them. Of the births in 2000 to women over age 30, more than two-thirds were to women age 30–34; over one-fourth were to women age 35–39; and one in 20 were to women over age 40.

Sources: Census Bureau, "Maternity Leave Arrangements: 1961–85," *Work and Family Patterns of American Women,* 1990, Table A; and National Center for Health Statistics, *National Vital Statistics Report* 49, no. 5, 2001b, Table 2.

Among women age 25–34, those who have their children early can lead very different lives from those who wait (or have no children at all). This division is socioeconomic (in terms of educational attainment and resultant differences in income) and racial. It is also heightened by racial differences in childbearing by married and unmarried women (the latter tend to get less support at home). Fully 22 percent of non-Hispanic white women who gave birth in 2000 were unmarried, compared with 69 percent of non-Hispanic black women and 43 percent of Hispanic women.

Although the birth rate among unmarried women of all ages in 2000 was below the peak reached in 1994, the number of such births was the highest ever recorded. Overall, about a third of U.S. births were to unmarried women, although rates varied substantially by race and ethnic origin (National Center for Health Statistics 2001b).

Table I-3 • First Births as a Percentage of All Live Births by Mother's Age, Race, and Hispanic Origin, 2000 (percent distributions)[1,2]

| | Number of First Births | Mother's Age | | |
		Under 25	25–34	35 and Over
All races	1,625,342	51.9	40.7	7.4
White, total	1,286,395	49.8	42.5	7.7
Non-Hispanic white	978,218	44.3	46.9	8.9
Black	231,392	72.0	23.4	4.6
Native American	14,532	77.5	19.5	3.0
Asian/Pacific Islander	93,024	26.6	62.6	10.9
Hispanic[3]	302,581	68.6	27.8	3.6

[1]Data are preliminary.
[2]Percentages may not total 100.0 due to rounding.
[3]People of Hispanic origin may be of any race.

Source: National Center for Health Statistics, *National Vital Statistics Report* 49, no. 5, 2001b, Table 2.

Women age 25–34 are far more likely than younger women to be married when they have children. Still, many women in this age group are raising children on their own or in other household arrangements. Three out of five (59.7 percent) had a child living with them in 2000 (including step- and adopted children), and nearly one in five (17.3 percent) was not currently married with a spouse present. In contrast, in 1975, four out of five young women (80.4 percent) had a child living with them, and all but roughly one in six (15.9 percent) were currently married with a spouse present. In both years, some of the unmarried women were divorced or widowed, but far more had never married in 2000 than in 1975. In 2000, nine percent of all women age 25–34 had children but had never married, compared with just over five percent in 1975 (see Table I-4).

The trend toward bearing and raising children outside of marriage has led some to say that, given a choice, women seem to prefer children to husbands. At the same time, there has been a notable increase in childlessness, suggesting that many women prefer not to have a child if they are not married. This fact could also suggest that women would rather forgo marriage and children. Yet ongoing surveys of women's preferences show no diminution in their desire for marriage and children, just in the price they are willing to pay for them. That is, women who can support themselves and their children are unlikely to marry simply to have children or to stay married if they think the marriage is a failure.

In 2000, nearly 20 percent of women age 40–44 were childless, compared with 10 percent in 1975 (Census Bureau 2001d). These women are assumed

Table I-4 • Women Age 25–34 with Children by Marital Status, 1975 and 2000 (in percentages)[1]

	Percentage with Children[2]	
	1975	*2000*
Total women age 25–34	80.4	59.7
Never married	5.3	9.0
Married, spouse present	64.5	42.4
Widowed	0.6	0.3
Divorced	5.4	4.9
Separated[3]	4.6	3.1

[1]Civilian household population.
[2]Living in household with own children under 18.
[3]Includes married, spouse absent.

Source: Special tabulations of the March 1975 and March 2000 Current Population Surveys, prepared by Deirdre Gaquin for the Women's Research and Education Institute (WREI), 2001.

to have completed their childbearing years. Today's young women seem likely to match that record, since 44 percent of women age 25–29 and 28 percent of women age 30–34 were childless in 2000 (see Table I-5).

There seems to be no one reason behind this notable increase in childlessness. However, the multiplicity of roles that young women undertake at the beginning of their adult lives, and the intensity of effort required to succeed at each of them, undoubtedly takes a toll. While many midlife women fear being squeezed or sandwiched between care for parents and care for children, the data show that few experience this squeeze at any one time, most have siblings to share it with, and it rarely lasts for long.

In contrast, young women and men age 25–34 are truly squeezed between the time and money demands of simultaneously investing in education, finding and climbing the first rungs of the career ladder, acquiring a life partner, establishing a home, and having and caring for children. No other age group bears such a complex burden, and today's younger women are aware that the future costs to them of postponing any one of these roles are considerable.

EDUCATION, WORK, AND MARRIAGE AND CHILDREN

The interplay between education, employment, and marriage and children dominates the lives of today's women age 25–34. As these factors shift and affect each other, they create changes in the life cycle as well as in the family. It

Table I-5 • Women without Children by Age, Selected Years 1976–2000[1]

Year Born	Percentage Childless at Age				Age in 2000
	25–29	30–34	35–39	40–44	
1931–1935	—	—	—	10.2	65–70
1936–1940	—	—	10.5	10.1	60–64
1941–1945	—	15.6	12.1	11.4	55–59
1946–1950	30.8	19.8	16.7	16.0	50–54
1951–1955	36.8	26.2	17.7	17.5	45–49
1956–1960	41.5	25.7	19.7	19.0	40–44
1961–1965	42.1	26.7	20.1	—	35–39
1966–1970	43.8	28.1	—	—	30–34
1971–1975	44.2	—	—	—	25–29

[1]In 1976 (the earliest year for which these data are available), women who had been born between 1946 and 1949 were age 25–29.

Source: Census Bureau, *Fertility of American Women: June 2000*, 2001c, Table H1.

used to be that marriage and children drove women's employment and education choices. For many, perhaps most in this age group, it's the other way around now, while for others nothing has changed. The difference lies in this age group's perception, or valuation, of the benefits to be derived from increased investment in their human capital as well as in their opportunities to make these investments effectively.

EDUCATIONAL BACKGROUND

Women age 25–34 are the first group to come of age since Americans became aware of the increased economic importance of education in obtaining well-paying jobs. This awareness is at the heart of this group's intense role juggling. While women's biology concentrates their childbearing in these years, their economic success for decades to come depends on their investment in education and on maintaining and furthering that investment in the work world.

The difference in the educational profile of today's younger women and that of their mothers' generation is striking. The proportion of women who have not completed high school is barely half what it was in 1975, and the proportion with "some" college has nearly doubled. (This category includes women with associate degrees and postsecondary vocational training.) Moreover, three out of 10 younger women now have bachelor's degrees or higher (see Figure I-5).

Racial and ethnic differences in educational attainment are stark among these young women. Over half of young Asian women have a bachelor's degree or higher, as do more than a third of non-Hispanic white women. In contrast, only a tenth of Hispanic women and fewer than a fifth of black women have reached this important milestone.

Given the widespread public understanding that high school dropouts are handicapped in today's economy, it is no surprise that only small percentages of younger white women (5.2 percent) and Asian women (6.3 percent) have less than a high school diploma. For young black women, high school completion is becoming routine. Still, one in eight is a high school dropout. And it is dismaying that more than a third of younger Hispanics are in this situation (see Table I-6).

WORK

Over 80 percent of women age 25–34 were working in 1999. Among those who did not work, 14 percent gave as the reason that they were taking care of their home and family (commonly referred to as "homemaking"). This is

Figure I-5 • Educational Attainment of Women and Men Age 25–34, 1975 and 2000 (percent distributions)[1]

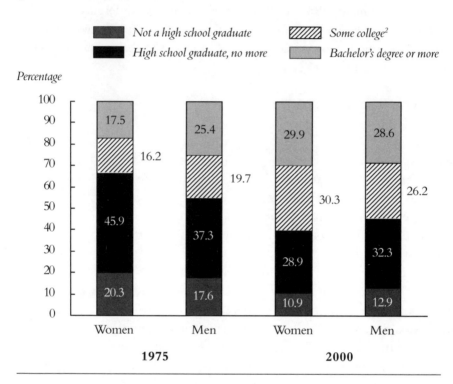

Source: Special tabulations of the March 1975 and March 2000 Current Population Surveys, prepared by Deirdre Gaquin for the Women's Research and Education Institute (WREI), 2001.

half the percentage of women who cited homemaking in 1975 (see Table I-7). (The proportion of men working declined slightly, from 97 to 94 percent, over this period.)

At the same time, only 11 percent of women age 35 and older in 2000 reported homemaking as their primary activity (not counting the 23 percent who said they were retired), indicating the concentration of domestic roles in the early adult ages. About two percent of women age 25–34 said schooling was their major activity, more than double the rate of 25 years earlier, while another two percent said they were ill or disabled.

Clearly, young women confront a broad array of sometimes conflicting roles. On one hand, their traditional family roles tend to be at peak intensity during this part of their lives. On the other hand, they need to invest in their

Table I-6 • Educational Attainment of Women and Men Age 25–34 by Race and Hispanic Origin, 2000 (percent distributions)[1]

	Not a High School Graduate	*High School Graduate, No More*	*Some College*[2]	*Bachelor's Degree or More*
Non-Hispanic white				
Women	5.2	28.5	30.8	35.5
Men	6.9	32.0	27.4	33.6
Non-Hispanic black				
Women	12.4	33.8	36.2	17.6
Men	11.2	42.1	28.5	18.1
Hispanic[3]				
Women	35.7	29.6	24.0	10.7
Men	41.2	30.5	19.7	8.6
Asian/Pacific Islander				
Women	6.3	17.8	24.6	51.3
Men	7.4	16.9	25.2	50.5
Native American				
Women	17.9	32.7	38.1	11.2
Men	25.9	37.4	22.2	14.5

[1]Percentages may not total 100.0 due to rounding.
[2]Includes two-year degrees.
[3]People of Hispanic origin may be of any race.

Source: Special tabulations of the March 1975 and March 2000 Current Population Surveys, prepared by Deirdre Gaquin for the Women's Research and Education Institute (WREI), 2001.

work lives in order to benefit later in the life cycle. One way for women to mitigate this contradiction is to limit their work experience by working part time, flexible schedules, or at home.

In 2000, 15 percent of employed women age 25–34 reported that they worked part time the previous year. This is roughly the same proportion as a quarter-century earlier. Part-time work in 2000 was more common for women in this age group than for other women; it was also nearly three times as common for women as for men in this age group. Similarly, as Chapter Two describes, flexible work schedules are relatively common for these young women, with nearly 20 percent reporting that they do some or all of their work at home.

However, most younger women do not want, are not able, or cannot afford to limit their work effort. In 2000, three in five women age 25–34 reported that they were employed full time, up from just one in three in 1975. (The increase

Table I-7 • Women Age 25–34 by Working Status and Reason for Not Working, 1975 and 2000 (percent distributions)[1]

	1975	2000
Worked previous year	63.2	80.9
Did not work previous year		
Caring for home or family	33.5	14.2
Ill or disabled	1.3	2.1
In school	0.8	1.9
Other	1.1	1.0
Total percentage	100.0	100.0
Total number (in thousands)	15,314	19,188

[1]Percentages may not total 100.0 due to rounding.

Source: Special tabulations of the March 1975 and March 2000 Current Population Surveys, prepared by Deirdre Gaquin for the Women's Research and Education Institute (WREI), 2001.

in the share of men in this age group who worked full time was less but still pronounced: from 76 percent to 84 percent.) In 1975, far more women age 25–34 said they were keeping house than said they were working full time.

Comparisons between 1975 and 2000 are inflected by differences across racial and ethnic groups, since the latter now account for a greater share of the population, especially among younger age groups. For instance, non-Hispanic white women are much more likely to work part time than are minority women. And Hispanic women, and to a lesser extent Asian women, are much less likely than non-Hispanic white women to be in the labor force.

These differences reflect the recent arrival of many people from distant countries and cultures. But they also reflect differences in education, family resources, cultural preferences, and employment barriers. For instance, black women have the greatest connection to the workforce of all women in the 25–34 age group: although they have the same labor force participation rates as non-Hispanic white women, black women are more likely to be employed full time. At the same time, black men have the lowest connection to the labor force of all men in this age group, with fewer than three in four employed full time.

FAMILY SITUATION

Women age 25–34 are more likely to work, no matter what their family situation, than women their age were in 1975. Even childless women who head their own households are slightly more likely to be working than was the case 25 years ago. Still, the most notable shift toward the work world is among women who have also chosen to marry and have children. In 1975, more than three-fourths of women in this age group had children, and over half of these mothers were not in the labor force. In 2000, only three-fifths of women in this age group had children, and all but 30 percent of these mothers were in the labor force.

Among childless married women in this age group, 85 percent were employed in 2000, up from 75 percent in 1975. The increase for married mothers was much larger: from less than 40 percent employed in 1975 to 65 percent employed in 2000. The increase was almost as pronounced for unmarried mothers maintaining their own household (who tended to be divorced or never married): from a little over half in 1975 to three-quarters in 2000.

Today, the tension between work and family works both ways, with some women postponing or even forgoing marriage and/or children in favor of work and career, while in the past they had postponed or forgone work and career in favor of marriage and children. Certainly the overwhelming majority of married women this age had children during both periods; the difference is that a smaller share of women were married in 2000. Research suggests that, these days, younger adults tend to marry when they are ready to have children, as society grants them the option of living with a partner without being married.

Not surprisingly, young women in unmarried partnerships are more likely to work than married women are. (The category of unmarried partnerships did not exist in 1975, as the phenomenon was less common.) Ninety percent of young women who are unmarried partners and have children are employed, as are nearly 80 percent of those who don't have children. About 70 percent have full-time employment, whether or not they have children (see Table I-8).

Part-time employment is highest for younger mothers when they are married or have partners. One in five women in this age group with children and a husband or partner is working part time. But marriage makes a difference. Fewer than half of young married mothers worked full time in 2000, and a third weren't in the labor force at all. In contrast, only one in 10 young mothers living with a partner was not in the labor force. Responses to questions in the National Survey of Families and Households have shown that unmarried partners tend to offer less support than husbands do when the children are not their own (Martin and Bumpass 1989).

The other group of young mothers with a large share outside the labor force—30 percent—is also in a potentially supportive situation, living with

Table I-8 • Employment Status of Women Age 25–34 by Household Relationship and Presence of Children, 1975 and 2000 (numbers in thousands)

	1975			2000		
	Total	With Children	Without Children	Total	With Children	Without Children
Wife in married-couple family	11,505	9,746	1,759	10,375	7,819	2,556
Percentage employed full time	27.6	21.6	61.0	52.8	45.5	75.2
Percentage employed part time	16.4	16.7	14.4	16.8	19.2	9.4
Percentage not in labor force	51.5	57.2	20.2	28.4	33.4	13.0
Unmarried householder[1]	2,436	1,506	930	4,901	2,526	2,375
Percentage employed full time	50.3	36.4	72.7	71.5	62.0	81.5
Percentage employed part time	15.5	16.1	14.6	11.1	12.8	9.3
Percentage not in labor force	28.0	40.1	8.4	13.3	19.4	6.8
Child or other relative of householder	1,108	509	599	2,256	748	1,508
Percentage employed full time	49.6	39.0	58.7	63.9	55.4	68.1
Percentage employed part time	12.1	11.4	12.7	10.8	11.0	10.7
Percentage not in labor force	31.7	40.7	24.1	21.9	29.9	18.0
Unmarried partner	(2)	(2)	(2)	663	111	552
Percentage employed full time	(2)	(2)	(2)	68.1	70.6	67.6
Percentage employed part time	(2)	(2)	(2)	12.5	19.2	11.2
Percentage not in labor force	(2)	(2)	(2)	14.9	10.2	15.9

[1] Includes never-married, formerly married, and separated women. [2] Data for unmarried partners not available for 1975.

Sources: Special tabulations of the March 1975 and March 2000 Current Population Surveys, prepared by Deirdre Gaquin for the Women's Research and Education Institute (WREI), 2001.

parents or other relatives. This living arrangement is also most common for childless younger women who are not in the labor force, either because they are continuing their education or because they need support for some other purpose. In contrast, young childless women who are maintaining their own households are most likely to be in the labor force and to be employed full time. Without a husband, partner, child, or other family member in the home, these women can concentrate on their economic role.

However, younger women who have children but lack husbands, partners, or other family members in the home need to fulfill multiple roles with little or no support. These younger mothers are not only likely to be in the workforce but to have a higher unemployment rate than other young mothers.

These patterns generally prevail across all racial and ethnic groups, but each group displays distinct differences. Young black wives have very high employment rates compared with other wives, especially if they are mothers. In general, mothers in this population group are more likely to be employed than most other mothers are, and those who are not employed tend to be living with a parent or another relative, or with a nonrelative, such as a friend or partner.

Young Hispanic mothers with family support, whether a husband, parent, or other relative, are far less likely to be employed than are other young mothers. In contrast, virtually all young childless Hispanic women who head their own households are employed. These women are breaking Hispanic traditions regarding both work and family. The same is true of young Asian women working and living on their own. However, young Asian mothers are far more likely to work than are young Hispanic mothers, married or not.

ECONOMIC STATUS

Education and family choices go a long way toward determining women's resources, both personal and familial, especially in terms of income. More diversity in these choices means that the standard measure of socioeconomic status—income—is also more diverse for women age 25–34 than ever before. In 2000, among women in this age group, those with the lowest household incomes were unmarried householders who were high school dropouts. These women's annual household income was only one-sixth that of women who were both college graduates and married, compared with more than one-fifth in 1975.

Since women who are married are less likely to work than those who are not, women's personal (as opposed to household) income is still highest in this age group for college graduates who are living on their own. However, education makes a much greater difference for young women's income than it used to. In 1975, single women householders who had not completed high school had an income nearly 40 percent of the income of women college graduates with the same living arrangement. By 2000, the income of single women householders was barely 25 percent of that of women with a college degree and a similar living arrangement.

In general, with or without higher education, married women had higher personal incomes on average in 2000 than in 1975. This fact reflects the rise in married women's employment as well as a general broadening of economic opportunities for women. At the same time, these broader opportunities mean that unmarried women are more likely to be able to support themselves, especially if they have invested in their education.

In this generation, where women and men tend to have roughly the same investment in education and work effort, the gap between women's and men's personal income is narrowing. Yet it is still significant. Looking at median personal income (from all sources), women age 25–34 only averaged 20 percent as much income as men their age in 1975, rising to 60 percent in 2000. This suggests that even well-educated women still improve their economic well-being through marriage, which in turn allows them to reduce their work effort, particularly when they have children.

Still, the data are unambiguous about the advantage that education confers on young women, particularly in the workplace but perhaps also in successful family outcomes, including opportunities for children. Whatever the choices they make about their multiple roles, women with more education have more opportunities from which to choose.

CONCLUSION

As they live the years between their twenty-fifth and thirty-fifth birthdays, today's younger women have a particular advantage over their mothers: a better understanding of their future, gained from their mothers' lives. When their mothers were in the 25–34 age group, they participated in the grand experiment often referred to as "having it all." That is, they sought to enjoy women's traditional roles while simultaneously exploiting their hard-won freedom to choose nontraditional opportunities.

Today's younger women have the same choices, but those who have the resources to choose one set of roles at a time do not have the same pressure: their mothers have shown them that women's increasingly longer lives provide the opportunity to "have it all" sequentially. The women who were age

25–34 in 1975 are the first to live a new midlife stage in which traditional gender roles are not very demanding. Their children are grown, and thanks to increases in life and health expectancy, their parents are largely still independent.

As a result, today's women age 45–64 are the first to have an extended working-age life stage without significant caregiving responsibilities (just as their mothers were the first to experience an extended retirement). These "20 new years," the product of twentieth-century health advances, were not anticipated by the women who are currently living them (Riche 2000). But today's younger women live their role-dense lives while watching their mothers adopt new, less complicated roles. With reasonable foresight and care, they can indeed "have it all."

NOTE

1. Unless otherwise noted, all data in this chapter come from special tabulations of the March 1975 and March 2000 Current Population Surveys, prepared by Deirdre Gaquin for the Women's Research and Education Institute (WREI). The Census Bureau conducts this survey each month for the Bureau of Labor Statistics so it can analyze and report unemployment across the nation. Each March the Census Bureau adds supplementary questions, known as the Annual Demographic File, so it can analyze demographic change among Americans, such as the ones described here.

Two

YOUNG WOMEN, EDUCATION, AND EMPLOYMENT

Marisa DiNatale and Stephanie Boraas

HIGHLIGHTS

THE DRAMATIC INCREASE in young women's educational attainment levels over the last 25 years and their growing presence in the workforce have changed the employment landscape and the meaning of what it is to be a woman age 25–34 today. Faced with opportunities not available to their counterparts in 1975, young women today are more likely to be in the labor force. They also have made significant headway in attaining higher-paying executive, managerial, and professional positions and in closing the earnings gap with men. Yet young women work more hours than they did a generation ago, and they continue to be disproportionately represented in such traditional "women's" occupations as kindergarten teachers and librarians. Key findings from this chapter include:

- About three-quarters of women age 25–34 were in the labor force in the year 2000, compared with a little over half in 1975.
- Young women today are more highly educated than their counterparts were in 1975. In 2000, 30 percent of women age 25–34 had completed four or more years of college, compared with 18 percent 25 years earlier.
- Young women have substantially closed the earnings gap with their male counterparts since 1979 (the first year for which comparable earnings data are available from the Current Population Survey). They earned 82 percent as much as young men in 2000 for full-time

work, compared with 68 percent in 1979. The shrinking earnings gap has many causes, including the shift of young women to higher-paying occupations and year-round work, their increasing educational attainment, and reduced incidences of gaps in their labor force participation. It's likely that these factors led to a rise in the real earnings of young women at the same time that young men were experiencing declines.

- Married women age 25–34, and particularly those with children, were far more likely to be in the labor force in 2000 than their counterparts were 25 years earlier.
- Young women were working more hours and more weeks out of the year in 1999 than their counterparts were 25 years ago. Black women were more likely than either white or Hispanic women to work full time and year round.
- In May 1997, 28 percent of women age 25–34—more than any other age group—had jobs with flexible schedules (those in which the beginning and ending times of work could be adjusted).
- Nearly one million women age 25–34 were displaced from a job between January 1997 and December 1999. When surveyed in February 2000, displaced young women were more than four times as likely as their male counterparts to have left the labor force.
- The vast majority of employed women age 25–34—83 percent—had health insurance coverage in February 2001. About 60 percent of women in this age group received it through their employers.
- Young black women who were working or looking for work were three times as likely as young white women to be living in poverty.
- Hispanic women age 25–34 were more likely than white women, but less likely than black women, to be part of the working poor.

INTRODUCTION

During the 1960s and 1970s, legislation and changing social mores dramatically altered young women's choices about their futures. Girls growing up in this period were influenced by both the conventions of their parents' generation and the new opportunities becoming available to them. In contrast, girls born in later years grew up in an era in which women were expected to combine market work and family responsibilities. Consequently, women age 25–34 in 2000 had a markedly different relationship to the labor market from their counterparts in 1975.

The first part of this chapter focuses on the major demographic and labor market indicators that are used to describe young women. These indicators show how young women and their relationship to the labor market have changed over the past quarter-century. The second part of the chapter focuses on issues facing young women in the labor market today.[1]

INDICATORS OF CHANGE

As a group, women age 25–34 in 2000 differed in a number of demographic and labor force characteristics from their counterparts of 1975.

EDUCATION

The educational attainment level of women age 25–34 improved dramatically between 1975 and 2000. In those 25 years, the share of women in this age group who had completed at least four years of college rose from 18 to 30 percent. At the same time, the share of men with that level of education edged up only three percentage points, to 29 percent. Meanwhile, the proportion of young women who had dropped out of high school fell from 20 percent to 11 percent (see Figure I-5 in Chapter One).

While white women continued to have the most schooling of the three major racial/ethnic groups in 2000, black women made large strides in educational attainment over the last quarter-century. In 1975, 32 percent of black women age 25–34 had completed fewer than four years of high school and just 10 percent had completed four or more years of college. In 2000, by contrast, just 13 percent of black women age 25–34 lacked a high school diploma, and 17 percent had college degrees.

Among young Hispanic women in the United States in 2000, however, a relatively high proportion (36 percent) had not completed high school. (This compares with about half in 1975.) About 11 percent had college degrees. More than half (55 percent) were foreign born and typically had limited education. In fact, in 2000, 50 percent of the foreign-born Hispanic women of this age group had not completed high school, compared with 19 percent of those born in the United States. Only nine percent had a bachelor's degree or higher, compared with 17 percent of those born in the United States.

The advances in educational attainment among young women during the last quarter-century were much sharper than those of their male counterparts. In 1975, the proportion of men age 25–34 with a college education exceeded that of their female contemporaries by a considerable margin. By 2000, however, the proportions of men and women in this age group who had college degrees were about equal. In the case of whites and Hispanics, women were slightly more likely to be college graduates than were men (see Table I-6 in Chapter One).

MARITAL STATUS AND MOTHERHOOD

Between 1975 and 2000, trends in marriage and family formation changed. Women age 25–34 in 2000 were less likely to be married than their counterparts were 25 years earlier. They were also less likely to be mothers. In 1975, more than three out of four women in this age group were married; by 2000, the proportion had dropped to three out of five. In addition, in 1975, just 11 percent had never married, with this proportion tripling, to 30 percent, by 2000 (Census Bureau 2001b).

The changing marital status of women also had an effect on family formation. In 1975, 76 percent of women age 25–34 had children. This proportion had declined to 60 percent by 2000. Also, as the age of childbearing rose, women in this group were far less likely to have older children but nearly as likely to have children under age three as their counterparts were a generation earlier (see Chapter One).

LABOR FORCE CHARACTERISTICS

Since 1975, the labor force participation rate (the proportion of the population that is either working or actively looking for work) of women age 25–34 has increased by about 20 percent. White women had the largest increase in participation, although black and Hispanic women also showed large gains (see Table II-1). In contrast, the labor force participation rate for men in the same age group drifted down from 95 to 93 percent, with black men showing a much more significant decline than whites.

The growing labor force participation rate of young women is related to a number of factors, the most prominent being their increasing rates of educational attainment and smaller likelihood of having married in their early twenties. In 1975, the median age at first marriage for women was 21.1 years; in 2000, it was 25.1 years (Census Bureau 2001a). A more detailed discussion of educational attainment and marital and family structure follows.

Labor force participation rates are strongly correlated with levels of educational attainment. In 2000, 86 percent of women age 25–34 with college degrees were in the labor force, compared with only 55 percent of those with less than a high school diploma, a difference of about 31 percentage points.

While the male labor force participation rate also correlated with education, the difference between those with a college degree and those with less

Table II-1 • Labor Force Participation of Women and Men Age 25–34 by Selected Demographic Characteristics, 1975 and 2000 (numbers are in thousands)[1,2]

Characteristic	Women				Men			
	Number		Participation Rate		Number		Participation Rate	
	1975	2000	1975	2000	1975	2000	1975	2000
Civilian labor force	8,304	14,787	54.2	77.1	13,692	17,091	95.3	93.3
Race and Hispanic origin[3]								
White	7,054	11,622	53.2	76.7	12,219	14,097	95.9	94.4
Black	1,083	2,298	62.8	80.6	1,216	1,984	91.2	87.7
Hispanic	384	1,784	46.6	63.6	686	2,658	94.1	94.1
Education[4]								
Not a high school graduate	1,260	1,141	40.8	54.7	2,371	2,053	92.3	86.0
High school diploma, no college	3,753	4,124	53.3	74.3	5,155	5,559	97.2	93.7
Some college/associate degree	1,434	4,592	57.5	79.0	2,638	4,474	93.8	94.3
Bachelor's degree or more	1,858	4,930	68.9	85.9	3,528	5,005	96.0	95.4
Marital status								
Married, spouse present	5,648	7,788	48.3	71.2	10,365	8,765	97.3	96.7
Unmarried, total	2,656	6,999	73.3	84.9	3,327	8,326	89.7	90.0
Never married	1,325	4,918	80.4	84.9	2,213	6,704	88.2	89.3
Divorced	796	1,295	76.8	87.7	626	991	92.7	94.4
Separated	486	734	57.9	81.7	471	612	92.8	92.2
Widowed	49	51	48.5	63.7	18	20	91.2	84.3

See footnotes at end of table.

(continued)

Table II-1 (continued)

| Characteristic | Women | | | | Men | | | |
| | Number | | Participation Rate | | Number | | Participation Rate | |
	1975	2000	1975	2000	1975	2000	1975	2000
Presence and age of children								
With children under age 18	5,281	8,054	45.4	70.1	(5)	6,855	(5)	96.5
Children age 6–17[6]	2,147	2,739	60.0	78.4	(5)	1,352	(5)	94.6
Children under age 6	3,134	5,315	38.9	66.5	(5)	5,504	(5)	96.9
Children under age 3	1,402	3,024	33.2	62.7	(5)	3,752	(5)	97.2
With no children under age 18	3,023	6,733	82.2	87.4	(5)	10,236	(5)	91.4

[1] Civilian population.

[2] Data for 1975 and 2000 are not precisely comparable because the Current Population Survey was redesigned in 1994.

[3] People of Hispanic origin may be of any race.

[4] Since 1992, data on educational attainment have been based on the highest diploma or degree received rather than the number of years of school completed. The 1975 equivalents of "not a high school graduate," "high school graduate, no college," "some college/associate degree," and "bachelor's degree or more" are "less than four years of high school completed," "four years of high school," "one to three years of college completed," and "four or more years of college," respectively.

[5] Data not available.

[6] None younger.

Sources: Bureau of Labor Statistics, Employment and Earnings, January 1976, Table 1, and January 2001, Table 5.

than a high school diploma was less pronounced. About 95 percent of young adult men with college degrees were in the labor force, compared with 86 percent of those with less than a high school education, a difference of only nine percentage points.

OCCUPATIONS

Women age 25–34 work in virtually every occupation, but they are more heavily represented in some occupations than in others (see Table II-2). Because of a change in the way occupations were classified in the Current Population Survey (CPS), a comparison with 1975 is not possible—1983 is the earliest year in which comparisons can be made. However, this analysis is still useful in examining the direction of any trends that may have emerged over the past couple of decades.

Since 1983, women have made headway into the higher-paying executive, administrative, and managerial occupations and into professional specialty occupations. They also are more likely to work in sales and service occupations.

Table II-2 • Employed Women and Men Age 25–34 by Occupation, 1983 and 2000 (percent distribution)[1]

Occupation	Women		Men	
	1983	*2000*	*1983*	*2000*
Executive, administrative, and managerial	9.2	15.5	11.4	12.8
Professional specialty	18.5	20.5	13.0	14.7
Technicians and related support	4.7	4.4	3.9	3.5
Sales	9.9	11.5	10.5	10.8
Administrative support, including clerical	30.2	22.6	5.9	5.8
Service	14.9	16.3	8.0	9.9
Precision production, craft, and repair	2.5	2.0	22.2	19.6
Operators, fabricators, and laborers	9.1	6.4	20.7	19.7
Farming, forestry, and fishing	1.0	0.8	4.3	3.2
Total percentage	100.0	100.0	100.0	100.0
Total employed (in thousands)	12,540	14,006	16,216	16,494

[1]Percentages may not total 100.0 due to rounding.

Sources: Bureau of Labor Statistics, *Labor Force Statistics Derived from the Current Population Survey, 1948–87*, 1988, Table B-18, and unpublished data from the 2000 Current Population Surveys (annual averages).

While the latter tend to be lower-paying jobs, men age 25–34 also are increasingly likely to be in these occupations.

Women made up 46 percent of all employed 25–34-year-olds in 2000, up from 44 percent in 1983. In both years, they represented about 80 percent of all workers in this age group in administrative support (clerical) jobs. The concentration of women in service occupations increased over the time period, from 59 percent of the total number of workers in such occupations in 1983 to 65 percent in 2000 (see Table II-3). In contrast, women continued to represent a smaller portion of employed 25–34-year-olds in manufacturing-related occupations—such as precision production, craft, and repair—where they comprised only about eight percent of workers in both years.

Among young workers in executive/managerial, professional, and technical occupations overall, about half were women in 2000. While the proportions of young women in professional specialty and technical occupations were about the same in 1983, there was considerable movement of women into executive, administrative, and managerial occupations over the next 17 years. Young women made up only about 38 percent of total employment in this age group and occupation in 1983. By 2000, however, the percentage had increased to 51 percent.

Nonetheless, it should be noted that, within these broad groups, women continued to be concentrated in some fairly traditional "women's" occupations. For instance, in 2000, women age 16 and older made up about 99 percent of kindergarten and preschool teachers, 85 percent of librarians, and 84 percent of legal assistants. These proportions were roughly the same in 1983. In contrast, while women overall still are underrepresented in some professional occupations, they have made substantial inroads. For example, the proportion of lawyers and engineers who are women has about doubled since 1983—to about 30 percent of lawyers and 10 percent of engineers—and those proportions are even higher among younger cohorts.

While women made up more than half of 25–34-year-olds in managerial and professional jobs in 2000, young black and Hispanic women were underrepresented in these occupations relative to their shares of total employment (see Table II-3). Black women represented only about six percent of total employment in executive, administrative, and managerial occupations, and Hispanic women held only four percent of these jobs in 2000. The corresponding figures for 1983 were two percent and one percent, respectively.

EARNINGS

In 1979 (the first year for which comparable data are available), median usual weekly earnings of full-time wage-and-salary workers age 25–34 were $440

Table II-3 • Employed People Age 25–34 by Occupation, Sex, Race, and Hispanic Origin, 2000

			Women		
				Percentage of Employed Who Are	
Occupation	Total Employed (in thousands)	As a Percentage of Total Employed	White	Black	Hispanic[1]
Total 25–34	30,501	45.9	36.2	7.1	5.6
Executive, administrative, and managerial	4,281	50.6	41.9	5.7	4.1
Professional specialty	5,300	54.2	44.0	5.9	3.3
Technicians and related support	1,196	51.8	41.6	7.4	5.2
Sales	3,386	47.4	38.4	6.4	5.3
Administrative support, including clerical	4,129	76.8	60.0	13.5	10.0
Service, private household	118	94.1	80.5	11.0	42.4
Protective service	632	16.6	10.1	6.0	1.3
Service, except protective and household	3,157	65.3	48.4	13.9	10.8
Precision production, craft, and repair	3,514	8.1	6.3	1.1	1.6
Machine operators, assemblers, and inspectors	1,743	34.0	24.7	6.0	9.2
Transportation and material moving	1,235	8.9	5.3	3.3	1.0
Handlers, equipment cleaners, helpers, and laborers	1,176	16.8	11.7	4.4	4.2
Farming, forestry, and fishing	634	17.4	16.6	0.5	5.5

[1]People of Hispanic origin may be of any race.

Source: Bureau of Labor Statistics, unpublished data from the 2000 Current Population Survey (annual averages).

for women and $653 for men (in 2000 inflation-adjusted dollars). During the 1980s and early 1990s, inflation-adjusted earnings of women age 25–34 increased slowly, while the earnings of their male counterparts decreased relatively rapidly (see Figure II-1). Since about 1993, however, changes in the earnings of men and women generally have been of similar size and have moved in the same direction. Despite the upturn in earnings that occurred for both men and women during the 1990s, men's earnings ($603 in 2000) remained below their inflation-adjusted 1979 level, while women's earnings ($493) rose. As a result of these trends, young women in 2000 earned approximately 81.8 percent as much as their male counterparts, compared with 67.4 percent in 1979.

Earnings of both women and men are higher for union members than for non-union members. Data from the CPS on union membership show that in 2000, median usual weekly earnings for women age 25–34 who worked full time and were not members of a union or represented by a union[2] were $483. Female union members in this age group saw earnings of $579 per week—a 20 percent increase. Men in this age group realized less of an earnings gain from joining a union—15 percent.

MARITAL STATUS AND MOTHERHOOD

Never-married women and divorced women had the highest labor force participation rates among women age 25–34 in both 1975 and 2000. Since 1975, however, the gap in the participation rates between never-married and divorced women and those who married has narrowed substantially. During that period, the labor force participation rate changed little for never-married women and grew by only about 11 percentage points for divorced women. In contrast, the participation rate for married women (spouse present) jumped by about 23 percentage points (see Table II-1).

In both 1975 and 2000, women age 25–34 who had no children under 18 were considerably more likely to be in the labor force than were those who were mothers. However, while the participation rate for childless women changed little over this period, the rate for women with children under age 18 grew by about 25 percentage points, to 70 percent in 2000. In fact, the labor force participation rate for women with children under age three almost doubled over the period, growing from 33 percent in 1975 to 63 percent in 2000.

While mothers age 25–34 were less likely to be labor force participants than their childless counterparts were, the reverse was true for men. Fathers in this age group were somewhat more likely to be in the labor force than were men with no children. Despite the fact that the labor force participa-

Figure II-1 • Median Usual Weekly Earnings of Full-Time Wage-and-Salary Workers Age 25–34 by Sex, 1979–2000 (in constant 2000 dollars)

2000 Dollars

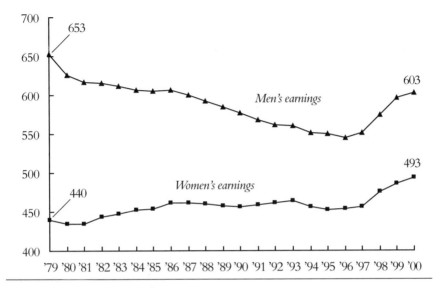

Source: Bureau of Labor Statistics, *Highlight of Women's Earnings in 2000*, 2001c, Table 13.

tion rates of mothers grew rapidly between 1975 and 2000, these rates still remain well below those of fathers. Clearly, raising children continues to have a greater impact on mothers' working lives than it does on fathers'.

UNEMPLOYMENT

In 2000, the unemployment rate for women age 25–34 was little different from that of men—4.0 percent compared with 3.4 percent, respectively. Both rates were at their lowest points in 25 years (see Figure II-2). A quarter of a century earlier, however, women's unemployment exceeded that of men by a little over two percentage points. The gap virtually disappeared in 1980, when men's unemployment shot up in response to a short but sharp recession, while women's unemployment did not rise as rapidly. The gap has remained quite narrow ever since, although the rate during recessionary periods has jumped much more sharply for men than it has for women.

Typically, economic downturns have a greater impact on men than they do on women because men are more likely to work in industries such as manufacturing and construction that are highly sensitive to changes in the business cycle. Women, on the other hand, tend to work in industries such

Figure II-2 • Unemployment Rates of Women and Men Age 25–34 , 1975–2000

Unemployment Rate

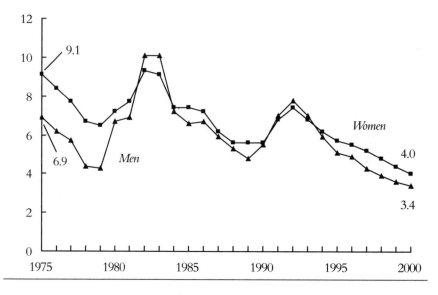

Sources: Bureau of Labor Statistics, *Employment and Earnings*, January 1976 through January 2001.

as services and government that are somewhat insulated from business cycles. Consequently, economic swings tend to be more evident in men's unemployment trends and more muted in women's.

WORK SCHEDULES

Young women spent more time during the year working in 1999 (the most recent year for which work experience data are available) than they did in 1975. Table II-4 shows that 81 percent of women age 25–34 worked at some time in 1999, compared with 64 percent in 1975. Moreover, of those with work experience, about 63 percent worked full time and year round in 1999, compared with less than half (46 percent) in 1975.[3]

Average weekly hours for young women at work in nonagricultural industries increased by 2.5 hours over the last quarter-century, rising from 35.4 in 1976 to 37.9 in 2000, while men's average weekly hours grew only slightly, from 43.2 hours to 43.9 hours. The increase in average hours worked by young women resulted from an increase in the number of those working full time. It also reflects both a decrease in the proportion of young women with short workweeks and an increase in the proportion with very long work-

Table II-4 • Women Age 25–34 with Work Experience by Race, Hispanic Origin, and Marital Status, 1975 and 1999 (numbers are in thousands)

| | 1975 | | | | 1999 | | | |
| | | | Percentage with Work Experience Who Usually Worked Full Time | | | | Percentage with Work Experience Who Usually Worked Full Time | |
	Total with Work Experience	As a Percentage of Population	Total	50–52 Weeks	Total with Work Experience	As a Percentage of Population	Total	50–52 Weeks
All races, total	10,141	63.9	74.3	45.5	15,517	80.9	80.3	62.9
Married, spouse present	6,936	58.4	68.8	38.3	8,372	76.5	75.7	57.6
Married, spouse absent	91	73.4	79.1	44.0	220	82.1	85.0	60.0
Widowed	65	59.1	84.6	46.2	51	63.0	76.5	60.8
Divorced	1,013	81.5	87.0	59.3	1,319	89.3	86.2	70.4
Separated	483	66.9	79.1	55.1	512	81.3	86.6	65.4
Never married	1,553	86.4	88.6	68.8	5,044	87.1	85.7	69.7
White, total	8,634	62.9	72.3	44.2	12,234	80.8	78.9	61.9
Married, spouse present	6,170	57.3	66.8	37.0	7,188	76.5	74.1	56.2
Married, spouse absent	67	72.0	77.6	41.8	156	83.9	82.7	57.7
Widowed	46	59.7	89.1	54.3	33	57.9	69.7	57.6
Divorced	849	81.6	87.3	58.5	1,086	89.2	86.1	71.4
Separated	296	70.3	77.0	43.2	342	79.4	86.5	63.7
Never married	1,205	90.5	88.4	71.1	3,429	88.8	85.7	70.7

(continued)

Table II-4 (continued)

| | 1975 | | | | 1999 | | | |
| | | | Percentage with Work Experience Who Usually Worked Full Time | | | | Percentage with Work Experience Who Usually Worked Full Time | |
	Total with Work Experience	As Percentage of Population	Total	50–52 Weeks	Total with Work Experience	As Percentage of Population	Total	50–52 Weeks
Black, total	1,267	70.4	85.6	53.0	2,387	83.8	86.9	70.0
Married, spouse present	615	71.6	86.2	50.4	725	82.7	86.6	73.0
Married, spouse absent	22	78.6	86.4	50.0	37	75.5	91.7	59.5
Widowed	17	56.7	70.6	23.5	18	78.3	88.9	66.7
Divorced	149	79.3	85.9	61.7	181	88.3	87.8	66.9
Separated	179	60.9	74.4	46.2	153	86.0	89.5	71.9
Never married	285	71.3	86.7	56.8	1,273	83.9	86.5	68.9
Hispanic, total[1]	(2)	(2)	(2)	(2)	1,844	65.7	82.2	60.0
Married, spouse present	(2)	(2)	(2)	(2)	1,038	60.2	80.3	55.4
Married, spouse absent	(2)	(2)	(2)	(2)	43	71.7	83.7	67.4
Widowed	(2)	(2)	(2)	(2)	11	64.7	90.9	54.5
Divorced	(2)	(2)	(2)	(2)	109	77.9	87.2	62.4
Separated	(2)	(2)	(2)	(2)	94	65.3	86.2	59.6
Never married	(2)	(2)	(2)	(2)	549	76.1	83.7	67.9

[1]People of Hispanic origin may be of any race.
[2]Data not available.

Sources: Bureau of Labor Statistics, unpublished data from the March 1976 and March 2000 Current Population Surveys.

weeks. In 1976, only about seven percent of young women worked 49 hours or more per week, and 21 percent worked fewer than 30 hours. By 2000, the proportion working very long workweeks had nearly doubled to 13 percent, while the proportion working fewer than 30 hours per week decreased to 17 percent.

Black women age 25–34 are more likely to work full time, year round, than are white women. In 1999, about 70 percent of the young black women who had work experience worked full time, year round, compared with 62 percent of their white counterparts. (The comparable proportion for Hispanic women was 60 percent.) In 1975, the proportions of those working full time, year round, were 53 percent for black women and 44 percent for white women.

MULTIPLE JOBHOLDING

Compared with young women in 1975, women age 25–34 in 2001 were more likely to hold two or more jobs. About six percent of all employed women in May 2001 held more than one job, compared with three percent 25 years earlier (see Table II-5). Interestingly, the multiple-jobholding rate for men in the 25–34-year-old age group was lower in 2001 than in 1975, and, whereas men were twice as likely as women to hold more than one job in 1975, there was little difference in these proportions in 2000.

CURRENT LABOR MARKET ISSUES

Throughout the 1980s and 1990s, the Bureau of Labor Statistics (BLS) developed measures for such labor force concepts as contingent and alternative work arrangements, worker displacement, and pension and health insurance coverage. Although these measures did not exist in 1975, a discussion of these work arrangements paints a broader picture of the labor market in which young women participate today.

ALTERNATIVE WORK ARRANGEMENTS
AND CONTINGENT WORKERS

In recent years, workers in alternative arrangements and contingent workers have become the focus of debate. (See box for definitions of alternative work arrangements and contingent workers.) Critics devalue the jobs that characterize these arrangements because they typically provide lower pay and lower rates of employer-provided pension and health care coverage (Jorgensen

Table II-5 • Multiple Jobholders Age 25–34 by Sex, May 1975 and May 2001
(numbers are in thousands)

| | 1975 | | | 2001 | | |
| | *Total Employed* | Multiple Jobholders | | *Total Employed* | Multiple Jobholders | |
		Number	*Percentage of Employed*		*Number*	*Percentage of Employed*
Women	7,574	248	3.3	13,680	781	5.7
Men	12,798	850	6.6	16,215	901	5.6

Sources: Bureau of Labor Statistics, unpublished data from the May 1975 and May 2001 Current Population Surveys.

1999). Some researchers, on the other hand, point out that such jobs may offer women flexibility and convenience that may not be available with traditional work arrangements. Also, there is some evidence that these arrangements may provide jobs to people who would otherwise be unemployed (Bureau of Labor Statistics 2001a, 1996b). In addition, it is important not to generalize about these types of jobs. For example, as pointed out in recent BLS analyses, while nearly half of on-call workers and temporary help agency workers would prefer regular employment, most consultants and independent contractors prefer their current arrangement. And pay, benefits, and other aspects of the jobs differ greatly among the various types of alternative arrangements.

In 1995, the BLS began collecting data on the prevalence of alternative work arrangements in a supplement to the CPS.[4] Data from the supplement clearly indicate that the incidence of such work arrangements is not widespread. Only about six percent of women age 25–34 are employed in the four alternative work arrangements, the most common being independent contracting (see Table II-6). In fact, since 1995, the proportion of young women working in alternative arrangements has edged down.[5]

Perhaps the arrangement that has received the most attention is the temporary help arrangement. This is largely because temporary help agency workers have been found to have the lowest median weekly earnings of all the arrangements and the lowest rates of health and pension benefit coverage.[6] While only a very small proportion of all employed women age 25–34 were temporary help agency workers, black and Hispanic women were somewhat more likely to be employed in this arrangement than white women were.

In contrast, young black and Hispanic women were somewhat less likely to be independent contractors than white women were. One interesting

---

ALTERNATIVE WORK ARRANGEMENTS

The Bureau of Labor Statistics defines four types of alternative work arrangements:

1. *Independent contractors:* These include consultants, freelance workers, and independent contractors, regardless of whether they are wage-and-salary workers or self-employed.
2. *On-call workers:* These include persons who are called into work only when they are needed.
3. *Temporary help agency workers:* These include workers who are paid by a temporary help agency but work temporarily at a client site.
4. *Contract company workers:* These workers are employees of a contract company who usually work for only one customer and at that customer's work site.

---

difference between male and female independent contractors is that men in this arrangement earn, on average, more than men in traditional arrangements do. Female independent contractors, on the other hand, earn less on average than their counterparts in traditional arrangements. Analysis of the data has shown that this is most likely due to the high percentage of female independent contractors who work part time.

Contingent workers are defined as those who do not have an explicit or implicit contract for long-term employment. The BLS defines three measures of contingent employment. The broadest measure and the one most cited, definition three, includes all wage-and-salary workers who do not expect their jobs to last, plus self-employed persons and independent contractors who have been employed in these arrangements for a year or less and expect to remain in them for a year or less.[7] (All the statements in this chapter relating to contingent work are based on definition three.)

As is the case with alternative work arrangements, the proportion of young women who are contingent workers is quite small and has been falling since the survey was first conducted in 1995. The percentages of white and black women age 25–34 who were likely to be contingent workers was roughly equal (about four percent for each), while Hispanic women were slightly more likely to be in this arrangement (6.5 percent). On average, contingent workers have lower pay and benefit coverage than workers do in traditional arrangements. In addition, because contingent workers view their jobs as short term, they may have an unstable employment arrangement and little attachment to their employers.

Table II-6 • Women Age 25–34 in Alternative and Traditional Work Arrangements and Contingent and Noncontingent Arrangements by Race and Hispanic Origin, February 2001 (percent distributions)[1]

	Workers in Arrangement as a Percentage of Employed Women Age 25–34			
Arrangement	Total	White	Black	Hispanic[2]
Contingent[3]	4.0	4.0	4.1	6.5
Noncontingent	96.0	96.0	95.9	93.4
Total percentage[4]	100.0	100.0	100.0	100.0
Alternative work arrangements				
Independent contractors	3.9	4.2	1.6	2.7
On-call	0.8	0.8	0.7	1.0
Temporary help agency	1.3	0.9	3.7	2.3
Contract firms	0.2	0.3	—	0.2
Traditional work arrangements	93.8	93.9	94.0	93.8
Total percentage	100.0	100.0	100.0	100.0

[1]Excludes day laborers.
[2]People of Hispanic origin may be of any race.
[3]Refers to those who fall under estimate 3 of contingency. Estimate 3 is the broadest measure of contingency and includes those who do not expect their job to last.
[4]Percentages may not total 100.0 due to rounding.

Source: Bureau of Labor Statistics, unpublished data from the February 2001 Current Population Survey.

WORK AT HOME AND FLEXIBLE SCHEDULES

Flexible work schedules are one way in which women address the challenge of meeting both work and family responsibilities. According to information collected in a May 1997 supplement to the CPS, about three million women age 25–34 who worked full time held jobs that allowed flexibility in their work schedules. (These are the most recent data available on the prevalence of flexible work hours and work at home.) Since altering the beginning and ending hours of work is often a requirement of part-time work, the following discussion of workers with flexible schedules is limited to those who usually work full time. In May 1997, about 28 percent of women age 25–34 reported that they had a flexible schedule on their job. This was about the same proportion as men in this age group (29 percent). Interestingly, women in this age group were more likely than those in other age groups to be able to vary their work hours (Bureau of Labor Statistics 2001b).

About 18 percent of all women age 25–34 who were employed during the survey reference period did at least some work at home. Of these, only about 29 percent of young women did so for pay, however. This percentage was only slightly higher than for young men (22 percent). The overwhelming majority of young women who worked at home were taking work home from the office for which they were not paid. The majority worked only partly at home, with just four percent reporting that they worked exclusively from home. Young women were slightly more likely to work at home than were men in the same age group (see Table II-7).

The 1997 CPS supplement showed that the prevalence of work at home among younger women differed greatly depending on race and Hispanic origin. While 20 percent of white women did some work at home, only 11 percent of Hispanic women and eight percent of black women in the same age group reported working at home.

Table II-7 • People Age 25–34 at Work by Prevalence of Working at Home, Sex, Race, and Hispanic Origin, May 1997 (numbers are in thousands)[1,2]

At Work	Women		Men	
	Number	*Percentage*	*Number*	*Percentage*
Total	13,792	100.0	16,414	100.0
Reporting work at home	2,498	18.2	2,358	14.5
Primary job partly at home	1,949	14.2	2,172	13.2
Primary job entirely at home	549	4.0	186	1.1
White	11,165	100.0	13,703	100.0
Reporting work at home	2,230	20.0	2,122	15.5
Black	1,850	100.0	1,735	100.0
Reporting work at home	151	8.2	108	6.2
Hispanic origin[3]	1,434	100.0	2,280	100.0
Reporting work at home	158	11.0	133	5.8

[1]Data are for workers whose primary jobs are in nonagricultural industries.
[2]Percentages are based on unpublished data on the number of people at work who responded to the question about work at home.
[3]People of Hispanic origin may be of any race.

Source: Bureau of Labor Statistics, unpublished data from the May 1997 Current Population Survey.

WORKER DISPLACEMENT

Nearly one million women age 25–34 lost or left their jobs between January 1997 and December 1999 because their plant or company closed or moved, there was insufficient work to do, or their positions or shifts were abolished.

In the latest CPS supplement on displaced workers, those who were displaced between January 1997 and December 1999 were asked questions about their employment status in February 2000. About 86 percent of the young women who were displaced said they were back in the labor force, compared with about 97 percent of their male counterparts. Women age 25–34 were the most likely of all displaced female workers to be re-employed. Moreover, of all displaced female workers age 25–54 (the prime working-age group), 25–34-year-olds were the least likely to be unemployed at the time of the survey. Young white women who had been displaced were more likely to be re-employed in February 2000 and less likely to be unemployed or out of the labor force than either their black or Hispanic counterparts.

The fact that young women were more likely than young men to have left the labor force after being displaced may mean that some women took the opportunity to begin a family or to pursue personal goals that did not involve work. The movement out of the labor market comes with a price, however. Research has shown that when women leave the labor force for extended periods of time to pursue family responsibilities, they return to lower wages that never quite catch up to the earnings potential of those who never left the workforce (Kletzer and Fairlie 2001).

WORKING POOR

For many women, economic gains over the past 25 years have narrowed the earnings gap with men and have led to more economic and financial independence. Nonetheless, nearly one million women age 25–34 in the labor force were classified as working poor in 1999 (see Table II-8). These are women who were in the labor force (working or looking for work) for at least 27 weeks in 1999 but whose income fell below the poverty threshold.[8] Women age 25–34 were somewhat more likely to be among the working poor than were their male counterparts in 1999 (seven percent versus five percent).

Black women of this age were far more likely to be among the working poor than were white or Hispanic women. Nearly 16 percent of the young black women who had been in the labor force for at least 27 weeks in 1999 were considered to be below the poverty level. This rate was nearly three times the rate for their white counterparts. A little over 10 percent of young Hispanic women were classified as working poor.

In contrast to young black women, black men in this age group were no more likely to be among the working poor than were white men (five per-

Table II-8 • People Age 25–34 in the Labor Force for 27 Weeks or More by Poverty Status, Race, and Hispanic Origin, 1999 (numbers are in thousands)

| | People Age 25–34 | | |
	Total	*Women*	*Men*
In labor force for			
27 weeks or more, total	30,695	13,967	16,728
White	24,839	10,975	13,865
Black	4,096	2,197	1,899
Hispanic[1]	4,178	1,620	2,558
Below poverty level	1,835	983	852
White	1,290	582	707
Black	433	340	93
Hispanic	486	172	315
Poverty rate[2]	6.0	7.0	5.1
White	5.2	5.3	5.1
Black	10.6	15.5	4.9
Hispanic	11.6	10.6	12.3

[1]People of Hispanic origin may be of any race.
[2]Number below the poverty level as a percentage of the total in the labor force for 27 weeks or more.

Source: Bureau of Labor Statistics, *Profile of the Working Poor, 1999*, 2001d, Table 2.

cent). (However, significant numbers of black men in this age group did not work for 27 weeks or more in 1999.) Hispanic men, however, were more than twice as likely to be among the working poor as were either white or black men.

HEALTH INSURANCE AND PENSION PLAN COVERAGE

Monetary earnings are only part of a worker's compensation. Health insurance and pensions are two other important components.

The rising costs of health care and prescription drugs in the United States have made health insurance a vital necessity for most people. While 83 percent of women age 25–34 who are wage-and-salary workers have health insurance from some source, young women in this age group are the most likely to be uninsured of all women age 25 and over (see Chapter Three). These data on health insurance and pension coverage come from the February 2001 supplement to the CPS. Although the rates of coverage for white and black women are close, white women are more likely than both their black and Hispanic counterparts to have coverage (see Table II-9).

About 60 percent of female wage-and-salary workers age 25–34 received health insurance through their main job.[9] Black women were the most likely to receive health insurance through their employer, followed by white and Hispanic women. Less than half of all Hispanic women received health insurance through their main job.

Pension plans—in the form of an employer-provided retirement plan, individual retirement account (IRA), or Keogh plan—are essential for future financial security. About half of all female wage-and-salary workers age 25–34 had a pension plan in February 2001. As with health insurance, the rates for white and black women were quite similar, at 50 percent and 48 percent respectively, while only 38 percent of Hispanic women reported having a pension plan.

Table II-9 • Female Wage-and-Salary Workers Age 25–34 by Health Insurance Coverage and Pension Coverage, February 2001 (numbers are in thousands)

Female Wage-and-Salary Workers	Total	White	Black	Hispanic[1]
Total	12,964	10,209	2,029	1,690
With health insurance coverage	10,775	8,555	1,622	1,160
Percentage of total	83.1	83.8	79.9	68.6
With coverage through main job	7,766	6,068	1,233	802
Percentage of total	59.9	59.4	60.8	47.5
With pension coverage	6,423	5,116	964	639
Percentage of total	49.5	50.1	47.5	37.8

[1]People of Hispanic origin may be of any race.

Source: Bureau of Labor Statistics, unpublished data from the February 2001 Current Population Survey.

CONCLUSION

Young women today face many of the same career choices and challenges as their peers did 25 years ago. While decisions about school, family, marriage, and careers often factor into one another, it is clear that today's young women are making somewhat different choices. In particular, they are spending more time at market work than their predecessors did. As a result, more women today are having to balance their roles as wives and mothers with their jobs.

As the above statistics indicate, compared with their counterparts in 1975, women age 25–34 today, particularly those who are married and have children, are much more likely to participate in the labor force. They also are more likely to have gone to college, to work more hours, and to pursue careers in higher-paying occupations. These decisions and opportunities, while rendering young women better off financially than they were 25 years ago, also present them with new and often difficult challenges as they attempt to prioritize their lives around work, marriage, and children.

Although women age 25–34 as a group earn more money (in real terms) today than they did in 1975, black and Hispanic women still lack parity with white women in earnings and benefits. Thus, while young women in general have made significant progress over the past quarter-century in gaining parity in the workforce, a significant gap remains, particularly for minority women.

NOTES

1. Most of the data in this chapter were derived from the Current Population Survey (CPS), a monthly sample survey of households conducted by the U.S. Census Bureau for the Bureau of Labor Statistics. For more information regarding the Current Population Survey, see *Current Population Survey: Design and Methodology*, Bureau of Labor Statistics Technical Paper 63, 2000. Where the CPS did not provide complete information, other sources were used.
2. Refers to members of a labor union or employee association similar to a union as well as to workers who report no union affiliation but whose jobs are covered by a union or an employee association contract.
3. Full-time, year-round workers are those who worked at least 50 weeks out of the calendar year and worked full time (35 hours or more) for the majority of weeks that they worked.
4. The first supplement on Contingent and Alternative Work Arrangements was conducted in February 1995. Subsequent supplements were conducted in February of 1997, 1999, and 2001.
5. In the February 1995 and 1997 Contingent and Alternative Work Arrangements supplements to the CPS, 7.5 percent of employed young women were working in one of the four alternative arrangements. In February 1999 and in February 2001, the percentage edged down to 6.3 percent.
6. In the February 1999 supplement, full-time female temporary help agency workers age 16 and over earned a median weekly salary of $331, compared with $474 for women in traditional arrangements. Earnings data for workers with traditional arrangements were not collected in the February 2001 supplement.
7. For a further discussion of BLS's estimates of contingency, see Bureau of Labor Statistics (1996a).

8. For information about how poverty is determined, see *Poverty in the United States: 1999* (Census Bureau 2000). For persons living with family members, the earnings thresholds used to define poverty status are defined in terms of total family income, including the earnings of other family members as well as income from other sources. For persons living alone or with nonrelatives, the earnings thresholds are based solely on their personal income.
9. Note that others might have been offered health insurance by their employers but declined coverage because they were covered by a spouse's policy or for other reasons.

Three

BABY BOOM TO GENERATION X: PROGRESS IN YOUNG WOMEN'S HEALTH*

Alina Salganicoff, Barbara Wentworth,
and Liberty Greene

HIGHLIGHTS

Overall, the health profile of young women today shows that significant gains have been made over the last 25 years—and that there is still much room for improvement. Changes in national policy, advances in science and medical research, and important shifts in culture and society have had a profound influence on women's health and access to care. This chapter examines the health and well-being of women age 25–34 today and discusses how these factors have changed over the last generation. Key findings from the chapter include:

*This chapter was undertaken with support of the Henry J. Kaiser Family Foundation, an independent national health care philanthropy that serves as a nonpartisan source of facts and analysis for policymakers, the media, the health care community, and the general public. The foundation is not associated with Kaiser Permanente or Kaiser Industries. The statements made and the views expressed are those of the authors and do not necessarily reflect those of the Foundation. The authors would like to thank Tina Hoff for her conceptual contributions to this chapter. We also appreciate the research guidance provided by Zoe Beckerman and Melissa Moore and the editorial assistance provided by Joan Strader.

- In the past 25 years, the share of young women with high cholesterol or hypertension has fallen, but the share of those who are overweight or obese has risen. Fewer than half of young women in the United States participate in regular physical activity and get adequate nutrition.

- Mental health conditions that disproportionately affect young women include major and postpartum depression, anxiety, and eating disorders. An estimated one in five women will experience a period of major depression in her lifetime, while an estimated one percent will be affected by anorexia nervosa and an estimated one to three percent will be affected by bulimia nervosa.

- Compared to 25 years ago, women today delay marriage and childbearing but initiate sexual activity earlier and have more sexual partners over the course of their lives.

- Overall contraceptive use has only increased slightly in the past 20 years, despite the availability of new and safer contraceptives. Condom use has doubled in this period, largely in response to the human immunodeficiency virus (HIV).

- Women now account for almost a quarter of new cases of HIV, up from seven percent in 1986. Women of color, particularly black and Hispanic women, have been disproportionately affected by this epidemic. Acquired immune deficiency syndrome (AIDS) is the leading cause of death among black women age 25–34.

- Since 1982, the overall rate of infertility has fallen for women. In 1995, 17 percent of women age 25–34 sought assistance with fertility testing, diagnosis, or treatment.

- Over the past 25 years, maternal and infant health has generally improved. Maternal and infant mortality has fallen significantly, and prenatal care use has increased due to public education and expansion of private and public coverage. Despite overall improvements, racial and ethnic disparities in maternal and infant mortality and prenatal care persist.

- The majority of young women get health coverage through employer-sponsored insurance. A sizable minority, mostly low-income women, are covered by Medicaid. Overall, one in five women age 25–34 is uninsured.

- Coverage rates among women of different races, ethnicities, and income levels can vary significantly. White and black women are most likely to have care through their own employer; Hispanic women have much lower rates of employer-based coverage and are the most likely of all three groups to be uninsured.

- In the last 25 years, managed care has become the dominant health care arrangement of both private and public coverage. Today, about three-quarters of women are enrolled in managed care plans.
- Most young women get preventive screening services, such as Pap smears, breast exams, and blood pressure checks. Less than half, however, are given blood cholesterol tests. Uninsured women have significantly lower levels of health care utilization and face formidable barriers to care.
- Women age 25–34 face a broad range of barriers to health care. Nearly one-third report they did not get needed care in the past year. A large minority of young women report that they lack control of decisions affecting their care and have concerns about the quality of care they receive. Cost is a barrier in filling prescriptions for one in five insured women and for nearly four in 10 uninsured women.
- During health care visits, physicians often do not raise topics that are important to sexually active young women. Only about a quarter of young women discussed alcohol and drug use, sexual history, and ways to protect themselves against sexually transmitted diseases (STDs) and HIV during their last gynecological visit.

INTRODUCTION

The early 1970s were a pivotal time for women's health in the United States. These years witnessed the awakening of a new movement among women. Women health care consumers were no longer willing to sit in the shadows while doctors, lawmakers, and manufacturers made unilateral decisions on their behalf. The events that occurred in this period set the stage for the women's health movement of today and shaped the health behaviors and attitudes of a new generation of women.

Changes in national policy, advances in science and medical research, and critical shifts in culture and society have had a profound influence on women's health and their access to care. Aspects of these changes, including reproductive rights, consumer activism, the rising prominence of women as key players in the health area, and new health technologies, significantly affected the lives and expectations of millions of young women (see Table III-1).

Compared with women 25 years ago, young women today have much broader reproductive choices that allow them better control of when and if they want to start a family. Such policy milestones as *Roe* v. *Wade*, the Pregnancy Discrimination Act, and the Family and Medical Leave Act and such research advancements as the advent of in vitro fertilization and new

Table III-1 • Time Line of Selected Milestones Affecting Women's Health

	Policy	Research	Society
1970	Title X of Public Health Service Act is enacted. This is first federal program dedicated to providing family planning services to underserved women.		
1971		Diethylstilbestrol (DES) is found to cause an array of problems both in women who had taken DES to prevent miscarriage and in their daughters.	First edition of *Our Bodies, Ourselves* is published by Boston Women's Health Collective.
1972	Supreme Court strikes down state laws prohibiting distribution of contraceptives to unmarried people. Title IX of Civil Rights Act is enacted, prohibiting sex discrimination in educational institutions receiving federal financial assistance.		Gloria Steinem launches *Ms. Magazine* and *Maude* addresses legal abortion, a first on national television.
1973	Supreme Court rules in *Roe v. Wade* that women's right to privacy applies to the choice to have an abortion, striking down state laws criminalizing abortion.		Sally Struthers as Gloria on *All in the Family* is victim of first attempted rape seen on television.
1974			A.H. Robbins halts sales of Dalkon Shield, an IUD that caused injury and, in some cases, death to women.

Year			
1974 *continued*			First Lady Betty Ford is diagnosed with breast cancer and becomes a leading advocate for breast cancer awareness and other women's health issues.
1976	Hyde Amendment passes, eliminating federal funding for abortion services with few exceptions.		
1978	Pregnancy Discrimination Act is enacted, amending Civil Rights Act of 1964 to prohibit workplace discrimination on basis of pregnancy.	In vitro fertilization is used successfully in Great Britain by Dr. Robert Edwards and Dr. Patrick Steptoe, leading to birth of Louise Brown.	
1981		CDC issues its first warning about a rare form of pneumonia in young gay men, later diagnosed as AIDS-related.	
1982		National Survey of Family Growth, a national survey on reproductive and maternal and child health, begins surveying all women of reproductive age, not solely women who have been married or have children.	Exercise video phenomenon is precipitated with the market release of *Jane Fonda's Workout.*
1983		CDC identifies female sexual partners of men with AIDS as a high-risk group for developing the disease.	First lesbian continuing character in daytime television is portrayed on "All My Children."

(continued)

	Policy	Research	Society
1988	Federal mandate requires Medicaid programs to provide health coverage to pregnant women and infants below the federal poverty level.		*Cagney & Lacey* features first date rape seen on television.
1989	Medicaid is expanded to require coverage of pregnant women and infants with incomes up to 133 percent of federal poverty level.		First condom sighting takes place on television in an episode of *Kate & Allie.*
1990		NIH establishes Office of Research on Women's Health, first office in U.S. Public Health Service dedicated to the state of women's health. FDA approves Norplant, a contraceptive implant that protects against pregnancy for up to five years.	Antonia Novello becomes first woman Surgeon General of the United States.
1991	National Breast and Cervical Cancer Early Detection Program is established, authorizing CDC to provide cancer screening services to underserved women.	NIH launches Women's Health Initiative, a long-term, national health study to advance research into preventive strategies for leading diseases and causes of death among women.	Bernadine Healy becomes first woman Director of NIH. Fox Network becomes first broadcast television network to air an advertisement for condoms.
1993	Family Medical Leave Act is enacted. Employees can take up to 12 weeks of unpaid, job-protected leave to care for a new child or a very ill family member.		

Year			
1996	Newborns and Mothers Health Protection Act is enacted, ending "drive-through deliveries" by requiring health plans to cover maternity stays of 48 to 96 hours. Personal Responsibility and Work Opportunity Reconciliation Act is enacted, repealing entitlement to cash assistance and eliminating automatic link between Medicaid and cash assistance.		
1997	Equity in Prescription Insurance and Contraceptive Coverage Act is first introduced in Congress. This bill would mandate insurance coverage of contraceptives by health insurers that cover prescription drugs.		
1998		FDA approves emergency contraception kits that can prevent pregnancy if used within 72 hours after unprotected sex.	Jane Henney becomes first woman appointed to be FDA commissioner.
1999		A *Journal of Pathology* article provides evidence that over 99 percent of cervical cancer cases are in women who also test positive for human papilloma virus.	
2000	Breast and Cervical Cancer Prevention and Treatment Act is passed, permitting states to offer Medicaid to uninsured women found through CDC screening to have breast or cervical cancer.	FDA approves mifepristone, the "abortion pill," a prescription alternative to surgical abortion during early stages of pregnancy.	

contraceptive options all changed and broadened the concept of reproductive rights for women.

The publication of books like *Our Bodies, Ourselves* and magazines like *Ms.* in the early 1970s, and women's activism around issues like the Dalkon Shield and the impact of diethystilbestrol (DES) on women and their daughters created a generation of women raised on consumer activism surrounding health. The idea that clinical research performed on men might not apply to women was gaining acceptance. The National Institutes of Health (NIH) established the Office of Research on Women's Health and launched the Women's Health Initiative.

Television reflected these societal shifts. Maude discussed abortion, Jane Fonda started an exercise video craze, Edith and Archie Bunker's daughter, Gloria, experienced an attempted rape, openly lesbian women became regular characters on daytime shows, and condoms were shown and discussed during prime time, mostly in response to AIDS, the deadly new epidemic that was spreading across the nation.

This chapter discusses the health and well-being of women age 25–34—today and over the past 25 years. The first section examines global indicators of health, including mortality and life expectancy. It also looks at changes in the prevalence of chronic conditions, health behaviors, and reproductive choices and health. The second section addresses young women's interactions with the health care system, focusing on the impact of insurance coverage, access to care, and content of care. The final section looks at the health-related accomplishments of young women today, the implications of these changes, and ways to assure that the health concerns of the next generation of women are addressed.

GENERAL HEALTH INDICATORS AND HEALTH-RELATED BEHAVIORS

Women in their mid-twenties to mid-thirties generally experience good health and have low rates of mortality and morbidity compared with later periods in their lives. Very often, however, health and related behaviors at this age set the stage for health concerns in midlife and old age. This section focuses on global indicators of health, health behaviors, and reproductive concerns facing women age 25–34 today and changes in these indicators over the past 25 years for this age group.

Life expectancy at birth, the average number of years a cohort of infants is expected to live, is a good way to gauge the health of a society. Life expectancy for women has increased among all races over the past 50 years. A woman born in 1950, who would have been 25 in 1975, was expected to live 71.1 years. Her daughter, born in 1975, had a life expectancy of 76.6 years. Disparities in life expectancy between white and black women have also been shrinking, but slowly. A white woman born in 1950 was expected to live an average of nine years longer than a black woman born the same year. By 1975, the disparity had diminished to six years but still persisted[1] (National Center for Health Statistics 1999).

The aggregate death rate for women age 25–34 is relatively low compared with older women and has fallen from 80.0 deaths per 100,000 women in 1977 to 66.9 deaths per 100,000 women in 1999 (National Center for Health Statistics 2001c). Among women age 25–34, significant variation is evident by race/ethnicity, with death rates as high as 127.4/100,000 for non-Hispanic black women and 124.2/100,000 for Native American women, which includes American Indians, Eskimos, and Aleuts. These death rates are twice as high as for non-Hispanic white women (58.6/100,000) and Hispanic women (51.8/100,000), and nearly four times as high as for Asian/Pacific Islander women (32.4/100,000) (National Center for Health Statistics 2001d).

The leading causes of death among women age 25–34 also vary by race/ethnicity but do not fully explain the disparities. Among all women in this age group, accidents are the leading cause of death, followed by malignant neoplasms, diseases of the heart, suicide, assault, and AIDS (see Table III-2). The most notable change in the leading causes of death among women age 25–34 is HIV, a disease that was nonexistent 25 years ago. Today, it is the number-one cause of death for black women and the fourth leading cause of death for Hispanic women (National Center for Health Statistics 2001d).

CHRONIC HEALTH PROBLEMS

Cardiovascular disease and diseases of the heart are among the top five causes of death among women age 25–34. These conditions also impair quality of life and, if not well managed, can lead to serious health problems later on in life. Among the risk factors for heart disease and stroke are hypertension, high cholesterol, diabetes, inadequate physical activity, diet, and obesity. One of the most revealing windows into the health status of the American public has been the National Health and Nutrition Examination Survey (NHANES), a nationally representative survey designed to collect information about the health and diet of people living in the United States. This unique study combines an in-home interview with a physical examina-

Table III-2 • Ten Leading Causes of Death for Women Age 25–34 by Race and Hispanic Origin, 1999

| Cause of Death | Total (all races) | | | Rank | | |
	Rank[1]	Percentage of Total Deaths[2]	Rate (per 100,000)	Non-Hispanic Women White	Non-Hispanic Women Black	Hispanic Women
All causes	—	100.0	66.9	—	—	—
Unintentional injuries (accidents)	1	21.8	14.6	1	2	1
Malignant neoplasms (cancers)	2	16.0	10.7	2	4	2
Heart disease	3	8.4	5.6	4	3	5
Suicide	4	7.1	4.8	3		6
Assault (homicide)	5	6.9	4.6	5	5	3
Human immunodeficiency virus (HIV)	6	6.4	4.3	8	1	4
Cerebrovascular diseases (e.g., stroke)	7	2.2	1.5	9	6	7
Diabetes mellitus	8	2.1	1.4	6	7	10
Congenital malformations, deformations, and chromosomal abnormalities	9	1.7	1.2	7		8
Pregnancy, childbirth, and the puerperium	10	1.4	0.9		9	9
Chronic liver disease and cirrhosis				10		
Chronic lower respiratory diseases					8	
Anemias					10	
All other causes	—	25.9	17.3	—		—

[1]Rank based on number of deaths.
[2]Percentages may not total 100.0 due to rounding.

Source: National Center for Health Statistics, *National Vital Statistics Report* 49, no. 11, 2001d, Tables 1 and 2.

tion and thus can provide a reliable national estimate of the prevalence of a wide range of chronic illnesses (National Center for Health Statistics 2001e).

In the 20 or so years between NHANES I (1971–1974) and NHANES III (1988–1994), hypertension rates among women age 20–34 have fallen from 11.2 percent in NHANES I to 3.4 percent in NHANES III. The prevalence of high cholesterol fell during the same period from 10.9 percent to 7.3 percent (National Center for Health Statistics 2000a).

A risk factor that has been on the rise, however, is the share of women age 20–34 who are overweight (body mass index [BMI] greater than or equal to 25). Obesity and overweight are associated with increased risk of diabetes, cardiovascular disease, osteoarthritis, and some cancers (Must et al. 1999). The percentage of women age 20–34 who are overweight rose from 25.8 percent in the period 1971 to 1974 to 37.0 percent in the period 1988 to 1994 (National Center for Health Statistics 2000a). Overweight and obesity rates are a particularly serious problem for black women, who experience these conditions at considerably higher rates than do white or Hispanic women (Must et al. 1999).

HEALTH BEHAVIORS

Health behaviors can have an important impact on women's health and well-being. Recent public health efforts have focused on raising awareness of how healthy behaviors can improve personal health. Exercise, nutrition, smoking, and alcohol and drug use can all have a very direct bearing on women's current and future health.

The effects of exercise on health have been well publicized. Health guidelines suggest regular physical activity to decrease risk for many chronic diseases and as an important component in weight control and obesity prevention (U.S. Department of Health and Human Services 1996). Despite these efforts, fewer than half of young women participate in vigorous physical activity at least two to four times per week (45.4 percent of those age 20–29 and 46.1 percent of those age 30–39). And more than a third (35.8 percent of women age 20–29 and 34.6 of women age 30–39) report that they do so rarely (U.S. Department of Agriculture 1997).

Good nutrition is also a critical element of good health, yet few women's diets meet the U.S. Department of Agriculture's Recommended Daily Allowances (RDA) of most vitamins and minerals. Most women fall below the RDAs on numerous important nutrients—including several that are essential to women's overall health. Young women attain peak bone mass at age 30 and remain stable until about age 40, after which calcium is lost from bones (Butler 1999). However, 83.1 percent of women age 20–29 and 74.7 percent of those age 30–39 do not meet the RDAs for calcium (U.S. Department of Agriculture 1997). Inadequate intake of folate among women of childbearing age has been linked to neural tube defects (Wald and Brower 1995), yet only half of women age 20–39 receive the RDAs of folate (52.4 percent of those age 20–29 and 52.0 percent of those age 30–39) (U.S. Department of Agriculture 1997). Iron deficiency in women can cause anemia, weakness, and headaches (National Research Council 1989), but almost three-quarters of young women do not receive the RDA of iron (74.1 percent of those age 20–29 and 73.4 percent of those age 30–39) (U.S. Department of Agriculture 1997). Anemia disproportionately affects black women and Hispanic women (Looker et al. 1997).

While men used to smoke at far greater rates than women, this "gender gap" has narrowed over the past several decades. Tobacco use contributes to more preventable deaths and disease than any other substance or behavior among women and is the leading cause of cancer death. In addition to disease risks from smoking that both men and women face—cancer, heart disease, and emphysema—there are gender-specific consequences and an increased risk of adverse reproductive outcomes. Tobacco use among women can lead to risks during pregnancy, increased complications from oral contraceptive use, menstrual dysfunction, and cervical cancer. Smoking is a major cause of coronary heart disease, particularly among women who use oral contraceptives. Women who smoke are also at increased risk for delayed conception as well as for primary infertility (no prior pregnancy) and secondary infertility (at least one prior pregnancy) (U.S. Department of Health and Human Services 2001). Although today's young women grew up with public service advertisements and health warnings on tobacco products, 30.5 percent of women age 26–34 report having smoked in the past month. This percentage is only nine points lower than what it was for women in this age group over 20 years ago. Differences in smoking rates within racial and ethnic subgroups are also evident; white women are more likely than black or Hispanic women to report ever smoking or smoking within the past month or year (Substance Abuse and Mental Health Services Administration 1999; National Institute on Drug Abuse 1997).

Nearly three-quarters of women age 26–34 (71.5 percent) reported using alcohol in the past year, including 14.1 percent who used it on 51 days or more. This share is down slightly from 1979, when 79.5 percent reported using alcohol in the past year. Rates of ever using alcohol and using alcohol in the past month have also fallen by five to seven percentage points over this period. Non-Hispanic white women were more likely to report alcohol use than black and Hispanic women (Substance Abuse and Mental Health Services Administration 1999; National Institute on Drug Abuse 1997).

MENTAL HEALTH

As a society, we are coming to accept that mental health is an integral part of overall health and not separate from physical health. While women are no more likely than men to experience mental illness, they are disproportionately affected by certain mental conditions—major depression, postpartum depression, anxiety, and eating disorders. Unfortunately, there are few sources of population-based estimates of the prevalence of mental health disorders among women—and even fewer that examine conditions for women age 25–34 (Misra 2001).

The National Comorbidity Survey, conducted from 1990–1994, was the first nationally representative mental health survey to provide estimates of prevalence and risk factors for selected psychiatric disorders (National Comorbidity Survey Program 2001). Researchers estimate that each year 13 percent of women will experience a diagnosable depressive disorder. About one in five women will experience an episode of major depression, twice the rate of men (Kessler 1998). The mean age of first onset of depression usually occurs in the mid-twenties, with the highest prevalence occurring between age 25 and 44 (American Psychiatric Association 1994). The National Comorbidity Survey estimated that 19.4 percent of women age 25–34 had experienced a major depressive episode in their lifetime and 4.3 percent of women age 25–34 had experienced a major depressive episode in the past 30 days (Blazer et al. 1994).

While drug and alcohol abuse is more common among men than women, a significant share of women struggle with these addictions. Patterns of illicit drug use have changed over the past 25 years. Slightly more women age 25–34 reported having tried an illicit drug (defined here as marijuana, cocaine, inhalants, hallucinogens, heroin, or prescription-type psychotherapeutics used for nonprescribed purposes) in 1998 than in 1979—44.9 percent in 1998 compared with 40.7 percent in 1979. However, fewer women reported recent use of illicit drugs. In 1979, 12.8 percent of young women reported using an illicit drug within the past month. By 1998, the percentage of 25–34-year-olds who reported using an illicit drug within the last month had decreased to 4.3 percent. White, non-Hispanic women were more likely to report having used an illicit drug during their lifetimes than were black or Hispanic women; however, black women were more likely to report more recent use, followed by whites and then Hispanics (Substance Abuse and Mental Health Services Administration 1999; National Institute on Drug Abuse 1997).

Eating disorders are also becoming more prevalent among women (Lucas et al. 1991; Kendler et al. 1991). Women represent 90 percent of individuals affected by eating disorders. An estimated 10 percent of women and girls are struggling with an eating disorder at any given time (National Eating Disorders Association 2001). Anorexia nervosa is estimated to affect about one percent of women (American Psychiatric Association 1994; Walters and Kendler 1995). Anorexia rates are highest among teen girls, but the disorder can affect women of any age (Halmi et al. 1991). The other main type of eating disorder, bulimia nervosa, is estimated to affect between one and three percent of women (Halmi 2000).

REPRODUCTIVE AND SEXUAL HEALTH

Over the past two and a half decades, interrelated social and demographic shifts have affected the sexual partnering, marriage, and childbearing patterns of young women. Today, women begin sexual relationships earlier and marry later than they did 25 years ago. In 1975, the median age at first marriage for women was 21.1 years; by 2000, it had risen to 25.1 years (Census Bureau 2001a). At the same time, the average age at which young women have their first sexual experience has fallen, according to the National Survey of Family Growth (NSFG), a nationally representative sample of women in their reproductive years. Current estimates put the average age at first intercourse for women age 25–34 at around 17 and a half years of age (National Center for Health Statistics 1997).

The combination of delayed marriage and earlier initiation of sexual activity results in an average gap of eight years between most women's first sexual experiences and their first marriage. Only 2.1 percent of women who married for the first time during 1965–1974 reported that they had had sex in the five years or more before their marriage compared with 56.1 percent of women who married for the first time during 1990–1995 (National Center for Health Statistics 1997). This delay, coupled with changes in attitudes around sex and the increased availability of contraceptives, has led to an increase in sexual partners among women (Laumann et al. 1994). Among women age 25–34, about half report having three or fewer lifetime sexual partners and about one in six report 10 or more partners (National Center for Health Statistics 1997). Data on the number of sexual partners are not available for the 1970s since the 1973 NSFG only surveyed women who had married (National Center for Health Statistics 2001f).

CONTRACEPTIVE USE

Given that women are delaying both marriage and childbirth and having earlier sexual experiences and more sexual partners, the importance of contraceptives in their lives cannot be overstated. It is notable that despite the significant changes in sexual behavior, there has been only a slight increase in the share of women age 25–34 who report using any contraceptives, from 66.7 percent in 1982 to 71.1 percent in 1995 (see Table III-3). Earlier data on contraceptive use were collected only for women who had married and are not comparable. Similar rates of increase are evident when comparing by race and ethnicity, with white women having the highest reported rates of contraceptive use (National Center for Health Statistics 2001a).

More significant changes are evident when comparing the contraceptive methods chosen by young women today with those used by their counter-parts in 1982, the first year when survey data included unmarried women. These shifts can be attributed to increased awareness of sexually transmitted

Table III-3 • Contraceptive Use among Women Age 25–34 by Race and Hispanic Origin and by Method of Contraception, 1982 and 1995 (in percentages)

	1982	1995
Percentage of women using any contraceptive[1]		
All races[2]	66.7	71.1
White	67.8	72.9
Black	63.5	66.8
Hispanic[3]	67.2	69.2
Percentage of contracepting women using methods		
Female sterilization	22.1	23.8
Male sterilization	10.1	7.8
Implant	★	1.3
Injectable	★	2.8
Birth control pill	25.7	33.3
IUD	9.7	0.8[4]
Diaphragm	10.3	1.7
Condom	11.4	21.1

[1]Methods of contraception used in month of interview. If multiple methods were reported, only the most effective method is shown. Methods are listed in the table in order of effectiveness.
[2]Includes Asian/Pacific Islanders and Native Americans, not shown separately (data not available).
[3]People of Hispanic origin may be of any race.
[4]May not be reliable due to standard error of 20–30 percent.

★These methods were not available in 1982.

Source: National Center for Health Statistics, *Health, United States, 2001,* Table 18, 2001a.

diseases, particularly HIV/AIDS, the introduction of such new contraceptive technologies as Norplant and injectables, and lifetime experiences with existing methods, among other factors.

One of the most notable changes over the past two decades has been the near doubling of the rates of condom use, largely in response to public awareness of HIV and the importance of prevention. During this period, use of the birth control pill also rose. Surgical sterilization rates remained high for women, while rates of male sterilization, a less complicated and less invasive procedure, fell. Meanwhile, the intrauterine device (IUD) and diaphragm have lost popularity: only a small fraction of women age 25–34 reported using either of these methods. However, only a small percentage of women in this age group use such newer methods as implants and injectables, despite the fanfare with which these methods initially were embraced (see Table III-3).

Young women today use contraceptives more consistently and earlier in their sexual lives than they did in the 1970s. Only half (49.0 percent) of women age 25–34 who first had intercourse in the 1970s reported using contraception at or before their first intercourse. Three-quarters (76.8 percent) of women who first had intercourse between 1990 and 1995 reported using contraception at first intercourse (National Center for Health Statistics 2000c). While these changes are encouraging, more than a third of all pregnancies among women age 25–34 remain unintended (Henshaw 1998).

Sexually Transmitted Diseases and HIV/AIDS

An estimated 15.3 million new cases of sexually transmitted diseases (STDs) occur annually in the United States. One in three sexually active individuals is estimated to have contracted an STD by age 24 (Alexander et al. 1998). STDs affect millions of people and can lead to long-term complications, including a variety of cancers, infertility, ectopic pregnancy and miscarriage, and chronic diseases. Because women are biologically more susceptible to infection than men if exposed to an STD, and because complications of these infections can be more severe for women than for men, women bear the greatest burden of STDs. In addition, STDs are less likely to produce symptoms in women or to be detected before serious problems develop (Eng and Butler 1997).

Women age 25–34 experience lower rates of such STD infections as gonorrhea and chlamydia than younger women do; rates peak for women at age 15–19. Rates of syphilis are considerably lower for this age group and have been falling in the past decade among both men and women (Centers for Disease Control and Prevention 2000, 2001).

The advent of HIV has had a dramatic effect on sexual behaviors in this country. Although initially considered to be a disease that largely afflicted gay men, significant numbers of women soon were infected. By the twentieth year of the HIV/AIDS epidemic, women accounted for 23 percent of new AIDS cases, up considerably from seven percent in 1986 (Centers for Disease Control and Prevention 1986, 1999). Women are estimated to constitute a fifth of the population living with AIDS (Centers for Disease Control and Prevention 1999), and AIDS is now the sixth leading cause of death for women age 25–34 (see Table III-2).

HIV/AIDS has had a disproportionate effect on women of color, particularly black and Hispanic women. While black women make up only 13 percent of the female U.S. population, they accounted for almost two-thirds (63 percent) of the new AIDS cases reported among women in 1999. Hispanics, who make up 11 percent of the female population, accounted for 18 percent of new cases (Centers for Disease Control and Prevention 1999; Itani and Kates 2001).

PREGNANCY AND CHILDBEARING

Along with marrying later in life, women are delaying childbirth. Between 1969 and 1994, the median age at first birth rose from age 21.3 to age 24.2 (Heck et al. 1997). Over the past 25 years, this trend has led to an increase in the pregnancy rate—defined as the number of pregnancies per 1,000 women—for women age 25–34. The pregnancy rate is calculated using a range of sources, including birth data from vital statistics, abortion data from the Alan Guttmacher Institute and the Centers for Disease Control and Prevention, and self-reported fetal loss data from the National Survey of Family Growth (National Center for Health Statistics 2000c).

The fertility rate (the rate of live births) increased most dramatically among women age 30–34, rising from 53.6 live births per 1,000 women in 1976 to 85.3 live births per 1,000 women in 1997. The fertility rate is higher among women age 25–29 than among women in their early thirties, but has changed only modestly over the past 20 years (see Table III-4).

While abortion was legal for women in the mid-1970s, the availability of and demand for abortion services grew considerably in the late 1970s and then increased modestly throughout the 1980s (National Center for Health Statistics 2000c). From 1976 to 1997, the induced abortion rate rose rapidly for women age 25–29, and increased modestly for women in their early thirties. The fetal loss rate, defined as spontaneous fetal losses from recognized pregnancies of all gestation periods, also increased moderately, although the reasons for this increase are not well understood (see Table III-4).

Table III-4 • Birth Rates and Childbearing Patterns among Women Age 25–34, 1975–1976 and 1997

	1975–1976		1997	
	25–29	*30–34*	*25–29*	*30–34*
Pregnancy rate per 1,000 women	150.8	82.2	171.3	124.2
Live birth rate	106.2	53.6	113.8	85.3
Induced abortion rate	24.1	15.0	33.3	18.1
Fetal loss rate	20.5	13.6	24.2	20.8
Birth rate per 1,000 unmarried women	27.5	17.9	56.2	39.0
Percentage of women who have had at least one live birth	68.9	84.8	56.5	73.8

Sources: National Center for Health Statistics, *Health, United States, 2001,* 2001a, Table 4, *National Vital Statistics Reports* 49, no. 4, 2001b, Table 1, *National Vital Statistics Reports* 48, no. 3, 2000b, Table 18, and *Vital and Health Statistics* Series 21, no. 56, 2000c, Table 3.

Indications of a trend toward delayed childbearing can also be seen in the decrease in the number of young women who have at least one live birth. Since 1975, there has been a reduction in the share of young women who have had at least one birth (see Table III-4). At the same time, there has been a dramatic increase in the proportion of women who experience their first birth after age 30—from 4.1 percent in 1969 to 21.0 percent in 1994 (Heck et al. 1997).

Changes in pregnancy rates and in age at first pregnancy have been accompanied by shifts in household structure and in childbearing patterns among unmarried women. Today, more women are having children outside of marriage. Between 1975 and 1997, the birthrate for unmarried women age 25–29 and for unmarried women age 30–34 more than doubled.

INFERTILITY

Delayed childbearing, new fertility drugs and technologies, and greater openness about infertility have led to an increased awareness in our society of fertility issues. Since 1982, the overall infertility rate among women has gone down. The primary infertility rate—among women with no prior pregnancy—has been stable, while the secondary infertility rate—among women with at least one prior pregnancy—has fallen. Among women age 25–34, 11.2 percent had impaired fecundity, defined as when a woman finds it difficult or impossible to get pregnant or carry a baby to term (National Center for Health Statistics 1997). A significant minority of women age 25–34 (17.1

percent) reported that, as of 1995, they had used some kind of infertility service at some point in their lives—medical advice, tests, drugs, surgery, or other treatments (National Center for Health Statistics 1997).

MATERNAL AND INFANT HEALTH

Over the past 25 years, maternal and infant health status has generally improved. This progress is attributable to a range of factors, including better nutrition, increased public education about the hazards of smoking and alcohol use during pregnancy, and the expansion of private and public coverage of prenatal care and childbirth (see "Health Insurance Coverage" section). Between 1970 and 1998, maternal mortality fell from 17 deaths/100,000 live births to 6.7/100,000 live births among women age 25–29, and from 31.6/100,000 live births to 7.5/100,000 live births among women age 30–34. However, there is still a large gap in maternal mortality rates between white women age 25–29 (4.9/100,000) and black women in this age group (17.2/100,000). The disparity is even greater for women age 30–34, with white women experiencing death rates of 4.9/100,000 compared with 27.7/100,000 for black women (National Center for Health Statistics 2000a).

Public education campaigns on the importance of prenatal care and Medicaid eligibility expansion for pregnant women have also contributed to improvements in infant and maternal well-being. Currently, Medicaid pays for over one-third of all births (National Governors Association 2001). Private insurance coverage of prenatal care and childbirth has also improved dramatically in response to federal legislation (see "Health Insurance Coverage" section). The percentage of women who receive prenatal care in the first trimester increased over the past decade or so. By 1998, a large majority of young women, 86.4 percent of 25–29-year-olds and 89.4 percent of 30–34-year-olds, received care in the first trimester. Few received late or no care, although these were the women at greatest risk for adverse perinatal outcomes. Care utilization, however, was not equal across racial and ethnic subgroups, with white women in both age groups more likely to receive early care than their black and Hispanic counterparts. Similarly, black and Hispanic women were more likely to receive late or no care than white women were (National Center for Health Statistics 2000b).

Low birthweight (LBW)—that is, infants born weighing less than 2,500 grams—has been associated with increased risk of infant mortality and developmental problems in children (Vohr et al. 1998). Part of the impetus behind expanding access to prenatal care was the prevention of LBW, driven by an Institute of Medicine report called *Preventing Low Birthweight* (Institute of Medicine 1985). About seven percent of infants born to women age

25–34 were classified as LBW in 1998. The proportion of LBW births has been rising since the early 1980s and is now at levels not seen since the early 1970s. This trend can be attributed in part to an increase in multiple births and in part to new medical technologies that can save preterm infants at younger ages and lower weights. The proportions of LBW infants born to Hispanic and white women are similar; rates for black women are much higher (National Center for Health Statistics 2000b). This difference holds true even when adjusting for differences in education, income, and other factors believed to influence birth weight (Collins and Butler 1997).

Although LBW rates are rising, infant mortality continues to fall, dropping among women of all ages from 20 deaths/1,000 live births in 1970 to 7.2 deaths/1,000 in 1998. As with maternal mortality, however, there is still a large gap in the infant mortality rate between whites and blacks (6.0 deaths/1,000 live births versus 14.3 deaths/1,000 live births, respectively) (National Center for Health Statistics 2001a).

YOUNG WOMEN AND THE HEALTH CARE SYSTEM

Access to health care is integral to ensuring that young women maintain their health and have healthy futures. In the United States, access to and use of health care is largely determined by health need, insurance coverage, scope of coverage, and availability of services. Other factors such as cultural practices, discrimination, and experiences with the health system also play a role. However, once women are in the door, the care they receive does not always meet recommended standards. Quality is uneven, and our ability to measure quality of care for services important to women is still in its infancy. This section reviews the role and scope of health coverage and the use of health care services among women age 25–34.

HEALTH INSURANCE COVERAGE

Health insurance coverage improves access to care for women. Women with coverage are more likely to report high rates of health care utilization and are less likely to encounter barriers to needed care than women who are uninsured (Salganicoff and Wyn 1999). Women obtain coverage through a variety of public and private sources. Most have private coverage, typically through employers—either their own or their spouse's. A small share of women has coverage through individually purchased policies, which can be costly, with high out-of-pocket costs and deductibles (Pollitz, Sorian, and Thomas 2001). Government programs, such as Medicare and Medicaid, are also important sources of coverage, particularly for women who are poor or disabled. Medicaid, the joint state and federal program for the poor, facilitates access to care for millions of low-income women. Medicare, primarily a program for the elderly, also benefits many nonelderly women with long-term disabilities. Most young women have coverage through private insurance or one of these public programs. However, nearly one in five lacks any coverage and is at high risk for experiencing barriers to care and poorer health outcomes.

Health care coverage for women has changed since the 1970s. Rates of employer-sponsored insurance have increased for women, particularly the growing ranks of young working women. In 1976, 79.2 percent of females had private coverage or Medicare, 6.6 percent received coverage under Medicaid, and 10.5 percent were uninsured (National Center for Health Statistics 1978). Information on trends in coverage of young women is not available because of differences in data collection and data analysis practices in the mid-1970s and today.

Employer-sponsored Insurance

Employer coverage rates for women have been uneven, declining from the late 1980s until 1993. Despite these vacillations, employer coverage remains the primary source of health insurance for women. Approximately two-thirds of women age 25–34 have employer-sponsored coverage, 45 percent through their own jobs and 22 percent through the employer of a spouse (see Table III-5). While the number of women in the workforce has grown in the last 25 years, women are more likely to work in lower-paying industries or in part-time jobs, employment situations that are less likely than high-wage industries and full-time positions to provide health insurance coverage (Wyn et al. 2001; Levitt et al. 2001). A growing share of women receive coverage in their own names (Employee Benefits Research Institute 1997, 1998, 2000, 2001). This shift is attributable in part to the rising number of young women who have entered the workforce since the 1970s, and in part to the increased costs of dependent coverage (Misra 2001). Women with dependent coverage are more vulnerable to losing coverage in the event of divorce or widowhood, or as a result of an employer raising family premium costs or abandoning dependent coverage altogether. Recent declines in the number of employers offering coverage to dependents, and increases in employee costs for family coverage, have reduced the share of women with this kind of coverage.

There are striking differences in rates of employer coverage by race and ethnicity. White women are most likely to have employer-sponsored coverage, followed by black and Hispanic women. White and black women

Table III-5 • Health Insurance Coverage of Women Age 25–34 by Race and Hispanic Origin and by Ratio of Income to Poverty Threshold, 2000

	Total Number (millions)	Total[1]	Employer Sponsored		Other Private	Other Public	Medicaid	Uninsured
			In Own Name	As Dependent				
Total women	19.0	100.0	45.1	22.3	3.8	1.3	8.5	18.9
Race or Hispanic origin								
White, non-Hispanic	12.3	100.0	47.5	26.3	4.4	1.4	6.2	14.1
Black, non-Hispanic	2.7	100.0	51.1	8.8	1.5	1.0	15.3	22.4
Hispanic[2]	2.8	100.0	31.2	17.1	2.2	1.4	12.6	35.5
Native American[3]	1.5	100.0	26.4	15.1	4.8	2.9	22.5	28.3
Asian/Pacific Islander	1.0	100.0	41.2	24.9	6.8	1.1	5.3	20.7
Ratio of income to poverty threshold[4]								
Less than 100 percent	3.1	100.0	12.1	4.0	6.0	1.5	33.6	42.8
100 to 199 percent	3.5	100.0	34.1	16.6	5.0	2.1	10.6	31.6
200 to 299 percent	3.6	100.0	50.6	24.8	3.7	1.5	3.0	16.4
300 percent and above	8.8	100.0	59.0	30.0	2.6	0.9	1.2	6.3

[1]Percentages may not total 100.0 due to rounding. [2]People of Hispanic origin may be of any race. [3]American Indian, Eskimo, and Aleut. [4]In 2000, 100 percent of the federal poverty threshold for a family of three was $13,738.

Source: Henry J. Kaiser Family Foundation estimates based on Urban Institute's analyses of the Census Bureau's March 2001 Current Population Survey, 2001c.

have similar rates of employer-sponsored coverage in their own names, reflecting their high workforce participation rates. However, fewer than one in 10 black women age 25–34 has employer-sponsored coverage as a dependent, a rate that is much lower than for other women. Hispanic women age 25–34 have much lower rates of employer-sponsored coverage overall (see Table III-5).

Hispanics are more likely to work in low-wage, nonunionized jobs that do not offer employer-sponsored coverage and less likely to be able to afford their share of premium costs and other related out-of-pocket costs for employer-based care (Schur and Feldman 2001). Nearly 60 percent of Hispanic women age 25–34 live in low-income households (below 200 percent of poverty) (Henry J. Kaiser Family Foundation 2001c). Poor women also have very limited access to employer-sponsored health coverage; just 16 percent of women age 25–34 with incomes below the federal poverty level have insurance through an employer, in contrast to 89 percent of women with incomes three times the poverty level or higher (see Table III-5).

Medicaid
Medicaid plays a critical role for low-income women, providing them with coverage for a broad range of health services, with minimal, if any, out-of-pocket costs for care. States determine Medicaid eligibility levels for young women within broad federal guidelines. In general, beneficiaries must be parents, pregnant, or disabled, and live in households with very low incomes; thus, women are most likely to qualify. The program has been successful in providing quality health coverage to low-income women (Rowland, Salganicoff, and Keenen 1999). Low-income women with Medicaid and low-income privately insured women are equally likely to receive preventive care, to have a regular source of care, and to have seen a physician in the past year (Salganicoff and Wyn 1999; Almeida, Dubay, and Ko 2001).

Overall, approximately nine percent of women age 25–34 are covered by Medicaid. Since Medicaid is means-tested, the program is particularly important for poor women and women in populations disproportionately affected by poverty. Among women age 25–34, Medicaid covers 34 percent of those who are poor, 13 percent of those who are Hispanic, and 15 percent of those who are black. It also covers more than one in 10 women in this age group who have an income between 100 percent and 199 percent of the poverty level (see Table III-5).

Over the last 25 years, Medicaid eligibility has both contracted and expanded in response to policy changes and economic climates. Reductions in eligibility were followed by fairly broad expansions for pregnant women from the mid-1980s to the early 1990s with decreases in enrollment after the passage of the Personal Responsibility and Work Opportunity Reconciliation Act (PRWORA), welfare reform, in 1996. The most notable expansions were the large-scale improvements in eligibility policies for pregnant women in the 1980s. By 1992, over half of the states had expanded their Medicaid eligibility levels beyond federal guidelines, and 22 states and the District of Columbia had raised eligibility levels for pregnant women and infants to 185 percent of the poverty level (U.S. Congress 1993). By 2000, 13 states covered pregnant women up to at least 200 percent of the poverty level or higher and 33 states provided coverage up to at least 185 percent of poverty or higher (National Governors Association 2001).

In more recent years, the federal government has allowed some states to extend eligibility through Section 1115 Medicaid research and demonstration waivers, which permit states to cover populations that were previously ineligible for Medicaid, such as poor single adults and low-income parents. Women's enrollment fell dramatically after Congress passed PRWORA, which severed the traditional link between cash assistance benefits and Medicaid (Wyn et al. 2001). Reductions in coverage were particularly hard on low-income women of reproductive age, who may not have known that they remained eligible for Medicaid even if they no longer qualified for cash benefits (Mann et al. 2002).

Uninsured Women

Medicaid expansions and improvements in workforce participation and employer-sponsored coverage in the last two and a half decades have failed to eradicate the problems faced by millions of uninsured women. Today, nearly one in five women age 25–34 lacks health coverage. This lack of coverage has significant implications for young women's access to health care. Compared with low-income women who have private coverage or those on Medicaid, uninsured women have the lowest rates of health care access and utilization and are the least satisfied with their care (Almeida, Dubay, and Ko 2001; Salganicoff and Wyn 1999).

In the 25–34 age group, 35 percent of Hispanic women, 22 percent of black women, and 14 percent of white women lack health coverage (see Table III-5). The problem is particularly acute among low-income women. Forty-three percent of poor women age 25–34 are uninsured, and nearly one-third of near-poor women in this age group (those with incomes between 100 percent and 199 percent of the poverty level) lack coverage. Most of these women cannot afford to purchase individual policies, and many are ineligible for Medicaid because they do not have children, are not pregnant or disabled, or do not financially qualify, despite their low incomes.

THE GROWTH IN MANAGED CARE

Managed care has grown from a small component of health insurance to the dominant source of coverage, both in private and public plans. In 1973, President Richard Nixon signed the Health Maintenance Organization Act, a law that helped pave the way for managed care's move into the job-based care market (Mitka 1998). From 1988 to 1998, managed care as a share of medium- and large-firm employer-based coverage grew from 29 percent to 52 percent, while conventional fee-for-service plans fell from 71 percent to 14 percent (Levitt, Lundy, and Srinivasan 1998). Medicaid managed care enrollment grew, as well, covering more than half of the Medicaid population by 1999, particularly low-income women and children. It is estimated that three-fourths of insured women currently receive care through some kind of managed care system (Collins et al. 1999).

Managed care was considered attractive for its potential to control costs and to improve access to care with reduced out-of-pocket costs through plans that focused on prevention and primary care. However, concerns about quality of service under managed care have become a major issue in national discourse. Critics have argued that these systems may encourage plans to undertreat patients and create barriers for needed specialist care, and that adequate mechanisms for monitoring quality of care may not be in place. In particular, poor and low-income women, such as those covered by Medicaid, may be vulnerable to these problems. Compared to the general population, these women tend to need more services, have unique care needs that may require specialist treatment, and lack the means to go out-of-plan for care (Salganicoff, Wyn, and Solis 1998; Rowland, Salganicoff, and Keenan 1999). In addition, research has found that women in managed care programs are not more likely to receive preventive care and are less satisfied with the care they receive and their choice of providers and access to care (Gonen 1998; Wyn, Collins, and Brown 1997).

Such concerns have led many states to pass legislation to loosen the tight control of managed care plans over service utilization. For example, 40 states mandated that plans provide patients with direct access (without a referral) to obstetricians and gynecologists, and 22 states mandated direct access to other specific types of specialists by the end of 2000 (Health Policy Tracking Service 2001). Congress has debated but has not passed federal legislation on consumer protections under managed care.

PROVIDING HEALTH BENEFITS THAT WOMEN NEED

Having health coverage is important, but it is also important to ensure that the services women need are included in their benefit packages. For young women, certain benefits, such as reproductive care, are particularly important; however, preventive and mental health care are cornerstones of good health for this population, as well.

Preventive Health Care

Aspects of preventive health that are important to young women include screening tests, such as Pap smears, clinical breast exams, and STD testing and treatment, in addition to regular checkups. Today, nearly all job-based plans cover an adult physical and an annual Ob/Gyn visit, with managed care plans offering the highest coverage rates (see Table III-6). Medicaid also covers physician visits and the abovementioned screening tests for women (Henry J. Kaiser Family Foundation 2001a).

Contraceptive Coverage

Contraceptive coverage is particularly important to young women. Although the birth control pill and other modern contraceptives became widely available in the 1960s, contraceptive coverage remains a benefit that many plans fail to provide. In 2001, just 64 percent of employer plans covered oral contraceptives, and only 41 percent provided comprehensive coverage of all methods of reversible contraception approved by the Food and Drug Administration (FDA) (Levitt et al. 2001). Federal legislation has been introduced in every Congress since 1997 to require health plans to cover contraceptive drugs if they cover other prescription drugs; however, no bills have been enacted (U.S. Library of Congress 2001). Public coverage of contraceptive services is more comprehensive. In 1970, Congress passed Title X of the Public Health Service Act, the law that first established federal funding for family planning (Alan Guttmacher Institute 2000b). In addition, Medicaid plays a critical role in financing family planning services for low-income women and covers prescription contraception comprehensively in nearly all states (Schwalberg et al. 2001).

Maternity and Prenatal Care

The state of health insurance coverage for maternity care has changed considerably in the last two and a half decades as more women have entered the workplace and as advocacy for women's health care needs has increased. In 1978, Congress passed the Pregnancy Discrimination Act as an amendment to Title VII of the Civil Rights Act of 1964. The law requires that all employer-sponsored health insurance cover pregnancy-related services on an equal basis with other medical needs, whether for an employee or for an employee's spouse (U.S. Library of Congress 2001). Maternity coverage increased dramatically within five years, from coverage in 57 percent of

Table III-6 • Percentage of Insured Workers with Coverage for Selected Benefits of Importance to Women by Type of Plan, 2001

			Type of Plan		
Benefits	All Plans	Conven-tional	HMO[1]	PPO[2]	POS[3]
Adult physicals	91	63	97	88	94
Prescription drugs	98	99	99	97	96
Outpatient mental	96	96	96	96	97
Inpatient mental	95	97	94	95	95
Annual Ob/Gyn visit	94	81	97	93	97
Prenatal care	97	97	98	96	97
Oral contraceptives	64	43	73	61	70
Reversible contraceptives[4]	41	27	45	39	47
Abortion	31	41	37	29	28
Sterilization	67	68	70	62	65

[1]Health maintenance organization.
[2]Preferred provider organization.
[3]Point-of-service plan.
[4]Includes oral contraceptives, implants, injectables, diaphragms, and IUDs.

Sources: Larry Levitt et al., *The Kaiser Family Foundation and Health Research and Education Trust Employer Health Benefits 2001 Annual Survey*, 2001, Exhibits 8.2 and 8.3.

policies in 1977 to coverage in 89 percent of policies in 1982 (Gold 1998). During the periods 1971 to 1975 and 1991 to 1995, the number of women who quit their jobs during pregnancy fell from over half of working women to just over a quarter, and the percentage of women who worked during and after their pregnancies increased significantly (Census Bureau 2001b). The Family and Medical Leave Act, enacted in 1993, subsequently affected maternity leave by mandating that employers with 50 or more workers provide 12 weeks of unpaid leave to employees (U.S. Library of Congress 2001).

Today, coverage for services like prenatal care is almost universal under employer-based plans (Levitt et al. 2001). Research indicates that insurance coverage is an important factor in women's use of such services. Compared to women with private insurance or Medicaid, uninsured women go to the doctor less frequently during pregnancy and are much more likely to report having never visited a physician while pregnant (Bernstein 1999). According to a report by the U.S. General Accounting Office in the mid-1980s, Medicaid improved women's access to prenatal care as they were enrolled in the program, although disparities persisted among subgroups of women by race and ethnicity (Kiely, Kogan, and Blackmore 1995). Nonetheless, a steady rise in the number of women receiving early prenatal care has accompanied these changes.

Fertility Care

As discussed earlier, a sizable minority of women age 25–34 have used some type of fertility service. Patient interest in infertility services remained steady during most of the 1970s until demand surged in the early 1980s, soon after the first successful birth resulting from in vitro fertilization in 1978 (National Center for Health Statistics 1985, 1997). Although such social factors as delayed childbearing also contributed to this change, the significant percentage of young women currently seeking fertility treatment indicates that infertility is an issue many of them confront (National Center for Health Statistics 1985). Fertility services, which can be extremely expensive, are not broadly covered by most insurance plans. In 2001, just 10 states required that private health plans mandate coverage of fertility benefits, with five of these states requiring coverage for in vitro fertilization (RESOLVE 2001). In addition, few states cover fertility drugs under Medicaid, limiting poor women's access to these services (Schwalberg et al. 2001).

Abortion

The Supreme Court's 1973 decision in *Roe* v. *Wade* dramatically altered women's access to abortions, the most common ambulatory surgery procedure among women of childbearing age (Picker Institute 1999; Alan Guttmacher Institute 2000a). The high court's decision established abortion as a woman's constitutionally protected right and thereby overturned any laws classifying abortion as a criminal act. The Supreme Court upheld the constitutional right to abortion in *Planned Parenthood* v. *Casey* in 1992; however, this decision also allowed states to place certain restrictions on abortion services, such as requiring parental notification or consent among minors or instituting a mandatory counseling session and subsequent waiting period. The decision also permitted state limitation on public funding for abortion (Alan Guttmacher Institute 2000c).

Because federal funding for abortion was effectively banned by the passage of the Hyde Amendment in 1977, restrictions on state funding in particular affect access to publicly funded abortion services (Alan Guttmacher Institute 2000c). Private and public programs do not widely cover abortion services: fewer than one-third of employer-sponsored plans provide abortion coverage (Levitt et al. 2001), and only 16 states provide Medicaid coverage for abortions termed "medically needy," which are outside the federal guidelines that require life endangerment, rape, or incest for public funding (Henry J. Kaiser Family Foundation 2001a).

Mental Health

Women in their reproductive years (between puberty and menopause) are the most likely of all women to have mental health needs (National Institute of Mental Health 2001). Insurance coverage for mental health services is therefore an issue of particular concern to women in this age bracket. The 1970s saw the growth of a strong consumer movement in support of mental health treatment, partially in response to public accounts by former patients about the inadequacies of the mental health system at that time (U.S. Department of Health and Human Services 1999). The Mental Health Systems Act, intended to provide states with federal support and assistance for mental health services, was passed in 1980 but then repealed the following year. Not until 1996 did Congress pass legislation to provide parity for mental health coverage and medical and surgical benefits. However, even this legislation applied only to lifetime and annual monetary limits; other charges, such as co-payments or deductibles, were not addressed, nor were additional limits on inpatient days or outpatient sessions (U.S. Library of Congress 2001). Today, 34 states have adopted their own parity laws, while Congress continues to debate federal legislation to require full parity (American Psychiatric Association 2001).

Although nearly all employer benefit plans provide coverage for inpatient and outpatient mental health services, nearly 98 percent of private plans placed more restrictions or costs on mental illness treatment than they did on other medical services in 1999 (Levitt et al. 2001; American Psychiatric Association 1999). A variety of community-based services are available to some women on Medicaid, depending on the policies in their state of residence; however, many states do not provide significant mental health coverage, and all states are prohibited from reimbursing psychiatric hospitals for services to nonelderly women (Bazelon Center for Mental Health Law 2000).

USE OF AND ACCESS TO HEALTH SERVICES

While young women are at a relatively healthy stage of life, they still have a substantial need for health and medical interventions. Preventive and screening services, routine gynecological care, and health education are important not just to address young women's current health needs but to help identify potential health problems that may arise in the future.

According to the Henry J. Kaiser Family Foundation's Survey of Women's Health (a nationally representative sample of nonelderly women in the United States conducted in 2001), most women age 25–34 (86 percent) have visited a physician in the past year (see Table III-7). Most also received such preventive screening services as Pap smears, breast exams, and blood pressure checks. Less than half, however, were given a blood cholesterol test, which can be vital in identifying high levels of cholesterol that can lead to heart disease and other circulatory conditions later in life.

Table III-7 • Access and Barriers to Health Care for Women Age 25–34, 2001 (percentages reporting)

		Women Age 25–34	
	Total	Insured	Uninsured
Utilization			
Physician visit in past 12 months	86	90	72
Blood cholesterol test in the past two years	42	47	26
Breast exam in the past two years	77	82	61
Pap smear in the past two years	86	90	76
Blood pressure check in the past two years	87	89	80
Access			
Have a usual source of care	78	87	48
In the past 12 months:			
Had a health problem and needed to see MD but didn't	31	26	45
Could not see specialist when thought one was needed	16	14	23
Not enough control over decisions affecting care	21	19	27
Concerns about quality of care received	26	25	30
Not enough doctors or clinics nearby	9	8	13
New doctor not accepting new patients	22	21	24
Did not fill prescription because of cost	25	21	38
Delayed or postponed care due to:			
Cost/affordability	28	16	65
Lack of insurance	25	13	62
Problem getting child care	10	8	14
Transportation problems	8	7	12
Finding time/taking time off from work	28	26	33
Could not get appointment with doctor wanted	24	24	24

Source: Henry J. Kaiser Family Foundation, "Survey of Women's Health," unpublished estimates, 2001b.

There remains a major gap in access and use of services by women with health insurance and by those without. As mentioned earlier, just under 20 percent of young women lack insurance. These women use significantly less health care and experience formidable barriers to care. Uninsured women are considerably less likely to have visited a physician in the past year or to have received recommended screening services (Almeida, Dubay, and Ko 2001; Salganicoff and Wyn 1999).

When examining access to care, an important factor associated with the use of services is the availability of a regular source of care. Uninsured women are significantly less likely than insured women to have a continuous relationship with a health care provider. In fact, less than half of uninsured women age 25–34 reported they had a regular source of care.

Despite overall high levels of physician visits, women age 25–34 confronted a range of barriers to health care. Nearly one-third reported that they had a health problem and needed care but didn't receive it. A large minority of women also reported that they lacked control over decisions affecting their care and had concerns about the quality of the care they received. Cost was still a barrier for filling prescriptions for one in five women with insurance and for nearly four in 10 women without coverage.

About one in four women age 25–34 also delayed getting care for a range of reasons, including costs, lack of insurance, difficulty in taking time off from work, or inability to schedule appointments with their preferred doctors. About one in 10 women in this age group delayed care because they had problems with child care or transportation. These access problems are more acute for women who are uninsured.

CONTENT AND QUALITY OF HEALTH CARE

In addition to measuring the volume of health care, it is informative to examine the content of care: the actual services that women receive once they get to a health care provider. As mentioned earlier, young women have a broad range of health needs but are especially reliant on reproductive health services. Most women age 25–34 should have routine gynecological visits at least every other year, and nearly three-fourths did so in 1999, according to a nationally representative survey of women conducted by the Henry J. Kaiser Family Foundation on reproductive health. Among women who visited a gynecologist in the past two years, most got a Pap smear or a breast exam and about half obtained a prescription for contraception, but fewer than one in 10 were advised to get an HIV or STD test, despite the prevalence of some STDs within this age group.

It is also helpful to consider the conversations that young women have with their physicians. According to the 1999 survey on reproductive health conducted by the Henry J. Kaiser Family Foundation, 60 percent of women reported discussing diet, exercise, and nutrition with their gynecologists. These topics were followed by discussion of cancers of reproductive organs and contraceptive options. About one-third of the women reported discussions about vitamins and other dietary supplements and about getting enough calcium in their diets. Significantly, only eight percent discussed emergency contraception, which was already FDA-approved at the time of the survey. This important contraceptive advance could be decisive in efforts to reduce rates of unintended pregnancy. Clearly, by these measures, physicians and women are not having the open dialogues necessary to communicate vital health information that can make a difference in the future health and well-being of women in this age group.

Health quality measurement is also in its early stages. Very limited techniques have been applied to measure quality of care. One of the most commonly used today is the Health Plan and Employer Data and Information Set (HEDIS). The National Committee for Quality Assurance (NCQA) developed this system in 1991 to use information provided by managed care plans to assess quality of care. Measures that are relevant to women age 25–34 include the share of a plan's membership that has had breast and cervical cancer screening, prenatal care in the first trimester, checkups after delivery, and chlamydia screening in the past year (although this measure is recommended only for women age 16–26) (National Committee on Quality Assurance 2000). The HEDIS system has a number of limitations for young women: it is used only by managed care plans, it measures only a small set of items, and it does not include any counseling services that may be important for women in this age group. To improve the ability of plans to monitor women's care, the NCQA appointed a Women's Health Measurement Advisory Panel in 1997 to develop new measures for possible inclusion in future editions of this system. Given the great variability in health care, poor information systems, fragmentation of care, and the limitations of current quality measurement systems, the arena of health care quality assurance merits significant attention in the future.

CONCLUSION

Overall, the health profile of young women today shows much progress compared with that of young women 25 years ago. But there is still a long road ahead. On some general health measures (life expectancy, hypertension, and high cholesterol), young women today appear to be better off than the women of their mothers' generation. Young women smoke and drink less and are less likely to use illicit drugs regularly than they were a generation ago. Despite public education and health trends and obsession with body image, young women today are heavier, many do not get the exercise they need, and few meet the dietary guidelines for good nutrition.

In the arena of reproductive health, there have been major shifts with far-reaching consequences, not only for women but for society as a whole. Today's young women are delaying marriage and childbirth but are becoming sexually active at younger ages and having more sexual partners. They have more reproductive choices, including better access to more effective contraceptives and to safe and legal abortions. They also receive greater social acceptance if they decide to have a child out of marriage or to forgo parenthood entirely. However, the landscape has new hazards. Women must now factor in the risks of acquiring a deadly virus, HIV, when they have sex. STDs are becoming more resistant to antibiotics. The number of abortion providers has fallen, while access to abortion services has become more difficult in many states, especially for poor women and teens.

In the area of health coverage and access, changes in the public and private health care markets have led to considerable change, for better and for worse. Although employer-based health coverage experienced a decline during the early 1990s, it has remained the primary source of care for women. Medicaid has also undergone significant reforms that have expanded the number of women who are eligible to receive care under the program, particularly low-income pregnant women. However, these expansions were enacted to protect infants, not mothers. Today, Medicaid coverage for pregnant women ends 60 days postpartum. Unless women qualify through another eligibility pathway, they lose coverage. And while states have more options than ever to expand coverage to low-income women, approximately one-third remain uninsured. The number of uninsured young women has increased as a result of declines in Medicaid enrollment attributable to the 1996 welfare reform legislation and the long-term erosion in employer-based coverage, along with economic changes in the health care marketplace.

While the medical community has made tremendous progress through sophisticated scientific breakthroughs such as mapping the human genome, significant numbers of young women are still not getting basic screening services at the rates recommended by leading health care groups. Uninsured women receive even lower standards of care. Social taboos still prevent women and their health care providers from having critical dialogues about sexual practices, drug and alcohol use, and violence. We may feel liberated, but today's population of women is still constrained by long-standing social inhibitions.

Let us hope that in 25 years we can look back on even more progress as we compare the health of young women with that of their mothers and grandmothers. An area that merits considerable attention is the persistent disparities in health status and access to care. Women of color, women who are poor, and women who are uninsured still fare considerably worse on a broad range of health measures. Much of the knowledge base on how to improve women's health is already there; we just need the commitment of adequate resources and the public will to make it happen.

NOTE

1. Data for the black population are not available before 1970. Data presented for 1950 are for the "nonwhite" population.

Four

INTEGRATING WORK AND LIFE: YOUNG WOMEN FORGE NEW SOLUTIONS

Jessica DeGroot and Joyce Fine

HIGHLIGHTS

For women in contemporary America, the years between their twenty-fifth and thirty-fifth birthdays are a time for making critical decisions affecting the balance in their work and personal lives. They decide whether to marry or not, whether to have children or not (or at least whether to defer child-bearing), and whether a full-time commitment to work can be reconciled with the demands of their lives outside of work.

The years between 25 and 35 are also those when women are likely to face key decisions about their future in the workplace. Today, the great majority of women in this age group work. In fact, most young women expect to hold paying jobs from the time they leave school until the time they retire. Unlike their mothers 25 years ago, contemporary young women assume they will work even when they have small children at home. Key findings from this chapter include:

- More than three-quarters of women age 25–34 work for pay, compared with just over half of women in this age group who were in the labor force 25 years ago.
- Young women today operate in a world based on an outdated concept of the ideal worker, which assumes that people come to work without any outside responsibilities, that they work at least 40 hours a week

with typical nine-to-five business hours, and that they do so throughout their working careers.

- Working full time or near full time outside the home makes it difficult for young women to manage their domestic lives as seamlessly as their mothers appeared to manage theirs. The fact that women remain disproportionately responsible for their children's lives, as well as for organizing their households, often leaves them stretched too thin, both at work and at home.

- Income, work opportunities, and work structure flexibility vary significantly depending on a young woman's education level. Young women with different levels of education face different opportunities and challenges as they try to balance work and family.

- In the new information age, in which work can be done 24 hours a day, seven days a week, young women—mothers and non-mothers—face significant challenges in finding time for their lives outside of work. However, today's new technology also provides an increasing number of young women with the tools to redesign their jobs and to create more time for other interests and commitments.

- Many young families are experimenting with nontraditional roles at home, with mothers and fathers sharing in the responsibilities of earning an income and caring for children.

- For young women to achieve a good balance between work and responsibilities outside of work, work at home must become a shared responsibility between the adults in the family. At the same time, paid work must be changed to fit within a new, twenty-first-century framework in which employees have time and energy to enjoy and manage the other important parts of their lives.

- It is also important that new work-life solutions be made equally accessible to young women (and men) with limited resources. Young families that cannot afford to cut back their work hours, or who fear for their job security if they ask for flexibility, must be assisted through responsive public policies that enable all families to reduce work obligations to create time to meet responsibilities at home.

INTRODUCTION

Jacqueline is a 28-year-old receptionist who works in a pediatrician's office from 8 A.M. to 4 P.M. five days a week. Her husband, a factory worker, typically works from 8 A.M. to 5 P.M. in a town about 40 minutes from their home. Their two-year-old daughter attends family day care in a neighbor's home from 7:45 A.M. to 4:30 P.M., Monday through Friday. Like many American women between the ages of 25 and 35, Jacqueline returned to work full time after a brief, one-month maternity leave. Although she enjoys her job, she would prefer to work fewer hours so that she could spend more time with her daughter. She does not do so because she and her husband earn just enough to pay their monthly bills. She is also afraid that if she requested a lighter schedule, her boss might say no and her job security would be threatened.

Mary, the doctor for whom Jacqueline works, is a 33-year-old woman who works long hours, including many Saturdays. Mary has been engaged for a year. Initially excited about marrying, Mary has been surprised to find herself procrastinating in making final wedding plans. She realizes that in addition to being busy at work, she is concerned about the changes that getting married will bring into her life. She knows that she will need to give up some flexibility, independence, and control over her time, especially since she and her fiancé hope to have children soon. Although she looks forward to starting a family, she sometimes worries that bringing children into her already busy life will be a *significant* challenge, and she struggles with the question of how to make it a welcome one.

Gloria is a 27-year-old single mother with an eight-year-old daughter and a six-year-old son. Gloria never finished high school, has been on and off welfare, and struggles to make a better life for herself and her children. Gloria is the person who cleans the office building where Mary and Jacqueline work. Coming in to work at night, Gloria sleeps while her children are in school. With her low salary and no health insurance, she lacks the income to pay someone to look after her children during her night shifts. Instead, she relies on relatives and friends but occasionally is forced to leave her children home alone.

Jacqueline, Mary, and Gloria's stories[1] illustrate the primary work-life challenge that women age 25–34 face: how to balance paid work with a full life outside of work. Sixty percent of women in this age group currently have children compared with approximately 80 percent of women age 35–44 (Census Bureau 2001). Although many are marrying and having children later than their mothers did, having children and managing their care is central to the lives of many young women in this age group (see Chapters One and Two). Even those who do not yet have children, or who do not expect to, find it difficult to balance work and outside commitments in today's overtime culture.

Despite the differences in their marital and parental status as well as their educational and financial attainments, Mary, Jacqueline, and Gloria share many core life experiences and expectations, not only with each other but also with the rest of their 25–34-year-old peers. In particular, they share the expectation that paid work will be an ongoing component of their adult lives, even while they are raising children (Bureau of Labor Statistics 1999).

More young mothers work today than worked 25 years ago, and more mothers work full time than in previous generations (see Chapter Two). Twenty-five ago, mothers typically did not work for pay while raising children, and, in general, they did not expect paid work to play a central, ongoing role in their lives. Often women in this generation quit working outside of the home once they had children. Even if they returned to work when their children were of school age, they often worked part days so that they could be home to meet their children at the end of the school day.

This chapter examines the work-life issues of three groups of young women. Jacqueline exemplifies one group, the 59.2 percent of women age 25–34 who are moderately educated. These are the young women who either have a high school diploma or who have taken some college courses beyond high school but do not have a baccalaureate degree (see Chapter One). Approximately three out of four of them have children (Census Bureau 2001).

Mary represents the second group, the 29.9 percent of women age 25–34 who are highly educated (see Chapter One). These young women have at least a four-year college degree; some have a graduate or professional degree. The percentage of young women with high levels of education is about half the percentage of young women with moderate levels of education. Compared with their moderately educated counterparts, young women like Mary are far less likely (41.5 percent) to have children (Census Bureau 2001).

Gloria exemplifies the third group of women highlighted in this chapter. Those without a high school diploma or GED make up almost 11 percent of women in the 25–34 age group (see Chapter One). They have a particularly strained work-life balance, largely because their lack of education and skills typically limits them to low-paying, low-status jobs. About 83 percent of these women have children, and the challenges they encounter lead to chronic work-life stress and related hardships (Census Bureau 2001).

While the three women described above lead very different lives, they all struggle with an outdated work-life paradigm. For the most part, our society has come to expect that women will work for pay throughout their lives but has failed to adequately address what this means in terms of changes in family life and how work gets accomplished. In particular, we continue to cling to old assumptions about the responsibilities of both female and male employees and about who should do the unpaid work of caring for families that women traditionally have done.

This chapter explores a range of issues that contribute to the complexity of young working women's lives. Since almost 60 percent of women age

25–34 are mothers, and even more will become mothers in the future, the chapter pays special attention to the challenges of working mothers. It examines how the work paradigm of a previous generation, designed with a homogeneous (male) workforce in mind, needs to be updated to suit today's heterogeneous workforce where nearly half the workers are women.

The chapter challenges outdated assumptions about the *ideal worker*, the *ideal mother*, and the *ideal father* and suggests that young women (and men) need to make two fundamental changes to create more integrated lives. First, to balance their lives and to have more of the relaxed, "quality" time at home that both men and women crave, they will need to change *how* they work (see Radcliffe Public Policy Center n.d.). Second, with support from outside resources when needed, parents must reinvent their roles at home so that caring for children becomes a shared obligation rather than primarily the responsibility of one parent.

CHALLENGES FACED BY YOUNG WORKING WOMEN

All young working women face challenges in trying to live a full life that includes paid work and outside commitments. However, these challenges differ based on a young woman's level of education.

HIGHLY EDUCATED WOMEN AND THE TIME DILEMMA

Young women in this category spend a great deal of time, money, and effort on their education. Most work hard to gain experience, to set a good track record, and to secure a place for themselves in their profession before interrupting their careers to have children. Many highly educated young women immerse themselves in their careers, working hard to get ahead, and leaving family concerns outside or on the periphery of their daily routines.

Highly educated women who are also mothers often fear that if they modify or rearrange their work schedules to create more time for their children, their careers will suffer. Many young women who have changed their schedules to accommodate family responsibilities have suffered career consequences. Others have returned to a job following a maternity leave only to find that their employer has replaced them with someone who was willing and able to put work before all other life priorities. Some young women who have taken extended maternity leaves have experienced difficulty finding a job that is similar in pay and status to the one they left. Too often, highly educated women face significant setbacks when they step off the career fast track. Thus, many defer family involvement—although this decision can have unforeseen consequences as infertility tends to increase around the age that a significant number of these women begin trying to have children (Drago and Varner 2001). A growing percentage of women in this age group ultimately forgo motherhood altogether (Census Bureau 2001).

Many highly educated young women face a dilemma that is acutely visible in such time-intensive careers as law, medicine, and consulting. These careers often demand a high level of job commitment, which translates into the expectation that workers have no significant responsibilities outside work.

One high-achieving young professional woman working for an international business-consulting firm insisted on taking her guaranteed two-week vacation, only to be told during her annual review that "perhaps she had a little too much time on her hands." The unspoken message was that her priorities were out of order. The norm for employees who had not yet made partnership at this organization was to prove their worth by skipping vacations altogether or by taking only an occasional long weekend.

Another young woman in the same organization was tired of working 70-hour weeks, including weekends. She took a 20 percent pay cut to stop working Saturdays and Sundays. Her supervisor, impressed that the woman was completing all of her work without coming in on weekends, suggested that her full salary be reinstated. The young woman refused. She saw the pay cut as her only insurance for not having to work on weekends, regardless of how much she achieved during the week.

Many highly educated young women in time-intensive careers postpone marriage and children until their careers are firmly established. They do this because they fear that attending to these important personal commitments will further exacerbate the challenges they face around time. With and without children, the pressure to put the rest of their lives on hold while they prove their worth on the job makes daily life hectic, with little time to date or to spend with spouses and children.

MODERATELY EDUCATED WOMEN AND THE TIME/INCOME CRUNCH

Jacqueline and her moderately educated peers tend to view the role of work in their lives somewhat differently from Mary and her highly educated peers. While work is important to them, these moderately educated young women experience less career track pressure. As a result, they may not be as worried about leaving the workforce temporarily or reducing their work involvement to tend to family matters. Yet Jacqueline and her peers confront their own set of challenges. For example, less skilled workers are easier to replace than highly skilled workers, which gives them less bargaining power and job security when they want to take maternity leave or reduce their work hours. Less skilled workers are more financially vulnerable than their highly educated counterparts. In addition, they experience a similar daily time crunch in managing work, family, errands, and other domestic responsibilities but often lack the resources to help alleviate the stress. Many cannot afford services that could save them time, such as regular domestic help to clean their homes, cook for them, and watch their children. Moderately educated women, therefore, face both a time crunch and an income crunch.

MINIMALLY EDUCATED WOMEN
AND THE WORK-FAMILY CRISIS

Young women in the minimally educated group experience the same challenges that moderately educated women face but to an even greater degree. These women are easily replaced by other workers and typically have no bargaining power at work regarding scheduling flexibility.

For example, a cleaning woman who works at an office building, like Gloria, must come in at night when the office workers are gone for the day. If she does not, her boss can quickly find someone else to fill her job. She does not have the option of changing her shift or working from home, and she cannot afford to reduce her work hours. Too often, she is forced to find a second job or to work overtime just to make ends meet. Typically, women in low-paying jobs that require minimal skills are expected to be available according to their job's schedule, with little thought for workers' needs.

The lack of work-life choices that young women with little education face is compounded by several factors (Garey 1999; Albelda 2001). First, they are the lowest paid workers in the labor force but are more likely to have children compared to women with more education. As a result, many young women with limited education need child care services, which they often cannot afford. Also, these young women typically have insufficient income to cover the food, clothing, and health care costs that children require.

Second, young women with little education and few skills are often required to work irregular hours, including late-night or especially long shifts, which are exhausting and do not correspond to typical child care hours. Third, these young women often work seasonal or sporadic hours, which lead to additional income and child care problems. Finally, women with little education frequently do not receive job benefits. This fact renders them vulnerable to expenses that employers cover for other workers, such as health care costs.

Thus, young women at the bottom of the educational ladder find themselves in a Catch–22 situation. They need to work, yet working itself presents additional problems. Finding a job that pays enough to cover the costs of working, including transportation and child care, with enough left over to live on is difficult. To help them break out of this cycle, many young women in these circumstances need help from external sources, including public programs.

IDEAL WORKER EXPECTATIONS

Young women operate in a world based on outdated concepts about the *ideal worker* (Williams 2000). In the old reality, men worked outside of the home and women worked inside the home, managing the family. What resulted was an artificial wall separating paid work from life at home.

This wall arose from the assumption that people came to work without any outside responsibilities, that they worked at least 40 hours a week with typical nine-to-five business hours five days a week (or more), and that they did so throughout their working careers. The ideal worker did not ask for, expect, seem to need, or even imagine working reduced hours for temporary periods to attend to such personal matters as child care, ailing parents, or a separate life passion.

Largely because of the large-scale influx of women into the labor force, the ideal worker norm has become increasingly gender-neutral—that is, it is open to anyone willing to put his or her career ahead of a life outside of work. Yet because women are also expected to perform more of the "work" at home, the ideal worker norm disproportionately affects their ability to get ahead at work.

Because many women cannot meet ideal worker standards throughout their careers, too often employers view them, consciously or unconsciously, as potential risks or poor long-term investments. Although most women having children today return to work soon after giving birth, questions often arise about how parenting will affect their work and whether they will demand changes in their schedules, miss work because of a sick child, or quit their job altogether. In other words, employers may not see working mothers as full team players.

The artifical wall separating work and home life also affects men. Very few families today have one parent who stays home full time since most working men are married to working women. The lives of both young women and young men are negatively influenced by old ideal worker expectations, which clash with today's realities and ultimately can wreak havoc on family life.

IDEAL PARENT EXPECTATIONS

While young women confront the ideal worker norm at work, they run into another set of challenges at home. Working full time or nearly full time outside the home makes it difficult for young women to manage their domestic lives as seamlessly as many of their mothers appeared to manage theirs. This fact often leaves them stretched too thin, both at work and at home. Despite many changes in men's roles at home, women remain disproportionately responsible for organizing their children's activities and managing household functions such as cooking, shopping, errands, and cleaning. Mothers generally are the ones who take off from work when children are sick or when backup care falls through, manage summer care and vacation days, and arrange their work schedules, wherever possible, to provide whatever parental time and direct care are needed.

The solid domestic ground of an earlier era has become more shaky. Young working women today often have one foot in the domestic/family camp and the other at work, and they must constantly redistribute their energy and focus to keep their lives on track. This complicated dance that young women are expected to perform (which inspired the term "supermom") leaves many of them exhausted from trying to do two full-time jobs. These young women manage a "second shift" at home after finishing a full day of paid work elsewhere (Hochschild 1990). As a result, women's stress and fatigue levels skyrocket, and their relationships with partners often become strained under the unrealistic expectation that they can and should "do it all."

Our cultural paradigm of parenting roles is based on outdated stereotypes, attributing different skills and weaknesses to mothers and fathers and distinct domains of responsibility. Usually, when a woman becomes a mother, her own expectations and those of others move her in the direction of a particular ideal. Regardless of her work situation, she faces internal and external pressures to become the *ideal mother*, a woman who puts the needs of her children and husband before her own needs as an individual.

While the ideal mother's identity is wrapped up in domesticity and her role as parent and homemaker, the *ideal father*'s realm is fiscal responsibility to his family. The ideal father is concerned that domestic routines go well and that the people at home are happy. However, he does not invest himself significantly in child care or other household chores. Instead, he immerses himself in work to provide financially for his family.

In contrast to the neutral gender of the ideal worker, the ideal mother and ideal father norms are deeply rooted in gender, and both young women and young men find it challenging to think differently about their gendered roles as parents. Before having children, they work hard to meet the demands of work. Suddenly, as new parents, regardless of their socioeconomic status, and often without even realizing it, these young couples fall into traditional patterns. Occasionally, both parents think creatively and negotiate new roles that suit their individual desires and priorities. But all too often, the father, the mother, or both parents hold onto very traditional assumptions about how they should behave.

BALANCING WORK AND FAMILY

Young women who are balancing work and family are caught by the force of these patterns and assumptions. They strive to be ideal workers in a world in which doing so still requires that they have minimal responsibilities outside of work. At the same time, they strive to be ideal mothers in a world in which mothers are now also expected to work outside of the home for pay. The arrival of a baby moves this dilemma to center stage. How can women achieve both ideals? Three potential outcomes can result from these competing demands.

In the first, the arrival of a child prompts parents to take on traditional roles: the women drop out of the workforce while the men assume sole financial responsibility for the family. In a variation of this approach, mothers significantly reduce their work hours so they can continue working while providing primary care for their children. As the mothers cut back on paid work, the fathers increasingly become the primary breadwinners, and both begin to conform to more stereotypical sex roles.

In a second, more contemporary outcome, both parents return to full-time work soon after the arrival of a baby and continue to aim to be ideal workers while using full-time child care. Some couples use this arrangement because of real financial need. Others do so because they cannot imagine any alternative or because they fear significant career ramifications if they choose to reduce their work hours.

The third outcome is relatively new and particularly timely.[2] Young working parents who have adopted this approach find it an excellent alternative to more widely practiced ways of tackling work and family responsibilities. These innovative couples challenge old ideal worker assumptions and reorganize their jobs to create more time for their lives outside work. Further distinguishing themselves from generations before them, they also experiment with new roles at home, sharing child care, domestic tasks, and fiscal responsibilities (DeGroot and Fine 2001). Below are two stories that exemplify this approach.

Holly is a 34-year-old woman who has completed two years of college. She is the mother of three children, age 11, nine, and one. She had her first child at 22, soon after marriage, and her second child when she was 25. Holly took a full year of maternity leave after the birth of each of her first two children before returning to work full time on a five-day, 6 A.M. to 2 P.M. schedule. Initially, she worked as a breakfast and lunch cook. Now she works as a pastry chef at a high-end grocery store. Her ex-husband, Sam, who is the father of her first two children, is a bartender. When they were married, Sam worked four 12-hour shifts from 4 P.M. to 4 A.M., totaling 48 hours each week.

Holly and Sam shared in the care of their children, with no outside help. Because they worked different hours, each was able to take responsibility for the children's care at different points in the day without needing to negotiate any changes in their work schedules. The difficulty with this arrangement was that they had little time to see each other and share each other's lives.

Holly and Cameron, her current partner, decided to avoid the extra strain that working opposite shifts puts on a relationship. Cameron works as a media support person, helping to meet the technical support needs of teachers at a local university. When Holly and Cameron's now–one-year-old daughter was born, Holly took a three-month paid leave by using a combination of six weeks' short-term disability coverage and "benefit hours" that she had accumulated over the past year. She and Cameron decided it would be better to combine Holly's shift work with a less-than-full-time schedule for him. Between the extra help from Cameron's mother on the day that Holly and Cameron's work schedules overlap and Cameron's reduced work hours, the couple feels that they have created a work/family balance with ample time for their daughter and their family. Although their financial situation is tight, Holly and Cameron agree that the extra time has been worth it. Holly and her ex-husband, Sam, continue to share in the care of their two school-age children.

Linda, a 34-year-old corporate consultant with an M.B.A, and Brad, a software company manager, both negotiated flexible work hours in their traditional nine-to-five jobs so that they could share the primary care of their two-year-old son, Sam. Even before marrying, Linda grappled long and hard with how to balance work and children and brought this issue up with Brad once it became clear that they were moving toward a committed relationship. Successful at work, they both truly enjoy what they do. Yet they are aware that other life involvements are also important to them. Once they started a family, Linda and Brad wanted to ensure that they would have both time with their children and time alone, as individuals and as a couple.

They made several deliberate decisions that have enabled them to realize their goals of balancing work and other life priorities. Linda and Brad saved money for a year so that they could take parental leave together when their child was born. They also arranged to work four days a week rather than five so they could spend more time with Sam. Now Linda stays at home on Tuesdays and Brad stays at home on Thursdays. The other three days of the week they use the support of a neighborhood child care center. Linda and Brad also take turns having one night to themselves every week, and once a month Linda's sister takes Sam overnight so that Linda and Brad can have time together as a couple.

ADAPTING TO OUR TIMES: CHANGING ROLES AT WORK AND AT HOME

For young women to achieve a good balance between work and responsibilities outside of work, significant changes need to occur in both of these realms. Work at home must become a shared responsibility between the adults in a family. At the same time, paid work must change to fit within a new, twenty-first-century framework in which employees have time and energy to enjoy and manage the other important parts of their lives.

REORGANIZING PAID WORK

Like the couples profiled above, many young women and their partners are reorganizing work to meet their personal needs. Women in the decade between 25 and 35 are beginning to recognize that the new information age allows them to approach employment in different ways. Whereas 25 years ago, most employees had to be physically present to do their work, this is no longer true for a wide range of jobs. Furthermore, for jobs that must be performed at the workplace, there are new approaches to help employees design flexible work options such as job-sharing, condensed workweeks, and part-time benefits.

Increasingly, employers and employees are experimenting with new ideas about *how* to do work and replacing the old definition of an ideal worker with a new twenty-first-century standard—the *integrated worker*. Instead of assuming that young women and men come to work free of outside responsibilities, insightful employers understand that most employees have important priorities outside of work. These employers also recognize that when workers change *how* they work in order to accommodate nonwork duties, they often develop solutions that make them more efficient employees (see Bailyn, Fletcher, and Kolb 1997; Friedman, Christensen, and DeGroot 1998). The story that follows illustrates this new approach.

Three years ago, Jane found herself dissatisfied with her work-life balance. At 27, she was rapidly progressing up the career ladder in one of the big 10 accounting firms but found that she had no energy and too little time to devote to her real passion: creative writing. Having majored in accounting and English in college, Jane realized that to continue to be happy at work, she needed to make time to focus on her writing. After several months of ruminating over how to do this, Jane approached her department's human resources manager. To Jane's delight, he was open to helping her work out a solution to accommodate her work and personal goals. Jane and the human resources manager agreed that she would reduce her client load from 12 to eight. This way, during the off-season in accounting, she would have time to devote to her creative writing projects, and during the busy seasons, she would put more hours into her paid work.

Halfway through the year on this new schedule, Jane realized that her job redesign needed some fine-tuning. The central assignments office had been calling her during her "writing time," asking her to take on additional work. Although Jane could have legitimately declined the work, as she had already completed her contractual tasks, she was wary that refusing the additional work might have a negative impact on her career.

Jane met again with her human resources manager, along with a member of the central assignments office. Together they developed a way to track Jane's hours so there would be no misunderstanding about when she was available for client work. Jane also suggested that she try using email and faxes to communicate with clients instead of always meeting with them in person.

The benefits of the new arrangement became apparent within the year. With fewer clients, Jane felt more focused at work and thus became more committed and effective. She could plan her time in advance and find better ways to get projects done. Jane felt satisfied with the changes she had made at work. Just as important, she had created enough time to complete a novel during her time outside of work. Three years later, still following this alternative work schedule, Jane was promoted to manager along with others in her work cohort (see Friedman, Christensen, and DeGroot 1998).

REORGANIZING DOMESTIC WORK

Just as many young women realize that the way work is organized affects their lives outside of work, they also are coming to understand that their domestic roles shape their ability to work outside the home. Many young couples are starting to share the previously separate roles of provider and primary parent. Once they do so, the concepts of the ideal mother and ideal father begin to change. The old notion of an ideal mother is replaced by the image of a woman with a broader vision of her capabilities and expectations of herself, who puts her family's needs and interests alongside her desire to work. Similarly, the old model of the ideal father changes into one of a man who invests his time and energy equally in his home life and his work life. In the new schema, both parents approach work and family in an integrated way, making both spheres of life a priority.

This new integrated parent model can apply to a single or a married parent, which is especially important today when 17.3 percent of women age 25–34 maintain a one-parent household. Whether or not their mothers and fathers are married, children benefit when parents share responsibility for their care. However, in single-parent households (and two-parent households), extended family and community resources provide important supplemental support, as the following story illustrates.

Pam is a 26-year-old registered nurse and single mother. Since her daughter, Amy, was born three years ago, Pam has rearranged her work and Amy's care several times in an effort to balance time with her daughter and time at work. After Amy's birth, Pam took a three-month maternity leave. Until Amy was one and a half, Pam alternated between working two and three 12-hour nursing shifts per week while relatives and friends cared for Amy. Pam left her job when a scheduling policy change required her to work some night shifts but soon returned as a case manager, working a typical nine-to-five, five-day-a-week schedule. When she started her new hours, Pam enrolled Amy full time at a child care center.

This arrangement lasted for about a year, until Pam again switched jobs, this time to become a case manager for an insurance company, where she knew there was an opportunity to work from home after one year of employment. The drawback of the new job was that it paid less. To supplement her income, Pam started working with patients privately in their homes. She now does home care full time because the pay is significantly better than the case manager work, and she often finishes her workday by mid-afternoon.

When Pam switched jobs to become a case manager, she also changed her child care arrangement. Although she liked the center, she was concerned about its high staff turnover rate. Pam's mother, who lives close by, now cares for Amy. Pam is very pleased with this setup because it allows her to spend more time with her daughter. Pam plans to enroll Amy in preschool soon and envisions spending after-school hours with her beginning around 3:00 P.M., rather than using extended day care.

Although Amy's father does not see her every week, he is a steady presence in her life and consistently contributes toward the cost of her care.

MAKING INTEGRATED LIVES AN OPTION FOR EVERYONE

Today's reality is that 70 percent of American women age 25–34 with children are in the labor force (see Chapter One). At the same time, if current trends continue, approximately 80 percent of women in this age group will have one or more children by the time they reach age 44 (Census Bureau 2001). This fact presents an opportunity for a new work-life template to enable contemporary and future generations of women and men to live integrated, satisfying lives. We recommend that individuals, businesses, and government take several steps to achieve this goal.

The first step, discussed earlier in the chapter, is to let go of the outdated concepts and behavior patterns for the ideal worker, the ideal mother, and the ideal father. If men's and women's careers and jobs continue to have markedly different trajectories once families have children, we will continue to hold ideals and expectations that are unrealistic given the demands of this new world and its new ways of working.

The second step is to make such solutions equally accessible to people of all financial and educational levels. Families that cannot financially afford to cut back their work hours, or that fear for their job security if they request flexibility, must be assisted through responsive, well-crafted public policies. These policies should enable all families to reduce work obligations to create time for meeting responsibilities at home.

Those with limited means should have the right to work reduced hours at different times in their work lives in order to care for children or seriously ill family members. To do so, they will need access to financial support, health insurance, and other important benefits when they are working less than full time.

One initiative that would ease the burden for parents of young children—especially those of limited means—is high-quality, universal preschool for three- and four-year-olds. There is ample evidence that children in this age group are socially ready to be with their peers and that they benefit from steady interaction with them.

The third step that will help young women and men to live more integrated lives is to hold all the different stakeholders—including individuals and families, employers, unions, and government—responsible for their part in the change process (Bailyn, Drago, and Kochan 2001). Starting at the individual and family levels, mothers and fathers will need to learn how to adopt a new approach to parenting, in which each is actively involved in the primary care of their children. At the employment level, organizations will need to eliminate outdated work practices and expectations, adopting in their place new norms that allow employees to work and have time for their lives outside of work. Unions must do their part in making flexibility an important part of their bargaining agenda. Finally, legislators must develop policies to support changes that allow for integrated lifestyles.

Through a combined effort, we can move beyond outdated work-life paradigms to create a new world in which workers, workplaces, families, and communities are more in sync with each other. Attaining this goal will benefit all of us. Workers, both women and men, will benefit from more integrated lives with more time for themselves, their families, and their communities. Workplaces will benefit from the retention of women workers and the higher productivity that results from more satisfied employees. And children will benefit from the attention of both parents rather than one. The combination of these changes will have ramifications for generations to come, for it is likely that children who grow up in shared parenting arrangements will forge similar solutions when they become adults and start families of their own.

NOTES

1. Jacqueline's, Mary's, and Gloria's stories are composites of women between the ages of 25 and 35. All other stories included in this chapter are the stories of real women's lives, and pseudonyms have been used to protect their privacy.
2. The authors work with the ThirdPath Institute, a nonprofit organization dedicated to teaching parents a new approach to work and family. Through workshops and educational materials, the Institute provides parents with practical hands-on information on how to redesign work and share in the care of their children.

Five

THE ECONOMICS OF YOUNG WOMEN TODAY

Lani Luciano

HIGHLIGHTS

THE STEADY DECREASE of employment discrimination has positioned many women age 25–34 to achieve the full financial self-determination denied to earlier generations of women. Yet the benefits of economic equality have not been distributed equally. This chapter examines the financial status of a generation of women equipped well, if not uniformly, to acquire wealth. How do their economic lives and prospects differ from those of their baby-boomer mothers and from men their age? What are their habits and attitudes regarding money, their strengths and weaknesses? What public and private policies will help determine their financial fates? Key findings from this chapter include:

- The earnings gap between men and women has been consistently smaller in the 25–34 cohort than in older age groups and has diminished over time, particularly for the well-educated. However, for the poorly schooled and minorities, substantial wage handicaps remain. Part-time workers, the self-employed, and those hired by small or low-wage businesses also may lack such vital workplace subsidies as health insurance and pension coverage.
- The true measure of economic self-sufficiency is not wages but financial assets that grow in value over time. Household consolidation, either through marriage or cohabitation, substantially increases young

women's wealth profile. Debts, however, such as the student loans that underpin many young women's professional aspirations, may significantly delay progress.

- Women's earnings are important in determining their families' standard of living. Yet absence from the workplace for child rearing or other family responsibilities reduces women's lifetime ability to accumulate individual assets, as do inadequate earnings. Those who lack savings opportunities in their early years face increasingly high barriers to the accumulation of personal wealth as they age. Many young women say they value financial security but lack of initiative, commitment, confidence, or skills often impede their financial progress.

- Unskilled women have few options for improving their economic situation or even maintaining it during financial setbacks. Elimination of public assistance as a permanent entitlement has forced some young mothers into a job market in which they are often ill-prepared to succeed. For these women, failure brings dire economic consequences.

- The future may hold some promising developments for improving low-income women's economic well-being, such as expanded tax credits and enactment of "living wage" laws. However, other, more ominous trends, such as the proposal to replace guaranteed Social Security benefits with self-directed accounts, may penalize low-earning, long-living females. In a social and political climate that increasingly emphasizes self-reliance, women whose individual circumstances or personal choices limit their ability to accumulate financial assets during their working years may face an impoverished old age.

INTRODUCTION

For women, the young adult years can be particularly significant to future financial security. Money earned and invested early in their working lives will compound over decades, growing steadily even during nonworking periods, such as time out for child rearing. Those who miss or are denied this early opportunity, however, may find it increasingly difficult to build sufficient assets as they age.

This chapter discusses how the financial lives and prospects of today's young women differ from those of their baby-boomer mothers and from men their age. It also looks at young women's habits and attitudes regarding money, their financial strengths and weaknesses, and public and private policies that will help determine their fiscal futures.

EARNINGS AND JOB BENEFITS

Young women today are much more likely to be self-supporting or to contribute substantially to their families' income than their mothers were. They are also, on average, better able to do so (see Table V-1).

CLOSING THE GAP

Throughout recent decades, earnings for women age 25–34 have been consistently nearer to the earnings of men in the same age group than they have been to the earnings of female workers as a whole. In addition, the wage gap between women and men has been shrinking faster for women age 25–34 than for older age groups.

In 1979 (the earliest year for which data are available), women wage-and-salary workers' full-time earnings were just 62.1 percent of men's; however, women 25–34 earned 67.4 percent as much as men in their age group. By 2000, the gap among young male and female workers had narrowed further. Young women's median weekly earnings were 81.9 percent of those of young men, while women of all ages made 73.6 percent of the earnings of men in all ages. (See Table 5–2 in the "Statistical Portrait" for the actual median weekly earnings in 2000.) For young part-timers—that is, people working fewer than 35 hours per week—pay in 2000 was nearly identical. Female

Table V-1 • Median Personal Income of Women Age 25–74 by Age, 1960–2000[1,2]

	Income When Age (2000 dollars)					Age in 2000
Year Born	25–34	35–44	45–54	55–64	65–74	
1926–1935	8,699	13,330	12,740	12,069	10,793	65–74
1936–1945	12,460	12,864	18,271	16,465		55–64
1946–1955	13,875	18,623	24,196			45–54
1956–1965	16,164	21,861				35–44
1966–1975	20,937					25–34

[1]The income shown in this table is personal income. In the case of a woman who lives alone, or who is the sole support of a family, her personal income constitutes the household's entire income.
[2]The CPI-U-RS was used to inflate the earnings series.

Source: Census Bureau, *Historical Income Tables,* Table P-8, <http://www.census.gov/hhes/income/histinc/p08.html>, 2001d.

workers age 25–34 had median wages of $211 per week, compared with $216 for men in their age group (Bureau of Labor Statistics 2001b).

In fields with a particularly large influx of women, the wage gap for full-timers may have been erased. A study of 2000 data from the Bureau of Labor Statistics found that, for women age 25–34 working full time in the 10 occupations with the greatest growth in female workers (veterinarians, public administrators, math/science teachers, chemistry teachers, industrial engineers, dentists, car salespeople, messengers, physician's assistants, and clergy), wage gaps are either nonexistent or women earn slightly more than men (Economic Policy Foundation 2001b).

WHO LAGS BEHIND?

The widening income inequalities that shadowed the early working lives of baby boomers in the 1970s and 1980s abated in the mid-1990s. However, global competition, immigration, the decline of unions, and the increasing use of temporary workers have kept a tight lid on the economic prospects of workers at the lowest economic rung (Census Bureau 2000a). (See Chapter Two for details about low-wage workers among women age 25–34.)

EDUCATION

The decline of employment discrimination has made higher education a greater determinant of female earning power than it once was, widening the gap between well-educated women and those with less schooling. However, even the best-educated women have not achieved overall wage parity with men.

In 1974, female college graduates age 25–34 working full time earned less than male high school graduates but roughly 30 percent more than female high school graduates (Blau, Ferber, and Winkler 1998). By 2000, the female baccalaureates earned considerably more than did male high school graduates, whose inflation-adjusted wages had declined, but still just 82 percent of male college graduates' wages. Compared with the earnings of female high school graduates, however, the well-educated women had pulled ahead by more than 50 percent, mainly because of stagnant wages for workers without advanced education (see Figure V-1).

Although lack of a college degree handicaps both sexes, the economic impact is more acute for women. In 2000, female high school graduates age 25–34 earned only 75 percent as much as male high school graduates— roughly the same as males without high school diplomas (Census Bureau 2000b).

Figure V-1 • Average Earnings of Women and Men Age 25–34 by Educational Attainment, 1975, 1980, 1985, 1990, 1995, and 2000

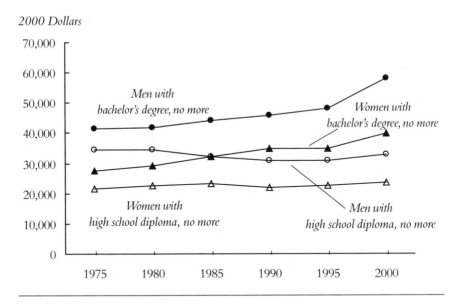

2000 Dollars

Source: Census Bureau, *Historical Income Tables,* Tables P32, P33, P34, and P35, <http://www.census.gov/hhes/income/histinc/>, 2001b.

Among women of the same age, education has not entirely eliminated wage disparities. This fact may be tied to race. In 2000, the median earnings of black female college graduates age 25–34 working full time, year round, were $30,888, while those of white female college graduates were $34,205. The median earnings of Hispanic female college graduates fell in between, at $32,396 (Census Bureau 2000b).

TIME AWAY FROM THE LABOR FORCE

Experts disagree about whether persistent wage gaps between the sexes mainly reflect a continuing bias in the workforce or women's generally more sporadic work lives, which may limit their opportunities for earnings advancement. Indeed, while mothers of young children are increasingly likely to work for pay (see Chapter One), full or partial absence from the workforce for child rearing or other family responsibilities significantly reduces their lifetime earnings.

An analysis of 1995 population-wide data showed that women's average earnings trended upward toward an economy-wide average wage (EWA)— the average of all wages of all workers—from age 16 through their early forties, but remained below the EWA throughout their working lives. In contrast, men's average wages rose above the EWA by their late twenties and didn't drop below it until retirement age (Employee Benefit Research Institute 2000a).

EMPLOYEE BENEFITS

Most employers are legally required to provide some financial subsidies to employees, including unemployment insurance, workers' compensation, and a 50 percent share of the payroll taxes that fund Social Security. Many voluntarily provide such additional subsidies as health insurance and retirement savings plans.

A worker with no employer-provided health insurance—usually a part-time or temporary employee, freelancer, or employee of a very small business—may still be covered by a spouse's insurance. If she isn't, she must either pay for her own insurance, at an annual cost well into four figures, or do without, which makes her vulnerable to crippling debt if she requires major medical care (see Chapter Three). Low-wage workers of Hispanic origin are the most likely to lack coverage.

Although young women age 25–34 have medical expenses averaging more than twice those of men their age, only 81.1 percent of these young women had health insurance coverage for part or all of 2000. In most cases, their insurance was through employers. Two-thirds of young women were covered through their own or their spouses' jobs, 9.8 percent were covered by Medicaid or another public program, and a mere 3.8 percent bought their own private coverage. Nearly one in five (18.9 percent) had no health insurance of any kind at any time during the year (see Table III-5 in Chapter Three).

Company-sponsored retirement savings plans offer several financial advantages to employees, including tax benefits and, in some cases, cash incentives. Part-time workers and employees of very small businesses are the least likely of all workers to be covered by company pension plans. Contract workers, such as freelancers or temps, are not covered at all.

In 1998, roughly 35 percent of all women age 27–35 (the cohort sample used in the study), including those not currently in the workforce, reported that they were covered by a company-sponsored pension. For currently employed workers, the percentage was higher and rising. In 1998, 45 percent of female workers age 27–35 reported having one or more workplace pensions, up from 41 percent in 1989 (Employee Benefit Research Institute 2000b).

The type of pension coverage has changed, however. (See discussion of policy implications at the end of the chapter.) In 1989, 25 percent of female workers age 27–35 were covered by a defined-benefit plan (the traditional pension arrangement in which an employer bears most or all of the cost and risk) and 25 percent had coverage under a defined-contribution plan (in which most of the cost and risk is borne by the employee). By 1998, only 13 percent of women age 27–35 had defined-benefit plans, while 34 percent had defined-contribution plans.

Although most young women with a defined-contribution plan in their workplace contribute to that plan, a greater percentage of young men take advantage of this opportunity for wealth accumulation. In 1989, 73 percent of women age 27–35 with a defined-contribution plan available to them actually contributed to the plan, the same percentage as men in that age group. By 1998, however, men age 27–35 were considerably more likely than women in that age group to contribute—86 percent of men compared with 76 percent of women (Employee Benefit Research Institute 2000b).

INCOME

Income is a broader measure of financial means than earnings. Income may include earnings, but it may also include other sources of monetary support, such as investment dividends and interest, business profits, government or private benefits, and material assistance from others. The median income for women age 25–34 has risen fairly steadily since the mid-1970s, increasing, in constant 2000 dollars, from $14,338 in 1975 to $20,937 in 2000. In contrast, the median income for men in that age group dropped from $31,323 to $30,634 over the same period (Census Bureau 2001b).

Between 1999 and 2000, median incomes for all people age 25–34 rose 1.2 percent. Because the percent change in median income for full-time, year-round workers age 25–34, both female and male, is considered statistically insignificant, it is not clear from the data available whether rising wages were the reason for the increase in overall income.

WORKING MOTHERS

Since the 1970s, the economic well-being of households has rested more and more on women, including the working mothers of young children. Between 1975 and 1996, for example, there was a net gain of nearly 19 percent in the real (inflation-adjusted) median income of married couples of all ages with minor children. With wives' earnings excluded, the median would have decreased by nearly two percent. By 1996, mothers' earnings accounted for 29 percent of median household income for married couples with children—more than twice that of 20 years before (Census Bureau 1998).

SINGLE MOTHERS

Of course, not all mothers are married, not all single mothers work, and not all single mothers who work are able to support their children adequately. Owing in large part to the passage of welfare reform in 1996, the percentage of single mothers who are working has increased from 75.2 percent to 81.9 percent[1] (Center on Budget and Policy Priorities 2001). Although the poverty rates of single working mother families have declined accordingly, they remain far higher than those of other families. In 2000, 25 percent of all single working-mother families were poor, compared with 5.1 percent of all families with children. Among single mothers who did not work, however, 74 percent were poor in 2000 (Census Bureau 2001c).

Although extreme financial need among households headed by women of all ages with no male present has declined steadily since 1991—when 47.1 percent were below the poverty level, compared with 32.5 percent in 2000—racial disparities remain. In 2000, more than 41 percent of families headed by black and Hispanic women with no spouse present were in poverty, compared with 27.5 percent of households headed by white women with no spouse present (Census Bureau 2001e).

NET WORTH[2]

Women age 25–34 are far more likely to be living with a spouse or partner than to be living alone (see Chapter One). This circumstance improves the financial standing of these households in two ways. Even if two can't live quite as cheaply as one, domestic consolidation provides some economies of scale. Just as important, women tend to marry or to partner with men who earn as much or more than they do. Couples thus are more likely than unattached single people to have disposable household income that they can invest in items of value—such as houses, cars, or stocks and bonds.

When it comes to households of which women age 25–34 are a part, those in married-couple and living-with-partner arrangements, with either one or two incomes, are by far the most prosperous—having total assets with a median value of $55,800 and $41,100 respectively in 1998 (see Table V-2). Single women reported household assets with a median value of $11,450—a little over half of the total assets reported by single male householders in the same age group.

The bulk of most Americans' current and likely future wealth rests on two sources: home equity and, increasingly, a tax-deferred retirement savings plan.

Table V-2 • Selected Assets and Debts of Women and Men Age 25–34 by Type of Household, 1998

	Two-Income Couple[1]		One-Income Couple[1]		Single Women		Single Men	
	Median Value (dollars)	Percentage with Asset or Debt	Median Value (dollars)	Percentage with Asset or Debt	Median Value (dollars)	Percentage with Asset or Debt	Median Value (dollars)	Percentage with Asset or Debt
Total assets	**41,140**	**94.9**	**55,840**	**96.2**	**11,450**	**89.2**	**21,260**	**92.6**
Liquid assets	7,550	90.0	5,200	84.8	3,050	82.8	3,801	89.3
Retirement accounts	7,500	49.0	10,500	33.7	6,100	31.5	8,000	44.3
Vehicle	9,700	80.2	8,900	82.3	4,400	60.3	7,400	69.8
Primary residence[2]	80,000	43.4	130,000	55.6	(3)	22.9	(3)	25.1
Home equity	17,000	—	26,000	—	(3)	—	(3)	—
Total debt	**24,270**	**100.0**	**39,200**	**100.0**	**9,970**	**100.0**	**10,400**	**100.0**
Home mortgage/ equity loan	66,000	36.6	81,000	52.2	(3)	16.4	(3)	18.5
Credit card debt(s)	1,600	56.2	2,400	40.4	1,500	41.4	1,400	52.8
Installment loan(s)[4]	10,000	62.1	7,200	60.4	7,700	48.4	8,900	53.5

[1]Includes married and partner couples.

[2]Total value of home including the amount secured by a loan.

[3]The sample of respondents was below the threshold considered statistically reliable.

[4]Includes student loans and car loans.

Source: Special analysis of the 1998 Federal Reserve's Survey of Consumer Finances, conducted by Mark Calabria and Darryl Getter for the Women's Research and Education Institute (WREI), 2001.

HOME OWNERSHIP

Married couples in which at least one partner is age 25–34 are more likely to own their own home than to rent, while unmarried individuals under 35 predominantly rent or live with their parents. Those who do own are more likely to be male than female. Between 1982 and 1997, home ownership among young single women held steady at 15 to 16 percent for those in the 25–29 age group, and at 29 to 30 percent for those in the 30–34 age group. Since 1997, however, home-ownership rates for single women have soared, reaching 21 percent for women age 25–29 and nearly 32 percent for the older cohort. Home-ownership rates for single men have increased as well, but not by as much. Among those age 25–29, the rates increased slightly from 23 percent in 1982 to a little over 27 percent in 2000. For the older cohort, home-ownership rates have increased from about 36 percent to 38 percent (Census Bureau 2001f).

In 1998, the median equity in a home owned by a one-income couple in which the woman was age 25–34 was $26,000. The median value of their primary residence was $130,000. For two-income couples, both home equity ($17,000) and value ($80,000) were lower. Unfortunately, the population of unmarried home owners is small, and we lack reliable information about their homes' median value and equity.

TAX-DEFERRED SAVINGS

To encourage workers to save a portion of their earnings for their nonworking years, the U.S. tax code allows them to open special retirement savings accounts and contribute money not subject to current taxation. These tax-advantaged plans include individual retirement accounts (IRAs), 401(k)s, Keoghs, and simplified employee pensions (SEPs). Some options are offered only through employers; others are available only to the self-employed. IRAs are available to anyone with earnings.

The decline in defined-benefit pensions—the kind funded entirely by employers—has made worker-funded plans increasingly important to workers' future financial security. Yet shorter job tenures, lower salaries, and risk-averse investing styles take their toll on women's ability to build retirement savings. In 1989, women age 27–35 with employer-sponsored defined-contribution plans had an average of $11,525 in their accounts, about equal to the account balances of men. However, the average account balance of the next age cohort (women age 36–44) was just $14,009 in 1989, compared with more than $40,000 for men in that age group (see Table V-3).

Table V-3 • Pension Accumulation by Women and Men Age 18–62 by Age, 1989 and 1998 (in 1998 dollars)

	Average Accumulated Defined-Contribution Balance		Women's Balance as a Percentage of Men's	Average Accumulated IRA Balance		Women's Balance as a Percentage of Men's
	Women	Men		Women	Men	
Total age 18–62 in 1989	16,372	41,149	40	17,053	26,576	64
Total age 18–62 in 1998	25,020	57,239	44	26,307	56,429	47
Age 18–26 in 1998	2,794	4,532	62	17,415[1]	8,009	217
Age 18–26 in 1989	4,140	3,607	115	2,073	2,554	81
Age 27–35 in 1998	11,875	28,152	42	10,260	22,956	45
Age 27–35 in 1989	11,525	11,912	97	7,866	9,183	86
Age 36–44 in 1998	23,074	50,761	45	20,874	33,614	62
Age 36–44 in 1989	14,009	40,349	35	12,249	21,897	56
Age 45–53 in 1998	45,412	72,621	63	33,816	64,826	52
Age 45–53 in 1989	15,768	65,081	24	25,501	29,226	87
Age 54–62 in 1998	25,557	123,625	21	38,579	105,482	37
Age 54–62 in 1989	47,362	82,113	58	22,025	47,708	46

[1]This large average balance may reflect the presence of a few large portfolios in a very small sample.

Source: Employee Benefit Research Institute, "Women and Pensions: A Decade of Progress?" *EBRI Issue Brief 227*, November 2000b, Table 2. Data used with permission.

Evidence suggests that today's young women workers, as they age, may fall even farther behind their male peers. In 1998, despite rising female wages, women age 27–35 had an average of just $11,875 in their workplace defined-contribution plan accounts, compared with $28,152 for men in that age group (Employee Benefit Research Institute 2000b).

Workers lacking access to company savings plans such as 401(k)s can get most of the same tax advantages through individual retirement accounts or special savings plans for the self-employed. However, participation rates in these self-initiated plans are much lower than they are for employer-sponsored programs. The percentage of employed women age 27–35 with IRAs rose only slightly between 1989 and 1998, from 15 percent to 18 percent, while the percentage of young males with IRAs dropped from 19 percent to 15 percent. These low rates of independent saving may reflect young people's financial ignorance, nonchalance about the future, lack of motivation, or reluctance to part with the contribution money. Aging may inspire second thoughts, however. By 1998, the percentage of IRA owners age 36–44 stood at 28 percent for females and 25 percent for males (Employee Benefit Research Institute 2000b).

OTHER ASSETS

Financial holdings other than homes or retirement savings accounts play only a minor role in the wealth of most adults age 25–34. Although technically assets, vehicles generally shrink in value over time, decreasing rather than increasing overall wealth. Liquid assets, such as checking accounts or bank passbook savings accounts, account for the remaining wealth of most young women who own assets. In 1998, single women reported liquid assets with a median value of $3,050, compared with liquid assets of $3,801 for single men. Women in one-income couple partnerships were slightly ahead, with $5,200 in liquid assets per household, while two-income couples had the most, $7,550. Additional categories of assets—such as securities held outside a tax-deferred plan, cash-value life insurance, or investment real estate—are held by too few young women to produce meaningful numbers.

MONEY MANAGEMENT

Accumulating wealth depends not just on the ability and opportunity to earn money but on managing it well. Although excessive spending and debt are significant barriers to financial security, the economic progress of young women is just as likely to be hampered by other factors, such as lack of initiative and commitment or risk-averse investing styles.

SPENDING

Households headed by a person under age 35 spend about the same percentage of their income on food, housing, and entertainment as do those headed by older consumers. They spend relatively more on clothes, services, and transportation and relatively less on health care and charity (Bureau of Labor Statistics 2000a). Within those spending categories, however, there are further distinctions. Young adults age 25–34 are more likely than are people age 35 and over to rent their housing, buy a car, and eat their food away from home (Bureau of Labor Statistics 2000b).

Although the spending patterns of single women age 25–34 do not differ markedly from those of single men in that age category, the percentage of after-tax income spent by single women and men varies tremendously. Indeed, during 1998 to 1999, single women spent 99.0 percent of their after-tax income, compared with 88.0 percent spent by single men. They spent 37.7 percent of their income on housing, compared with 30.2 percent spent by men, and 5.7 percent on food at home, compared with 4.1 percent spent by men. Even clothing and shoes did not account for much difference—an average of 6.1 percent for women compared with 4.3 percent for men. Perhaps surprisingly, single women spent 8.2 percent on car purchases, significantly more than the 5.1 percent spent by men. Possibly reflecting cultural norms, men spent more on entertainment (5.2 percent compared with 4.2 percent spent by women) and dining out (7.0 compared with 5.3 percent spent by women) (Bureau of Labor Statistics 2000b).

Households with at least one partner age 25–34 spent, on average, considerably more on car purchases than single individuals in that age group did—$12,519, compared with $3,500. However, they spent just $1,776 on entertainment, not much more than single men spent. Couples spent an average of $2,890 at home and $2,250 away (Bureau of Labor Statistics 2000a, 2001a).

DEBT

Household debt levels rose steadily during the 1980s and 1990s, reaching an aggregate all-time high of more than 100 percent of average household income in 2000 (BCA Research 2001). For unmarried adults age 25–34, debt is likely to consist principally of installment financing, such as education and car loans and credit card balances. In 1998, households consisting of single women age 25–34 reported a median debt of $9,970, somewhat less than that of single men in the same age group, who reported median debt of $10,400. These women reported installment loans totaling a median $7,700 and credit card balances of a median $1,500. Debt for their male counterparts was similarly distributed. Total median debt for both one- and two-income couples age 25–34 was considerably higher—$39,200 and $24,270 respectively, reflecting a higher rate of home ownership than that of singles (see Table V-2).

Ratios of debt to income, however, are not similar among single people. In 1997, the debts of single women in the younger half of our cohort constituted a median 32 percent of their incomes, compared with 27 percent for single males in that age group—probably a reflection of women's generally lower salaries. Yet the debts of single women in the older half of the cohort constituted, on average, a smaller proportion of their income, nine percent, compared with single men in the same age group, whose debts equaled an average of 37 percent of their income.

Several factors may account for the wide post-30 gap, including single men's higher rate of home ownership and the resulting mortgage liabilities. It's undeniable, however, that steeply rising education costs and shrinking financial aid grants, along with the growing pursuit of advanced degrees, have increased debt burdens for the younger half of the 25–34 age cohort. A 1998 study of men and women who had student loans—the majority of whom were under 30 and female—found that the median student loan balance in 1997 was $13,000. Medians for previous studies are not available, but the averages reveal a trend. In 1997, the average student loan balance was $18,800, compared with $8,200 in 1991 and $7,500 in 1987 (Nellie Mae 1998).

For 25 percent of college graduates who attended four-year private institutions, student loan debt in 1997 was greater than their current annual incomes, as it was for 40 percent of the people who had borrowed for graduate study in medicine, law, or business. Forty percent of all borrowers said that student loan debt had caused them to delay home-buying, up from 25 percent in 1991; 22 percent said their loans had caused them to delay having children, up from 12 percent in 1991 (Nellie Mae 1998).

ATTITUDES AND BEHAVIORS

While earning handicaps may play a role in women's ability to amass wealth, so may the ways in which they think and act regarding money. Unlike many baby boomers who claimed to disdain money in their young adulthoods, roughly the same percentage of today's young women say they highly value financial security as say they do not. In a survey of males and females age

21–34 (median age 27.5), 49 percent of women ranked financial security as very important, compared with just 31 percent of men in that age group (see Table V-4). They consistently ranked such goals as buying a home, paying off debts, and saving for retirement higher than did men their age. Still, 44 percent of women (and 48 percent of men) asserted that it was more important to spend than to save, while 41 percent of women (and 47 percent of men) claimed that the more they spent, the better they felt about themselves. Forty-eight percent of women described themselves as living paycheck to paycheck, compared with 38 percent of men, and nearly half said they expected to have 30 pairs of shoes before they had $30,000 in retirement savings (OppenheimerFunds, Inc. 2001).

Next to commitment and favorable market conditions, investing skill is the most important determinant of success in financial management. As the looming retirement of baby boomers has caused the popular press to focus on financial topics, many young adults have become more sophisticated about investing. For example, back in 1989, a third of men and women age 27–35 put the bulk of their retirement funds into bonds, which over time typically produce far lower returns than stocks. By 1998, only 16 percent of

Table V-4 • Financial Attitudes of Women and Men Age 21–34, 2001 (in percentages)

	Women	*Men*
Goals considered very important:		
Buying a home	52	47
Paying off debts	65	56
Saving for retirement	48	45
Providing security for self	49	31
Felt strongly or somewhat strongly that:		
Money is for spending, not for saving	44	48
The more things I own, the better I feel	41	47
I will not be able to live better than my parents	32	33
Described themselves as living paycheck to paycheck	48	38
Expected to acquire 30 pairs of shoes before saving $30,000 for retirement	47	(1)

[1] Question was asked of women only.

Source: OppenheimerFunds, Inc., *Gen X Retirement Survey*, 2001.

women age 27–35 with retirement-fund investments were still investing mainly in bonds, while 48 percent were mainly investing in stocks; by comparison, only 43 percent of men in that age group were investing mainly in stocks. The remaining women spread their holdings evenly across both investment categories (Employee Benefit Research Institute 2000b).

POLICY IMPLICATIONS

Today's young women grew up in an era of generous social spending that now seems at an end. Those who are ill-prepared to earn, save, and manage money throughout their working years may face increasing economic disadvantages as they age. For these vulnerable women, the direction of public and private policies regarding pensions, health coverage, wages, and taxation will largely determine whether they face an impoverished old age.

SOCIAL SECURITY AND MEDICARE

Few young adults realize that changes to Social Security law in the 1980s have already altered the program significantly for them. Workers born after 1960 are not eligible to receive full pension benefits at age 65, as their grandparents were, or even at age 66, as most baby boomers are. To receive their full entitlement, young workers will have to wait until age 67. Recent proposals to partially privatize the Social Security program, if enacted, also are likely to affect mainly the young. Privatization would allow workers to take part of what they pay in Social Security payroll taxes—money that is used to pay current beneficiaries—and invest it in personal accounts similar to IRAs and 401(k)s. As with other defined-contribution plans, however, most of the cost and risk burden of these private accounts would fall on individuals.

The Employee Benefit Research Institute calculated the effect of privatizing Social Security on two cohorts—workers born in 1962 (i.e., those somewhat older than our age group) and workers born in 1982 (i.e., those somewhat younger than our age group). Assuming that a worker who has wages equal to the economy-wide average contributes two percent to a private account, as is currently proposed, and achieves a historically reasonable 8.12 percent average annual rate of return, someone born in 1982 could expect to accumulate a median $117,258 over a 44-year career. Based on prevailing gender wage patterns, however, a woman would accumulate a median account balance of $88,370, almost 25 percent less than the overall median, while a man's account would reach a median of $137,863, nearly 20 percent above the median (Employee Benefit Research Institute 2000a).

Time away from the workforce would penalize women further. Under the current Social Security system, an absence from the labor force of up to five years will have little impact on a worker's future benefits. Privatized accounts make workforce absences costly, although the impact differs according to the timing and length of the absence. Using the assumptions in the above example, the average wage-earning woman who dropped out of the workforce between age 26 and 30 would accumulate a median of $72,733 in her private account. If she stayed away until age 35, she'd have just $57,957 at the end of her career (Employee Benefit Research Institute 2000a). What's more, unlike current government-guaranteed benefits, the future worth of privatized payments would be uncertain, subject to erosion from inflation, management fees, or investment losses, and thus likely to cause further disadvantage to those with smaller accumulations.

It's possible that a privatized system also would lead to cutbacks in non-retirement Social Security benefits by shrinking the current program's revenues. Payments now available to survivors and the disabled—the equivalent of private-sector insurance policies—are particularly important to low-wage earners who cannot afford private coverage and to racial minorities who have higher rates of premature death and disability than those of the general population.

Proposals to turn Medicare—the health insurance safety net for elders—into a free-market voucher program are also likely to harm women more than men. Instead of providing health insurance directly to seniors, as traditional Medicare does, a voucher plan would provide a fixed subsidy that seniors would use to purchase private health insurance on the open market. Seniors likely to require a lot of medical services—that is, the oldest, sickest, and frailest beneficiaries, mainly long-lived females—would be undesirable customers to cost-conscious health insurers. Without strict regulatory oversight, these vulnerable individuals would find it impossible to obtain health coverage at an affordable price and possibly at any price.

While younger women may not easily envision themselves as physically frail or victimized by future public policies that leave them to fend for themselves, the experience of their own mothers may provide an unwelcome preview of what to expect. The unusually large size of the baby-boom generation, along with recent strides in extending longevity, is likely to produce an unexpected and possibly unsustainable burden on the current Medicare system. Shortfalls in financial and physical support for the elderly may fall hardest on their traditional caregivers, their daughters.

PRIVATE PENSIONS

The predominant type of pension plan offered by employers has changed significantly over the last two decades. Defined-contribution plans are on the rise and defined-benefit plans are waning, a shift that may or may not be advantageous to women, depending on individual circumstances.

Defined-benefit plans—the traditional form of pension coverage—guarantee workers a specific future payment, based mainly on salary and the number of years with an employer. Once an employee has fully vested in, or secured her entitlement to, a pension (generally after about five years), the size of her future payment grows with both her earnings and her time on the job. If she changes jobs or drops out of the workforce before vesting, she may get no pension at all. If she returns to work later and is covered under a new defined-benefit plan, she must begin vesting all over again. This factor, plus lower salaries, invariably has resulted in women having fewer and more meager pensions than men. With increasing job turnover among all workers, however, the disadvantages of defined-benefit plans may no longer fall harder on women than on men.

In the 1980s, a quirk in the tax law gave rise to defined-contribution plans, in which employees set aside a tax-deferred portion of their salaries, typically up to six percent, sometimes matched, at least in part, by the employer. A worker is immediately vested in her own contributions and generally is entitled to any employer-matched funds within a year or so. If she leaves work or changes jobs, she can take her vested account balance with her. She may even cash out her savings, an unwise but often tempting option. Unlike the fixed entitlement from a defined-benefit plan, however, the amount of retirement income available from a defined-contribution plan depends entirely on how much money a worker (and often her employer) is able to contribute to her account and its subsequent investment performance. Those with long job tenures, high salaries, and good investment skills are better positioned for success than the less advantaged.

EFFECTS ON LOW-WAGE WORKING WOMEN

America's image as a land of plenty often obscures the fact that, even by tough government standards, a significant number of citizens qualify as poor. Although women age 25–34 comprise less than 22 percent of the total nonelderly female population, they constitute nearly 26 percent of nonelderly females who are poor.

In the 25–34 age group, roughly 13 percent of women report incomes below the federal poverty line, compared with 7.7 percent of men. Another 4.4 percent are "near poor," with incomes that fall below 125 percent of the poverty line. Black and Hispanic women are more likely than whites to have low incomes. Among the poor or near poor, nearly one-quarter are black and nearly one-quarter are Hispanic. These disparities guarantee that policies that negatively affect low-wage workers are hardest on young females, especially minorities.

TAXATION

Prevailing politics govern the U.S. tax code's treatment of wealth. High rates at the upper margins of income during the 1960s and 1970s fell sharply during the Reagan years and have remained historically low.

Over this period, however, one tax provision has consistently favored the poor. Since 1975, the federal government has offered an Earned Income Tax Credit (EITC), a subsidy that allows low-paid workers to receive a tax rebate on their earnings, even if they owe no income taxes. Although singles can qualify for the benefit, subsidies are largest for working parents, capped at $3,888 for families with two children and $2,353 for families with one. The program has been expanded repeatedly, especially as welfare has fallen into disrepute, and is likely to continue. Currently, roughly one tax return in six claims the EITC (Center on Budget and Policy Priorities 2000a).

Depending on where a low-wage worker lives, state income tax policies can be punishing or nurturing. In 1999, 20 states imposed at least some tax on a family of four with an earned income of $17,028, ranging from $555 in Kentucky to $2 in North Carolina. Thirteen states imposed no tax on such a family, and the remainder offered refundable tax credits ranging from $20 in Maryland to $1,222 in Minnesota (Center on Budget and Policy Priorities 2000b). Although trends seem to indicate that state EITC programs will spread, states' future fiscal health, as well as their social agendas, will ultimately steer policy.

Fiscal concerns are also likely to determine the direction of the payroll tax that funds Social Security benefits. Most workers pay 7.65 percent for Social Security (and Medicare) levied on earnings below $84,900 (the maximum in 2002). The total levy of 15.3 percent, of which employers pay half, falls most heavily on low-wage earners. Although low-wage earners ultimately receive a proportionately larger Social Security benefit than high-wage earners do, many legislators acknowledge the tax's crippling effect on the ability of the poor to save and invest. (Indeed, the EITC was conceived to offset the regressive Social Security tax.) As a result, there has been recent talk of a rate cut. However, payroll taxes seem far more likely to rise than fall over coming years, as projected Social Security trust fund deficits kick in.

LIVING WAGE

In 1994, Maryland passed the nation's first ordinance requiring city contractors to pay their employees an hourly wage more closely related to living costs than the $5.15 legal minimum and indexed to rise with inflation. Since then, "living wage" ordinances have been passed in 62 jurisdictions in 24 states. The average living wage is $9.66 per hour, and some ordinances mandate health insurance benefits, as well. Although most laws apply only to government contractors, a few apply to other employers, such as public schools or recipients of property tax abatements (Economic Policy Foundation 2001a).

The living wage movement has intensified the perennial debate over whether a wage floor helps or hurts workers by reducing the number of employers who can afford to hire them. However, as long as the impact of a living wage is confined mainly to government, ordinances are likely to continue to materialize while affecting relatively few workers.

LIFE AFTER WELFARE

If numbers are the measure of success, state and federal welfare reform programs have been successful, reducing public assistance rolls nationwide by more than 50 percent since 1994. Although reform implicitly, if not explicitly, promised job training, child care, and other fail-safe features, it has not distributed these benefits uniformly, and the loss of cash support has had a harsh effect on some women, especially the mentally or physically disabled and hard-core unemployables.

Even for former welfare recipients fully committed to working, earning enough to support a family remains problematic. In Wisconsin, the first state to enact radical reform, the average earnings of former welfare recipients who worked year round showed a real increase of 94 percent between 1990 and 1998. Even so, total earnings for former welfare recipients in the state averaged just $16,389 in 1998 (Wisconsin Policy Research Institute 2001).

Although not time-limited the way cash payments are, noncash benefits, such as Medicaid and food stamps, remain means-tested. A low-wage earner who leaves the welfare rolls may earn too much to qualify for these vital benefits and yet be unable to afford health insurance or adequate food without them. As a result, many ex-recipients may find themselves more financially strapped than ever and thus still unable to lift themselves and their families from poverty.

In the long run, welfare reform stands to deliver a better life to future generations of women and their children by encouraging self-reliance and self-esteem, modeling work habits, defeating racial stereotypes, and promoting marriage. However, the transition is likely to impose the heaviest burden on the first generation of women to struggle toward freedom from dependency, more than one-third of whom are age 25–34. Indeed, these young mothers in their prime childbearing years comprise the largest group of women over age 15 receiving public assistance, both today and historically. How well they cope will be a measure of both their individual resilience and society's compassion.

CONCLUSION

With employment equality nearly achieved, young women are now able to attain financial equality, an opportunity that comes with a lifetime responsibility to earn, save, invest, and manage money. How well they handle this challenge ultimately will determine the scope of their financial freedom and, in some cases, their personal freedom, as well.

For some, the path to economic success will be smooth. Many young women who pursue a career will become financially self-sufficient mainly through their own efforts. Those who focus their talents primarily at home also may play a major role in sustaining and improving their families' standards of living. For others, though, the path to financial self-reliance will be strewn with setbacks and obstacles, some insurmountable. Young women who lack the personal and professional assets to succeed in the job market face discouraging prospects. In an era of limited social support, their economic future may be dim.

NOTES

1. Editors' note: In 2000, more than one-third of single mothers were age 25–34. Of these, 74.5 percent were employed (Census Bureau 2001a).
2. Unless otherwise identified, data in this section and the section entitled "Money Management" are from a special analysis of the 1998 Federal Reserve Board's Survey of Consumer Finances, conducted by Mark Calabria and Darryl Getter for the Women's Research and Education Institute (WREI), 2001.

Six

TAKING IT FROM HERE: POLICIES FOR THE TWENTY-FIRST CENTURY

Cynthia B. Costello and Vanessa R. Wight

AS THE CHAPTERS in this volume have shown, young women today live in a world that differs, in many important respects, from the world their mothers lived in at a comparable age. Some differences are the result of important policy reforms of the 1960s and 1970s, such as laws requiring employers and educational institutions receiving federal dollars to make jobs and programs open to girls and women, and policies making credit available, for the first time, to women in their own names. Also during this period, abortion was legalized and birth control became widely available—with far-reaching implications for young women.

Not all women have benefited equally from these changes, however. As this book illustrates, there are marked differences between the haves and the have-nots among women age 25–34. Those with education, especially a college degree or more, typically land in professional and managerial jobs with good pay and benefits and the income that comes from working in these jobs over time. These women are more likely to defer childbearing until their mid-twenties or later—which gives them an opportunity to establish themselves in careers, and perhaps start saving for the future, before taking on family responsibilities. Of course, these young women face continuing gender disparities in pay and opportunities for advancement compared with their male peers. And many experience considerable stress as they strive to climb the career ladder while juggling child care and other responsibilities outside of work.

Young women with limited education face a quite different set of challenges. Unless they acquire an education and develop skills and competencies along the way, they end up in low-wage, dead-end jobs. More likely than their better-off contemporaries to have children at a young age—and to have them alone—many of these young women have high expenses and little income with which to cover them. They are also more likely than others in their age group to lack benefits—especially health insurance and pension coverage— and to have greater health problems. Without income to save and invest, the future financial security of young women in these circumstances is uncertain.

This final chapter of *The American Woman 2003–2004* looks at policies that might improve the lives of young women in the years ahead: What educational and employment initiatives could open doors for them? What reforms might help them balance their jobs and their commitments outside of work? What changes are needed to enhance their health and well-being? And finally, how can young women be assured greater financial security over time?

EDUCATION: OPENING DOORS

We already know that access to education has a profound impact on young women's lives—increasing not only their employment opportunities and earning potential but also their long-term financial well-being. Completing high school is fundamental to women's future success. Given the chance and a good environment that encourages high school completion, these girls are likely to take the next step. The women who attend college and earn a bachelor's degree are more likely to get better jobs and have higher earnings than both their male and female contemporaries who lack a college degree.

Young women with little education tend to work in jobs that require little or no skills. These are women—a good number of them without high school diplomas—who serve fast food, work as nurses' aides in hospitals and nursing homes, or clean office buildings at night. Women of color—especially black and Hispanic women—make up a disproportionate share of this group.

In this country, each generation has required more education than the last to make a good living. Gone are the days when young adults could enter the labor market with a high school degree, or less, and expect to move up in a company and earn a better income along the way. Today, a college degree is the entry ticket to a good job. That three out of 10 young women now have a bachelor's degree or higher is good news. But women still have a long way to go—especially Hispanic women, a relatively high proportion of whom do not complete high school, much less attain a bachelor's degree.

Perhaps it is time to rethink the requirements of an educated citizenry. In the nineteenth century, this country established a universal public education system to give children the basic literacy and math skills required of a rapidly developing industrial economy. If most of the "good jobs" in our information-based, service economy now require a college degree, shouldn't an important policy goal be to ensure access to a college education for every young person who wants it? And shouldn't financial support—in the form of scholarships and low-cost loans—be offered to young women and men who cannot otherwise afford higher education?

Affirmative action continues to play an important role in opening the doors of higher education to those who might not otherwise have the chance to attend college or vocational education programs. Starting in the 1970s, affirmative action laws paved the way to higher education for many women and minorities. Title IX of the Education Amendments prohibited sex discrimination in education and athletic programs in schools, colleges, and universities that received federal aid. Before the passage of Title IX in 1972, qualified women were denied admission to law schools, medical schools, and business administration and other professional programs. They were also discouraged from applying for nontraditional training in postsecondary vocational education programs. In the three decades since the passage of this important legislation, women have made significant progress in the attainment of college and professional degrees. Moreover, increased access to school-related athletic programs on both secondary and postsecondary levels has had a tremendous impact on women's ability to achieve—in sports and academics.

Unfortunately, recent reversals in affirmative action law threaten to undermine this progress—particularly for women of color. In 1996, California passed Proposition 209 prohibiting preferential treatment on the basis of race or gender in education, employment, or contracting. Two years later, there was a 57 percent decrease in underrepresented minority students—both women and men—admitted to the University of California at Berkeley and a 36 percent decrease in underrepresented minorities admitted to the University of California at Los Angeles (Matosantos and Chiu 1998).

Also in 1996, the Texas Fifth Circuit Court of Appeals ruled, in *Hopwood* v. *Texas,* that race could not be used as a factor in college admissions. Shortly after this ruling, the Texas attorney general banned the use of race and ethnicity in determining financial aid, fellowships, recruitment, and retention. The effect on the enrollment rates of minority women at the University of Texas Law School has been dramatic, decreasing the number of black women enrolled in the school by 55 percent and the number of Hispanic women by 28 percent (National Council of Women's Organizations 2000).

This change in policy represents a step backward. Originally designed to help level the playing field—and to provide higher education opportunities to members of previously excluded groups—affirmative action is still needed to ensure women and minorities access to college admission and professional and vocational education programs.

Reforms also are needed to correct the continuing gender disparities in such scientific and technical disciplines as engineering and the physical sciences. That men receive more than eight out of 10 bachelor's degrees in engineering, and six out of 10 in the physical sciences, underscores the problem. Policies should address what the higher education community can do to recruit young women into these fields. They also should examine how our nation's primary and secondary school systems are preparing—or failing to prepare—girls for careers in science and math.

While policies still are needed to enhance young women's access to postsecondary education, it is important to remember that more than one in 10 women age 25–34 have not graduated from high school. More than one in three Hispanic women (36 percent) lack a high school diploma. For these women, higher education is not even on the radar screen. Strengthening our nation's high school equivalency (GED) programs for young adults—both women and men—should be a national priority. It is also important that such programs be linked to the community college system and that young women who earn high school diplomas be encouraged to continue their education.

Community colleges have long been the bedrock of higher education for those with limited resources. The flexibility of these programs and their lower costs make it possible for lower-income individuals to acquire college credits and work toward an associate's, and in many cases a four-year, degree. Acquiring even a two-year associate's degree can make a big difference in job opportunities and earnings for young women.

While the focus in this book is on women in their young adult years, education policy is most effective when it takes a cradle-to-college approach. Today's children quickly become tomorrow's young adults, and those who face educational disadvantages at a young age have a difficult time catching up later on. Hardly a month goes by without a warning that our nation's schools are in "crisis." Ignoring the educational deficiencies in our public education system today will only create greater challenges down the road as young people without basic literacy and math skills find themselves poorly equipped to get good jobs and move up the career ladder.

WORKPLACE REFORMS: BREAKING THROUGH
THE GLASS CEILING

Labor market policy can play a major role in expanding opportunities for young women. Compared to their mothers' generation, young women today have many more career choices—for example, in law, medicine, and business. That young women now represent nearly half of the recent law school graduates underscores this change. So does the selection of Carleton Fiorina a few years back to head the corporate giant Hewlett-Packard and the appointment by Democratic and Republican administrations alike of women to leadership positions in government.

And yet, for all the progress that has occurred, young women entering the labor market find that gender still limits how far they can go in the world of work. Women are underrepresented among senior partners in law firms and in the more prestigious medical specialties, such as surgery. At the very top of our nation's corporations, it is still unusual to see a female chief executive officer. Women of color are woefully underrepresented in high-level corporate positions. And, of course, we have yet to see a woman elected president or vice president of the United States.

For young women to make further progress, both public and private workplace policies need to change. It is hard to believe that, before 1963, when the mothers of today's young women were entering the labor force, it was entirely legal to discriminate against women in employment. That started to change with passage of the Equal Pay Act of 1963, guaranteeing equal pay for equal work, and Title VII of the Civil Rights Act of 1964, prohibiting employment discrimination on the basis of race, color, religion, sex, or national origin. Statutes soon followed requiring that federal contractors take affirmative action to ensure that applicants be considered for employment and treated during their tenure without regard to race, color, religion, sex, or national origin. In 1978, the Pregnancy Discrimination Act was passed amending the Civil Rights Act to encompass pregnancy, childbirth, or related medical conditions. These laws have made a difference, opening formerly closed doors to women and persons of color and supporting their career advancement. As long as women and minorities are underrepresented in top positions and certain jobs and professions, affirmative action must be protected.

Employers have an important role to play in expanding opportunities for young women. A strong commitment from an organization's top management can make the difference between a culture that promotes young women's advancement and one that does not. For example, top executives can provide strong support for diversity programs designed to identify and groom women and minorities with high potential for positions of responsibility. The strongest of these programs set diversity targets and hold managers accountable for meeting them.

Networking and mentoring programs also can be effective. While promising young male employees—especially white male employees—often are integrated into the network of powerful men, young women typically must create their own networks. Doing so is not an easy task in workplaces where most of the top managers are men. Companies can encourage networking opportunities for young women by establishing women's leadership programs. Another approach is to proactively link talented young women with more senior managers through mentoring programs. Able young women and minorities have a better chance to climb the career ladder when the leadership of an organization demonstrates a real and visible commitment to promoting them.

WORK-FAMILY POLICIES: THE UNFINISHED AGENDA

There is probably no issue more important to young women than work-family policy. Many of the obstacles young women face in the workplace stem from their family responsibilities. Despite increased family involvement by men, the care of children and the running of households remain, for the most part, in women's hands. And, of course, many young women handle these responsibilities by themselves. While some progress has occurred in the work-family policy arena, much remains to be done.

Passage of the Family and Medical Leave Act (FMLA) in 1993 was a major step forward in work-family policy. Under FMLA, women and men who work for organizations with more than 50 employees are guaranteed unpaid leave for the birth or adoption of a child or the care of a sick relative. Still, millions of people are unable to take advantage of FMLA because they work for small employers, work too few hours, or have insufficient job tenure to qualify. Millions more cannot afford to take leave without pay. Family leave policy must be broadened to include both small employers (for whom many young women work) and paid leave for those who cannot otherwise afford to take time off for caregiving.

Smart employers realize that the typical young worker is no longer a man with a wife at home. Today, this young worker is just as likely to be a woman, and a woman of color at that, and someone with child care responsibilities. A number of companies are helping employees better integrate their jobs and their lives outside of work through flexible work hours, work-at-home options, on-site child care centers, and dependent care referral programs. Some of the most progressive companies give work groups license to design their own jobs to promote smoother work-life integration and, in doing so, find that productivity increases as a result.

Still, most workplaces are not models of work-family integration. The fact that women now represent close to half of the American workforce has not fundamentally changed a culture of work that continues to reward those who put in long hours and place jobs above family and other outside commitments. Those who opt for reduced work hours or flexible work schedules are often penalized for these choices—considered less "serious" employees and poorer candidates for advancement. Only by addressing this culture head on—and by challenging the assumption that long work hours translate into high productivity—will we make substantial progress in redesigning work to enable young women and men to truly balance their jobs and their lives outside of work.

Inequities exist in access to work-family policies and programs. The young women who need "family-friendly" and "flexible" policies the most are often those who are the least likely to find them in their jobs. These are the women with low earnings and little education who tend to work in *in-flexible* jobs without basic benefits. Consider the young woman who cleans office buildings at night or who serves fast food. Typically, she cannot vary her work hours, and, because her job provides no paid sick or vacation time, she cannot take time off when needed. Even for young women without children, such jobs can be a challenge. For young mothers, a child's illness or a breakdown in child care arrangements can cause serious problems.

The child care system in this country is woefully inadequate. In recent years, the federal government increased its funding of the child care block grant program. Yet many young women cannot find affordable child care in their communities or near their jobs. Moreover, questions have been raised about the quality of child care typically available to working parents. Many young women piece together a patchwork of care that includes relatives, neighbors, some organized child care, and, all too often, leaving young children with older siblings or even alone. These unstable arrangements often break down, jeopardizing children's safety and security and women's ability to keep jobs. Provision of quality, affordable child care to all women who need it would enhance their employment stability while providing children with important early education.

Although not typically considered a work-family benefit, paid sick and vacation time is critical to women's ability to work and care for their children. That the majority of low-wage jobs lack paid sick and vacation time causes considerable hardship for many young women (Heymann et al. 2002). The children of parents in these jobs have more chronic health problems and learning disabilities than those from higher-income families. FMLA allows for unpaid leave in the event of a prolonged family illness, but it does not cover leave for the type of episodic illnesses—such as flu, ear infections, or strep throat—that are far more common. Many working mothers cope with the lack of leave time available at work by quitting their jobs when they or their children are sick. The establishment of a minimum standard for paid sick leave and vacation time in employment should be a national priority.

GAINING FINANCIAL SELF-SUFFICIENCY: CLOSING THE GAP

In the past, the most disadvantaged young women—mostly poor single mothers—received income support from the federal government in the form of Aid to Families with Dependent Children (AFDC). When Congress eliminated AFDC and substituted the Temporary Assistance to Needy Families (TANF) program in 1996, federal policy shifted from providing long-term income support for needy women and children to requiring mothers to work. The verdict is still out on the long-term impact of this change, but many young women report that they are not receiving the help they need to become financially self-sufficient. Helping young women attain self-sufficiency will require a combination of approaches: providing them with career ladders, increasing the minimum wage, enhancing the Earned Income Tax Credit, enacting pay equity legislation, and expanding the number of unionized jobs in the sectors where women work.

That young women in low-wage jobs typically do not have a career ladder is a major obstacle to self-sufficiency. A young woman serving fast food hamburgers or changing beds in a hospital has nowhere to go unless she acquires some additional education. Job training may be an alternative, but many such programs have only a small impact on career mobility and earnings. Programs funded under the Job Training Partnership Act in the 1980s and 1990s have been criticized as having a limited impact on the most disadvantaged women—particularly those of Hispanic origin (Pérez and Rodriguez 1996). More recently, the Workforce Investment Act (WIA) of 1998 was designed to bring all the elements of job training—including literacy and employment skills—under one roof in a "one-stop center." It is too early in the implementation of WIA to draw any firm conclusions about whether it will be more effective than previous job-training approaches.

Training is a realistic alternative to higher education only when it is linked to a job with real earnings potential and a promise of career advancement. Some vocational education programs do move lower-income young women into better jobs, especially those that train women for nontraditional jobs as, for example, firefighters, mechanics, and computer technicians. These programs are underfunded, however, and will require additional support to reach more than a small proportion of the young women who could benefit from them.

The low pay in many of the service-sector and part-time jobs where young women work is a stumbling block to self-sufficiency. The minimum wage was last increased in 1997 from $4.75 to $5.15. Because the minimum wage is not adjusted for inflation, it loses value in real terms over time: the real value in 2000 dollars of the minimum wage was 30 percent below its peak in 1968 and 24 percent below its level in 1979 (Economic Policy Institute 2000). Even at twice the minimum wage, a young woman working full time, year round, would earn only $21,424 a year before taxes—hardly enough to support herself, much less one or more children. A minimum wage increase and an inflation provision would help the many young women, particularly minorities, who work in low-wage jobs.

Improvements in the Earned Income Tax Credit (EITC) also could enhance the financial prospects of young women with low incomes. EITC, which was designed to help relieve the payroll tax burden of low-income workers and families, is not without its own limitations. Central to EITC's success is the fact that it is refundable; most low-income workers who owe little or no taxes still can qualify for the credit. However, the program falls short of reaching many young women and families in need. The benefits do not increase for families with more than two children, and the credit phases out as a worker's wages increase. Some policy experts advocate that a single credit combining the EITC with the Child Tax Credit and the dependent exemption could assist low-income working women with more than two children at home.

Pay equity legislation aimed at closing the earnings gap between women and men is another needed reform that would increase young women's earnings. Although the earnings gap is narrowest among 25–34-year-olds, it begins to widen as women reach their peak earning years. The result is a lifetime of lost earnings and potential savings. Pay equity legislation builds on the progress that resulted from passage of the Equal Pay Act of 1963. While that act requires employers to pay a man and woman hired to do the same job the same wage, many young women work in jobs that are held mostly by women (such as teaching, nursing, and clerical positions). Pay equity legislation would require employers to pay the same wage to employees who work in jobs with comparable educational and skill requirements.

Expanding the number of jobs covered by union contracts could help young women improve their wages, benefits, and perhaps their job flexibility as well. In 2001, about 11 percent of women age 25–34 were members of a union or worked in a job that was covered by a union. Compared with women in nonunion jobs, those in union jobs have higher wages and better benefits. They also have some protection from employer sanctions through the union grievance process. In recent years, the percentage of young women covered by unions has declined (Bureau of Labor Statistics 2001). In one encouraging development, the American Federation of Labor-Congress of Industrial Organizations (AFL-CIO) has launched an aggressive organizing drive targeted at the service sector where many young women work.

IMPROVING THE HEALTH OF YOUNG WOMEN

The ability of young women to get needed health care services is tied directly to whether they have health insurance coverage. Nearly one in five young women—many of them employed in service-sector and part-time jobs—has no insurance coverage at all, while many more have private plans that require hefty deductibles and copayments. Many do not receive the preventive and screening services, reproductive services (including prenatal care, contraceptives, and abortion), and mental health services that are critical to women in this age group. The last time the country engaged in a serious debate about health care reform was almost a decade ago. It is time to move this issue to center stage once again.

The majority of young women today receive their health care through managed care plans. A number of states now mandate that such plans provide women with direct access to obstetricians and gynecologists (rather than requiring women to get referrals to these providers). It is now time for Congress to pass legislation guaranteeing all women access to these providers and other specialists for treatment of particular conditions and diseases. Policies also should address whether women are receiving critical services through managed care plans, such as comprehensive screening (including screening for STDs and HIV/AIDS), reproductive services, adequate provider counseling, and mental health services.

In the absence of comprehensive health insurance coverage, many young women with low incomes receive health care services through government programs. Medicaid provides prenatal care to millions of young women and health care to their children. The National Breast and Cervical Cancer Early Detection Program provides Pap smears and mammograms to many young women who would otherwise go without these critical services. And community health centers make a broad array of health care services available to young women with limited resources. Although vitally important, all of these programs reach only a small proportion of the young women who need them, and increased funding is needed to broaden their reach.

Public education efforts focused on promoting healthy behaviors in women age 25–34 are a smart investment of public dollars. This is a time when changed behaviors can have a long-term impact on women's health.

Smoking, inadequate exercise, poor diet, substance abuse, and lack of contraceptive use and protection against HIV/AIDS stand out as issues that require public policy attention. Public programs should showcase positive role models of young women making healthy choices and provide an array of supports to help them develop healthy behaviors.

The fact that young women today start having sex earlier, and have more sexual partners before marriage than their mothers did, makes access to the full range of reproductive services central to their health. With overall contraceptive use having increased only slightly over the last 20 years, it is imperative that public education efforts target young women (and men) through community organizations, workplaces, educational institutions, community health centers, and providers' offices.

Protection of a woman's right to choose is as important today as it was 25 years ago. It is easy to forget that, before 1973, abortion was illegal in this country in all but a few states. The Supreme Court ruling in *Roe* v. *Wade* applied women's right to privacy to the choice to have an abortion. A backlash against this decision was reflected in the passage of the Hyde Amendment in 1976, eliminating federal funding for abortion services with few exceptions. Subsequent judicial and legislative decisions have further eroded women's access to abortion. Pregnancy prevention is preferable to abortion—and young women who do not wish to have children need reinforcement for using contraception every time they have sex. It is also critical that, in the age of the deadly HIV virus, young women be supported in insisting that their partners protect themselves with condoms. Still, unintended pregnancies will occur, and women should have the option of abortion should they need one.

Public policy should encourage health care providers to adopt a comprehensive approach to health care for young women. Young women require screening for a number of conditions and diseases—including STDs, HIV/AIDS, cervical cancer, heart disease, diabetes, mental health problems, and eating disorders. They also would benefit from counseling on health behaviors such as smoking, drinking and drug use, nutrition and exercise, and contraceptive use. It is important that public policy support health plans and providers in expanding preventive and screening services to young women by, for example, incorporating counseling on STDs, contraception, and healthy behaviors into office visits.

Finally, the federal government should support research on the health status, conditions, and diseases that disproportionately affect young women and the prevention strategies that can enhance young women's health and well-being. The establishment of the Office of Research on Women's Health at the National Institutes of Health (NIH) in 1991 was a milestone in focusing attention on the need for women's health research. A number of women's health studies are currently under way at NIH and other federal agencies. Still, we know far too little about what works in health promotion and disease prevention in young women. We need additional research on what motivates young women to adopt healthy behaviors (including the use of birth control that protects them from pregnancy as well as from STDs and HIV/AIDS) and on barriers to change and ways to help young women overcome them.

RETIREMENT SECURITY: STRENGTHENING THE THREE-LEGGED STOOL

While it is difficult for young women to think ahead to retirement, it is important that they do so. The fact that young women today represent a smaller birth cohort and are having children later than young women who came before them has implications for their retirement security. As today's young women move into middle age, many will find themselves sandwiched between caring for children and providing assistance to aging parents. Policies are needed to support women, and men, as they seek to balance work and caregiving responsibilities that span multiple generations. When the young women of today become old themselves, those who for one reason or another did not have their own children may lack family support when they need it. Young women have a strong stake in retirement policies that take these factors into account.

A secure retirement is based on a three-legged stool of pension income, Social Security, and individual savings. All three are closely tied to a woman's marital status, work history, and earnings over time. For young women who work in high-paying jobs with a clear promotional track and good retirement benefits, accumulating a nest egg is an attainable objective; it is a far more challenging one for those who work in low-wage, dead-end jobs without pension plans.

Employer-provided pensions are a critical foundation of women's retirement security. In the past, a woman relied on her husband's pension—sharing his retirement benefit and collecting a spousal benefit if he died first. Today, later marriage and higher divorce rates, coupled with higher labor force participation, are prompting young women to look to their own jobs for pension security. In recent years, women's pension coverage through their own jobs has increased. Despite this, women are still disproportionately lacking coverage, and black and Hispanic women are even more likely than their white counterparts to go without.

A significant number of employers, especially small businesses and service-sector employers, do not offer pension plans to their workers. Even if they do, women often do not qualify for coverage because of part-time hours or insufficient job tenure. Among those who do qualify for coverage, many do not have enough income to contribute to the plan—because of low earnings, high debt, or excessive spending. Policies should help young women save and contribute to pension plans when they have them and expand pension coverage to those who work part time, have short job tenure, or work for small employers.

The Economic Growth and Tax Relief Reconciliation Act, passed by Congress in 2001, contains a number of provisions that may encourage young women to save, or save more, for retirement. The tax package raises the ceiling on what an individual can contribute to a defined contribution plan from $10,500 to $15,000 (phased in over five years) and allows people age 50 and older to contribute an additional $5,000 over their personal ceiling or plan limit. For those who can afford it, the new ceiling offers young women an opportunity to expand their retirement contributions and earnings over time. Because cash flow problems make it difficult for many young women to contribute fully to their pension plans, the increased contribution limit for those 50 and over may allow young women today an opportunity to "catch up" later when their earnings and ability to contribute could be higher.

Several provisions in the tax package are particularly important for young women who have shorter job tenures than their male counterparts (often due to absence from the workforce for childbearing and child rearing). The act decreases the vesting requirement in 401(k) plans and improves the portability of defined contribution plans. Decreasing the vesting requirement from five to three years should increase women's retirement earnings by giving them access to their employer's contribution after a shorter period of time. The improved portability provision may encourage young women to roll over their retirement account into a tax-deferred savings vehicle when they change jobs rather than cashing it out and spending it.

An important provision in the new law that could help some low-wage working women is a nonrefundable tax credit for contributions to retirement savings vehicles such as individual retirement accounts (IRAs). Intended as an aggressive savings option, the provision allows a nonrefundable tax credit of up to $2,000 for low- to middle-income individuals who contribute to an IRA, a Roth IRA, or another qualified retirement plan. However, this tax credit may not be as helpful to many poor and near-poor women who lack the income to deposit up front into a retirement plan. Also, it does not apply to those women who do not pay taxes because their incomes are too low. The law would be improved if it provided direct funds to low-wage workers, earmarked for investment in a retirement savings account.

Young women have a strong stake in preserving the second leg of the retirement stool—Social Security—because many of them will rely heavily on the program as a principal source of income in their later years. Three out of four women age 65 and older living alone receive at least half of their income from Social Security, and 40 percent are either completely dependent or almost completely dependent on the benefit as their source of income (Social Security Administration 2002).

Created at a time when men were the primary breadwinners, working women today face particular disadvantages under the Social Security system. Women receive only 76 percent of the median benefit awarded to their male counterparts (Social Security Administration 2001). Women's lower benefits are the result of lower lifetime earnings and time out of the workforce. Proposals to count women's caregiving years by replacing the "zero years" practice with a "family service credit" would enhance the financial security of many women when they retire. Given the high divorce rates and women's longer life expectancies, increasing the divorced spouses' benefit and the widows' benefit would also improve women's retirement prospects.

Privatization of Social Security is a popular idea in some policy circles, but young women should be wary of what it could mean for them in retirement. Under the current Social Security system, benefits are guaranteed, constant, and annually adjusted to the cost of living. Furthermore, women who worked mostly in low-wage occupations, where minority women are concentrated, receive Social Security benefits that represent a higher percentage of their pre-retirement wages than is the case for their higher-wage counterparts. Conversely, individual retirement accounts depend on the amount that is contributed, fluctuate with the health of the economy, rarely offer cost-of-living adjustments, and do not award benefits based on a progressive benefit formula—that is, they do not compensate for a lifetime of lower earnings. Preserving the solvency of the Social Security trust fund is critical to ensure that the baby-boomer parents of today's young women receive a guaranteed and constant benefit when they retire—and that the system remains strong when these young women age into retirement themselves.

The third leg of the retirement stool—private savings—is one of the biggest challenges of all. The accumulation of debt during their early working years, including student loans and home mortgages, leaves many young women with little left over to save. And for those with low earnings, making ends meet is hard enough. Many of the policy options discussed in this chapter could enhance the ability of young women to save—from policies designed to increase women's wages and incomes to those aimed at adding benefits, such as health insurance, pension coverage, and paid sick leave and vacation time.

A number of policy changes in the last 25 years have improved the lives of young women significantly. Many were the result of the advocacy efforts of a generation of feminists who came of age in the 1960s and 1970s—the mothers of today's young women—and started a revolution that had as its goal gender equity for women in American society. Those efforts produced a broad range of reforms, from affirmative action to equal pay to reproductive choice.

Young women have benefited from the changed policy landscape they inherited from their mothers. As a generation, they have more choices and broader opportunities than their mothers had. However, they face a new set of challenges, highlighted in this volume—from the stress that comes from trying to "do it all," to the absence of affordable, quality child care, to the deadly health risks associated with HIV/AIDS. And, of course, it is the young women with the lowest levels of education and income who face the greatest obstacles.

In the early twenty-first century, young women find themselves heirs to their mothers' unfinished agenda. Now it is up to them to chart their own policy course for the future—a course that is likely to include many of the same issues for which their mothers fought. However, it is also important that young women put their own stamp on such efforts, crafting and supporting policies that move them toward equality, give them better options, and improve their financial security. Young women have a strong stake in a future characterized by equality and opportunity—and a future that provides the societal supports that will enable them to live full, satisfying, and healthy lives. To achieve these goals, young women will have to take risks and act boldly and imaginatively. On this last point, we have no doubt that they will rise to the challenge.

AMERICAN WOMEN TODAY:
A STATISTICAL PORTRAIT

DEMOGRAPHICS

THIS SECTION PRESENTS basic statistics about the people who live in the United States, with particular attention to those who are female. Some projections about the U.S. population in years to come are included here, as are some data from past years. Here, as in every section of the "Statistical Portrait," each table and figure is accompanied by a sentence or two intended to help the reader make sense of the numbers.

Readers interested in the implications of the numbers should find much to think about. Take, for example, Figure 1-11, which shows that between 1980 and 2000, the proportion of women age 20–24 who were single rose from just over half to nearly three-quarters. The figure also shows that among women in every age group between 25 and 55, the never-married proportion was roughly twice as large in 2000 as it had been just two decades earlier.

While the majority of women ultimately will marry, the trend toward later first marriage is evidence that young women today have more alternatives than did women of earlier generations. And, to the extent that later marriages mean later childbearing and may mean fewer children, the trend also suggests the need to recognize how heavily our society depends on family members to care for its old people. As the women now young grow old, there will surely be fewer family members to call upon for assistance. Findings include:

- Except in the Hispanic population, where the ratio is very close to 50/50, females predominate to some extent in every racial and ethnic group in the United States. This is because women typically live longer than their male contemporaries (see Tables 1-1 and 1-2 and Figure 1-1). The older the age group, the more disproportionately female it is (see Figure 1-15).

- The baby boomers, now in middle age, make a distinct bulge in the age distribution profile of the U.S. population. Even in 2033, enough boomers will remain to swell the ranks of the elderly to an unprecedented degree (see Figure 1-2).

- Projections are that by 2033, one in every five Americans will be of Hispanic origin; one in every 14 will be of Asian/Pacific Islander descent (see Figure 1-5).

- Over 14 million of the women and girls who live in America emigrated from other countries. Most who came to the United States before 1980 are whites of non-Hispanic origin; most who came after 1980 are of Hispanic or Asian/Pacific Islander origin (see Figure 1-7).

- Over roughly the next three decades, life expectancy is projected to increase for both sexes, but it will continue to be longer for women than for men (see Table 1-2).

- Fertility rates declined in the last decade of the twentieth century, although the Hispanic fertility rate remains by far the highest. The rates for blacks and Native Americans virtually converged, as did the Asian/Pacific Islander and white rates (see Figure 1-9 and Table 1-3).

- Over time, longer life expectancies and declining fertility rates push median ages upward. Between now and 2033, the median age for U.S. women overall is projected to increase by nearly three years, that of men by two and a half. Non-Hispanic white females are and will continue to be the "oldest" group (see Table 1-4).

- Today's typical first-time bride is three years older than her 1980 counterpart and nearly five years older than her 1960 counterpart (see Figure 1-10).

- In 1975, two-thirds of all American *households* consisted of married couples. By 2000, that proportion had shrunk to slightly over half (see Figure 1-13). Still, as of 2000, more than three-quarters of American *families* were married-couple families (see Table 1-6).

- Most men over 65 are living with a spouse; most women over 65 are not. Asian/Pacific Islanders are the older women most likely to live with a spouse—46 percent do (see Figure 1-16).

Table 1-1 • Population of the United States by Race, Hispanic Origin, and Sex, July 1, 2003 (projected)[1]

The 144-plus million females who live in the United States constitute just over half (51 percent) of the country's population. Females predominate to some extent in every group shown here except among Hispanics, where the ratio is very close to 50/50.

	Number
All races	
Females	144,530,000
Males	138,269,000
White, non-Hispanic	
Females	101,129,000
Males	97,235,000
Black, non-Hispanic	
Females	18,226,000
Males	16,430,000
Native American, non-Hispanic[2]	
Females	1,079,000
Males	1,041,000
Asian/Pacific Islander, non-Hispanic	
Females	6,155,000
Males	5,583,000
Hispanic[3]	
Females	17,940,000
Males	17,979,000

[1]Resident population of the 50 states and the District of Columbia.
[2]American Indian, Eskimo, and Aleut.
[3]People of Hispanic origin may be of any race—in other words, Hispanic origin is not a *racial* category; *see* Figure 1-6. Until fairly recently, most of the government sources that presented data by race and Hispanic origin included persons of Hispanic origin both in the racial category to which they belonged (most are white) *and* in the category "persons of Hispanic origin." Today, some of these sources present data by Hispanic and non-Hispanic origin; that is, persons of Hispanic origin, whatever their race, are shown by origin but not by race, and persons not of Hispanic origin are shown by race.

Source: Census Bureau, *Population Projections of the United States by Age, Sex, Race, Hispanic Origin, and Nativity: 1999 to 2100*, 2000, Table NP-D1-A.

Figure 1-1 • Population of the United States by Age and Sex, July 1, 2003 (projected)[1]

Males outnumber females in the age groups under 30, but after 30 the balance tips the other way. Because women typically live longer than their male contemporaries, the older the age group, the more disproportionately female it is (see Table 1-2 and Figure 1-15).

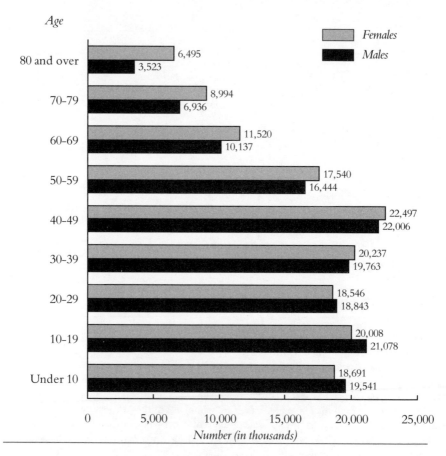

[1]Resident population of the 50 states and the District of Columbia.

Source: Census Bureau, *Population Projections of the United States by Age, Sex, Race, Hispanic Origin, and Nativity: 1999 to 2100*, 2000, Table NP-D1-A.

Figure 1-2 • Population of the United States in 2003 and 2033 by Age and Sex (projected) (percent distributions)

The baby boomers, now in their forties and fifties, make a distinct bulge in the age distribution profile of the U.S. population. By 2033, death will have reduced their numbers considerably. However, enough will remain to swell the ranks of the elderly to an unprecedented degree.

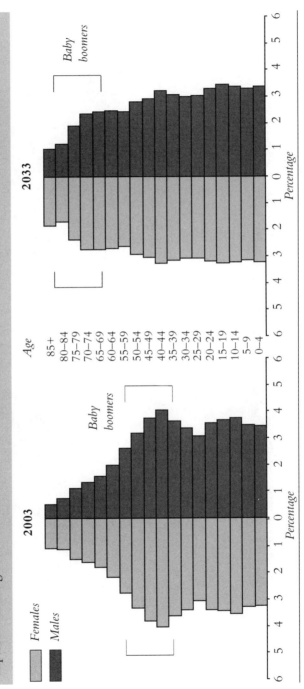

Source: Census Bureau, *Population Projections of the United States by Age, Sex, Race, Hispanic Origin, and Nativity: 1999 to 2100*, 2000, Table NP-D1-A.

Figure 1-3 • Population of the United States in 2003 by Age, Sex, and Hispanic Origin (projected) (percent distributions)

These figures show how today's Hispanic and non-Hispanic populations are distributed by age and sex. The Hispanic figure is a traditional "pyramid," largely because the Hispanic fertility rate has been comparatively high. The non-Hispanic distribution, forming a pyramid only above its baby-boomer midsection, reflects decades of low fertility rates.

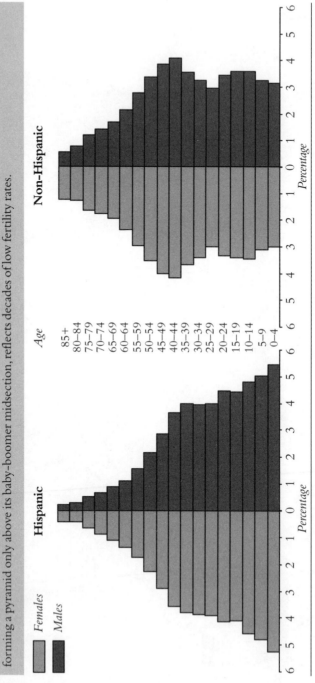

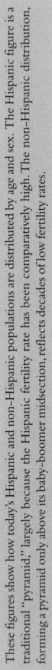

Source: Census Bureau, *Population Projections of the United States by Age, Sex, Race, Hispanic Origin, and Nativity: 1999 to 2100, 2000,* Table NP-D1-A.

Figure 1-4 • Population of the United States in 2033 by Age, Sex, and Hispanic Origin (projected) (percent distributions)

By 2033, the age distribution of the Hispanic population will still form a pyramid, albeit less exaggerated than in 2003. Half the Hispanic population will be younger than 30. In the non-Hispanic population, however, decades of low fertility rates, coupled with baby boomers living long lives, will produce a barrel-shaped distribution in which nearly half the people will be over 40.

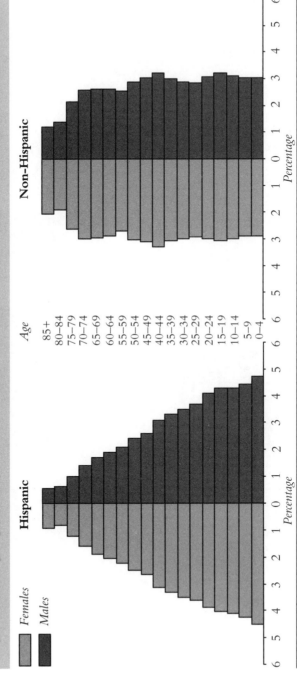

Source: Census Bureau, *Population Projections of the United States by Age, Sex, Race, Hispanic Origin, and Nativity: 1999 to 2100*, 2000, Table NP-D1-A.

Figure 1-5 • Population of the United States by Race and Hispanic Origin, 2003 and 2033 (projected) (percent distributions)[1]

The U.S. population is expected to grow by about 76 million (27 percent) between now and 2033. People of Hispanic origin and Asian/Pacific Islanders—children born in this country as well as immigrants—will account for close to two-thirds of the growth. As a result, by 2033, one in every five Americans will be of Hispanic origin; one in every 14 will be of Asian or Pacific Islander descent.

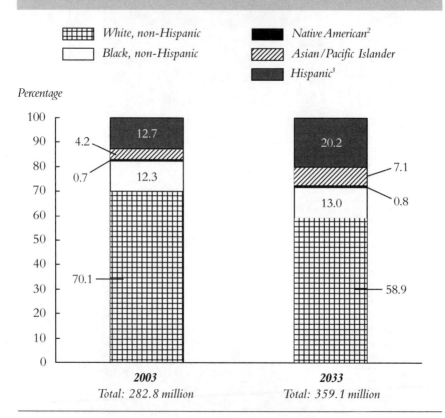

	White, non-Hispanic		Native American[2]
	Black, non-Hispanic		Asian/Pacific Islander
			Hispanic[3]

2003
Total: 282.8 million

2033
Total: 359.1 million

[1]Resident population of the 50 states and the District of Columbia.
[2]American Indian, Eskimo, and Aleut.
[3]People of Hispanic origin may be of any race. In this figure, Hispanics are not included in the racial categories. *See* Figure 1-6 and footnote to Table 1-1.

Source: Census Bureau, *Population Projections of the United States by Age, Sex, Race, Hispanic Origin, and Nativity: 1999 to 2100*, 2000, Table NP-D1-A.

Figure 1-6 • U.S. Hispanic Population by Race, 2003 and 2033 (projected)

As the pie figure below shows, every race is represented among Hispanics in this country. Still, 91 percent are white, and projections are that while their numbers will more than double between now and 2033, their racial mix will change hardly at all.[1] However, as can be seen in the bar figure, the Hispanic proportion of every racial group *will* change over the next three decades.

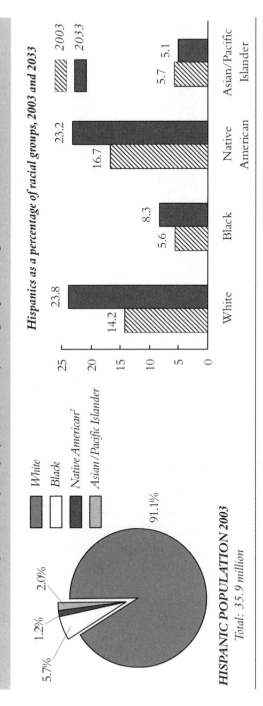

Hispanics as a percentage of racial groups, 2003 and 2033

Legend: 2003, 2033

White: 14.2 (2003), 23.8 (2033)
Black: 5.6 (2003), 8.3 (2033)
Native American: 16.7 (2003), 23.2 (2033)
Asian/Pacific Islander: 5.7 (2003), 5.1 (2033)

Pie chart legend: White, Black, Native American[2], Asian/Pacific Islander

White 91.1%, Black 5.7%, Native American 1.2%, Asian/Pacific Islander 2.0%

HISPANIC POPULATION 2003
Total: 35.9 million

[1]The racial mixes for 2003 and 2033 are the same if the percentages are rounded to the nearest whole number.
[2]American Indian, Eskimo, and Aleut.

Source: Census Bureau, *Population Projections of the United States by Age, Sex, Race, Hispanic Origin, and Nativity: 1999 to 2100,* 2000, Table NP-D1-A.

Figure 1-7 • Foreign–Born Females by Year of Entry and Race and Hipanic Origin

Altogether, more than 14 million of the women and girls who live in the United States are foreign-born—that is, they emigrated from other countries. Non-Hispanic white women account for 55 percent of the women who came to this country in the years before 1970 (a period when U.S. immigration laws strongly favored people of European origin), but since then women of Hispanic origin have been predominant, constituting nearly half of all foreign-born females who came here in the last decade of the twentieth century.

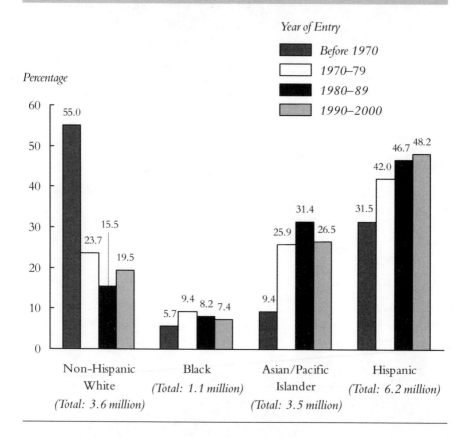

Sources: Census Bureau, *The Asian and Pacific Islander Population in the United States: March 2000 (Update)*, 2001, Table 8, *The Black Population in the United States: March 2000*, 2001, Table 8, and *The Hispanic Population in the United States: March 2000*, 2001, Table 8.3.

Figure 1-8 • Foreign–Born and U.S.-Born Females by Age, 2000 (percent distributions)

The age distribution of foreign-born women and girls differs noticeably from that of females born in the United States. Most obvious is that the proportion of U.S.-born females who are under age 15 is over three times the comparable proportion of foreign-born females (22.7 percent versus 6.7 percent). Nearly as noticeable are the comparatively large proportions of foreign-born females in the 25–34 and 35–44 age groups.

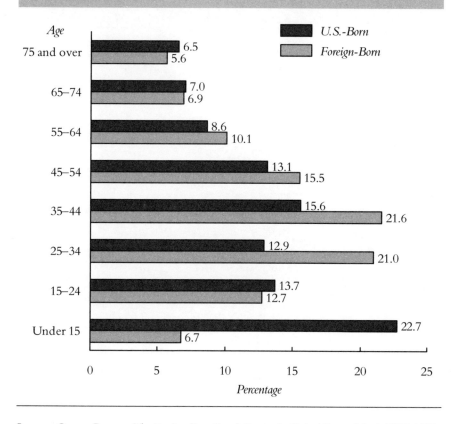

Source: Census Bureau, *The Foreign-Born Population in the United States: March 2000*, 2001, Tables 1.1 and 2.1.

Table 1-2 • Life Expectancy at Birth and at Age 65 by Sex, Race, and Hispanic Origin, 2003 and 2035 (projected)

Over roughly the next three decades, life expectancy is projected to increase for both sexes in all of the groups shown here, but it will continue to be longer for women than for men.

| | *Life Expectancy (years of life remaining)* | | | |
| | *At Birth* | | *At Age 65* | |
	Females	*Males*	*Females*	*Males*
All races				
2003	80.4	74.6	19.9	16.5
2035	84.8	79.1	23.1	19.3
Non-Hispanic				
White				
2003	80.6	75.2	19.8	16.4
2035	84.7	79.1	22.8	19.1
Black				
2003	76.0	69.2	18.5	15.0
2035	82.2	75.6	22.2	18.3
Native American[1]				
2003	82.9	73.9	25.0	19.7
2035	87.6	80.0	26.9	21.8
Asian/Pacific Islander				
2003	86.7	81.1	24.8	20.8
2035	88.5	83.4	26.1	22.3
Hispanic[2]				
2003	84.1	77.6	22.8	19.4
2035	87.0	81.2	24.9	21.4

[1] American Indian, Eskimo, and Aleut.

[2] People of Hispanic origin may be of any race. In this table, Hispanics are included in the racial categories as well as in the Hispanic category. *See* Figure 1-6 and footnote to Table 1-1.

Source: Census Bureau, *Population Projections of the United States by Age, Sex, Race, Hispanic Origin, and Nativity: 1999 to 2100*, 2000, Table NP-D5.

Figure 1-9 • U.S. Fertility Rates by Race and Hispanic Origin, 1950–1999 (number of births per 1,000 women age 15–44 in specified group)[1,2]

> Fertility rates declined in the last decade of the twentieth century in every group shown here, although the Hispanic fertility rate remains by far the highest. The rates for blacks and Native Americans virtually converged, as did the overall, Asian/Pacific Islander, and white rates (see Table 1-3).

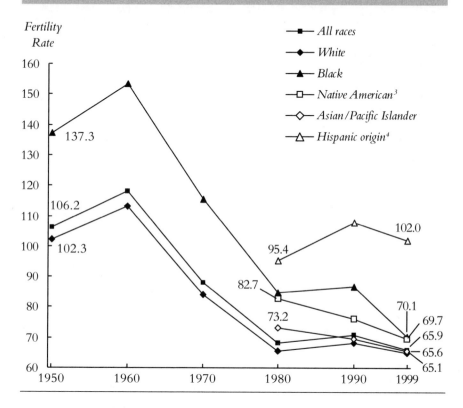

[1]Data for Native Americans, Asian/Pacific Islanders, and persons of Hispanic origin are not available for the years 1950, 1960, and 1970.
[2]After 1970, rates are based on the mother's race. Earlier rates were based on the child's race.
[3]American Indian or Alaska Native.
[4]People of Hispanic origin may be of any race. *See* Figure 1-6 and footnote to Table 1-1.

Sources: Census Bureau, *Statistical Abstract of the United States: 1980*, 1980, Table 88; National Center for Health Statistics, *Health, United States, 2000*, 2000, Table 3, and *National Vital Statistics Report* 49, no. 1, 2001, Tables 3 and 8.

Table 1-3 • U.S. Fertility Rates by Race and Hispanic Origin, 1999 (number of births per 1,000 women age 15–44 in specified group)[1,2]

The convergence in 1999 of fertility rates tracked in Figure 1-9 makes it hard to distinguish one from another. The first set of numbers in this table shows the 1999 rates by race. From the second set of numbers, by Hispanic/non-Hispanic origin, one can see that the fertility rate for non-Hispanic whites is about eight percentage points lower than for whites when Hispanics are included.

	Fertility Rate
By race	
All races	65.9
White	65.1
Black	70.1
Native American	69.7
Asian/Pacific Islander	65.6
By Hispanic/non-Hispanic origin	
White, non-Hispanic	57.7
Black, non-Hispanic	73.0
Hispanic	102.0
Mexican	111.6
Puerto Rican	77.7
Cuban	51.2
Other Hispanic origin	92.6

[1]Rates for white, non-Hispanic and black, non-Hispanic are for 1998.
[2]Rates are by race and Hispanic origin of mother.

Sources: National Center for Health Statistics, *Health, United States, 2000,* 2000, Table 3, and *National Vital Statistics Report* 49, no. 1, 2001, Tables 3 and 8.

Table 1-4 • Median Ages of the U.S. Population by Sex, Race, and Hispanic Origin, July 1, 2003, and July 1, 2033 (projected)

Over time, longer life expectancies and declining fertility rates push median ages upward. Between now and 2033, the median age of U.S. women overall is projected to increase by nearly three years, that of men by two and a half. Non-Hispanic white females will continue to be the "oldest" group—currently more than half are over 40; by 2033, just about half will be over 45.

| | Median Age in Years | | | |
| | 2003 | | 2033 | |
	Female	Male	Female	Male
All races	37.6	35.1	40.4	37.6
Non-Hispanic				
White	40.6	38.3	44.9	42.0
Black	33.0	29.3	39.1	35.1
Native American[1]	29.7	28.1	34.6	33.3
Asian/Pacific Islander	33.9	31.9	36.7	34.0
Hispanic[2]	27.6	26.0	31.0	29.1

[1] American Indian, Eskimo, and Aleut.
[2] People of Hispanic origin may be of any race. In this table, Hispanics are not included in the racial categories. *See* Figure 1-6 and footnote to Table 1-1.

Source: Census Bureau, *Population Projections of the United States by Age, Sex, Race, Hispanic Origin, and Nativity: 1999 to 2100*, 2000, Table NP-D1-A.

Table 1-5 • Marital Status by Sex, Race, and Hispanic Origin, 2000 (percent distributions)[1]

Unless she or he is black, the typical American adult is married and living with a spouse. However, in all of the groups shown here, the widowed proportion is much higher among the women than among the men and the never-married proportion is lower. These differences are attributable, in part, to the difference in the age distribution of women and men (see Figure 1-1).

Marital Status	All Races		White		Black		Asian/Pacific Islander		Hispanic[2]	
	Women	Men	Women	Men	Women	Men	Women	Men	Women	Men
Married, spouse present	53.8	58.3	57.2	60.9	30.8	40.0	58.2	56.4	53.0	53.1
Married, spouse absent	3.8	3.2	3.1	2.7	7.7	6.5	4.9	5.8	7.6	6.6
Widowed	10.5	2.7	10.8	2.7	10.3	3.1	6.9	1.3	6.7	1.6
Divorced	10.8	8.8	10.7	8.9	12.5	10.3	5.6	3.5	8.9	6.4
Never married	21.1	27.0	18.1	24.9	38.7	40.2	24.4	33.1	23.8	32.3
Total percentage[3]	100.0	100.0	100.0	100.0	100.0	100.0	100.0	100.0	100.0	100.0
Total number (in millions)	104.9	96.9	86.6	81.5	13.3	10.7	4.1	3.8	10.7	10.4

[1]Persons age 18 and over.

[2]People of Hispanic origin may be of any race. In this table, Hispanics are included in the racial categories as well as in the Hispanic category. See Figure 1-6 and footnote to Table 1-1.

[3]Percentages may not total 100.0 due to rounding.

Source: Census Bureau, America's Families and Living Arrangements: March 2000, 2001, Table A1.

Figure 1-10 • Median Age at First Marriage by Sex, 1900–2000

Today's typical first-time bride, who has recently celebrated her twenty-fifth birthday, is three years older than her 1980 counterpart and nearly five years older than her 1960 counterpart. She is also closer in age to the typical bridegroom than the first-time brides of earlier decades.

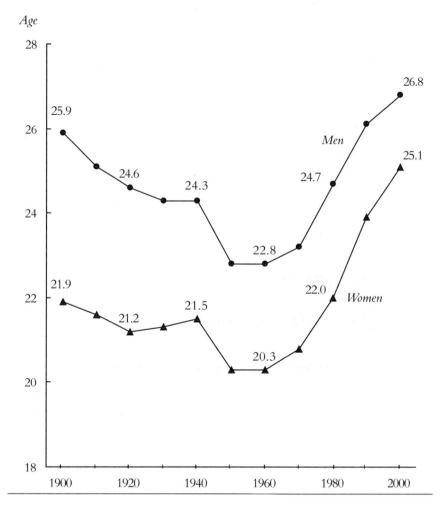

Source: Census Bureau, *America's Families and Living Arrangements: March 2000*, 2001, Table MS-2.

Figure 1-11 • Never-Married Women by Age, 1980 and 2000

"Dramatic" is often over used, but it seems the right word to characterize the changes in women's lifestyles suggested by this figure. In 1980, only a hair over 50 percent of women age 20–24 were single (never married), compared with nearly three-quarters in 2000. Among women in every age group between 25 and 55, the proportion who had never married was roughly twice as large in 2000 as it had been just two decades earlier.

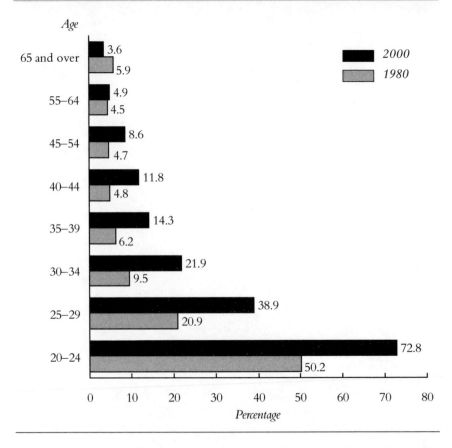

Sources: Census Bureau, *America's Families and Living Arrangements: March 2000*, 2001, Table A1, and unpublished data from the March 1980 Current Population Survey.

Figure 1-12 • The Divorce Rate, 1950–1999

After declining gradually for nearly two decades, the divorce rate—the number of divorces in a given year per 1,000 persons in the population—appears to have leveled off.

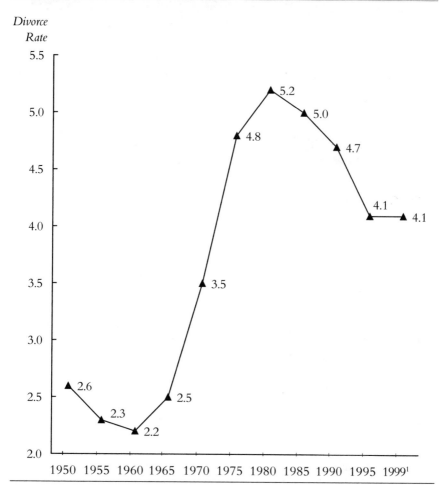

'For the 12 months ending with December 1999. The rate does not include data for California, Colorado, Indiana, and Louisiana.

Sources: Census Bureau, *Statistical Abstract of the United States: 2000*, 2000, Table 77; and National Center for Health Statistics, *National Vital Statistics Report* 48, no. 19, 2001, Table 1.

Figure 1-13 • Households by Type, 1975 and 2000 (percent distributions)[1]

Over the last quarter of the twentieth century, the number of American households grew by 30 percent, and the proportions in the "mix" of household types changed noticeably. For example, in 1975, two-thirds of all households consisted of married couples. By 2000, that proportion had shrunk to slightly over half.

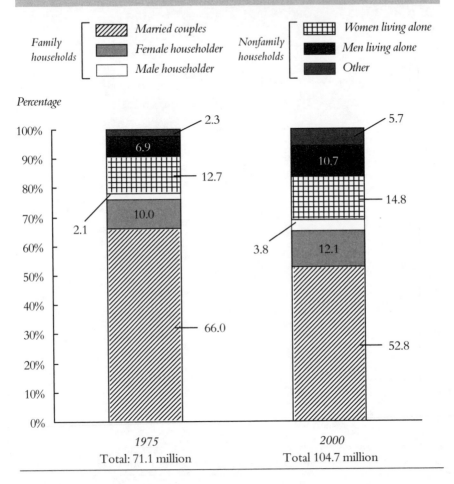

[1]Percentages may not total 100.0 due to rounding.

Sources: Census Bureau, *America's Families and Living Arrangements: March 2000*, 2001, Tables H1 and HH-1, and unpublished data from the March 1975 Current Population Survey.

Table 1-6 • Families by Family Type, Race, and Hispanic Origin, 1975 and 2000 (percent distributions)[1]

> The married-couple family is still the predominant American family type, except in the black community. Nevertheless, as of 2000, families headed by single house-holders—whether female or male—accounted for larger proportions of the families in every group shown here than was the case in 1975.

Family Type	1975	2000
All races[2]		
Married couple	84.1	76.8
Wife in paid labor force	37.0	47.7
Wife not in paid labor force	47.1	29.1
Female head, no spouse present	13.3	17.3
Male head, no spouse present	2.6	5.9
Total percentage	100.0	100.0
Total number (in thousands)	56,245	72,383
White		
Married couple	86.8	80.8
Wife in paid labor force	37.3	49.6
Wife not in paid labor force	49.5	31.3
Female head, no spouse present	10.8	13.8
Male head, no spouse present	2.4	5.4
Total percentage	100.0	100.0
Total number (in thousands)	49,873	60,218
Black		
Married couple	60.0	48.7
Wife in paid labor force	34.1	33.7
Wife not in paid labor force	25.9	14.9
Female head, no spouse present	35.9	42.7
Male head, no spouse present	4.1	8.6
Total percentage	100.0	100.0
Total number (in thousands)	5,586	8,812

See footnotes at end of table.

(continued)

Table 1-6 (continued)

Family Type	1975	2000
Asian and Pacific Islander		
Married couple	(3)	82.6
Wife in paid labor force	(3)	(3)
Wife not in paid labor force	(3)	(3)
Female head, no spouse present	(3)	11.2
Male head, no spouse present	(3)	6.2
Total percentage	(3)	100.0
Total number (in thousands)	(3)	2,663
Hispanic[4]		
Married couple	75.9	67.9
Wife in paid labor force	31.6	38.3
Wife not in paid labor force	44.3	29.5
Female head, no spouse present	20.9	22.6
Male head, no spouse present	3.3	9.5
Total percentage	100.0	100.0
Total number (in thousands)	2,499	7,728

[1]Percentages may not total 100.0 due to rounding.

[2]Includes Native Americans, not shown separately (data not available).

[3]Data for Asian/Pacific Islanders are not available for 1975 or for 2000 for the categories "wife in paid labor force" and "wife not in paid labor force."

[4]People of Hispanic origin may be of any race. In this table, Hispanics are included in the racial categories as well as in the Hispanic category. *See* Figure 1-6 and footnote to Table 1-1.

Source: Census Bureau, *Historical Income Tables,* <http://www.census.gov/hhes/income/histinc/>.

Figure 1-14 • Children's Living Arrangements by Race and Hispanic Origin, 2000 (percent distributions)[1]

Most white and Hispanic children live in two–parent families; most black children do not. A black child is not only the most likely to be living with a single parent (nearly always the mother) but also the most likely to be living with someone other than a parent.

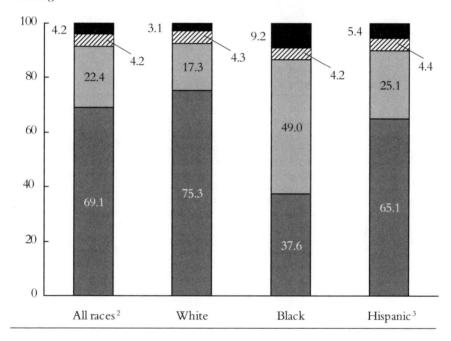

Percentage

[1]Percentages may not total 100.0 due to rounding.
[2]Includes Asian/Pacific Islanders and Native Americans, not shown separately (data not available).
[3]People of Hispanic origin may be of any race. In this figure, Hispanics are included in the racial categories as well as in the Hispanic category. *See* Figure 1-6 and footnote to Table 1-1.

Source: Census Bureau, *America's Families and Living Arrangements: March 2000*, 2001, Tables CH-1, CH-2, CH-3, and CH-4.

Figure 1-15 • Ratio of Women to Men in the Population by Age, 1999 (number of women per 100 men in a given age group)

This figure makes starkly clear just how overwhelmingly female the elderly population is (see also Figure 1-1). Among the oldest old—people age 90 and over—there are nearly three women for every man.

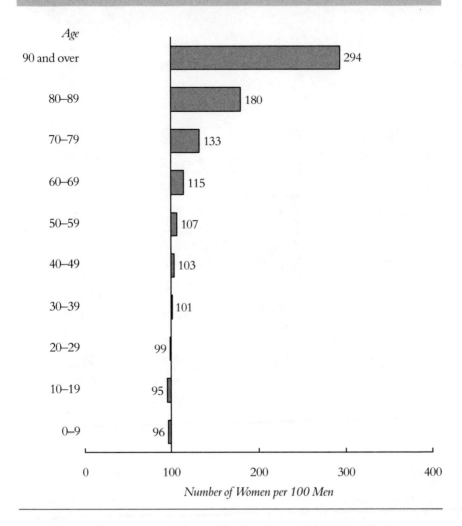

Source: Census Bureau, *Statistical Abstract of the United States: 2000*, 2000, Table 13.

Figure 1-16 • Living Arrangements of Women and Men Age 65 and over, and of the Women by Race and Hispanic Origin, 2000 (percent distributions)[1,2]

Most men age 65 and over are living with a spouse; most of their female contemporaries are not. Asian/Pacific Islanders (A/PI) are the older women most likely to live with a spouse—46 percent do. This might be because Asian/Pacific Islander men typically live longer than men in any other group (see Table 1-2).

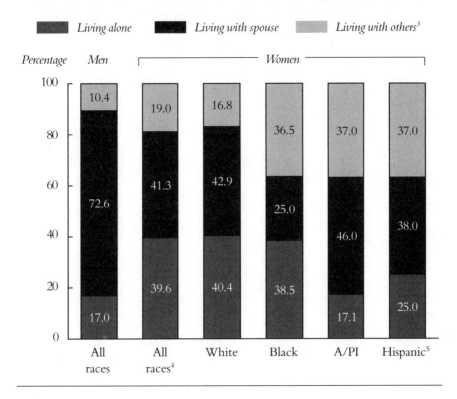

[1]Percentages may not total 100.0 due to rounding.
[2]Noninstitutional population.
[3]Most of these women live with family members, either in their own households or in the family members' households.
[4]Incudes Native Americans, not shown separately (data not available).
[5]People of Hispanic origin may be of any race. In this figure, Hispanics are included in the racial categories as well as in the Hispanic category. *See* Figure 1-6 and footnote to Table 1-1.

Source: Census Bureau, *America's Families and Living Arrangements: March 2000*, 2001, Table A2.

Table 1-7 • Living Arrangements of Women and Men Age 65 and over, and of the Women by Age, Race, and Hispanic Origin, 2000 (numbers are in thousands, percent distributions)[1,2]

This table shows what a difference advancing age makes in women's living situations. Unless she is black or Hispanic, a "young-old" woman (age 65–74) is more likely than not to be living with a spouse. Once past 75, however, the odds change: for example, if she is Asian/Pacific Islander (A/PI), she is most likely living with other family members; if she is white, she is most likely living alone.

	Living Alone	Living with Spouse	Living with Others[3]	Total Percentage	Total Number
Women					
Age 65 and over	39.6	41.3	19.0	100.0	18,736
Age 65–74					
All races[4]	30.6	52.9	16.5	100.0	9,748
White	30.6	55.3	14.0	100.0	8,435
Black	34.8	31.4	33.9	100.0	963
A/PI	15.3	56.0	28.7	100.0	275
Hispanic[5]	21.3	43.4	35.3	100.0	662
Age 75 and over					
All races	49.4	28.8	21.8	100.0	8,988
White	50.5	29.9	19.6	100.0	8,110
Black	43.6	16.2	40.2	100.0	697
A/PI	20.4	27.2	52.4	100.0	147
Hispanic	31.6	28.4	40.0	100.0	370
Men					
Age 65 and over	17.0	72.6	10.4	100.0	13,884

[1]Percentages may not total 100.0 due to rounding.
[2]Noninstitutional population.
[3]Most of these women live with family members, either in their own households or in the family members' households.
[4]Includes Native Americans, not shown separately (data not available).
[5]People of Hispanic origin may be of any race. In this table, Hispanics are included in the racial categories as well as in the Hispanic category. *See* Figure 1-6 and footnote to Table 1-1.

Source: Census Bureau, *America's Families and Living Arrangements: March 2000*, 2001, Table A2.

Section 2

EDUCATION

THE INCREASING EDUCATIONAL ATTAINMENT of American women in general is documented in this section, as are the troubling gaps between the educational "haves" and the "have-nots." "Gulf" might be a better word to characterize the educational difference between the typical Asian/Pacific Islander woman and the typical woman of Hispanic origin: nearly 41 percent of Asian/Pacific Islander women in the United States are college graduates, about four times the comparable percentage of Hispanic women. (Among women age 25–34, the multiple is five.)

Education's power to broaden horizons and encourage ambition is difficult to quantify, although it can certainly be felt in Sara Perez's case (see "Two Generations: A Mother and Daughter Talk about Their Lives"). But this book contains abundant evidence of education's effect on women's earning power (see especially Table 5-7 of this "Statistical Portrait" but also Chapters One and Two). For example, it is surely no accident that, of all women in the United States, Asian/Pacific Islanders have the highest annual earnings. Findings include:

- Of all women in the United States, Asian/Pacific Islander women are the most likely to have a bachelor's degree and the most likely to have a graduate degree (see Table 2-1 and Figure 2-1).
- In the over-25 population as a whole, the percentage of women with college degrees is smaller than the percentage of men, but the gap has been closing. It has closed altogether in the 25–34 age group (see Table 2-2).
- Asian/Pacific Islander and white women are more likely to be college graduates than black or Hispanic women, but black women have made the greatest strides proportionally: the percentage of college graduates among them doubled between 1980 and 2000. Hispanic women have

made some progress but are still the least likely to have a four-year degree (see Figure 2-2).

- Women from Mexico and other Central American countries, who account for about 30 percent of all foreign-born women age 25 and over in the United States, constitute over half of the foreign-born women who lack even a high school diploma. Close to half (47.5 percent) of all college-educated foreign-born women came here from Asia (see Figure 2-3).

- Undergraduate student bodies became more diverse during the 1990s, but the "mix" differed somewhat depending on sex. A larger proportion of the women than of the men were black; a larger proportion of the men than of the women were Asian/Pacific Islander (see Table 2-3).

- Business is the universal and unisex favorite college major, but otherwise, women's choices of majors are quite different from men's. For example, engineering, which ranks third in popularity among men, makes the top 10 only among Asian/Pacific Islander women (see Table 2-4).

- Women earn the majority of undergraduate and master's degrees, and women's predominance at these levels is expected to grow over the current decade. Men are still more likely to earn professional and doctoral degrees, although the gap has been shrinking (see Table 2-5).

- Women are better represented at nearly every degree level in nearly every field—including engineering and computer sciences—than they were two decades ago. However, it is still true that most of the people who earn degrees in engineering, computer sciences, and the physical sciences are men (see Table 2-6).

- Over the last two decades of the twentieth century, women's share of professional degrees in all fields increased significantly but nowhere more dramatically than in pharmacy and veterinary medicine, where women now take two-thirds of the degrees (see Table 2-7).

Table 2-1 • Educational Attainment of Women and Men Age 25 and over by Race and Hispanic Origin, 2000 (in percentages)

Many Hispanics of both sexes are at a severe educational disadvantage compared with other Americans.

	No High School	Some High School, No Diploma	High School Diploma or More	Percentage with Some College, No Degree	Associate Degree, No More	Bachelor's Degree or More	Postgraduate Degree[1]	Number (in thousands)
All races[2]								
Women	6.8	9.1	84.0	17.7	8.4	23.6	7.3	91,620
Men	7.1	8.7	84.2	17.4	7.1	27.8	10.0	83,611
White								
Women	6.7	8.3	85.0	17.6	8.6	23.9	7.4	76,167
Men	6.9	8.2	84.8	17.2	7.3	28.5	10.2	70,900
Black								
Women	6.2	15.5	78.3	20.1	7.6	16.7	5.3	11,157
Men	8.1	13.2	78.7	19.9	5.8	16.3	4.8	8,879
A/PI[3]								
Women	10.5	6.1	83.4	12.4	6.6	40.7	11.3	3,527
Men	6.1	5.7	88.2	12.8	7.4	47.5	19.7	3,140
Hispanic[4]								
Women	27.4	15.1	57.5	13.9	5.5	10.5	3.3	8,785
Men	27.2	16.2	56.6	13.0	4.5	10.7	3.4	8,365

[1]Includes master's, professional, and doctorate degrees. [2]Includes Native Americans, not shown separately (data not available). [3]Asian/Pacific Islander. [4]People of Hispanic origin may be of any race. *See* Figure 1–6 and footnote to Table 1–1.

Source: Census Bureau, *Educational Attainment in the United States: March 2000 (Update)*, 2000, Table 1.

Figure 2-1 • Educational Attainment of Women Age 25 and over by Race, 2000 (percent distributions)

Compared with her counterparts of other races, the typical Asian/Pacific Islander woman in this country is far more likely to have a bachelor's degree and far more likely to have a graduate degree. (At least in part, this is because a substantial proportion of women college graduates who have emigrated to the United States are from Asia [see Figure 2-3].)

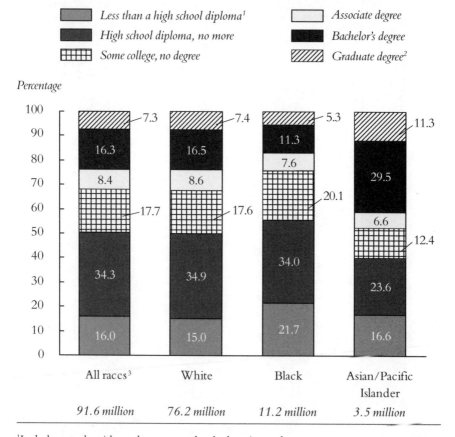

Percentage

[Legend:]
- Less than a high school diploma[1]
- High school diploma, no more
- Some college, no degree
- Associate degree
- Bachelor's degree
- Graduate degree[2]

	All races[3]	White	Black	Asian/Pacific Islander
Graduate degree	7.3	7.4	5.3	11.3
Bachelor's degree	16.3	16.5	11.3	29.5
Associate degree	8.4	8.6	7.6	6.6
Some college, no degree	17.7	17.6	20.1	12.4
High school diploma, no more	34.3	34.9	34.0	23.6
Less than a high school diploma	16.0	15.0	21.7	16.6
	91.6 million	76.2 million	11.2 million	3.5 million

[1]Includes people with an elementary school education or less.
[2]Includes professional degrees.
[3]Includes Native Americans, not shown separately (data not available).

Source: Census Bureau, *Educational Attainment in the United States: March 2000 (Update)*, 2000, Table 1.

Table 2-2 • Educational Attainment of Women and Men Age 25 and over by Age, Race, and Hispanic Origin, 2000 (in percentages)

While an education gender gap still exists in the overall population of adults age 25 and up (see Table 2-1), the gap has closed in the youngest 10-year cohort. Only in the case of non-Hispanic blacks are women age 25–34 less likely than their male counterparts to have at least a bachelor's degree, and even in that case the difference is very small.

	High School Graduate or More		*Bachelor's Degree or More*	
	Women	*Men*	*Women*	*Men*
All races[1]				
Total 25 and over	84.0	84.2	23.6	27.8
25–34	89.1	87.1	29.9	28.6
35–44	89.1	88.1	26.6	27.4
45–54	89.0	88.9	28.2	32.3
55–64	81.4	82.1	19.5	27.9
65 and over	69.5	69.6	11.4	21.4
Non-Hispanic white				
Total 25 and over	88.4	88.5	25.5	30.8
25–34	94.8	93.0	35.5	33.6
35–44	93.5	92.3	29.0	30.4
45–54	93.5	93.1	30.6	35.3
55–64	86.7	87.1	21.2	30.5
65 and over	74.4	73.8	12.0	23.2
Non-Hispanic black				
Total 25 and over	78.7	79.1	16.8	16.4
25–34	87.6	88.7	17.6	18.1
35–44	87.0	89.4	19.4	17.4
45–54	83.8	81.5	20.6	19.6
55–64	71.5	63.7	13.3	13.9
65 and over	47.6	44.8	8.2	7.6

See footnotes at end of table.   *(continued)*

Table 2-2 (continued)

	High School Graduate or More		Bachelor's Degree or More	
	Women	*Men*	*Women*	*Men*
Asian/Pacific Islander[2]				
Total 25 and over	83.4	88.2	40.7	47.6
25–34	93.8	92.6	51.2	50.4
35–44	87.8	89.6	44.0	52.2
45–54	86.3	90.3	41.4	47.8
55–64	69.2	88.5	32.9	44.3
65 and over	57.0	70.4	15.2	32.2
Hispanic[3]				
Total 25 and over	57.5	56.6	10.6	10.7
25–34	64.3	58.9	10.8	8.6
35–44	64.2	59.9	13.6	11.2
45–54	56.4	58.4	11.8	14.2
55–64	45.8	48.5	5.8	11.0
65 and over	34.9	41.0	5.2	9.3

[1]Includes Native Americans, not shown separately (data not available).

[2]Educational attainment data for Asian/Pacific Islanders were not available by Hispanic/ non-Hispanic origin. According to Census Bureau projections, as of mid-2000 about six percent of Asian/Pacific Islanders were of Hispanic origin.

[3]People of Hispanic origin may be of any race.

Source: Census Bureau, *Educational Attainment in the United States: March 2000 (Update)*, 2000, Table 3.

Figure 2-2 • Women Age 25 and over Who Have a Bachelor's Degree or More by Race and Hispanic Origin, 1980, 1990, and 2000 (in percentages)

Although Asian/Pacific Islander women and white women are more likely to be college graduates than black or Hispanic women, it is black women who have made the greatest strides proportionally: the percentage of college graduates among them doubled in two decades, from 8.3 percent in 1980 to 16.7 percent in 2000. Hispanic women have made some progress but are still the least likely to have a four-year degree.

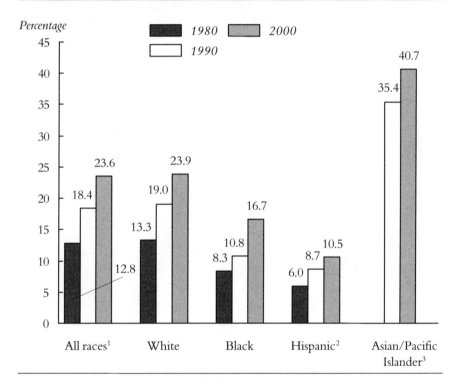

[1]Includes Native Americans, not shown separately (data not available).
[2]People of Hispanic origin may be of any race. In this figure, Hispanics are included in the racial categories as well as in the Hispanic category. *See* Figure 1-6 and footnote to Table 1-1.
[3]Data for Asian/Pacific Islanders are not available for 1980.

Sources: Census Bureau, *Educational Attainment in the United States: March 2000 (Update)*, 2000, Table 1, and *Statistical Abstract of the United States: 2000*, 2000, Table 249.

Figure 2-3 • Educational Attainment of Foreign-Born Women Age 25 and over by World Region of Birth, 2000 (percent distributions)

Women from Mexico and other Central American countries, who account for about 30 percent of all foreign-born women age 25 and over in the United States, constitute over half of the foreign-born women who lack even a high school diploma and only about seven percent of those who are college graduates. Close to half (47.5 percent) of all college-educated foreign-born women in this country came from Asia.

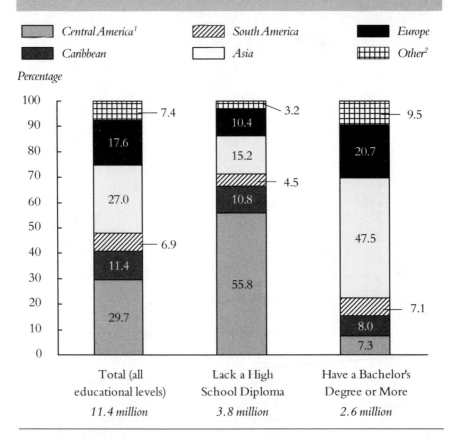

¹The majority of Central Americans are from Mexico.
²From Africa, Oceana, Bermuda, and Canada.

Source: Census Bureau, *The Foreign-Born Population in the United States: March 2000,* 2001, Tables 3.5 and 4.5.

Table 2-3 • Undergraduate Enrollment of Women and Men by Race and Hispanic Origin, 1990, 1995, and 1997 (percent distributions)[1]

Undergraduate student bodies became more diverse during the 1990s but the "mix" differed somewhat depending on sex. For example, a larger proportion of the women than of the men were black; a larger proportion of the men than of the women were Asian/Pacific Islander.

	Women			Men		
	1990	*1995*	*1997*	*1990*	*1995*	*1997*
Non-Hispanic						
White	78.4	72.9	71.3	79.6	74.5	73.3
Black	10.8	12.3	12.7	8.5	9.6	9.9
Asian/Pacific Islander	3.8	5.3	5.6	4.8	6.4	6.8
Native American[2]	0.9	1.1	1.1	0.8	1.0	1.0
Hispanic[3]	6.1	8.5	9.3	6.2	8.4	9.1
Total percentage[4]	100.0	100.0	100.0	100.0	100.0	100.0
Total number (in thousands)	6,487	6,707	6,768	5,254	5,257	5,266

[1]Fall enrollment of undergraduates (excluding non–U.S. citizens) in accredited institutions of higher education.
[2]American Indians and Alaska Natives.
[3]People of Hispanic origin may be of any race.
[4]Percentages may not total 100.0 due to rounding.

Source: National Center for Education Statistics, *Digest of Education Statistics, 2000,* 2001, Table 208.

Table 2-4 • Ten Most Popular Majors among Bachelor's Degree Recipients by Sex, and by Race and Hispanic Origin of Women, Academic Year 1997/98 (in rank order)[1]

Except for business, the universal and unisex favorite, women's choices of majors are quite different from men's.

Major Field	Men Total	Women Total	Non-Hispanic Women				Hispanic Women[4]
			White	Black	A/PI[2]	NA[3]	
Business and management[5]	1	1	1	1	1	1	1
Education	5	2	2	4	9	2	4
Health professions and related sciences		3	3	3	4	4	5
Social sciences and history	2	4	4	2	3	3	2
Psychology	8	5	5	5	5	5	3
Biological and life sciences	4	6	7	6	2	7	8
English language and literature/letters	10	7	6	9	8	9	9
Communications	7	8	9	8			
Visual and performing arts	6	9	8		6	10	6
Liberal arts and sciences, general studies, and humanities		10	10	10		6	
Public administration and services				7		7	
Multi/interdisciplinary studies					10		
Foreign languages and literature							7
Engineering	3				7		
Computer and information sciences	9						10

[1]Excludes non-U.S. citizens on temporary visas. [2]Asian/Pacific Islander. [3]American Indian/Alaska Native. [4]Hispanics may be of any race. [5]Includes business management and administrative services, business, marketing and distribution, and consumer and personal services.

Source: National Center for Education Statistics, *Digest of Education Statistics 2000,* 2001, Table 266.

Table 2-5 • Recipients of Postsecondary Degrees by Sex, 1977/78, 1997/98, and Projected 2009/10

Women's major share of undergraduate and master's degrees is expected to grow over the current decade, and women are expected to continue narrowing men's lead in earning professional degrees. Women's share of doctoral degrees is not, however, expected to grow appreciably during the current decade.

Degree	1977/78	1997/98	Percent Change 77/78– 97/98	Projected 2009/10
Associate, total number	412,246	558,555	35.5	611,000
Number of women	207,528	340,942	64.3	387,000
Women as a percentage of degree recipients	50.3	61.0	—	63.3
Bachelor's, total number	921,204	1,184,406	28.6	1,324,000
Number of women	433,857	664,450	53.1	776,000
Women as a percentage of degree recipients	47.1	56.1	—	58.6
Master's, total number	311,620	430,164	38.0	439,000
Number of women	150,408	245,789	63.4	264,000
Women as a percentage of degree recipients	48.3	57.1	—	60.1
Professional, total number[1]	66,581	78,598	18.0	81,600
Number of women	14,311	33,687	135.4	38,400
Women as a percentage of degree recipients	21.5	42.9	—	47.1
Doctoral, total number	32,131	46,010	43.2	47,100
Number of women	8,473	19,346	128.3	20,000
Women as a percentage of degree recipients	26.4	42.0	—	42.5

[1]First professional degrees (i.e., in law, medicine, etc.).

Source: National Center for Education Statistics, *Digest of Education Statistics, 2000,* 2001, Table 248.

Table 2-6 • Women Awarded Bachelor's, Master's, and Doctoral Degrees in Selected Fields, 1977/78 and 1997/98 (in percentages)[1]

Women are better represented at nearly every degree level in nearly every field than they were two decades ago.

| | Women Awarded | | | | | |
| Field | Bachelor's Degrees | | Master's Degrees | | Doctoral Degrees | |
	1977/78	1997/98	1977/78	1997/98	1977/78	1997/98
Biological/life sciences	38.4	55.1	35.4	52.4	24.1	42.5
Business	27.3	48.5	16.9	38.6	8.5	31.4
Computer and information sciences	25.7	26.7	18.7	29.0	7.7	16.3
Education	72.5	75.2	67.8	76.4	39.0	63.2
Engineering and related fields	6.7	16.9	5.3	19.9	2.3	12.2
English language and literature/letters	62.8	66.8	64.6	66.1	45.9	59.1
Health professions	80.5	82.1	70.2	77.7	38.5	62.5
Mathematics	40.2	46.5	31.8	41.0	14.9	25.7
Physical sciences	21.3	38.4	16.9	35.9	10.0	25.2
Psychology	59.0	74.4	54.6	73.1	37.6	67.5
Social sciences and history	40.5	49.2	33.1	46.7	24.3	40.8
Visual and performing arts	62.0	58.7	52.1	58.8	36.7	51.3
All fields	47.1	56.1	48.3	57.1	26.4	42.0

[1]The numbers from which these percentages were calculated include nonresident alien recipients. In most cases, excluding nonresident aliens from the calculations slightly increases women's share of degrees.

Source: National Center for Education Statistics, *Digest of Education Statistics, 2000*, 2001, Tables 248, 279, 281, 283, 284, 285, 287, 290, 291, 292, 294, 296, and 298.

Table 2-7 • Women Awarded First Professional Degrees in Selected Fields by Race and Hispanic Origin, 1978/79 and 1997/98 (percent distributions)[1]

Over the last two decades of the twentieth century, women's share of professional degrees in all fields increased significantly but nowhere more dramatically than in pharmacy and veterinary medicine, where women now take two-thirds of the degrees.

	Dentistry		Law		Medicine		Pharmacy		Veterinary Medicine	
	1978/79	*1997/98*	*1978/79*	*1997/98*	*1978/79*	*1997/98*	*1978/79*	*1997/98*	*1978/79*	*1997/98*
Non-Hispanic										
White	82.8	60.6	89.9	75.6	86.0	65.7	75.6	66.5	94.1	92.8
Black	8.8	7.7	6.5	10.5	8.0	11.0	4.6	8.8	3.6	2.0
Asian/Pacific Islander	5.7	26.8	1.4	7.3	3.2	17.5	19.3	22.3	0.2	2.2
Native American[2]	0.3	0.3	0.4	1.0	0.4	0.9	—	0.1	1.4	0.6
Hispanic[3]	2.4	4.7	1.8	5.6	2.4	5.0	0.5	2.2	0.6	2.4
Total percentage[4]	100.0	100.0	100.0	100.0	100.0	100.0	100.0	100.0	100.0	100.0
Degrees awarded to women	628	1,430	9,998	17,293	3,377	6,346	217	2,387	494	1,433
As a percentage of all degrees	11.7	37.8	28.5	44.4	23.0	41.6	35.8	67.2	29.0	65.7

[1]Data exclude non-U.S. citizens on temporary visas. [2]American Indian/Alaska Native. [3]Hispanics may be of any race. [4]Percentages may not total 100.0 due to rounding.

Sources: National Center for Education Statistics, *Digest of Education Statistics, 1982,* 1982, Table 110, and *Digest of Education Statistics, 2000, 2001,* Table 275; and U.S. Department of Education, Office of Civil Rights, *Data on Earned Degrees Conferred by Institutions of Higher Education by Race, Ethnicity, and Sex, Academic Year 1978–1979,* 1981, Table 9.

Section 3

HEALTH

THIS SECTION LOOKS AT TOPICS related to women's reproductive health as well as statistics on chronic disease, disability, and leading causes of death. It also includes some data about behavior (smoking) or conditions (obesity) that put women's health at risk.

For a woman of childbearing age and even beyond, reproductive health is central to general health. This is a fact of life for women, whether or not they want or expect to bear children. Disorders of the reproductive system also can compromise the ability of women who want children to become pregnant. So any increase in the incidence of sexually transmitted diseases is worrisome, and the incidence of chlamydia, most of whose victims are female, has soared.

For women who bear children, prenatal care beginning early in pregnancy can head off long-term health problems for the mother as well as the baby-to-be. Although pregnant women of all races are increasingly likely to receive this care, Native American, black, and Hispanic women remain less likely than women of other races to receive it. Findings include:

- The typical American woman is having her children later and choosing to do so. Pregnancies among women in the 30–34 age group in 1996 (the most recent year for which data are available) were more than double the number in 1976, and a larger percentage went to term (see Table 3-1).
- Abortions in 1997 were more likely than in earlier years to have been performed very early in pregnancy—55.4 percent were performed in the first eight weeks, compared with, for example, 51.6 percent in 1990 (see Table 3-2).
- Even though an increasing percentage of black mothers have received early prenatal care, the troublingly high incidence of low birthweight

among the babies of black mothers compared with other babies has persisted (see Figures 3-1, 3-2, and 3-3).

- Between the late 1980s and the late 1990s, mortality rates declined among U.S. infants of all races. However, a black baby born in 1996–98 was more than twice as likely as a white baby to die in the first year, just as had been the case in 1986–88 (see Table 3-3).
- Heart disease and cancer are the two leading causes of death for men and for women of all races. Diabetes ranks fourth for women of all races except white (see Table 3-4).
- Women are much more likely to get breast cancer than lung cancer but much more likely to die of lung cancer, which is the leading cause of cancer death in women (see Table 3-5).
- As of 1988–94 (the latest period for which data are available), close to one in four white women and four in 10 black women were obese, up from fewer than one in six and one in three, respectively, in 1976–80 (see Figure 3-4). Obesity is a major cause of diabetes, one of the leading five causes of death for women (see Table 3-4). Obesity also is linked with coronary artery disease and high blood pressure.
- Relatively fewer women in every age group were current smokers in 1999 than in 1979. Still, it is troubling that more than one-quarter of women in both the 18–24 and 35–44 age groups are smokers (see Figure 3-5).
- There were far fewer new AIDS cases in 2000 than in 1995, but a larger percentage of them were females, who accounted for nearly one in four AIDS cases newly reported in 2000, up from less than one in five of the cases reported just five years earlier (see Table 3-6).
- Severe disability is more prevalent among black people of both sexes than among their counterparts in other racial groups, but—regardless of race—is more common among people age 65 and over than among younger people and most common among elderly women (see Table 3-7).

Table 3-1 • Pregnancy Outcomes by Age of Woman, 1976 and 1996 (numbers are in thousands)

The dry statistics in this table reflect a significant change since 1976 in the typical American woman's life pattern—specifically, that she is having her children later and choosing to do so. (See also Chapter One.) While the overall number of pregnancies in 1996 was around 1.2 million (25 percent) greater than the number in 1976, the increase occurred entirely in the age groups over 25. Pregnancies among women in the 30–34 age group in 1996 were more than double the 1976 number, and a larger proportion went to term. The pattern was similar but even more striking in the 35–39 and 40-and-over age groups.

| | 1976 | | | 1996 | | |
| | | Outcome[1] (in percentages) | | | Outcome[1] (in percentages) | |
Age	*Number of Pregnancies*	*Live Births*	*Abortions*	*Number of Pregnancies*	*Live Births*	*Abortions*
Under 15	32	37.5	50.0	26	42.3	38.5
15–19	1,073	52.1	33.8	893	55.1	29.6
20–24	1,644	66.4	23.8	1,570	60.2	27.6
25–29	1,381	70.4	16.0	1,617	66.2	19.7
30–34	602	65.1	18.3	1,312	68.4	14.9
35–39	214	54.2	26.6	683	58.6	16.4
40 and over	56	46.4	37.5	140	53.6	23.6
Total	5,002	63.3	23.6	6,240	62.4	21.9

[1]The balance of the pregnancies ended in miscarriage or stillbirth.

Source: National Center for Health Statistics, *Vital and Health Statistics* 21, no. 56, 2000, Table 2.

Table 3-2 • Legal Abortions by Week of Gestation, 1972, 1980, 1990, and 1997[1]

Abortions in 1997 were more likely than in the earlier years shown here to have been performed very early in pregnancy—more than 55 percent were done in the first eight weeks, compared with, for example, less than 52 percent in 1990. On the other hand, the percentages performed relatively late in the second trimester (16 weeks or more) were also slightly higher in 1997 than in either 1980 or 1990.

| | *Percent Distributions* | | | |
Week of Gestation	*1972*	*1980*	*1990*	*1997*
8 weeks or less	34.0	51.7	51.6	55.4
9–10 weeks	30.7	26.2	25.3	22.0
11–12 weeks	17.5	12.2	11.7	10.7
13–15 weeks	8.4	5.1	6.4	6.2
16–20 weeks	8.2	3.9	4.0	4.3
21 weeks or more	1.2	0.9	1.0	1.4
Total percentage	100.0	100.0	100.0	100.0
Total number	586,760	1,297,606	1,429,577	1,186,039

[1]Week of gestation is calculated from last menstrual period.

Source: Centers for Disease Control and Prevention, *Abortion Surveillance—United States, 1997* 49, no. SS-11, 2000, Table 1.

Figure 3-1 • Prenatal Care for Mothers with Live Births by Race and Hispanic Origin, 1970–1999 (in percentages)[1,2]

Since 1990, the percentage of mothers receiving prenatal care early in their pregnancies has increased in all of the groups shown here. However, black, Hispanic, and, especially, Native American women are still less likely to receive such care than white and Asian/Pacific Islander women.

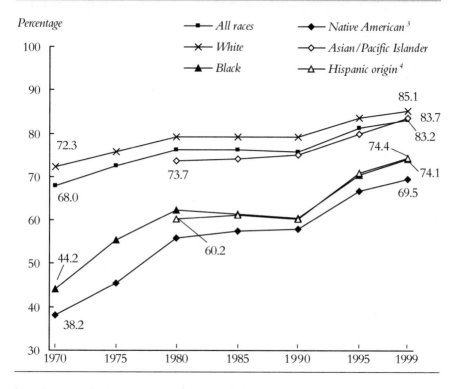

[1]Care began in the first trimester.
[2]Data for Asian/Pacific Islanders and people of Hispanic origin are not available for the years 1970 and 1975.
[3]American Indian or Alaska Native.
[4]People of Hispanic origin may be of any race. *See* Figure 1-6 and footnote to Table 1-1.

Source: National Center for Health Statistics, *Health, United States, 2001*, 2001, Table 6.

Figure 3-2 • Low-Birthweight Births by Mothers' Race and Hispanic Origin, 1970–1999 (in percentages)[1]

The troublingly high incidence of low birthweight among the babies of black mothers has persisted over the three decades shown here, even though, over the same period, an increasing percentage of black mothers received early prenatal care (see Figure 3-1). Low-birthweight babies are more fragile than babies of normal weight and more likely to die in the first year of life.

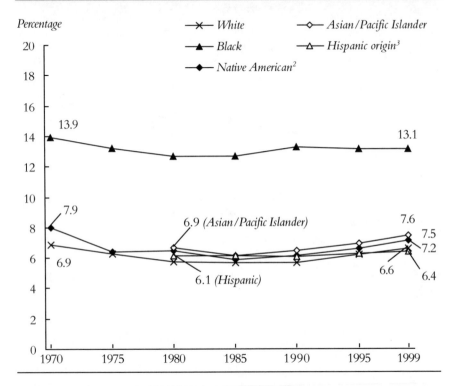

[1]Data for Asian/Pacific Islanders and people of Hispanic origin are not available for the years 1970 and 1975.
[2]American Indian or Alaska Native.
[3]People of Hispanic origin may be of any race. *See* Figure 1-6 and footnote to Table 1-1.

Source: National Center for Health Statistics, *Health, United States, 2001,* 2001, Table 12.

Figure 3-3 • Low–Birthweight Births in 1999 by Mothers' Race and Hispanic Origin (low–birthweight births as a percentage of all live births)

Thirteen percent—more than one in seven—of all infants born to black mothers in 1999 were low-birthweight babies; that is, they weighed less than 2,500 grams (about five and one-half pounds). This is nearly twice the incidence of low birthweight (6.6 percent) among the babies of white mothers, for example.

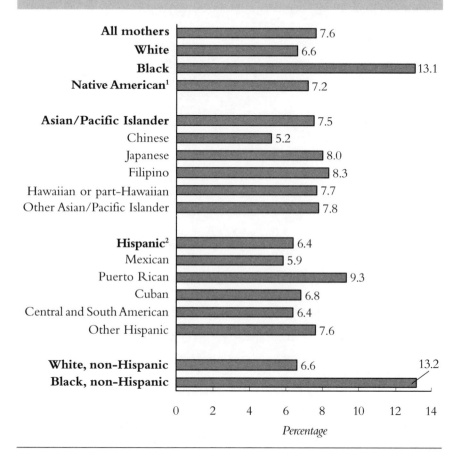

[1]American Indian or Alaska Native.
[2]People of Hispanic origin may be of any race. *See* Figure 1-6 and footnote to Table 1-1.

Source: National Center for Health Statistics, *Health, United States, 2001*, 2001, Table 12.

Table 3-3 • Infant Mortality Rates for Babies Born in the United States in 1986–88 and 1996–98 by Mothers' Race and Hispanic Origin (number of infant deaths in the first year of life per 1,000 live births)

Over the decade between the late 1980s and the late 1990s, mortality rates declined among U.S. infants of all races, including blacks. However, a black baby born in 1996–98 was more than twice as likely as a white baby to die in the first year, just as had been the case in 1986–88.

	Infant Mortality Rate	
	1986–88	1996–98
All races	9.8	7.2
White	8.2	6.0
Black	17.9	13.9
Native American[1]	13.2	9.3
Asian/Pacific Islander	7.3	5.2
Chinese	5.8	3.4
Japanese	6.9	4.3
Filipino	6.9	5.9
Hawaiian and part-Hawaiian	11.1	8.2
Other Asian/Pacific Islander	7.6	5.5
Hispanic[2]	8.3	5.9
Mexican	7.9	5.8
Puerto Rican	11.1	8.1
Cuban	7.3	4.7
Central and South American	7.5	5.2
Other Hispanic	9.0	6.8
White, non-Hispanic	8.1	6.0
Black, non-Hispanic	17.9	13.9

[1] American Indian or Alaska Native.
[2] People of Hispanic origin may be of any race. In this table, Hispanics are included in the racial categories as well as in the Hispanic category. *See* Figure 1-6 and footnote to Table 1-1.

Source: National Center for Health Statistics, *Health, United States, 2001*, 2001, Table 20.

Table 3-4 • Ten Leading Causes of Death by Sex and by Race and Hispanic Origin of Females, 1999 (in rank order)

Heart disease and cancer are the two leading causes of death for men and for women, regardless of race.

Cause of Death	Males Total	Females Total	Non-Hispanic Females White	Black	A/PI[1]	NA[2]	Hispanic Females[3]
Heart disease	1	1	1	1	2	1	1
Malignant neoplasms (cancers)	2	2	2	2	1	2	2
Cerebrovascular diseases (e.g., stroke)	3	3	3	3	3	5	3
Chronic lower respiratory diseases	5	4	4	7	6	7	6
Diabetes mellitus	6	5	8	4	4	4	4
Influenza and pneumonia	7	6	5	9	7	8	7
Unintentional injuries (accidents)	4	7	7	5	5	3	5
Alzheimer's disease		8	6				
Nephritis, nephritic syndrome, and nephrosis (diseases of the kidney)	10	9	9	6	8	9	10
Septicemia		10	10	8	10	10	
Suicide	8						
Chronic liver disease and cirrhosis	9					6	9
HIV/AIDS				10			
Essential (primary) hypertension and hypertensive renal disease					9		
Certain conditions originating in the perinatal period[4]							8

[1] Asian/Pacific Islander. [2] American Indian or Alaska Native. [3] Hispanics may be of any race. [4] Conditions causing the death of newborns.

Source: National Center for Health Statistics, Health, United States, 2001, 2001, Table 32.

Table 3-5• Incidence and Death Rates among Women from Selected Cancers by Cancer Site and Race, 1998 (rates per 100,000 women)

Women are much more likely to get breast cancer than lung cancer but much more likely to die of lung cancer, which is the leading cause of death from cancer in women. Other statistics in this table give rise to puzzling questions. For example, why is breast cancer in black women more lethal than in white women, although it is white women who are more likely to get breast cancer? Why are black women more likely than white women to get lung cancer but, apparently, no more likely than white women to die from it?

	Incidence[1]			Death Rate[2]		
	All Races	White	Black	All Races	White	Black
Breast	118.1	121.3	99.2	22.7	22.2	29.6
Lung and bronchus	43.4	44.8	47.9	34.6	35.3	34.7
Uterus (except cervix)	21.8	22.9	16.1	3.3	3.1	5.7
Ovary	13.9	14.4	10.3	7.2	7.5	6.2
Cervix	7.5	6.7	10.5	2.5	2.2	4.9

[1]Cancer diagnosed in 1998.
[2]Age adjusted.

Source: National Cancer Institute, *SEER Cancer Statistics Review, 1973–1998*, 2001, Tables IV-2, IV-3, V-3, VII-3, XV-3, XV-6, and XX-3.

Figure 3-4 • Overweight and Obesity among White and Black Women Age 20–74, 1976–80 and 1988–94 (in percentages)

As of 1988–94 (the latest years for which data are available), close to one in four white women and four in 10 black women were obese, up from fewer than one in six and one in three, respectively, in 1976–80. Obesity is not only a major factor in the onset of diabetes, one of the top five causes of death for women (see Table 3-4), but is also associated with coronary artery disease and high blood pressure.

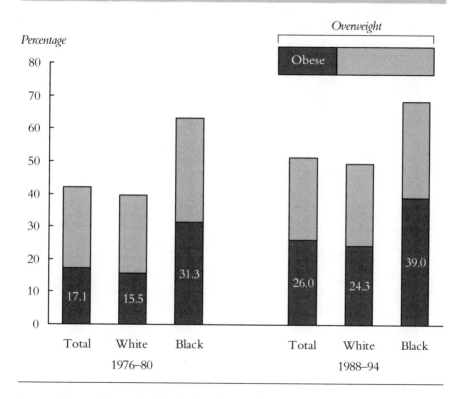

Source: National Center for Health Statistics, *Health, United States, 2001*, 2001, Table 69.

Figure 3-5 • Women Smokers by Age, 1979 and 1999 (current smokers as a percentage of all women in their age group)

Relatively fewer women in every age group were current smokers in 1999 than in 1979. As a result, mortality rates among women from lung cancer should decline in the long run. Still, it is troubling that more than one-quarter of women in both the 18–24 and 35–44 age groups are smokers.

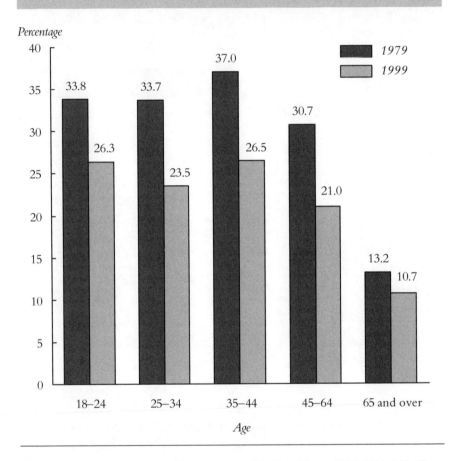

Percentage

Source: National Center for Health Statistics, *Health, United States, 2001*, 2001, Table 60.

Figure 3-6 • Reported Cases of Certain Sexually Transmitted Diseases in the United States, 1950–2000 (both sexes)[1]

Gonorrhea, syphilis, and chlamydia are the three most prevalent sexually transmitted diseases. Chlamydia was first reported in 1984 (a year not shown on this figure); since then, the number of reported cases has soared. Most chlamydia victims are female (see Table 3-6). Untreated, the infection can have serious long-term consequences for their reproductive health, including sterility and ectopic pregnancy.

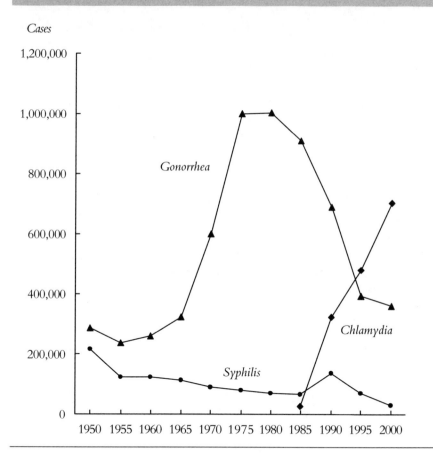

[1]Number of cases reported by state health departments.

Source: Centers for Disease Control and Prevention, *Sexually Transmitted Disease Surveillance, 2000,* 2001, Table 1.

Table 3-6 • Newly Reported Cases of HIV and AIDS and Certain Other Sexually Transmitted Diseases in the United States, 1995 and 2000[1,2]

More than 21,000 new cases of HIV were reported in 2000, exceeding the number reported in 1995 by about 6,600 (around 44 percent), and the female percentage of new HIV cases was up, as well, from 28.2 percent to 31.5 percent. There were far fewer new AIDS cases in 2000 than in 1995, but, again, a larger percentage of them were female; indeed, females accounted for nearly one in four AIDS cases newly reported in 2000, up from less than one in five (18.8 percent) of the cases reported just five years earlier.

	1995		2000	
	Total Number of Cases	Percentage Female	Total Number of Cases	Percentage Female
HIV[3]	14,864	28.2	21,476	31.5
AIDS	73,380	18.8	41,960	24.9
Chlamydia trachomatis	449,653	85.4	702,093	80.2
Gonorrhea	392,213	48.1	358,995	49.8
Syphilis	68,947	49.8	31,575	45.8

[1]Genital herpes and nonspecific pelvic inflammatory disease (PID) are omitted because only partial data are available.
[2]HIV/AIDS can also be transmitted by means other than sexual contact, such as, for example, blood transfusions or infected hypodermic needles.
[3]Includes only people with HIV infection who have not developed AIDS.

Sources: Centers for Disease Control and Prevention, *HIV/AIDS Surveillance Report* 7, no. 2, 1995, Tables 10, 22, and 23, *HIV/AIDS Surveillance Report* 12, no. 2, 2001, Tables 10, 12, and 18, *Sexually Transmitted Disease Surveillance, 1995,* 1996, Table 2, and *Sexually Transmitted Disease Surveillance, 2000,* 2001, Table 2.

Table 3-7 • Incidence of Disability among People Age 15 and over by Sex, Age, Race, and Hispanic Origin, 1997 (numbers are in thousands)

> While severe disability is more prevalent among black people of both sexes than among their counterparts in other racial groups, the incidence of severe disability is significantly higher—regardless of race—among people age 65 and over than among people under 65, and is highest of all among elderly women. (At least in part, this can be attributed to the fact that such a large proportion of the oldest old are women—see Figures 1-1 and 1-2.)

| | *Women* | | | *Men* | | |
| | *Total Number* | *Percentage with Disability* | | *Total Number* | *Percentage with Disability* | |
		Any	*Severe*		*Any*	*Severe*
All races[1]						
15–24	18,235	9.8	5.1	18,663	11.6	5.4
25–64	70,768	20.0	12.5	68,331	18.1	11.5
65 and over	18,565	57.5	41.2	13,498	50.4	32.8
White, non-Hispanic						
15–24	12,071	10.2	4.9	12,236	12.3	5.0
25–64	51,982	19.4	11.5	51,372	17.8	10.6
65 and over	15,655	56.1	39.0	11,414	48.6	30.1
Black						
15–24	2,904	11.4	6.8	2,685	12.7	8.3
25–64	9,081	24.9	18.7	7,457	25.2	20.0
65 and over	1,611	67.4	53.8	1,048	61.4	48.6
Asian/Pacific Islander						
15–24	720	3.5	2.1	733	7.1	2.5
25–64	2,664	14.7	8.7	2,307	11.1	6.8
65 and over	357	65.3	52.0	288	59.4	45.7
Hispanic[2]						
15–24	2,481	7.4	4.6	2,917	7.9	4.7
25–64	6,872	18.9	13.4	7,094	14.1	10.0
65 and over	904	58.8	50.9	686	54.9	42.0

[1]Includes Native Americans, not shown separately (data not available).
[2]People of Hispanic origin may be of any race. *See* Figure 1-6 and footnote to Table 1-1.

Source: Census Bureau, *Americans with Disabilities: 1997,* Table 1, 2001.

Section 4

EMPLOYMENT

WOMEN'S STEADILY INCREASING commitment to the paid labor force and to full-time work is certainly one of the biggest, longest-running, and most important stories in recent American history—a story warranting the 26 tables and figures devoted to it here.

In this section is a wealth of information about women and work, beginning with statistics about the steady growth in female labor force participation over the second half of the twentieth century.

The steady increase in women's labor force participation has not, however, produced major changes in women's patterns of employment compared with men's. Women workers still are more concentrated than men in certain industries and occupations, much as they were decades ago. While women have had considerable success in entering some traditionally male occupations—notably the white-collar professions, such as law and medicine—few women have penetrated the highly paid blue-collar trades. Findings include:

- At the midpoint of the twentieth century, only one-third of the U.S. labor force was female; by the end of the century, that proportion was approaching one-half (see Figure 4-1).
- In 1950, slightly more than one in every three women were working or looking for work; by 2000, that proportion had reached three in every five (see Table 4-1).
- Over the last several decades, labor force participation increased among black, white, and Hispanic women, although black women retained their longtime lead and Hispanic women lagged somewhat (see Table 4-4).
- Compared with unemployment rates in the 1980s, the rates were low in the 1990s, especially at the end of the decade. But even in that boom period, unemployment was much higher among black and

Hispanic workers than among white workers (see Table 4-5 and Figure 4-2).

- Between 1990 and 2000, the tilt toward employment in the service-producing sector of the economy grew steeper for men as well as women. Nevertheless, women still are far more concentrated in the service sector than men, and especially so in the services industry (see Table 4-7).

- Women are half again more likely than men to be government workers and more than twice as likely to work for a private nonprofit entity. Men, on the other hand, heavily predominate among self-employed workers (see Table 4-8).

- Although the number of men in labor unions dropped by nearly a million (nine percent) between 1990 and 2000, the number of union women increased by about half a million (eight percent) (see Table 4-9).

- In 1990, the typical employed woman was more likely to be in an administrative support job than in a managerial or professional job. In 2000, the reverse was true (see Table 4-10).

- Black women are noticeably overrepresented among women clergy and social workers. Asian/Pacific Islander women are overrepresented among physicians and computer programmers (see Table 4-13).

- The growth in labor force participation by mothers has been steadiest among the mothers of school-age children; by 2000, nearly four in every five were in the workforce. Labor force participation by the mothers of toddlers (children under age three) declined slightly between 1998 and 2000 (see Figure 4-6).

- Between 1975 and 2001, the amount of time that women spent at paid work increased from a little over 34 hours a week to more than 36 hours a week (see Figure 4-8).

Figure 4-1 • Women in the Labor Force, 1950–2000 [1]

At the midpoint of the twentieth century, only one-third of the U.S. labor force was female; by the end of the century, that proportion was approaching one-half (47 percent). The number of women in the labor force increased by more than 350 percent over the period.

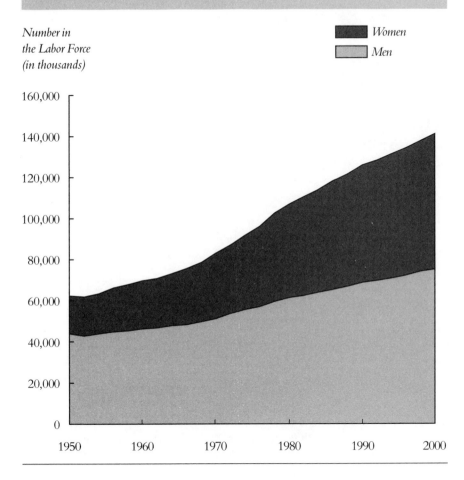

*Number in
the Labor Force
(in thousands)*

■ *Women*
□ *Men*

[1]Civilians age 16 and over.

Sources: Bureau of Labor Statistics, *Employment and Earnings*, January 2001, Table 9, and *Handbook of Labor Statistics*, 1989, Table 2.

Table 4-1 • Women's Labor Force Participation, 1950–2000[1]

Women's labor force participation rate nearly doubled between 1950, when slightly more than one in every three women was working or looking for work, and 2000, when that proportion was three in every five.

Year	Women's Labor Force Participation Rate	Women as a Percentage of Total Labor Force	Year	Women's Labor Force Participation Rate	Women as a Percentage of Total Labor Force
1950	33.9	29.6	1976	47.3	40.5
1951	34.6	30.7	1977	48.4	41.0
1952	34.7	31.0	1978	50.0	41.7
1953	34.4	30.8	1979	50.9	42.1
1954	34.6	30.9	1980	51.5	42.5
1955	35.7	31.6	1981	52.1	43.0
1956	36.9	32.2	1982	52.6	43.3
1957	36.9	32.5	1983	52.9	43.5
1958	37.1	32.7	1984	53.6	43.8
1959	37.1	32.9	1985	54.5	44.2
1960	37.7	33.4	1986	55.3	44.5
1961	38.1	33.8	1987	56.0	44.8
1962	37.9	34.0	1988	56.6	45.0
1963	38.3	34.4	1989	57.4	45.2
1964	38.7	34.8	1990	57.5	45.2
1965	39.3	35.2	1991	57.4	45.3
1966	40.3	36.0	1992	57.8	45.4
1967	41.1	36.7	1993	57.9	45.5
1968	41.6	37.1	1994	58.8	46.0
1969	42.7	37.8	1995	58.9	46.1
1970	43.3	38.1	1996	59.3	46.2
1971	43.4	38.2	1997	59.8	46.2
1972	43.9	38.5	1998	59.8	46.3
1973	44.7	38.9	1999	60.0	46.5
1974	45.7	39.4	2000	60.2	46.6
1975	46.3	40.0			

[1]Civilians age 16 and over.

Sources: Bureau of Labor Statistics, *Employment and Earnings*, January 2001, Tables 1 and 2, and *Handbook of Labor Statistics*, 1989, Table 2.

Table 4-2 • Women's Labor Force Participation Rates by Age and Five-Year Birth Cohort, Selected Years, 1955–2000

Shown here is labor force participation over time by women in each of nine five-year birth cohorts. Reading down, one can compare participation at the same age by women of different cohorts. Reading across, one can track participation by women of the same cohort as they aged. With only one exception, participation at every age has been higher in each successive cohort than in its predecessors, although, so far, age 45–49 has been the "high water mark" of labor force participation.

Labor Force Participation at Age

Year Born	25–29	30–34	35–39	40–44	45–49	50–54	55–59	60–64	65–69	Age in 2000
1931–35	35.6	38.2	49.2	56.7	62.1	60.8	55.3	38.0	19.4	65–69
1936–40	38.9	44.7	55.0	66.1	67.8	66.9	59.5	40.1		60–64
1941–45	45.2	51.9	64.9	71.9	74.8	70.7	61.2			55–59
1946–50	57.3	64.1	71.7	77.6	77.2	74.1				50–54
1951–55	66.7	70.3	75.5	78.1	79.1					45–49
1956–60	71.4	73.4	76.3	78.7						40–44
1961–65	73.8	75.0	75.8							35–39
1966–70	74.9	75.6								30–34
1971–75	77.1									25–29

Sources: Bureau of Labor Statistics, *Employment and Earnings*, January 1986, Table 3, January 1991, Table 3, January 1996, Table 3, and January 2001, Table 3, and *Labor Force Statistics Derived from the Current Population Survey, 1948–87,* 1988.

Table 4-3 • Labor Force Participation by People Age 55 and over by Sex and Age, 1990, 1998, and 2000 (numbers are in thousands)

Older women are much less likely to be in the labor force than either their younger "sisters" (see Table 4-2) or their male contemporaries. (One possible explanation is that, traditionally, women have married men four or five years older than they. Many wives may want—or be encouraged—to retire when their husbands retire.) Nevertheless, between 1990 and 2000, labor force participation increased somewhat in all the five-year age cohorts of women age 55 and over. It is interesting to note that participation by both sexes in the 65–69 age group was around two percentage points higher in 2000 than in 1998. In 2000, for the first time, workers between 65 and 72 could collect the full Social Security benefits to which they were entitled without any offset for their earnings.

	In the Labor Force					
	1990		*1998*		*2000*	
	Number	*Percent*	*Number*	*Percent*	*Number*	*Percent*
Women						
Age 55–59	3,059	55.3	3,885	61.3	4,181	61.2
60–64	2,016	35.5	2,077	39.1	2,219	40.1
65–69	941	17.0	907	17.8	969	19.4
70–74	365	8.2	445	9.3	472	9.9
75 and over	196	2.7	255	2.9	321	3.5
Men						
Age 55–59	4,014	79.8	4,609	78.4	4,856	77.1
60–64	2,771	55.5	2,644	55.4	2,718	54.8
65–69	1,192	26.0	1,204	28.0	1,288	30.1
70–74	534	15.4	623	16.5	682	17.9
75 and over	307	7.1	413	7.5	469	8.0

Sources: Bureau of Labor Statistics, *Employment and Earnings*, January 1991, Table 3, January 1999, Table 3, and January 2001, Table 3.

Table 4-4 • Labor Force Participation Rates by Sex, Race, and Hispanic Origin, 1970, 1980, 1990, 2000, and Projected 2010[1]

In the population as a whole (i.e., of all races), women's labor force participation rose and men's declined over the last three decades of the twentieth century; these trends are projected to continue during the present decade. The increase for women reflected growing participation by women in all the groups shown here, although black women retained their longtime lead and Hispanic women lagged somewhat. The drop in participation among men overall, on the other hand, was largely the effect of the trend among non-Hispanic white men. Hispanic men were the most likely to be in the labor force.

| | *Labor Force Participation Rates* | | | | |
	1970	*1980*	*1990*	*2000*	*2010*
Women					
All races	43.3	51.5	57.5	60.2	62.2
White	42.6	51.2	57.4	59.8	61.6
Non-Hispanic white	(2)	51.3	57.8	60.3	62.0
Black	(2)	53.2	58.3	63.2	66.2
Asian and other[3]	(2)	55.4	57.4	58.9	60.9
Hispanic[4]	(2)	47.4	53.1	56.9	59.4
Men					
All races	79.7	77.4	76.4	74.7	73.2
White	80.0	78.2	77.1	75.4	73.8
Non-Hispanic white	(2)	78.0	76.5	74.7	72.9
Black	(2)	70.6	71.1	69.0	68.2
Asian and other	(2)	74.5	74.9	74.9	74.8
Hispanic	(2)	81.4	81.4	80.6	79.0

[1]Civilians age 16 and over.
[2]Data not available.
[3]Includes Native Americans, not shown separately (data not available).
[4]People of Hispanic origin may be of any race. In this table, Hispanics are included in the racial categories as well as in the Hispanic category. *See* Figure 1-6 and footnote to Table 1-1. (Data by Hispanic origin are not available for years before 1980.)

Sources: Bureau of Labor Statistics, *Handbook of Labor Statistics*, 1989, Table 5, and "Labor Force Projections to 2010: Steady Growth and Changing Composition," *Monthly Labor Review* 124, no. 11, 2001, Table 3.

Table 4-5 • Unemployment Rates by Sex, Race, and Hispanic Origin, 1975–2001[1]

Compared with unemployment rates in 1975 and in the 1980s, the rates were low in the 1990s, especially at the end of the decade. But even in that boom period, unemployment was much higher among black and Hispanic workers than among white workers.

Year	All Races[2] Women	Men	White Women	Men	Black Women	Men	Hispanic[3] Women	Men
1970	5.9	4.4	5.4	4.0	(4)	(4)	(4)	(4)
1975	9.3	7.9	8.6	7.2	14.8	14.8	(4)	(4)
1980	7.4	6.9	6.5	6.1	14.0	14.5	10.7	9.7
1985	7.4	7.0	6.4	6.1	14.9	15.3	11.0	10.2
1990	5.4	5.6	4.6	4.8	10.8	11.8	8.3	7.8
1995	5.6	5.6	4.8	4.9	10.2	10.6	10.0	8.8
2000	4.1	3.9	3.6	3.4	7.2	8.1	6.7	4.9

[1]Civilians age 16 and over.
[2]Includes Asian/Pacific Islanders and Native Americans, not shown separately (data not available).
[3]People of Hispanic origin may be of any race. In this table, Hispanics are included in the racial categories as well as in the Hispanic category. *See* Figure 1-6 and footnote to Table 1-1.
[4]Data not available.

Sources: Bureau of Labor Statistics, *Employment and Earnings,* January 1991, Table 5, January 1996, Table 5, and January 2001, Table 5, and *Handbook of Labor Statistics*, 1989, Table 28.

Figure 4-2 • Unemployment Rates of White, Black, and Hispanic Women, 1980–2000[1]

Even though both black and Hispanic women's unemployment rates in 2000 were lower than at any other time over the two decades shown here, they were still a good deal higher than white women's rates—in the case of black women, exactly double (7.2 versus 3.6).

Unemployment Rate

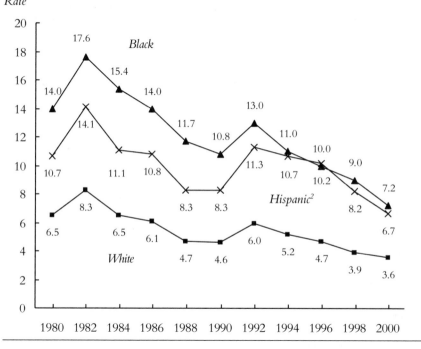

[1]Unemployed women as a percentage of the female civilian labor force age 16 and over.
[2]People of Hispanic origin may be of any race. In this figure, Hispanics are included in the racial categories as well as in the Hispanic category. *See* Figure 1-6 and footnote to Table 1-1.

Sources: Bureau of Labor Statistics, *Employment and Earnings*, January 1991, Tables 3 and 40, January 1993, Tables 3 and 40, January 1996, Table 5, January 1997, Table 5, January 1999, Table 5, and January 2001, Table 5, and *Handbook of Labor Statistics*, 1989, Table 28.

Table 4-6 • Labor Force Participation and Unemployment Rates by Veteran Status, Sex, Race, and Hispanic Origin, 2000 (numbers are in thousands)[1]

In every group shown here, labor force participation among women veterans is higher than among women who are not veterans. The reverse is true among men. (It should be borne in mind, however, that the majority of male veterans served in World War II or the Korean conflict, and are now past retirement age. The majority of women veterans are much younger—most entered military service after the all-volunteer force was created in 1973.) With the notable exception of white women, vets of both sexes in the several racial/ethnic groups shown here had lower unemployment rates in 2000 than their nonveteran counterparts.

	Women		Men	
	Veterans	*Not Veterans*	*Veterans*	*Not Veterans*
All races[2]				
Total number	1,555	99,523	23,138	69,441
Percentage in the labor force	66.6	60.8	58.4	82.7
Unemployment rate	4.2	3.6	2.8	3.4
White				
Total number	1,249	82,321	20,386	57,764
Percentage in the labor force	63.7	60.2	57.5	83.9
Unemployment rate	4.3	3.1	2.6	2.9
Black				
Total number	263	12,394	2,281	7,835
Percentage in the labor force	80.7	65.3	64.8	75.0
Unemployment rate	3.3	6.3	4.2	7.6
Hispanic[3]				
Total number	65	10,106	892	8,943
Percentage in the labor force	66.3	58.6	68.4	85.7
Unemployment rate	2.5	5.9	2.9	4.3

[1]People age 20 and over.
[2]Includes Asian/Pacific Islanders and Native Americans, not shown separately (data not available).
[3]People of Hispanic origin may be of any race. In this table, Hispanics are included in the racial categories as well as in the Hispanic category. *See* Figure 1-6 and footnote to Table 1-1.

Source: Bureau of Labor Statistics, unpublished data from the 2000 Current Population Survey (annual averages).

Figure 4-3 • Women Employed Year Round and Less Than Year Round by Full- or Part-Time Status, 1980 and 2000 (percent distributions)

Not only did the number of employed women grow by more than 19 million between 1980 and 2000, but the proportion who worked year round, full time, increased from a minority in 1990 (less than 45 percent) to the substantial majority in 2000 (nearly 59 percent). The percentage of women working year round, part time, increased only slightly.

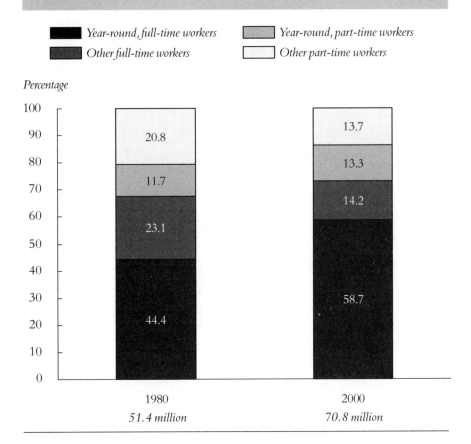

Sources: Census Bureau, *Money Income of Households, Families, and Persons in the United States: 1991,* 1992, Table B-16, and unpublished data from the March 2001 Current Population Survey, Table PINC-05, <http://ferret.bls.census.gov/macro/032001/perinc/>.

Table 4-7 • Employed People by Industry and Sex, 1990 and 2000 (percent distributions)

Between 1990 and 2000, the tilt toward employment in the service-producing sector of the economy grew steeper for men as well as women—in the goods-producing sector, only construction employed a larger share of people in 2000 than in 1990. Nevertheless, women are still far more concentrated in the service sector than men, and especially so in the services industry.

	Women		Men	
Industry	1990	2000	1990	2000
Agriculture	**1.3**	**1.4**	**3.9**	**3.4**
Goods-producing sector	**14.2**	**11.9**	**34.1**	**31.0**
Mining	0.2	0.1	1.0	0.6
Construction	1.2	1.5	10.9	11.8
Manufacturing				
Durable goods	6.2	5.4	14.3	12.1
Nondurable goods	6.6	4.9	7.9	6.5
Service-producing sector	**84.4**	**86.6**	**62.1**	**65.6**
Transportation and public utilities	4.3	4.4	9.0	9.6
Wholesale trade	2.5	2.6	5.2	5.2
Retail trade	19.0	18.2	14.7	15.1
Finance, insurance, and real estate	8.8	8.1	5.2	5.0
Services[1]	45.3	49.0	23.0	26.1
Public administration	4.5	4.3	5.0	4.6
Total percentage[2]	**100.0**	**100.0**	**100.0**	**100.0**
Total number (in thousands)	53,479	62,914	64,435	72,293

[1]Includes private households.
[2]Percentages may not total 100.0 due to rounding.

Sources: Bureau of Labor Statistics, *Employment and Earnings*, January 1991, Table 25, and January 2001, Table 17.

Table 4-8 • Government, Private-Sector, and Self-Employed Workers by Sex, 2000

The majority of employed women and men work for private, for-profit concerns, but women are slightly less concentrated therein than men (67.2 percent versus 72.5 percent). Women are about half again more likely than men to be government workers (17.2 percent versus 11.4 percent) and more than twice as likely to work for a private nonprofit entity—indeed, nearly 69 percent of all workers in that sector are women. Men, on the other hand, heavily predominate among self-employed workers.

	Percent Distribution		Percentage Female
	Women	Men	
Private, nonprofit	7.7	3.0	68.8
Private, for profit	67.2	72.5	44.6
Government	17.2	11.4	56.8
Federal	2.3	2.6	43.9
State	4.9	3.3	56.3
Local	10.0	5.5	61.3
Self-employed, unincorporated	1.8	4.5	26.1
Self-employed, incorporated	6.0	8.5	37.9
Without pay	0.1	0.1	62.2
Total percentage[1]	100.0	100.0	—
Total number employed (in thousands)	62,917	72,292	46.5

[1]Percentages may not total 100.0 due to rounding.

Source: Bureau of Labor Statistics, unpublished data from the 2000 Current Population Survey (annual averages).

Table 4-9 • Labor Union Membership by Sex, Race, and Hispanic Origin, 1990 and 2000 (numbers are in thousands)

Although the number of men in labor unions dropped by nearly a million (nine percent) between 1990 and 2000, the number of union women increased by about half a million (eight percent). Proportionately, the increase in union membership over the period was greatest (14 percent) among black women, who now account for close to half of all black union members.

	Total Employed[1]		Union Members[2]		Women as a Percentage of Union Members	
	1990	*2000*	*1990*	*2000*	*1990*	*2000*
Women						
All races[3]	49,077	57,933	6,175	6,680	36.9	41.1
White	41,605	47,350	4,884	5,183	35.4	39.6
Black	5,875	7,843	1,060	1,208	44.0	48.5
Hispanic[4]	3,312	5,725	415	582	34.3	37.5
Men						
All races	54,828	62,853	10,564	9,578	—	—
White	47,515	53,105	8,914	7,911	—	—
Black	5,541	6,701	1,350	1,282	—	—
Hispanic	4,869	7,884	794	972	—	—

[1]Wage-and-salary workers age 16 and over.
[2]Employed members of labor unions or employee associations similar to unions.
[3]Includes Asian/Pacific Islanders and Native Americans, not shown separately (data not available).
[4]People of Hispanic origin may be of any race. In this table, Hispanics are included in the racial categories as well as in the Hispanic category. *See* Figure 1-6 and footnote to Table 1-1.

Sources: Bureau of Labor Statistics, *Employment and Earnings*, January 1991, Table 57, and January 2001, Table 40.

Table 4-10 • Employed Women and Men by Occupation, 1990 and 2000 (percent distributions)[1]

In 1990, the typical employed woman was more likely to be in an administrative support job than in a managerial/professional job. In 2000, the reverse was true. But women are still more concentrated than men in a few occupations.

Occupation	Women		Men	
	1990	*2000*	*1990*	*2000*
Managerial and professional	**26.2**	**32.3**	**25.8**	**28.4**
Executive, administrative, and managerial	11.1	14.2	13.8	15.0
Professional specialty	15.1	18.1	12.0	13.5
Technical, sales, and administrative support	**44.4**	**40.0**	**20.1**	**19.8**
Technicians and related support	3.5	3.6	3.0	2.9
Sales occupations	13.1	12.9	11.2	11.4
Administrative support, including clerical	27.8	23.5	5.9	5.4
Service occupations	**17.7**	**17.5**	**9.8**	**10.0**
Private household	1.4	1.2	(2)	(2)
Protective service	0.5	0.7	2.6	2.7
Other service	15.8	15.6	7.1	7.3
Precision production, craft, and repair	**2.2**	**2.1**	**19.4**	**18.7**
Operators, fabricators, and laborers	**8.5**	**6.9**	**20.6**	**19.3**
Machine operators, assemblers, and inspectors	6.0	4.3	7.5	6.4
Transportation and material moving occupations	0.8	0.9	6.8	6.9
Handlers, equipment cleaners, helpers, and laborers	1.6	1.7	6.2	6.0
Farming, forestry, and fishing	**1.0**	**1.1**	**4.4**	**3.7**
Total percentage[3]	**100.0**	**100.0**	**100.0**	**100.0**
Total employed (in thousands)	53,479	62,915	64,435	72,293

[1]Employed people age 16 and over.
[2]Less than 0.05 percent.
[3]Percentages may not total 100.0 due to rounding.

Sources: Bureau of Labor Statistics, *Employment and Earnings*, January 1991, Table 21, and January 2001, Table 10.

Table 4-11 • Employed Women by Occupation, Race, and Hispanic Origin, 2000 (percent distributions)[1,2]

Compared with black and Hispanic women workers, white and Asian/Pacific Islander (A/PI) women are more heavily concentrated in just two broad occupational categories—managerial and professional, and technical, sales, and administrative support. Taken together, these occupations account for close to three-quarters of all employed white women and over 70 percent of A/PI women. A/PI women are the most likely to be managers or professionals (38.7 percent); Hispanic women the least likely (17.8 percent). Considerably higher percentages of black and Hispanic women than of their white and A/PI counterparts are in service occupations.

Occupation	White	Black	A/PI[3]	Hispanic[4]
Managerial and professional	**33.4**	**24.8**	**38.7**	**17.8**
Executive, administrative, and managerial	14.8	10.7	19.1	8.9
Professional specialty	18.6	14.1	19.6	8.9
Technical, sales, and administrative support	**40.5**	**38.6**	**32.5**	**37.2**
Technicians and related support	3.5	3.7	4.2	2.7
Sales occupations	13.2	10.9	12.0	12.1
Administrative support, including clerical	23.7	24.0	16.3	22.5
Service occupations	**16.4**	**25.2**	**17.7**	**26.2**
Private household	1.2	1.4	1.7	4.0
Protective service	0.6	1.6	—	0.6
Other service	14.6	22.1	16.0[5]	21.6
Precision production, craft, and repair	**2.1**	**2.1**	**2.7**	**3.3**
Operators, fabricators, and laborers	**6.4**	**9.1**	**8.1**	**13.6**
Machine operators, assemblers, and inspectors	3.9	5.5	6.3	9.7
Transportation and material moving occupations	0.8	1.4	0.3	0.6
Handlers, equipment cleaners, helpers, and laborers	1.6	2.2	1.5	3.3

See footnotes at end of table.   *(continued)*

Table 4-11 (continued)

Occupation	White	Black	A/PI	Hispanic
Farming, forestry, and fishing	**1.3**	**0.2**	**0.4**	**1.8**
Total percentage[6]	**100.0**	**100.0**	**100.0**	**100.0**
Total number (in thousands)	51,780	8,154	2,450	6,014

[1]Employed women age 16 and over.
[2]Data were not available for Native Americans.
[3]Data for the Asian/Pacific Islanders are from the March 2000 Current Population Survey.
[4]People of Hispanic origin may be of any race. In this table, Hispanics are included in the racial categories as well as in the Hispanic category. *See* Figure 1-6 and footnote to Table 1-1.
[5]Includes protective service workers, if any.
[6]Percentages may not total 100.0 due to rounding.

Sources: Bureau of Labor Statistics, *Employment and Earnings*, January 2001, Table 10, and unpublished data from the 2000 Current Population Survey (annual averages); and Census Bureau, *The Asian and Pacific Islander Population in the United States: March 2000 (Update)*, 2001, Table 12.

Table 4-12 • Women Employed in Selected Occupations, 1990 and 2000[1]

Women's presence in certain once–male-dominated professions—medicine and dentistry, for example—increased significantly between 1990 and 2000 and ebbed a bit in some female-dominated professions—nursing and elementary school teaching, for example. But the workers in such skilled blue-collar occupations as auto mechanic and carpenter are still overwhelmingly men (see also Table 4–14).

Occupation	Number of Women (in thousands)		Women as a Percentage of Total Employed	
	1990	2000	1990	2000
Airplane pilots and navigators	6	5	5.1	3.7
Architects	26	51	18.4	23.5
Automobile mechanics	7	11	0.8	1.2
Carpenters	18	25	1.3	1.7
Clergy	31	51	9.6	13.8
Computer programmers	214	185	36.0	26.5
Data processing equipment repairers	18	53	11.4	15.4
Dental assistants	185	210	98.7	96.4
Dentists	15	31	9.5	18.7
Economists	50	74	43.8	53.3
Editors and reporters	146	161	52.0	55.8
Financial managers	218	393	44.3	50.1
Lawyers and judges	157	275	20.8	29.7
Librarians	160	198	83.3	85.2
Managers, medicine and health	116	58.6	66.5	77.9
Mechanical engineers	17	22	5.4	6.3
Physicians	111	201	19.3	27.9
Registered nurses	1,581	1,959	94.5	92.8
Social workers	385	599	68.2	72.4
Teachers, elementary school	1,283	1,814	85.2	83.3
Teachers, postsecondary	288	420	37.7	43.7
Telephone installers/repairers	22	39	11.3	13.1
Welders and cutters	24	29	4.0	4.9

[1]Civilians age 16 and over.

Sources: Bureau of Labor Statistics, *Employment and Earnings,* January 1991, Table 22, and January 2001, Table 11, and unpublished data from the 2000 Current Population Survey (annual averages).

Table 4-13 • Women Employed in Selected Occupations by Race and Hispanic Origin, 2000[1] (numbers are in thousands)

> Black women are noticeably overrepresented among the women in several of the occupations shown here, including members of the clergy and social workers. "Other" women (see note) are overrepresented among physicians and computer programmers. White women are overrepresented among, for example, editors and reporters and librarians.

Occupation	Number of Women (all races)	Percentage of Employed Women Who Are			
		White	*Black*	*Other*[2]	*Hispanic*[3]
All occupations	62,915	82.3	13.0	4.7	9.6
Clergy	51	74.5	21.6	3.9	—
Computer programmers	185	75.1	10.8	14.1	2.2
Data processing equipment repairers	53	69.8	20.8	9.4	5.7
Dental assistants	210	91.9	4.8	3.3	10.0
Economists	74	81.1	6.8	12.2	2.7
Editors and reporters	161	90.7	6.2	3.1	3.7
Financial managers	393	90.3	6.6	3.1	6.1
Lawyers and judges	275	84.0	9.5	6.5	5.5
Librarians	198	89.9	7.1	3.0	7.1
Managers, medicine and health	585	85.3	10.4	4.3	5.0
Physicians	201	69.2	10.9	19.9	4.0
Registered nurses	1,959	84.1	9.8	6.1	2.7
Social workers	599	74.8	21.7	3.5	8.2
Teachers, elementary school	1,814	86.8	11.1	2.1	5.6
Teachers, postsecondary	420	84.5	8.8	6.7	4.3

[1]This table is intended to complement the preceding one. However, eight of the occupations shown in Table 4-12 are omitted here because they employ too few women on which to calculate reliable racial breakdowns.

[2]Other was derived by subtracting whites and blacks from the total. Most women in the "other" category are Asian/Pacific Islanders, since there are only about 422,000 Native American women between the ages of 20 and 64, compared with more than four million Asian/Pacific Islander women in that age group.

[3]People of Hispanic origin may be of any race. *See* Figure 1-6 and footnote to Table 1-1.

Source: Bureau of Labor Statistics, unpublished data from the 2000 Current Population Survey (annual averages).

Table 4-14 • Women Employed in Selected Nontraditional Technical and Trade Occupations, 1990 and 2000[1,2]

> The last decade of the twentieth century saw small increases in women's representation in this assortment of traditionally male (and generally well-paying) occupations, but women are still exceedingly rare in most of them.

Occupation	Number of Women (in thousands)		Women as a Percentage of Total Employed	
	1990	*2000*	*1990*	*2000*
Aircraft engine mechanics	3	8	2.8	6.1
Electrical and electronic equipment repairers	61	115	8.6	11.5
Electricians	12	24	1.7	2.7
Firefighters	2	7	1.2	3.0
Heating, air conditioning, and refrigeration mechanics	1	4	0.5	1.2
Industrial machinery repairers	15	22	3.0	4.2
Industrial truck and tractor equipment operators	25	40	5.7	7.0
Machinists	19	31	3.9	6.3
Painters, construction and maintenance	31	36	5.6	5.8
Plumbers, pipefitters, and steamfitters	4	7	0.9	1.3
Police and detectives, public service	57	68	12.1	12.1
Truck drivers[3]	102	146	3.9	4.7

[1]Civilians age 16 and over.

[2]"Nontraditional" occupations are defined by the U.S. Department of Labor as those in which less than 25 percent of the workers are women.

[3]For 1990, we aggregated "truck drivers, heavy" and "truck drivers, light."

Sources: Bureau of Labor Statistics, *Employment and Earnings,* January 1991, Table 22, and January 2001, Table 11, and unpublished data from the 2000 Current Population Survey (annual averages).

Figure 4-4 • Employed Women and Men in Alternative Work Arrangements, February 2001 (percent distributions)[1]

Several million more men than women were in alternative work arrangements as of early 2001, and these men were considerably more likely than their female counterparts to be independent contractors, although this arrangement accounted for the majority of both sexes. Women were more likely than men to be in "on call" arrangements (substitute teachers would fall into this category) or to work for "temp" agencies.

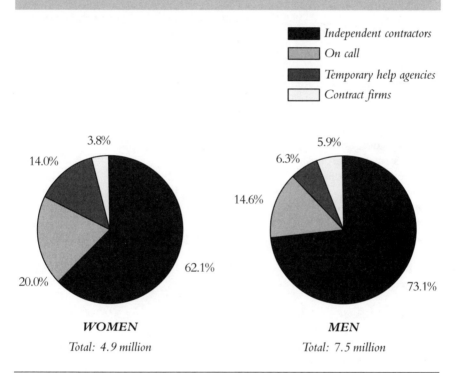

■ *Independent contractors*
▨ *On call*
▨ *Temporary help agencies*
□ *Contract firms*

3.8%
14.0%
20.0%
62.1%

WOMEN
Total: 4.9 million

5.9%
6.3%
14.6%
73.1%

MEN
Total: 7.5 million

[1]Excludes day laborers.

Source: Bureau of Labor Statistics, unpublished data from the February 2001 Current Population Survey.

Table 4-15 • Self-Employed and Wage-and-Salary Workers by Sex and Occupation, 2000 (percent distributions)[1]

A self-employed woman is about eight times as likely as her male counterpart to be in a service occupation (29.4 percent versus 3.8 percent); a self-employed man is nearly 17 times as likely as his female counterpart to be in a construction trade (21.9 percent versus 1.3 percent). In both cases, self-employed workers are much more likely than their wage-and-salary counterparts to be in these occupations.

Occupation	Percent Distribution of Self-Employed Workers		Percent Distribution of Wage-and-Salary Workers	
	Women	Men	Women	Men
Managerial and professional	**34.6**	**35.9**	**32.6**	**28.7**
Executive, administrative, and managerial	15.3	20.2	14.3	15.0
Professional specialty	19.3	15.7	18.3	13.7
Technical, sales, and administrative support	**29.4**	**19.7**	**40.9**	**20.5**
Technicians and related support	0.7	0.9	3.7	3.2
Sales occupations	20.5	18.0	12.6	11.3
Administrative support, including clerical	8.2	0.8	24.5	6.0
Service occupations	**29.4**	**3.8**	**17.1**	**10.9**
Personal service occupations	23.9	2.1	2.8	0.8
All other service occupations	5.5	1.7	14.3	10.1
Precision production, craft, and repair	**3.5**	**30.4**	**2.1**	**18.4**
Construction trades	1.3	21.9	0.2	7.4
All other precision production, craft, and repair	2.2	8.6	1.9	11.0
Operators, fabricators, and laborers	**2.7**	**8.7**	**7.2**	**20.8**
Farming, forestry, and fishing	**0.4**	**1.5**	**0.2**	**0.8**
Total percentage[2]	**100.0**	**100.0**	**100.0**	**100.0**
Total number (in thousands)	3,417	5,256	58,554	64,574

[1]Excludes persons self-employed in the agricultural industry.
[2]Percentages may not total 100.0 due to rounding.

Source: Bureau of Labor Statistics, unpublished data from the 2000 Current Population Survey (annual averages).

Table 4-16 • Government and Private-Sector Employment and Self-Employment in Selected Occupations by Sex, 2000

Among workers in general, women are considerably more likely than men to be government employees (17.7 percent versus 11.8 percent) and a little less likely to be self-employed (5.6 percent versus 7.5 percent). Among the workers in this sampling of managerial and professional occupations, these differences by gender are more pronounced, especially in the legal profession.

	Percentage Employed in			
	Private Industries[1]	*Gov't.*[1]	*Self-Employed*	*Total Number*
Total, all occupations[2]				
Women	76.7	17.7	5.6	61,149
Men	80.7	11.8	7.5	69,763
Executive, administrative, and managerial occupations				
Women	78.5	15.6	5.9	8,895
Men	78.8	11.3	9.9	10,758
Health-diagnosing occupations (e.g., physicians, dentists, veterinarians, podiatrists)				
Women	72.5	12.8	14.7	265
Men	70.9	6.8	22.2	721
Lawyers and judges				
Women	54.7	30.8	14.5	275
Men	60.9	17.4	21.8	651

[1] Wage-and-salary workers.
[2] Excludes workers in private households and unpaid family workers.

Source: Bureau of Labor Statistics, unpublished data from the 2000 Current Population Survey (annual averages).

Figure 4-5 • Children with Mothers in the Labor Force by Children's Age, 1970, 1980, 1990, and 2000 (in percentages)

In 1970, most children had mothers who stayed at home full time. Nowadays, most children—even preschool children—have mothers in the paid workforce. Unquestionably a revolutionary change, this is by now an established reality (a reality to which, many working parents would agree, America's schools and workplaces have been slow to adapt).

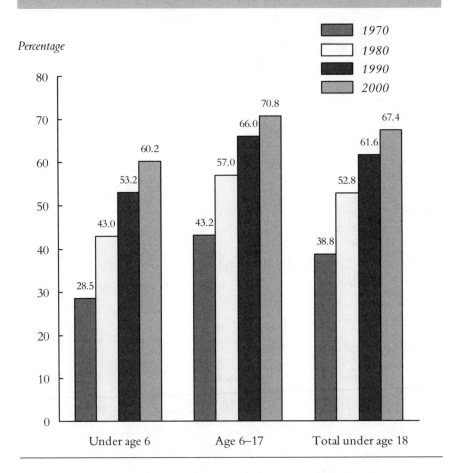

Sources: Bureau of Labor Statistics, *Handbook of Labor Statistics,* 1989, Table 59, and unpublished data from the March 1990 and March 2000 Current Population Surveys.

Figure 4-6 • Labor Force Participation Rates of Mothers with Children under 18 by Children's Age, 1980–2000[1]

Figure 4-5 plots the growth over three decades in the percentage of children whose mothers are in the paid labor force. This figure tracks the increase in labor force participation by mothers over the latter two of those decades. The upward trend has been steadiest among the mothers of school-age children; by 2000, nearly four in every five (79 percent) were in the workforce. Late in the 1990s, labor force participation by the mothers of toddlers (children under three) declined slightly.

Labor Force Participation Rate

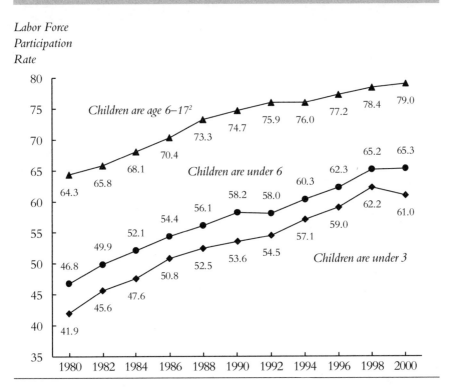

[1]Includes women of all marital statuses.
[2]None younger than six.

Sources: Bureau of Labor Statistics, *Handbook of Labor Statistics*, 1989, Table 56, and unpublished data from the March 1990, 1992, 1994, 1996, 1998, and 2000 Current Population Surveys.

Table 4-17 • Employment Status of Mothers with Children under Age 18 by Children's Age, 1980, 1990, and 2000

Whatever her child's age, in 2000 the typical American mother was considerably more likely to be in the labor force—i.e., working or looking for work—than were her counterparts in 1990 and 1980. But the proportion of employed mothers who worked full time did not change much in 20 years, and the working mothers of toddlers were a little less likely to be full time than their counterparts in 1990.

	Mothers (numbers in thousands)		
	1980	*1990*	*2000*
With children under 18	31,431	33,262	35,395
Number in the labor force	17,790	22,196	25,795
Percentage in the labor force	56.6	66.7	72.9
Number employed	16,526	20,865	24,693
Number employed full time	11,750	15,226	18,202
As a percentage of employed	71.1	73.0	73.7
With children 6–17 (none younger)	17,499	17,123	19,604
Number in the labor force	11,252	12,799	15,479
Percentage in the labor force	64.3	74.7	79.0
Number employed	10,640	12,133	14,931
Number employed full time	7,757	9,146	11,441
As a percentage of employed	72.9	75.4	76.6
With children under six	13,970	16,139	15,792
Number in the labor force	6,538	9,397	10,316
Percentage in the labor force	46.8	58.2	65.3
Number employed	5,886	8,732	9,763
Number employed full time	3,997	6,081	6,761
As a percentage of employed	67.9	69.6	69.3
With children under three	8,508	9,737	9,293
Number in the labor force	3,565	5,216	5,670
Percentage in the labor force	41.9	53.6	61.0
Number employed	3,167	4,823	5,350
Number employed fulltime	2,074	3,314	3,544
As a percentage of employed	65.5	68.7	66.2

Sources: Bureau of Labor Statistics, *Handbook of Labor Statistics*, 1989, Table 56, and unpublished data from the March 1990 and March 2000 Current Population Surveys.

Figure 4-7 • Employment Status of Mothers with Children under Age 18 by Children's Age, 2000 (percent distributions)[1]

The older her children, the more likely a mother is to be in the labor force, and the more likely she is to work full time. In 2000, close to three in five (58.4 percent) of women with children age 6–17 worked full time; only one in five (21 percent) was out of the labor force entirely. The situation was quite different among the mothers of small children (under three): they were marginally less likely to be working full time (38.1 percent) than to be out of the labor force altogether (39 percent).

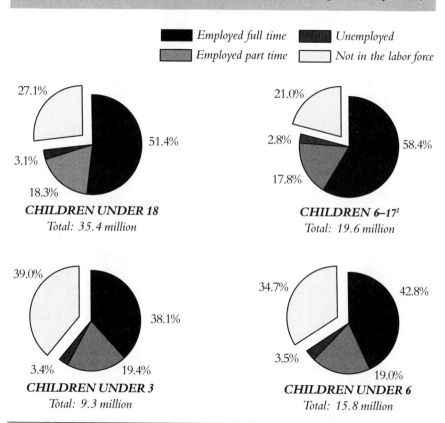

Employed full time   Unemployed
Employed part time   Not in the labor force

27.1%
51.4%
3.1%
18.3%
CHILDREN UNDER 18
Total: 35.4 million

21.0%
2.8%
58.4%
17.8%
CHILDREN 6–17[2]
Total: 19.6 million

39.0%
38.1%
3.4%   19.4%
CHILDREN UNDER 3
Total: 9.3 million

34.7%   42.8%
3.5%
19.0%
CHILDREN UNDER 6
Total: 15.8 million

[1]Percentages may not total 100.0 due to rounding.
[2]None younger than six.

Source: Bureau of Labor Statistics, unpublished data from the March 2000 Current Population Survey.

Table 4-18 • Child-Care Arrangements for the Young Children of Working Mothers by Race and Hispanic Origin, 1995 (in percentages)[1,2]

Of the 10-plus million young children (under five) with working mothers, nearly half (47.5 percent) were looked after by relatives—mostly fathers and/or grandparents—while their mothers worked. The children of black mothers are the most likely to be cared for in either family day care or organized day-care centers.

| | | *Percentage Using Arrangement* | | | |
| | *All* | *Non-Hispanic* | | | |
Care Provided by	*Races*	*White*	*Black*	*Other*[3]	*Hispanic*[4]
Relatives					
Father	18.2	19.1	10.5	20.8	20.2
Grandparent	17.4	16.7	18.8	24.9	18.0
Sibling or other relative	6.0	4.3	12.0	9.9	9.2
Mother while she works[5]	5.9	6.6	2.6	8.1	3.9
Nonrelatives					
Family day care	17.2	17.7	19.9	14.5	10.7
Other	14.0	13.9	13.1	14.5	15.8
Organized facilities					
Day-care center	19.4	18.9	26.9	11.1	17.5
Nursery/preschool[6]	8.1	7.7	12.4	8.8	5.1
Other[7]	3.2	2.9	2.2	4.2	6.1
Total number of children (in thousands)	10,047	7,359	1,253	433	1,002

[1]Primary care arrangements for children under age five.
[2]Percentages add to more than 100.0 because some children have more than one "primary" arrangement.
[3]Asian/Pacific Islanders and Native Americans.
[4]People of Hispanic origin may be of any race. *See* Figure 1-6 and footnote to Table 1-1.
[5]Includes mothers working at home or away from home.
[6]Includes children in Head Start.
[7]Includes children in kindergarten and school-based activities, children caring for themselves, and children with "no regular arrangements."

Source: Census Bureau, *Who's Minding the Kids? Child Care Arrangements: Fall 1995,* 2000, Table 4A.

Figure 4-8 • Weekly Hours Worked by Sex, 1975–2001[1,2]

Over the last quarter-century or so, the amount of time that women spent at paid work gradually increased (not always steadily, however—economic cycles played a role). The typical woman worker spent more than 36 hours a week at her paid job in 2001, compared with a little over 34 hours in 1975. Men still typically work more hours than women, but—after allowing for economic cycles—the trend for men is essentially flat.

Hours Worked

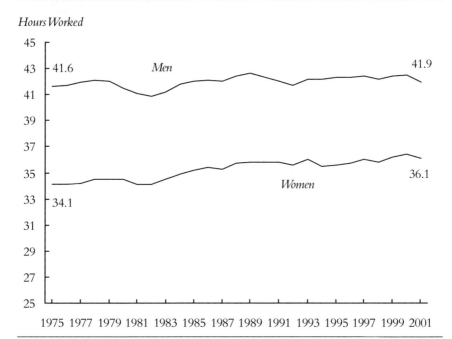

[1]Workers age 16 and over.
[2]Data for 1994 and later years are not directly comparable with data for earlier years because of Current Population Survey redesign.

Source: Bureau of Labor Statistics, unpublished data from the Current Population Survey (annual averages).

Section 5

EARNINGS AND BENEFITS

THIS SECTION USES TWO MEASURES of earnings: the median weekly earnings of full-time workers and the median annual earnings of full-time workers who worked year round. By either measure, and taking inflation into account, the earnings of America's working women have been increasing. However, black women continue to earn considerably less than Asian/Pacific Islander and white women do, and Hispanic women have the lowest earnings of all.

Between the mid-1980s and 1993, when men's earnings were dropping as women's earnings were increasing, the female-to-male earnings ratio (also called the "earnings gap" or "wage gap") narrowed; 1993 saw the lowest point to date. After that, as men's earnings began to recover, the narrowing trend stalled and the wage gap widened slightly.

Benefits are a central component of the compensation package in any job. Lack of health insurance continues to be a major problem, especially for Hispanics. Whether female or male, Hispanic workers are the least likely to have health insurance through their own jobs. And Hispanic women are less likely than black or white women to be in an employer-provided pension plan. Findings include:

- Asian/Pacific Islanders were the highest earners of all women who worked year round, full time (including non-Hispanic white women). Hispanic women had the lowest annual earnings of all year-round, full-time workers (see Figures 5-3 and 5-4).
- At least since 1975, the earnings gap has been narrowest among workers age 25–34. In 2000, the ratio of female to male earnings was nearly 82 percent (81.8), compared with 68.4 percent among workers age 55–64 (see Figure 5-2).
- Education makes a significant difference in women's earnings: in 2000, women with a bachelor's degree who worked year round, full time,

earned more than twice as much as their counterparts who had not finished high school (see Table 5-7).

- Among women who work year round, full time, 58 percent of white women and nearly 53 percent of black women are in an employer- or union-provided pension plan, while only about 39 percent of Hispanic women are. Pension plan coverage is the exception among part-time workers, even if they work year round (see Table 5-8).

- Most women age 18–64 who have private health insurance are in an employer-provided group plan, and most are covered through their own jobs. Roughly two-thirds of the women who worked year round, full time, in 2000 had health insurance through their own jobs. Among Hispanic women, however, not quite 53 percent had health insurance through their own jobs (see Figure 5-6 and Table 5-9).

- While, in general, males are more likely than females to lack health insurance coverage, the reverse is true in the 55–64 age group, where about one in seven women had no health insurance coverage of any kind in 2000 (see Figure 5-8).

- Close to one in five women workers, compared with roughly one in seven men, took a leave for family or medical reasons during the 18-month period preceding the Labor Department's 2000 Family Leave Survey. People with children were the most likely to take the leave; workers with family incomes at the low end of the income scale were less likely than better-off workers to take the leave, which is unpaid (see Table 5-11).

Figure 5-1 • Median Weekly Earnings by Sex, 1975–2000[1,2]

The female-to-male earnings ratio (also called the "earnings gap" or "wage gap") narrowed between the mid-1980s and 1993 (its narrowest point to date) because men's earnings were dropping as women's were rising. After that, as men's earnings began to recover, the gap widened slightly.

2000 Dollars

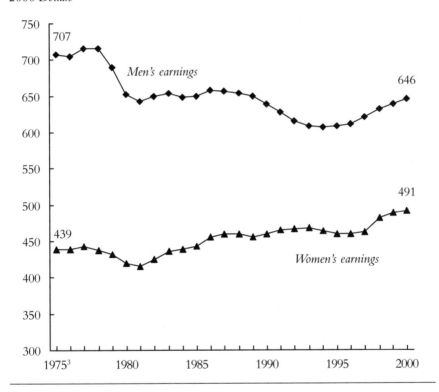

[1]Median usual weekly earnings of full-time wage-and-salary workers age 16 and over.
[2]The CPI inflation calculator at http://www.bls.gov was used to inflate the earnings series.
[3]Data for 1975–1978 are based on the May Current Population Surveys.

Sources: Bureau of Labor Statistics, *Employment and Earnings*, January 1991, Table 54, January 1993, Table 54, January 1995, Table 37, January 1996, Table 37, January 1997, Table 37, January 1999, Table 37, and January 2001, Table 37, *Handbook of Labor Statistics*, 1989, Table 41, and unpublished data from the May 1975 through May 1978 Current Population Surveys.

Table 5-1 • Median Weekly Earnings by Sex, and Female-to-Male Earnings Ratios, 1975, 1980, 1985, and 1990–2000[1]

Taking inflation into account, women's earnings were 11.8 percent higher in 2000 than they had been in 1975; men's earnings were 8.6 percent lower. But in the 1990s, men began regaining the lost ground (see also Figure 5-1).

	Median Earnings		Ratio of Women's
	Women	*Men*	*to Men's Earnings*[2]
Current dollars			
1975 (May)	137	221	62.0
1980	201	312	64.4
1985	277	406	68.2
1990	346	481	71.9
1991	366	493	74.2
1992	380	501	75.8
1993	393	510	77.1
1994	399	522	76.4
1995	406	538	75.5
1996	418	557	75.0
1997	431	579	74.4
1998	456	598	76.3
1999	473	618	76.5
2000	491	646	76.0
2000 dollars[3]			
1975	439	707	62.0
1993	468	608	77.1
2000	491	646	76.0
Percent change (2000 dollars)			
1975–2000	+11.8	-8.6	—
1993–2000	+4.9	+6.3	—

[1]Median usual weekly earnings of full-time wage-and-salary workers age 16 and over.
[2]Calculated on current dollars.
[3]The CPI inflation calculator at http://www.bls.gov was used to inflate 1975 and 1993 dollars.

Sources: Bureau of Labor Statistics, *Employment and Earnings*, January 1991, Table 54, January 1993, Table 54, January 1995, Table 37, January 1996, Table 37, January 1997, Table 37, January 1999, Table 37, and January 2001, Table 37, *Handbook of Labor Statistics*, 1989, Table 41, and unpublished data from the May 1975 Current Population Survey.

Figure 5-2 • Female-to-Male Earnings Ratios among Workers Age 25–64 by Age, 1975–2000[1,2]

At least since 1975, the earnings gap has been narrowest among workers age 25–34: the female-to-male earnings ratio in that age group was nearly 82 percent in 2000 (see also Chapter Two). However, the most consistent gains between 1980 and 2000 were in the 45–54 age group. (In 2000, these were baby boomers.)

Earnings Ratio

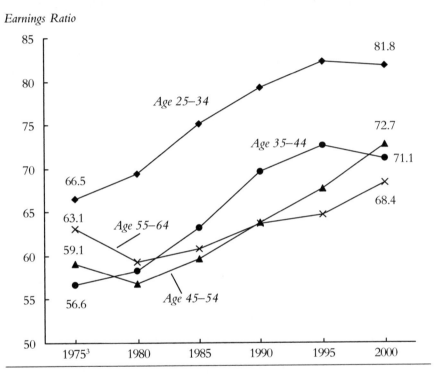

[1]Based on usual median weekly earnings of full-time wage-and-salary workers.
[2]The editors elected to focus on the earnings of workers age 25–64. We omitted the 16–24 group (where the earnings ratio was around 91 percent in 2000) because many of these workers have yet to finish their education. We omitted the group age 65 and over because large standard errors accompany the earnings data for these workers (relatively few people in this age group are employed full time).
[3]May 1975.

Sources: Bureau of Labor Statistics, unpublished data from the May 1975 Current Population Survey and the 2000 Current Population Survey (annual averages).

Table 5-2 • Median Weekly Earnings by Sex, and Female-to-Male Earnings Ratios among Workers Age 25–64 by Age, 2000[1,2]

Figure 5-2, which looks at workers by 10-year age group, shows that the earnings gap is narrowest among workers age 25–34. As this table shows, the gap is considerably narrower in the younger half of that age group than in the older half (84.7 percent versus 79.0 percent).

| | Median Weekly Earnings (2000 dollars) | | |
Age	Women	Men	Earnings Ratio
16 years and over	491	646	76.0
25 years and over	515	700	73.6
25–29	482	569	84.7
30–34	505	639	79.0
35–39	515	716	71.9
40–44	525	748	70.2
45–49	563	762	73.9
50–54	568	804	70.6
55–59	512	752	68.1
60–64	489	703	69.6

[1]Median usual weekly earnings of full-time wage-and-salary workers.
[2]The editors elected to focus on the earnings of workers between 25 and 65. We omitted the group between 16 and 25 (where the earnings ratio was around 91 percent in 2000) because many of these workers have yet to finish their education. We omitted the group age 65 and over because large standard errors accompany the earnings data for these workers (relatively few people in this age group are employed full time).

Source: Bureau of Labor Statistics, unpublished data from the 2000 Current Population Survey (annual averages).

Table 5-3 • Median Weekly Earnings by Sex, and Female-to-Male Earnings Ratios by Race and Hispanic Origin, 1975–2000[1]

The earnings gap shrank to some degree in all the groups shown here over the last quarter of the last century and narrowed *relatively* the most (by about 13 percentage points) among whites. Still, the gap was consistently narrowest among black and Hispanic workers and widest among white workers.

	Median Weekly Earnings (2000 dollars)					
	1975[2]	1980	1985	1990	1995	2000
All races[3]						
Women	439	420	443	459	459	491
Men	707	652	650	639	608	646
Earnings ratio	62.0	64.4	68.2	71.8	75.5	76.0
White						
Women	442	422	450	468	469	500
Men	720	667	667	655	640	669
Earnings ratio	61.3	63.3	67.4	71.4	73.3	74.7
Black[4]						
Women	416	387	403	406	401	429
Men	554	510	487	474	464	503
Earnings ratio	75.1	75.8	82.9	85.6	86.4	85.3
Hispanic[5]						
Women	(6)	(6)	366	369	345	364
Men	(6)	(6)	472	424	395	414
Earnings ratio	—	—	77.6	87.0	87.1	87.9

[1]Median usual weekly earnings of full-time wage-and-salary workers age 16 and over.
[2]May 1975.
[3]Includes Asian/Pacific Islanders and Native Americans, not shown separately (data not available).
[4]"Black and other" in 1975.
[5]People of Hispanic origin may be of any race. In this table, Hispanics are included in the racial categories as well as in the Hispanic category. *See* Figure 1-6 and footnote to Table 1-1.
[6]Data on earnings of Hispanic workers by sex were not available for 1975 and 1980.

Sources: Bureau of Labor Statistics, *Employment and Earnings,* January 1986, Table 54, January 1991, Table 54, January 1996, Table 37, and January 2001, Table 37, *Handbook of Labor Statistics,* 1989, Table 41, and unpublished data from the May 1975 Current Population Survey.

Table 5-4 • Median Weekly Earnings of Full-Time Wage-and-Salary Workers in Selected Occupations by Sex, 2000

In most of the occupations shown here for which both women's and men's median earnings are available, women earned less than men. Even when there are earnings data for only one sex, inferences can be drawn. For example, in the case of airplane pilots/navigators, the median for both sexes is higher than the median for men, which suggests that the handful of women in this occupation (only 3.1 percent) generally earn more than the men. In the case of architects, on the other hand, the median for both sexes is lower than for men only, which suggests that— at least among those architects who are wage-and-salary workers—women generally earn less than men.

| | | Earnings | | Women as a Percentage of |
Occupations	Both Sexes	Women	Men	Workers[1]
Airplane pilots and navigators	1,283	(2)	1,272	3.1
Architects	1,052	(2)	1,126	21.4
Automobile mechanics	533	(2)	538	0.8
Carpenters	533	(2)	533	0.6
Clergy	700	(2)	716	13.4
Computer programmers	944	868	968	26.0
Data processing equipment repairers	676	638	692	16.7
Dental assistants	414	417	(2)	96.4
Economists	876	785	1,148	48.2
Editors and reporters	742	718	795	51.0
Financial managers	965	787	1,201	49.4
Lawyers and judges	1,314	1,054	1,448	29.3
Librarians	667	657	(2)	85.5
Managers, medicine and health	743	676	1,039	76.0
Mechanical engineers	1,126	(2)	1,128	8.0
Physicians	1,340	899	1,553	31.2

See footnotes at end of table.

(continued)

Table 5-4 (continued)

Occupations	Earnings			Women as a Percent-age of Workers[1]
	Both Sexes	Women	Men	
Registered nurses	790	782	890	91.2
Social workers	602	589	637	71.3
Teachers, elementary school	718	701	860	83.2
Teachers, postsecondary	939	805	1,020	38.5
Telephone installers/ repairers	763	(2)	776	12.5
Welders and cutters	519	(2)	523	5.8

[1]Full-time wage-and-salary workers. *See* Table 4-12 in the Employment Section for women's representation among all workers in these occupations (i.e., including workers who are other than full-time wage-and-salary workers, such as self-employed workers and part-time workers).

[2]Full-time wage-and-salary workers of this gender in this occupation are too few for a reliable estimate of median earnings.

Source: Bureau of Labor Statistics, *Employment and Earnings,* January 2001, Table 39.

Table 5-5 • Female-to-Male Earnings Ratios by Occupation, 1990, 1995, and 2000[1]

While the earnings gap shrank between 1990 and 2000 for full-time wage-and-salary workers in most of the occupational categories shown here, and, overall, was more than four percentage points narrower in 2000 than in 1990 (76 percent compared with 71.8 percent), the narrowing took place largely in the first half of the decade. After that, the trend stalled.

| | Earnings Ratio | | |
Occupation	1990	1995	2000
All occupations	71.8	75.5	76.0
Managerial and professional specialty	69.9	73.0	71.3
Executive, administrative, and managerial	65.4	68.4	67.7
Professional specialty	74.2	76.4	74.2
Technical, sales, and administrative support	66.9	68.9	69.0
Technicians and related support	73.2	74.9	71.1
Sales occupations	57.8	57.0	59.5
Administrative support, including clerical	75.5	78.5	79.8
Service occupations	71.9	73.9	76.3
Protective service	84.9	79.3	75.9
All other service occupations[2]	84.6	88.0	88.0
Precision production, craft, and repair	64.8	69.5	70.9
Mechanics and repairers	96.2	102.2	96.6
Construction trades	82.1	78.9	79.3
Precision production occupations	59.1	60.7	64.2
Operators, fabricators, and laborers	69.3	71.9	72.1
Machine operators, assemblers, and inspectors	66.5	70.3	71.7
Transportation and material moving occupations	75.1	73.4	72.9
Handlers, equipment cleaners, helpers, and laborers	81.2	86.6	81.2
Farming, forestry, and fishing	82.1	84.7	84.7

[1]Usual median weekly earnings of full-time wage-and-salary workers.
[2]Excluding workers in private households.

Sources: Bureau of Labor Statistics, *Employment and Earnings,* January 1991, Table 56, January 1996, Table 39, and January 2001, Table 39.

Table 5-6 • Median Annual Earnings of Year-Round, Full-Time Workers by Sex, Race, and Hispanic Origin, 1975–2000[1,2]

Unlike the preceding tables and figures, which are based on the usual median *weekly* earnings of full-time wage-and-salary workers, this table and the earnings tables and figures that follow are based on the *annual* earnings of full-time workers who worked year round, including but not limited to wage-and-salary workers. Among women of all races who met these criteria, median real annual earnings increased fairly steadily between 1975 and 2000, but the gains were far from uniform across racial/ethnic groups. White women saw the largest increase—$6,758 (32 percent), Hispanic women the smallest—$2,276 (12.5 percent). Asian/Pacific Islander women, for whom only relatively recent data are available, were the highest earners among women. Men lost ground in some of the years shown here. By 2000, however, all but Hispanic men had more than made up the lost ground.

	Median Annual Earnings (2000 dollars)					
	1975	1980	1985	1990	1995	2000
Women						
All races[3]	21,297	22,279	23,978	25,451	25,260	27,355
White	21,322	22,438	24,242	25,741	25,725	28,080
Non-Hispanic white	(4)	(4)	(4)	26,138	26,568	29,604
Black	20,539	21,235	21,958	23,163	23,203	25,117
Asian/Pacific Islander	(4)	(4)	(4)	27,379	27,933	31,156
Hispanic[5]	18,251	19,259	20,052	20,122	19,288	20,527
Men						
All races	36,207	37,033	37,131	35,538	35,365	37,339
White	37,048	38,118	38,462	37,082	36,124	38,869
Non-Hispanic white	(4)	(4)	(4)	38,690	38,628	41,157
Black	27,549	26,955	26,825	27,110	27,429	30,409
Asian/Pacific Islander	(4)	(4)	(4)	34,365	35,452	40,946
Hispanic	26,714	26,977	26,168	24,570	22,882	24,638

[1]For the years before 1990, data are for civilian workers only.
[2]The Census Bureau used the CPI-U-RS to inflate the earnings series.
[3]Includes Native Americans, not shown separately (data not available).
[4]Data were not available for 1975, 1980, and 1985.
[5]People of Hispanic origin may be of any race. In this table, Hispanics are included in the racial categories as well as in the Hispanic category. *See* Figure 1-6 and footnote to Table 1-1.

Source: Census Bureau, *Historical Income Tables–People*, P-38, P-38A, P-38B, P-38C, P-38D, and P-38E, <http://www.census.gov/hhes/income/histinc/>.

Figure 5-3 • Median Annual Earnings of Year-Round, Full-Time Workers by Sex and Race, 1975–2000[1,2,3]

As of 2000, Asian/Pacific Islander men had overtaken white men as America's highest earners (although non-Hispanic white men were still slightly ahead—see Table 5-6). Asian/Pacific Islander women were the highest earners of all women—in fact, they earned slightly more than black men.

2000 Dollars

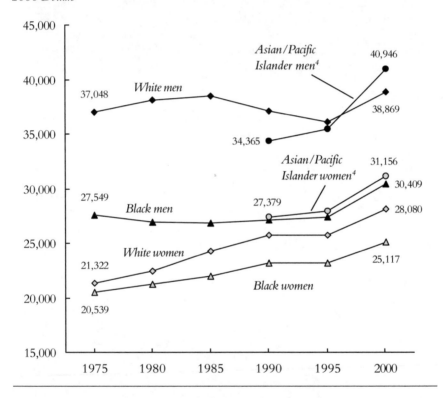

[1]Before 1990, data are for civilian workers only.
[2]The Census Bureau used the CPI-U-RS to inflate the earnings series.
[3]Includes Native Americans, not shown separately (data not available).
[4]Data for Asian/Pacific Islanders are not available for years before 1988.

Source: Census Bureau, *Historical Income Tables–People*, P-38A, P-38B, and P-38C, <http://www.census.gov/hhes/income/histinc/>.

Figure 5-4 • Median Annual Earnings of Year-Round, Full-Time Workers by Sex and Hispanic Origin, 1975–2000[1,2]

Hispanic women have the lowest annual earnings of all year-round, full-time workers. At least since 1975, Hispanic men have had much lower earnings than men overall, although for about half of that period the median for Hispanic men was higher than for women overall. However, between 1985 and 1990, the median for Hispanic men dropped below the median for women overall.

2000 Dollars

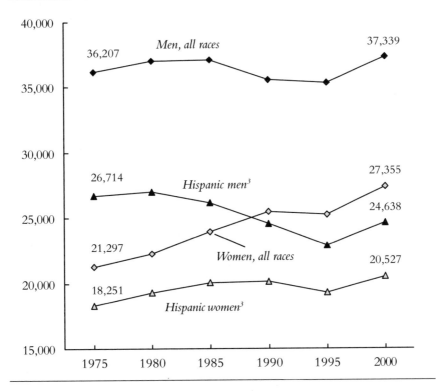

[1]Before 1990, data are for civilian workers only.
[2]The Census Bureau used the CPI-U-RS to inflate the earnings series.
[3]People of Hispanic origin may be of any race. *See* Figure 1-6 and footnote to Table 1-1.

Source: Census Bureau, *Historical Income Tables–People*, P-38 and P-38D, <http://www. census.gov/hhes/income/histinc/>.

Table 5-7 • Women's Median Annual Earnings by Educational Attainment, 1991 and 2000 (in 2000 dollars)[1,2,3]

Overall, women working year round, full time, in 2000 earned 10 percent more in real—i.e., inflation-adjusted—dollars than similarly employed women earned in 1991. However, the earnings edge conferred by college and academic (as opposed to professional) postgraduate degrees is clear: women with bachelor's, master's, or doctoral degrees gained far more than women with less education. On the other hand, they also gained more in relative terms than women with professional degrees, even though the latter remained the highest earners.

	1991	2000	Percent Change
Total, all levels	26,347	28,977	+10.0
Less than ninth grade	14,413	15,399	+6.8
Some high school, no diploma	16,768	17,209	+2.6
High school graduate or GED	22,347	23,719	+6.1
Some college, no degree	26,417	27,190	+2.9
Associate degree	29,555	30,178	+2.1
Bachelor's degree, no more	34,252	38,208	+11.5
Master's degree	41,024	47,049	+14.7
Doctorate	49,756	55,620	+11.8
Professional degree	52,769	56,103	+6.3

[1]Earnings of year-round, full-time workers age 25 and over.
[2]The year 1991 is the earliest for which data comparable to 2000 data are available.
[3]The Census Bureau used the CPI-U-RS to inflate the earnings from 1991.

Source: Census Bureau, *Historical Income Tables–People*, P-24, <http://www.census.gov/hhes/income/histinc/>.

Table 5-8 • Pension Plan Coverage by Workers' Sex and Work Experience, and by Race and Hispanic Origin of Women, 2000[1]

Unless they are Hispanic, women who work year round, full time, are likely to be in an employer-provided pension plan, but pension plan coverage is the exception among part-time workers, even if they work year round.

| | | Percentage | |
	Number (in thousands)	With Pension Plan Offered at Work	Worker Included in Plan
Total with work experience[2]			
Women, all races[3]	70,818	56.8	42.7
White	58,122	57.1	43.1
Non-Hispanic white	51,470	59.1	44.9
Black	9,331	57.9	42.4
Hispanic[4]	7,010	41.8	28.9
Men, all races[3]	79,176	57.1	46.2
Year-round, full-time			
Women, all races	41,595	66.8	56.8
White	33,159	67.7	58.1
Non-Hispanic white	29,288	70.2	60.6
Black	6,390	65.3	52.7
Hispanic	4,084	49.5	39.2
Men, all races	58,762	63.4	55.8
Year-round, part-time			
Women, all races	9,416	41.7	23.1
White	8,373	42.2	23.9
Non-Hispanic white	7,633	43.3	24.9
Black	669	39.8	18.3
Hispanic	771	31.6	14.3
Men, all races	4,548	36.4	15.6

[1]"Pension plan" refers to an employer- or union-provided pension or retirement plan.
[2]Total includes workers who did not work year round.
[3]Includes Asian/Pacific Islanders and Native Americans, not shown separately (data not available).
[4]People of Hispanic origin may be of any race. *See* Figure 1-6 and footnote to Table 1-1.

Source: Census Bureau, Current Population Survey, March 2001, Table NC8, <http://ferret.bls.census.gov/macro/032001/noncash/nc8_000.htm>.

Figure 5-5 • Women Workers in Employer-Provided Pension Plans and Women Workers with Employer-Provided Health Insurance by Employer Size, 2000 (percent distributions)

Although they are less than half of all employed women, women who work for employers with 1,000 or more employees account for more than half of women in a pension plan or with health insurance coverage through their own jobs.

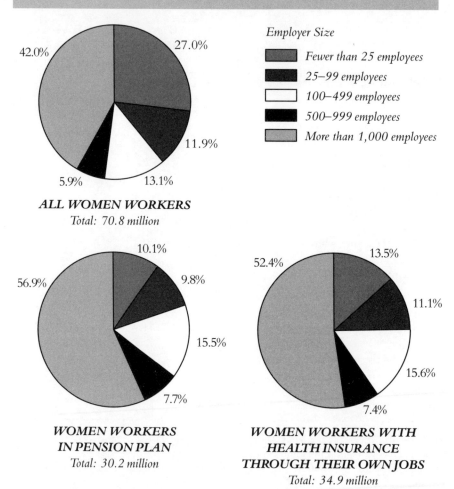

Employer Size

Fewer than 25 employees
25–99 employees
100–499 employees
500–999 employees
More than 1,000 employees

ALL WOMEN WORKERS
Total: 70.8 million

**WOMEN WORKERS
IN PENSION PLAN**
Total: 30.2 million

**WOMEN WORKERS WITH
HEALTH INSURANCE
THROUGH THEIR OWN JOBS**
Total: 34.9 million

Source: Census Bureau, Current Population Survey, March 2001, Tables NC7 and NC8, <http://ferret.bls.census.gov/macro/032001/noncash/nc7_000.htm> and <.../ nc8_000.htm>.

Table 5-9 • Year-Round, Full-Time Workers Covered by Health Insurance through Their Own Jobs by Sex, Race, and Hispanic Origin, 2000 (numbers are in thousands)[1]

Roughly two-thirds of the women and men who worked year round, full time, in 2000 had health insurance through their own jobs (the percentage was somewhat higher—72.1 percent—among non-Hispanic white men). Among Hispanic workers, coverage was much less widespread: scarcely more than half of the men and not quite 53 percent of the women had health insurance through their jobs.

	Total Number of Workers	*With Health Insurance through Own Jobs[2]*	
		Number	*Percentage*
All races[3]			
Women	41,595	27,430	65.9
Men	58,762	40,417	68.8
White			
Women	33,159	21,897	66.0
Men	49,974	34,591	69.2
Non-Hispanic white			
Women	29,288	19,851	67.8
Men	43,513	31,367	72.1
Black			
Women	6,390	4,336	67.9
Men	5,804	3,823	65.9
Hispanic[4]			
Women	4,084	2,157	52.8
Men	6,766	3,398	50.2

[1] Workers age 15 and over.
[2] With employer-provided group health insurance in their own names.
[3] Includes Asian/Pacific Islanders and Native Americans, not shown separately (data not available).
[4] People of Hispanic origin may be of any race. In this table, Hispanics are included in the racial categories as well as in the Hispanic category. *See* Figure 1-6 and footnote to Table 1-1.

Source: Census Bureau, Current Population Survey, March 2001, Table NC7, <http://ferret.bls.census/gov/macro/032001/noncash/nc7_000.htm>.

Figure 5-6 • Women Age 18–64 with Private Health Insurance by Age and Source of Coverage, 2000 (percent distributions)[1,2]

Most women age 18–64 who have private health insurance (as distinct from coverage by a government plan such as Medicare or Medicaid) are in employer-provided group plans, and most are covered through their own jobs. Except for the 18–24 group (many of whom may be students), the women most likely to have individual insurance policies (usually more expensive than group coverage) are over 60 but not yet 65—i.e., not quite old enough for Medicare.

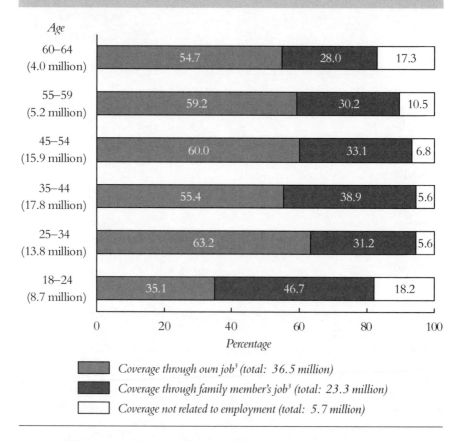

Age

60–64 (4.0 million)	54.7	28.0	17.3
55–59 (5.2 million)	59.2	30.2	10.5
45–54 (15.9 million)	60.0	33.1	6.8
35–44 (17.8 million)	55.4	38.9	5.6
25–34 (13.8 million)	63.2	31.2	5.6
18–24 (8.7 million)	35.1	46.7	18.2

Percentage

■ Coverage through own job[3] *(total: 36.5 million)*
■ Coverage through family member's job[3] *(total: 23.3 million)*
☐ Coverage not related to employment *(total: 5.7 million)*

[1]Percentages may not total 100.0 due to rounding.
[2]Women with coverage for all or part of the year.
[3]Coverage related to current or past employment.

Source: Census Bureau, Current Population Survey, March 2001, Table 24, <http://ferret.bls.census.gov/macro/032001/pov/new24_000.htm>.

Figure 5-7 • Health Insurance Coverage for People of All Ages by Sex and Type of Insurance, 1990 and 2000 (in percentages)[1,2]

The overall "profile" of health insurance coverage or lack of it in 2000 does not appear to be very different from what it had been a decade earlier. Nevertheless, there were four million more uninsured people in 2000 than there had been in 1990.

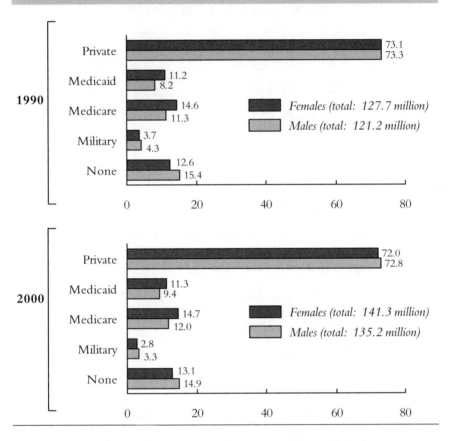

[1] The "insured" had coverage for all or part of the year; the uninsured had no coverage at any time during the year.

[2] Percentages for each sex total more than 100.0 percent because some insured had coverage from more than one source.

Source: Census Bureau, *Health Insurance Historical Tables*, Table HI-2, <http://www.census. gov/hhes/hlthins/historic/index.html>.

Figure 5-8 • People with and without Health Insurance Coverage by Age and Sex, 2000

In general, males are more likely than females to lack health insurance coverage. In the 55–64 age group, however, the reverse is true. About one in seven women in this age group (15.2 percent) had no health insurance coverage of any kind in 2000. (See Figure 5-6 for information about sources of private health insurance coverage for women age 18–64.)

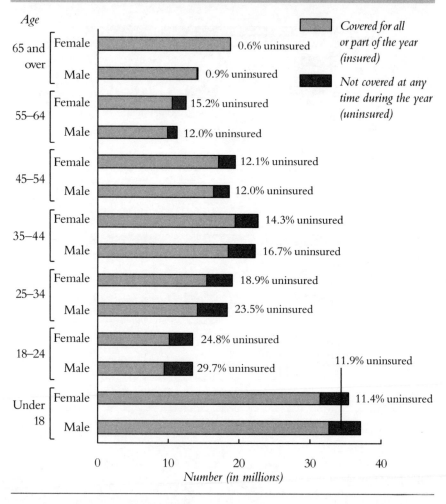

Source: Census Bureau, *Health Insurance Historical Tables*, Table HI-2, <http://www.census.gov/hhes/hlthins/historic/index.html>.

Table 5-10 • People without Health Insurance Coverage by Family Relationship and by Sex and Work Experience, 1995 and 2000

As was the case in 1995, the majority of uninsured people in 2000 were male. However, the female proportion of the population without health insurance coverage edged up from 46.6 percent to 47.9 percent between 1995 and 2000. More wives (but fewer husbands) were uninsured in 2000 than in 1995. Fewer children were uninsured in 2000 than in 1995; minor children's representation among the uninsured dropped from 23.0 percent to 20.5 percent.

	Number of Uninsured (in thousands)		Percentage of Uninsured	
	1995	2000	1995	2000
Total uninsured	40,388	38,464	100.0	100.0
Females	18,837	18,426	46.6	47.9
Males	21,551	20,038	53.4	52.1
People living in families, total	32,315	30,633	80.1	79.6
Wives	5,593	5,673	13.8	14.7
Husbands	5,129	4,890	12.7	12.7
Female householders	2,153	2,436	5.3	6.3
Children under age 18	9,287	7,872	23.0	20.5
Children over age 18	6,174	5,301	15.3	13.8
Other[1]	3,979	4,461	9.9	11.6
People in unrelated subfamilies	383	323	0.9	0.8
People not living in families, total	7,691	7,509	19.0	19.5
Unrelated females	2,890	2,863	7.2	7.4
Unrelated males	4,801	4,646	11.9	12.1
People of working age (16–64)	31,629	31,124	78.3	80.9
Women working full time, year round	4,241	4,885	10.5	12.7
Other female workers	5,228	5,092	12.9	13.2
Women who did not work	4,989	5,005	12.3	13.0
Men working full time, year round	7,713	8,189	19.1	21.3
Other male workers	6,168	4,944	15.3	12.9
Men who did not work	3,289	3,010	8.1	7.8

[1]Could include male householder with no spouse present, as well as other relatives.

Sources: Census Bureau, Current Population Survey, March 1996, Table 24, <http://ferret.bls.census.gov/macro/031996/pov/24_000.htm>, and Current Population Survey, March 2001, Table 24, <.../032001/pov/new24_000.htm>.

Table 5-11 • Employees Who Took Leave for Family or Medical Reasons by Selected Characteristics, 2000 (in percentages)

Close to one in five women, compared with roughly one in seven men, took a leave for family or medical reasons during the 18-month period preceding the Labor Department's 2000 Family Leave Survey. Not surprisingly, people with children were the most likely to take leave (24.4 percent). Also not surprisingly, since this kind of leave is usually unpaid, workers with family incomes at the low end of the income scale were less likely to take the leave than better-off workers.

	Percentage Taking Leave
All employees	16.5
Women	19.8
Men	13.5
Age	
18–24	11.2
25–34	20.2
35–49	16.6
50–64	17.0
65 or older	11.6
Marital status	
Currently married or living with partner	18.5
Formerly married	20.0
Never married	9.2
Presence of children under age 18 in household	
One or more children	24.4
No children	11.3
Annual family income	
Less than $20,000	16.5
$20,000 to less than $30,000	16.2
$30,000 to less than $50,000	18.3
$50,000 to less than $75,000	19.9
$75,000 to less than $100,000	16.8
$100,000 or more	18.1

Source: Bureau of Labor Statistics, "Family and Medical Leave: Evidence from the 2000 Surveys," *Monthly Labor Review* 124, no. 9, 2001, Table 4.

Section 6

ECONOMIC SECURITY

THE LAST FIVE YEARS of the twentieth century saw income gains for families of every type even after taking inflation into account. Still, in 2000 as in earlier years, married couples with working wives (most are two-earner couples) continued to have by far the highest incomes. There were significant differences in median family income by race and Hispanic origin, with Asian/Pacific Islander couples and non-Hispanic white couples having substantially higher median incomes than black couples and Hispanic couples (who had the lowest incomes of all couples). Families headed by women had by far the lowest incomes overall.

Across all family types, families that include children under 18 are more likely to be poor than families that do not include minor children. A single-parent family is more likely to be poor than a married-couple family of the same race or origin with children, and a single-mother family is the most likely to be poor. In fact, between 1995 and 2000, the income gap between married couples with children and families consisting of single women with children grew even wider. Findings include:

- Poverty rates are higher for females than for males at every age and among people of every race and origin. In certain age groups (age 25–34, and age 75 and over) women are almost twice as likely as men to be poor. Overall, almost a quarter of black and Hispanic women, compared with about 10 percent of white women, live in poverty (see Table 6-5).
- Both the number and the percentage of women receiving public assistance were strikingly lower in 2000 than they had been in 1995, and the real median income from public assistance was nearly two-thirds lower. In all likelihood, this was largely the result of the implementation of the Personal Responsibility and Work Opportunity

Reconciliation Act of 1996, often referred to as the "welfare reform" bill (see Table 6-2).

- The paycheck is the most common and the largest source of personal income for women age 25–64. Overall, in 2000, close to four-fifths of those who had personal income from any source had wage-or-salary income, and the proportions were even larger among black and Hispanic women. By contrast, only 6.5 percent of women were receiving child support (see Table 6-3).

- Older women typically have fewer sources of income and receive fewer dollars from these sources than older men. For example, in 2000, less than 30 percent of women age 65 and up, compared with over 44 percent of men, had income from a retirement plan based on their own employment, and the women's median income from that source was only 56 percent of the median for men (see Table 6-4).

- Elderly women—especially women 75 or over—had much higher poverty rates than their male contemporaries. And women who live alone were the most economically vulnerable of America's elderly: overall, one in every three was either poor or close to it, with an income under 125 percent of poverty (or less than $10,325 a year). The percentages in or close to poverty were considerably higher among those who were black or Hispanic (see Figure 6-5 and Table 6-7).

- Compared with people who rent, people who own their own homes are less likely to be poor. However, whether they own or rent and whether they live alone or with others, female householders are more likely to be poor than their male and married-couple counterparts (see Table 6-8).

Figure 6-1 • Median Family Income by Family Type, 1980–2000[1]

The last five years of the twentieth century saw income gains for families of every type, even after taking inflation into account (as this figure does). Even couples without working wives and male-headed families more than recovered the ground they had lost since 1980. Still, married couples with working wives (most are two-earner couples) continued to have by far the highest annual income; families headed by women continued to have by far the lowest.

2000 Dollars

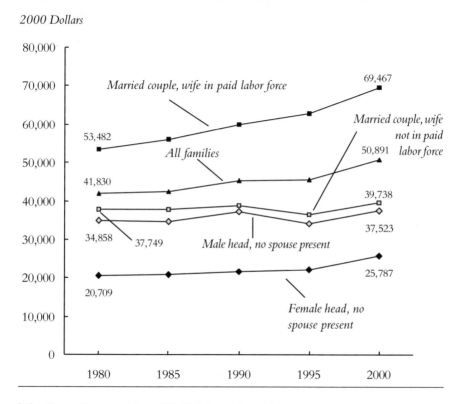

[1]The Census Bureau used the CPI-U-RS to inflate the income series.

Source: Census Bureau, *Historical Income Tables–Families*, Table F-7, <http://www.census. gov/hhes/income/histinc/>.

Table 6-1 • Median Family Income by Race and Hispanic Origin and by Family Type, 1980, 1990, and 2000[1]

Families of every type in the groups shown here had incomes with more purchasing power in 2000 than in 1990, but married couples had by far the greatest gains. Black and non-Hispanic white couples' income showed similar percentage increases (about 17 percent) between 1990 and 2000, although the 2000 median for non-Hispanic white couples was still substantially higher than for black couples. Asian/Pacific Islander couples had the highest median income; Hispanic couples had the lowest. (It is hard to avoid the conclusion that the key to this disparity lies in the educational disparity—see Section 2, especially Table 2-1 and Figure 2-1.)

	Median Income (2000 dollars)		
	---	---	---
	1980	*1990*	*2000*
White			
All families	43,583	47,398	53,256
Married couple	46,761	51,784	59,953
Wife in paid labor force	54,197	60,664	70,462
Wife not in paid labor force	38,661	39,522	40,145
Female-headed, no spouse present	23,694	25,073	28,371
Male-headed, no spouse present	37,270	39,251	39,427
Non-Hispanic white			
All families	(2)	49,098	56,442
Married couple	(2)	53,074	62,046
Wife in paid labor force	(2)	(2)	72,390
Wife not in paid labor force	(2)	(2)	41,924
Female-headed, no spouse present	(2)	26,838	30,231
Male-headed, no spouse present	(2)	40,915	41,294
Black			
All families	25,218	27,506	34,204
Married couple	36,995	43,378	50,741
Wife in paid labor force	45,356	51,408	59,423
Wife not in paid labor force	24,711	26,107	30,369
Female-headed, no spouse present	14,774	15,568	20,395
Male-headed, no spouse present	24,985	28,052	31,278

See footnotes at end of table.   *(continued)*

Table 6–1 (continued)

	Median Income (2000 dollars)		
	1980	*1990*	*2000*
Asian/Pacific Islander			
All families	(2)	54,243	61,501
Married couple	(2)	59,380	66,848
Wife in paid labor force	(2)	(2)	(2)
Wife not in paid labor force	(2)	(2)	(2)
Female-headed, no spouse present	(2)	29,002	30,543
Male-headed, no spouse present	(2)	(2)	52,112
Hispanic[3]			
All families	29,281	30,085	35,050
Married couple	34,544	35,946	40,631
Wife in paid labor force	43,076	44,654	50,448
Wife not in paid labor force	27,956	27,179	28,675
Female-headed, no spouse present	13,990	15,297	21,006
Male-headed, no spouse present	26,468	29,203	32,852

[1]The Census Bureau used the CPI-U-RS to inflate the income series.
[2]Data are not available.
[3]People of Hispanic origin may be of any race. In this table, Hispanics are included in the racial categories as well as in the Hispanic category. *See* Figure 1-6 and footnote to Table 1-1.

Source: Census Bureau, *Historical Income Tables–Families*, Tables F-7A, F-7B, F-7C, and F-7D, and F-7E, <http://www.census.gov/hhes/income/histinc/>.

Figure 6-2 • Median Income of Families with Children by Family Type, 1980–2000[1]

Like families overall, families of every type that included children had more real income in 2000 than in 1995 (see Figure 6-1). But single-parent families continued to lag way behind married couples with children, and the yawning income gap between the latter and families consisting of a single women with children grew even wider.

2000 Dollars

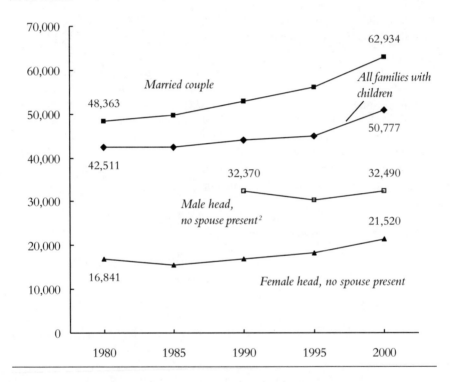

[1]The Census Bureau used the CPI-U-RS to inflate the income series.
[2]Data not available for 1980 or 1985.

Source: Census Bureau, *Historical Income Tables–Families*, Table F-10, <http://www.census.gov/hhes/income/histinc/>.

Table 6-2 • Women Age 15 and over with Income from Earnings, SSI, and Public Assistance, 1995 and 2000 (numbers are in thousands)[1]

Both the number and the percentage of women receiving public assistance were strikingly lower in 2000 than they had been in 1995, and real median income from public assistance was nearly two-thirds lower ($2,520 versus $6,958). It is probably not coincidental that the Personal Responsibility and Work Opportunity Reconciliation Act of 1996, often referred to as the "welfare reform" bill, went into effect during the period shown in this table.

| | 1995 | | 2000 | | Median Income from Source (2000 dollars) | |
	Number	Percentage	Number	Percentage	1995	2000
Total women with income from any source	96,007	100.0	99,974	100.0	13,620	16,188
With earnings	65,557	68.3	70,718	70.7	18,837	20,309
With SSI[2]	3,120	3.2	2,894	2.9	7,430	5,057
With public assistance[3]	4,239	4.4	1,874	1.9	6,958	2,520

[1]WREI used the CPI-U-RS to inflate the 1995 income.

[2]SSI (Supplemental Security Income) includes federal, state, and local welfare agency payments to low-income people who are 65 years old or over or people of any age who are blind or disabled.

[3]Public assistance includes cash assistance payments low-income people receive, such as Aid to Families with Dependent Children (AFDC), Temporary Assistance to Needy Families (TANF), general assistance, and emergency assistance.

Sources: Census Bureau, Current Population Survey, March 1996, Table PINC-11, <http://ferret.bls.census.gov/macro/031996/perinc/11_000.htm>, and March 2001, Table PINC-08, <.../032001/perinc/new08_000.htm>.

Table 6-3 • Sources of Personal Income for Women Age 25–64 by Race and Hispanic Origin, 2000[1]

The paycheck is both by far the most common and the largest source of personal income for women age 25–64: overall, in 2000, 78.7 percent of those who had personal income from any source had wage-or-salary income, and the proportions were even larger among black and Hispanic women.

| | Women with Income from Source | | Median Income from Source (dollars) |
	Number (in thousands)	Percentage	
Total with income[2]			
All races	67,628	100.0	21,324
White	55,355	100.0	21,484
Black	8,901	100.0	20,619
Hispanic origin[3]	6,388	100.0	15,309
Wage and salary			
All races	53,253	78.7	24,096
White	43,351	78.3	24,395
Black	7,292	81.9	22,349
Hispanic origin	5,207	81.6	16,842
Self-employment[4]			
All races	4,310	6.4	7,274
White	3,797	6.9	7,161
Black	273	3.1	10,069
Hispanic origin	258	4.0	6,666
Unemployment compensation			
All races	1,907	2.8	1,982
White	1,482	2.7	1,944
Black	337	3.8	2,160
Hispanic origin	224	3.5	1,913
Social Security			
All races	4,458	6.6	6,709
White	3,581	6.5	6,720
Black	739	8.3	6,758
Hispanic origin	353	5.5	6,436

See footnotes at end of table. (continued)

Table 6-3 (continued)

| | Women with Income from Source | | Median Income from Source (dollars) |
	Number (in thousands)	Percentage	
Child support			
All races	4,394	6.5	3,613
White	3,500	6.3	3,888
Black	797	9.0	2,512
Hispanic origin	401	6.3	2,989
Public assistance			
All races	1,355	2.0	2,881
White	864	1.6	3,178
Black	420	4.7	2,295
Hispanic origin	348	5.4	4,097
Interest			
All races	38,497	56.9	1,404
White	33,796	61.1	1,411
Black	2,935	33.0	1,338
Hispanic origin	2,058	32.2	1,350
Dividends			
All races	14,711	21.8	1,553
White	13,357	24.1	1,556
Black	701	7.9	1,578
Hispanic origin	503	7.9	1,534

[1]The income shown in this table is personal income. In the case of a woman who lives alone, or who is the sole support of a family, her personal income constitutes the household's entire income.
[2]Totals comprise women who had personal income from any source in 2000. However, not every source of income is detailed in this table.
[3]People of Hispanic origin may be of any race. In this table, Hispanics are included in the racial categories as well as in the Hispanic category. *See* Figure 1-6 and footnote to Table 1-1.
[4]Excludes farm self-employment, from which 736,000 women age 25–64 had income in 2000.

Source: Census Bureau, Current Population Survey, March 2001, Table PINC-08, <http://ferret.bls.census.gov/macro/032001/perinc/new08_000.htm>.

Table 6-4 • Sources of Personal Income for People Age 65 and over by Sex, and for Women Age 65 and over by Race and Hispanic Origin, 2000[1]

Older women typically have fewer sources of income and receive fewer dollars from them than older men. For example, under 30 percent of women age 65 and up have "other retirement income"—i.e., from a pension or other plan based on their own employment—compared with over 44 percent of men, and women's median income from that source ($5,870) is 56 percent of the median for men.

	With Income from Source		Median Income from Source (dollars)
	Number (in thousands)	Percentage	
With income from any source[2]			
Women, all races	18,320	100.0	10,898
White women	16,196	100.0	11,221
Black women	1,612	100.0	8,678
Hispanic women[3]	989	100.0	7,524
Men, all races	13,937	100.0	19,167
Earnings			
Women, all races	2,312	12.6	8,554
White women	2,041	12.6	8,739
Black women	215	13.3	7,242
Hispanic women	89	9.0	8,903
Men, all races	3,247	23.3	16,572
Social Security			
Women, all races	16,928	92.4	7,819
White women	15,078	93.1	7,959
Black women	1,471	91.3	6,910
Hispanic women	844	85.3	6,388
Men, all races	12,688	91.0	11,053
Supplemental Security Income (SSI)			
Women, all races	864	4.7	3,160
White women	560	3.5	2,950
Black women	189	11.7	2,419
Hispanic women	191	19.3	3,896
Men, all races	343	2.5	3,574

See footnotes at end of table.

(continued)

Table 6-4 (continued)

	With Income from Source		Median Income from Source (dollars)
	Number (in thousands)	Percentage	
Survivor benefits			
Women, all races	1,569	8.6	5,648
White women	1,443	8.9	5,652
Black women	96	6.0	4,785
Hispanic women	56	5.7	4,871
Men, all races	195	1.4	7,128
Other retirement income[4]			
Women, all races	5,413	29.6	5,870
White women	4,927	30.4	5,837
Black women	420	26.1	6,043
Hispanic women	153	15.5	4,527
Men, all races	6,159	44.2	10,420
Property income[5]			
Women, all races	10,844	59.2	2,026
White women	10,243	63.2	2,042
Black women	398	24.7	1,608
Hispanic women	286	28.9	1,773
Men, all races	8,701	62.4	2,186

[1]The income shown in this table is personal income. In the case of an individual who lives alone, or who is the sole support of a family, personal income constitutes the household's entire income.

[2]Totals comprise people who had income from any source in 2000. However, not every source of income is detailed in this table.

[3]People of Hispanic origin may be of any race. *See* Figure 1-6 and footnote to Table 1-1.

[4]Includes retirement income from company or union, federal government, military, state or local government, railroad, annuities, or IRA, Keogh, or 401(k).

[5]Includes property income from interest, dividends, and rents, royalties, estates, or trusts.

Source: Census Bureau, Current Population Survey, March 2001, Table PINC-08, <http://ferret.bls.census.gov/macro/032001/perinc/new08_000.htm>.

Figure 6-3 • Female Social Security Recipients Age 62 and over by Entitlement Status, 1975 and 2000[1,2,3]

Many women who are eligible for Social Security retirement benefits based on their own earnings are also eligible for benefits based on their husbands' earnings, but they are not entitled to both benefits. However, they may elect whichever is larger.[4] Dually entitled workers (almost always women) are workers who paid FICA taxes on their own earnings for at least 10 years (40 quarters) but elected the wife's or widow's benefit—to which they would have been entitled had they never paid a nickel in FICA taxes—because it was larger.

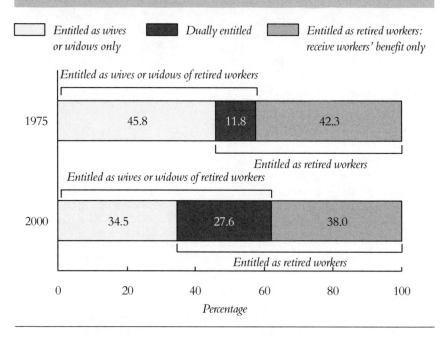

Entitled as wives or widows only　　Dually entitled　　Entitled as retired workers: receive workers' benefit only

[1]As of December for both years.
[2]Data include retired workers, disabled workers, women entitled as parents, and disabled widows and mothers.
[3]Percentages may not total 100.0 due to rounding.
[4]Technically, the benefit for a dually entitled worker comprises the benefit based on her own earnings plus an amount equal to the difference between her own benefit and what she is entitled to as a wife or widow.

Source: Social Security Administration, *Social Security Bulletin, Annual Statistical Supplement, 2001 (Draft)*, 2001, Table 5.A14, <http://www.ssa.gov/policy/>.

Table 6-5 • Poverty Rates of Individuals by Sex, Age, Race, and Hispanic Origin, 2000 (numbers are in thousands)

Poverty rates are higher for females than for males at every age and among people of every race and origin shown here.

	Females			Males		
	Total	*In Poverty*		*Total*	*In Poverty*	
	Number	*Number*	*Percentage*	*Number*	*Number*	*Percentage*
Total, all ages, all races	140,976	17,701	12.6	134,940	13,437	10.0
Under 18	35,101	5,776	16.5	36,831	5,857	15.9
18–24	13,489	2,326	17.2	13,473	1,567	11.6
25–34	18,989	2,472	13.0	18,451	1,420	7.7
35–44	22,603	2,158	9.5	22,177	1,520	6.9
45–54	19,462	1,319	6.8	18,578	1,122	6.0
55–64	12,532	1,354	10.8	11,252	887	7.9
65 and over	18,799	2,296	12.2	14,179	1,063	7.5
65–74	9,691	1,017	10.5	8,187	575	7.0
75 and over	9,108	1,279	14.0	5,992	488	8.1
White	114,694	12,043	10.5	111,299	9,248	8.3
Non-Hispanic white	98,692	8,418	8.5	95,187	6,154	6.5
Black	19,071	4,617	24.2	16,677	3,284	19.7
Asian/Pacific Islander	5,819	634	10.9	5,538	591	10.7
Hispanic[1]	16,854	3,873	23.0	16,864	3,283	19.5

[1]People of Hispanic origin may be of any race. *See* Figure 1-6 and footnote to Table 1-1.

Source: Census Bureau, *Poverty in the United States: 2000,* 2001, Table 2.

Figure 6-4 • Poverty Rates of Families with Children by Family Type, 1975–2000[1]

Between 1995 and 2000, as family incomes rose (see Figures 6-1 and 6-2, and Table 6-1), poverty rates for families with children fell. In relative terms, the drop was steepest—nine percentage points—for female-headed families. Nevertheless, in 2000, nearly one in three (32.5 percent) of these families was poor, a poverty rate double that for male-headed families and more than five times that for married-couple families.

Poverty Rate

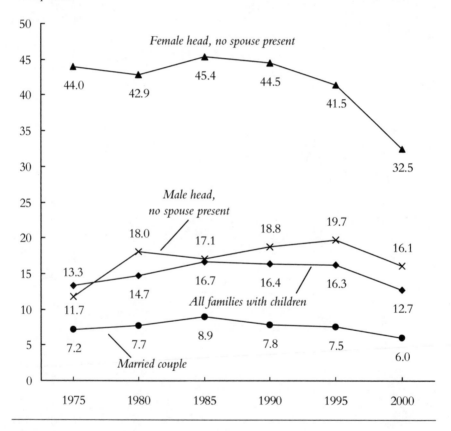

[1]Family households that include related children under 18.

Source: Census Bureau, *Historical Poverty Tables*, Table 4, <http://www.census.gov/hhes/poverty/histpov/hstpov4.html>.

Table 6-6 • Poverty Rates of Families by Family Type, Presence of Children, and Race and Hispanic Origin, 2000

A family of any type that includes children under 18 is more likely to be poor than a family of the same type, race, and Hispanic/non–Hispanic origin that does not include minor children. Among families with children, a single-parent family is more likely to be poor than a married-couple family of the same race or origin, and a single-mother family is the most likely to be poor.

| | *Percentage in Poverty* | | | |
| | *All Family Types* | *Married- Couple Families* | *Families with* | |
			Female Head[1]	*Male Head[1]*
All families, all races[2]	8.6	4.7	24.7	11.5
Families with children[3]	12.7	6.0	32.5	16.1
Families without children	4.3	3.6	8.3	6.3
White families	6.9	4.4	20.0	10.2
Families with children	10.3	5.8	27.5	14.6
Families without children	3.6	3.2	6.2	5.0
Non-Hispanic white families	5.3	3.3	16.9	9.6
Families with children	7.7	3.8	23.9	13.8
Families without children	3.2	2.9	5.3	4.5
Black families	19.1	6.1	34.6	16.2
Families with children	24.9	6.3	41.1	21.7
Families without children	9.0	5.8	15.0	10.5
Hispanic[4] families	18.5	14.1	34.2	12.6
Families with children	22.9	16.9	41.4	17.0
Families without children	8.7	7.9	12.8	6.9

[1] With no spouse present.
[2] Includes Asian/Pacific Islanders and Native Americans, not shown separately (data not available).
[3] Family households that include related children under age 18.
[4] People of Hispanic origin may be of any race. In this table, Hispanics are included in the racial categories as well as in the Hispanic category. *See* Figure 1-6 and footnote to Table 1-1.

Source: Census Bureau, *Historical Poverty Tables*, Table 4, <http://www.census.gov/hhes/poverty/histpov/hstpov4.html>.

Figure 6-5 • Poverty Rates of People Age 65 and over and 75 and over by Sex, 1990–2000

The poverty rate for elderly women drifted generally downward during the last decade of the twentieth century (although a slight up-tick was apparent between 1999 and 2000). Still, in 2000 as in 1990, elderly women—especially women 75 or over—had much higher poverty rates than their male contemporaries.

Poverty Rate

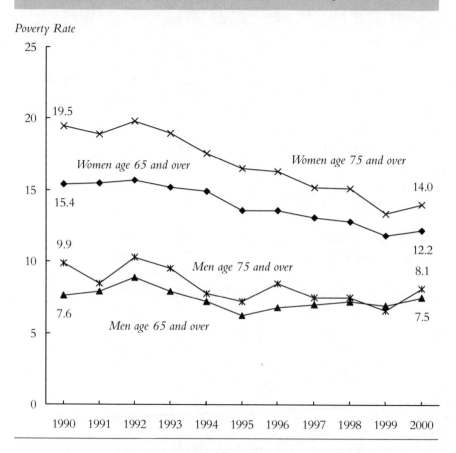

Sources: Census Bureau, *65+ in the United States,* 1996, Table 4-4, *Income, Poverty, and Valuation of Noncash Benefits: 1993,* 1995, Table 8, *Income, Poverty, and Valuation of Noncash Benefits: 1994,* 1996, Table 9, *Poverty in the United States: 1990,* 1991, Table 6, *Poverty in the United States: 1991,* 1992, Table 6, *Poverty in the United States: 1995,* 1996, Table 2, *Poverty in the United States: 1996,* 1997, Table 2, *Poverty in the United States: 1997,* 1998, Table 2, *Poverty in the United States: 1998,* 1999, Table 2, *Poverty in the United States: 1999,* 2000, Table 2, and *Poverty in the United States: 2000,* 2001, Table 2.

Table 6-7 • Women Age 65 and over Living Alone by Ratio of Income to Poverty
Level and Race and Hispanic Origin, 2000 (in percentages)

Women who live alone are the most economically vulnerable of America's
elderly. Overall, in 2000, more than 1.5 million of them (about one in every five)
were downright poor; one in every three was either poor or very close to it—
i.e., with an annual income under 125 percent of poverty or less than $10,325 a
year.[1] While white women were typically in a considerably less precarious
situation than black or Hispanic women (well over half of whom had incomes
below 125 percent of poverty), most white elderly women who lived alone were
hardly on easy street—more than four million of them (over three in every five)
had incomes of less than $16,520 (or twice the poverty threshold).

Women Age 65 and Over Living Alone	Race and Hispanic Origin			
	All Races[2]	White	Black	Hispanic[3]
Percentage with income below				
100 percent of poverty	21.3	18.9	43.1	37.7
125 percent of poverty	34.7	32.5	54.4	58.5
150 percent of poverty	47.3	45.3	65.8	69.2
200 percent of poverty	64.0	62.5	79.1	80.8
Total number (in thousands)	7,449	6,706	641	298

[1]The poverty threshold for a single person age 65 and over was $8,259 in 2000.
[2]Includes Asian/Pacific Islanders and Native Americans, not shown separately (data not
available).
[3]People of Hispanic origin may be of any race. In this table, Hispanics are included in the racial
categories as well as in the Hispanic category. *See* Figure 1-6 and footnote to Table 1-1.

Source: Census Bureau, *Poverty in the United States: 2000,* 2001, Table 2.

Table 6-8 • Economic Status of Householders by Tenure, Type of Household, and Sex of Householder: Selected Measures, 1999

Compared with people who rent, people who own their homes are less likely to be poor—indeed, in 1999, owner households of every type had higher median incomes than their renter counterparts. Female householders, whether owners or renters, whether in households of at least two persons or in one-person households, are more likely to be poor than their male and married-couple counterparts. Women householders are also more likely to be elderly—indeed, well over half (58 percent) of female owners who live alone and close to one-third (33.1 percent) of female renters who live alone are at least 65 years of age.

	Percentage		Median (dollars)	
Owner households	*In Poverty*	*Age 65/+*	*Income*	*Home Value*
Of two or more persons				
Married couples	5.7	19.3	58,776	122,384
Other/female householder	16.1	21.7	29,592	90,206
Other/male householder	7.5	14.4	41,900	98,256
Of one person				
Female householder	20.3	58.0	17,942	87,844
Male householder	10.6	29.1	33,934	87,718

	Percentage		Median (dollars)	
Renter households	*In Poverty*	*Age 65/+*	*Income*	*Housing Costs*
Of two or more persons				
Married couples	16.1	8.3	34,735	7,776
Other/female householder	35.6	4.7	16,872	6,852
Other/male householder	15.5	3.0	24,685	7,788
Of one person				
Female householder	28.8	33.1	15,335	6,192
Male householder	19.5	13.0	23,411	6,180

Source: Census Bureau and Department of Housing and Urban Development, *American Housing Survey for the United States in 1999,* 2000, Tables 3-9, 3-20, 3-22, 4-9, 4-20, and 4-21.

Section 7

WOMEN IN THE MILITARY

WOMEN HAVE OFFICIALLY SERVED in the U.S. military for over a century—since 1901. During most of this time, their service, although of great value to their nation, was limited to ancillary roles and was constrained by law and policy. In 1973, this began to change, when the expiration of the Selective Service Act brought the draft to an end. The era of the all-volunteer force has resulted in slow but steady growth in the numbers of women serving in the military—from under two percent in 1972 to about 15 percent at the start of 2002—and the movement of women into an increasing number of military occupations.

In 1991, women's extraordinarily fine service during the Persian Gulf War—more than 41,000 deployed to the combat zone—opened the way for the repeal of laws that prevented them from serving on aircraft with combat missions or as permanent crew members aboard combat ships (destroyers, aircraft carriers, etc.). Today, more than 10,000 Navy and Marine Corps women serve aboard combat ships; women of all the services are involved in combat air missions as pilots, navigators, and crew members; and women are serving in peacekeeping operations around the world. Their presence in military actions, such as the war in Afghanistan, is no longer considered remarkable; in fact, it is routine.

Now that women are serving in air and sea units with combat missions and also in combat support occupations that bring them routinely into combat zones, they face dangers that only men faced previously. Navy women were among those detained by China in 2001 after the incident in which a damaged U.S. Navy patrol plane was forced to land in Chinese territory. Two women sailors were among those killed during the terrorist attack on USS *Cole* in 2000, and a woman Marine in an aircrew was the first American female casualty of the war in Afghanistan.

While every Department of Defense service has had one woman serving at the three-star level (lieutenant general/vice admiral), the senior woman on active duty at the start of 2002 is a Navy vice admiral. She was the first woman to be promoted to three-star rank in any service and remains the most senior woman ever to serve on active duty.

In spite of women's gains in the military, however, it remains the only profession in this country in which discrimination based on sex is mandated. Women are banned by national policy from serving in certain units and occupations for no other reason than that they are female. They may not serve in occupations or units whose principal mission is ground combat—these include infantry, armor, most field artillery, and special forces, such as SEALS and rangers. Women also are barred from serving aboard submarines—except in the case of short cruises for training or other temporary duty—because of privacy considerations.

Men, on the other hand, have to register for the draft while women do not. The most recent test of the male-only draft before the Supreme Court occurred in 1981 in *Rostker v. Goldberg*, when the constitutionality of excluding women was upheld. Since that time, many more military units and occupations have opened to women. Given these circumstances, one question that requires more debate is whether men and women should have different responsibilities as citizens with respect to military service. Findings include:

- Women currently constitute nearly 15 percent of U.S. service personnel, but they are not spread evenly through the services or the ranks. The Marine Corps has the smallest percentage of women and the Air Force, the largest (see Table 7-1).
- As of the beginning of 2002, minority women—the majority of them black—accounted for roughly half of all female enlisted personnel in the Department of Defense services overall (the comparable percentage for men was less than one-third). In the Army, where nearly 74,000 women serve, over 46 percent of enlisted women and over 23 percent of women officers are black (see Table 7-1).
- All occupations and positions in the Coast Guard are open to women, as are 99 percent of those in the Air Force. Ninety-six percent of Navy occupations and 91 percent of Navy positions are open to women. However, although most Army and Marine Corps occupations are open to women, a third of Army positions and nearly two-fifths of Marine Corps positions are closed to them (see Figure 7-3).
- Military women (like civilian women workers) are more concentrated than men in a few occupations—for example, administration and

health care occupations account for about half of the women, compared with less than 20 percent of the men. However, since many more occupations and positions are open to women coming into the services now than was the case before 1993/1994, this could change over time (see Figure 7-4).

Table 7-1 • Active-Duty Servicewomen by Branch of Service, Rank, Race, and Hispanic Origin, September 30, 2001

As of September 30, 2001, women in the military (including the Coast Guard) numbered 207,340—14.8 percent of the total active force. The Air Force has the highest percentage of women, the Marine Corps the lowest. The Army has the highest percentage of black women; the Marine Corps has the highest percentage of women of Hispanic origin. The Navy and the Coast Guard have higher percentages of women officers than of enlisted women; the reverse is true of the other services.

Service and Rank[1]	Number of Women	Women as a Percentage of Total Personnel	Percent Distribution of Women[2]			
			White	Black	Hispanic	Other
Total DOD forces[3]						
Enlisted	171,865	14.9	48.0	35.3	9.3	7.4
Officers	31,824	14.7	71.7	16.0	3.9	8.4
Army						
Enlisted	62,827	15.7	36.9	46.5	9.4	7.2
Officers	11,038	14.5	64.0	23.2	4.7	8.1
Navy						
Enlisted	44,630	14.0	47.9	31.6	11.7	8.8
Officers	7,981	14.9	75.4	11.3	4.9	8.4
Marine Corps						
Enlisted	9,552	6.2	54.0	22.8	16.8	6.4
Officers	978	5.4	74.0	12.9	6.7	6.4
Air Force						
Enlisted	54,856	19.6	59.7	27.7	6.2	6.4
Officers	11,805	17.3	76.2	12.6	2.3	8.9
Coast Guard						
Enlisted	2,864	10.2	75.4	11.5	7.2	5.9
Officers	787	11.3	80.2	7.2	5.6	7.0

[1]Officers include warrant officers.
[2]Percentages may not total 100.0 due to rounding.
[3]Defense Department (DOD) forces do not include the Coast Guard, which, in peacetime, is part of the Department of Transportation.

Source: U.S. Department of Defense, Defense Manpower Data Center, unpublished data, September 30, 2001.

Figure 7-1 • Active-Duty Servicewomen in the Department of Defense Services by Officer/Enlisted Status, 1972–2001 (in percentages)[1]

Since 1972, the year before the beginning of the all-volunteer force, the percentage of women in the enlisted ranks has grown almost ninefold and in the officer ranks has more than tripled.

Percentage

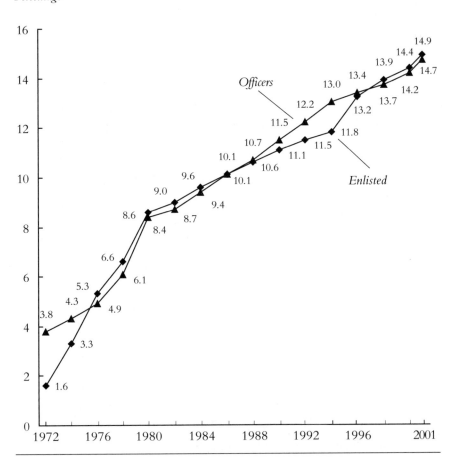

[1]Does not include the Coast Guard, which, in peacetime, is part of the Department of Transportation.

Source: U.S. Department of Defense, Defense Manpower Data Center, unpublished data, August 1997, May 31, 1999, March 31, 2000, and September 30, 2001.

Figure 7-2 • Women in Senior Enlisted and Officer Pay Grades by Branch of Service, Selected Years, 1972–2001 (in percentages)

A key measure of women's status in the military is their growing seniority. These charts depict women as a percentage of the three senior enlisted pay grades and as a percentage of pay grade O6 (colonel or Navy captain). (More women are also now reaching the flag and general officer ranks—as of September 2001, there were 33 women generals and admirals on active duty in the Department of Defense services.)

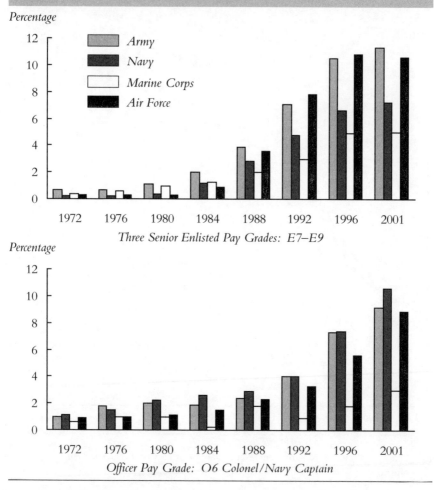

Three Senior Enlisted Pay Grades: E7–E9

Officer Pay Grade: O6 Colonel/Navy Captain

Source: U.S. Department of Defense, Defense Manpower Data Center, unpublished data, August 1997 and September 30, 2001.

Table 7-2 • Active-Duty Servicewomen by Pay Grade Grouping and Branch of Service, September 30, 2001[1]

Women are gaining seniority in both officer and enlisted pay grades. It takes 20 years to reach the more senior ranks, so the percentages of women among senior officer and enlisted personnel are roughly equivalent to the percentages of women in the junior officer and enlisted ranks in the early 1980s. For an idea of women's future representation in the senior ranks, look at the percentage of women in the junior ranks now: these range from around six percent of junior enlisted Marines to between 20 and 24 percent of junior Air Force officers and enlisted personnel.

Service and Pay Grade Grouping	Number of Women	Women as a Percentage of Total Personnel in Pay Grade
Army		
Officers, total	11,038	14.5
General (O7–O10)	11	3.5
Senior (O6)	330	9.2
Midgrade (O4–O5)	3,031	13.4
Junior (O1–O3, W1–W5)	7,666	15.5
Enlisted, total	62,827	15.7
Senior (E7–E9)	5,556	11.3
Midgrade (E5–E6)	17,517	14.1
Junior (E1–E4)	39,754	17.5
Navy		
Officers, total	7,981	14.9
Flag (O7–O10)	11	5.1
Senior (O6)	352	10.6
Midgrade (O4–O5)	2,519	14.6
Junior (O1–O3, W1–W5)	5,099	15.5
Enlisted, total	44,630	14.0
Senior (E7–E9)	2,431	7.2
Midgrade (E5–E6)	13,500	10.7
Junior (E1–E4)	28,699	18.1

See footnote at end of table.

(continued)

Table 7-2 (continued)

Service and Pay Grade Grouping	Number of Women	Women as a Percentage of Total Personnel in Pay Grade
Marine Corps		
Officers, total	978	5.4
General (O7–O10)	1	1.2
Senior (O6)	19	3.0
Midgrade (O4–O5)	135	2.6
Junior (O1–O3, W1–W5)	823	6.8
Enlisted, total	9,552	6.2
Senior (E7–E9)	672	5.0
Midgrade (E5–E6)	2,147	5.9
Junior (E1–E4)	6,733	6.4
Air Force		
Officers, total	11,805	17.3
General (O7–O10)	10	3.7
Senior (O6)	329	8.9
Midgrade (O4–O5)	3,561	14.2
Junior (O1–O3, W1–W5)	7,905	20.3
Enlisted, total	54,856	19.6
Senior (E7–E9)	3,997	10.6
Midgrade (E5–E6)	18,541	16.5
Junior (E1–E4)	32,318	24.8
Coast Guard		
Officers, total	787	11.3
Flag (O7–O10)	2	6.1
Senior (O6)	10	3.1
Midgrade (O4–O5)	153	8.2
Junior (O1–O3, W1–W5)	622	13.0
Enlisted, total	2,864	10.2
Senior (E7–E9)	270	7.5
Midgrade (E5–E6)	1,064	9.5
Junior (E1–E4)	1,530	11.6

[1]Excludes women selected for, but not yet actually serving in, each pay grade grouping as of September 30, 2001.

Source: U.S. Department of Defense, Defense Manpower Data Center, unpublished data, September 30, 2001.

Table 7-3 • Women as a Percentage of Personnel in Each Military Pay Grade, Department of Defense Services (DOD), September 30, 2001

Women, just under 15 percent of the total armed forces, constitute a smaller share of personnel in the senior pay grades than in the more junior ones. Women's presence in the senior ranks today reflects women's overall presence in the armed services 15 to 20 years ago (see Table 7-2).

Pay Grade	Total DOD[1]	Army	Navy	Marine Corps	Air Force
Officers					
O7–O10	3.6	3.5	5.1	1.2	3.7
O6	9.2	9.2	10.6	3.0	8.9
O5	12.4	12.9	13.4	3.0	12.9
O4	13.7	13.8	15.4	2.4	15.0
O3	16.4	16.0	15.6	5.2	19.7
O2	18.4	20.4	16.0	7.8	21.8
O1	18.5	20.2	17.1	9.2	20.6
W5	2.0	11.3	(2)	6.3	(3)
W4	3.0	3.3	10.7	4.3	(3)
W3	5.4	5.2	4.5	7.2	(3)
W2	8.8	9.6	6.8	6.2	(3)
W1	7.2	7.3	(2)	6.6	(3)
Enlisted					
E9	7.1	7.7	4.4	2.9	11.7
E8	9.5	11.1	6.9	5.9	11.8
E7	9.7	11.7	7.7	5.0	10.3
E6	10.5	12.1	8.5	5.2	12.5
E5	14.7	15.6	12.4	6.2	19.0
E4	17.6	17.1	17.4	6.9	24.5
E3	17.7	18.1	20.6	6.5	24.1
E2	17.2	18.2	17.3	6.6	32.0
E1	15.5	16.9	15.3	4.8	22.4

[1]Does not include the Coast Guard, which, in peacetime, is part of the Department of Transportation.
[2]Navy personnel who are warrant officers serve in pay grades W2, W3, and W4 only.
[3]The Air Force has no personnel in the warrant officer ranks.

Source: U.S. Department of Defense, Defense Manpower Data Center, unpublished data, September 30, 2001.

Figure 7-3 • Positions and Occupations Currently Open to Active-Duty Women by Branch of Service, 2001 (in percentages)

With the exception of a few Navy positions on minesweepers that were opened to women in the late 1990s, the positions and occupations available to military women have not changed since 1994. The term "position" refers to a particular job in a given unit. For example, the occupation of hospital corpsman is open to Navy women, but the position of hospital corpsman aboard a submarine is closed to them. The occupations and units closed to women are those whose primary mission is ground combat, i.e., infantry, armor, special forces/SEALs, and most artillery. Women also may not serve as permanent members of submarine crews because of close living quarters.

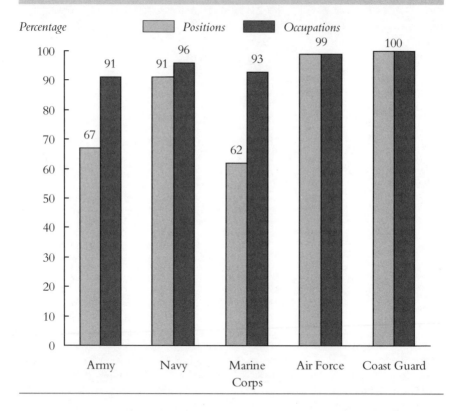

Source: U.S. Department of Defense, Office of the Assistant Secretary of Defense for Public Affairs, Public Affairs News Release no. 449–94, July 29, 1994, and Office of the Chief of Naval Operations, 1999.

Figure 7-4 • Occupational Profile of Active-Duty Enlisted Personnel in the Department of Defense Services by Sex, 2001 (percent distributions)[1,2]

Most midgrade and senior women currently on active duty entered military service before the 1993/1994 changes to the combat restriction laws, which opened new occupations and positions to them. That explains to some extent the disproportionate numbers of women in health care and administration. It will be interesting to see if these proportions change now that women entering military service have more options.

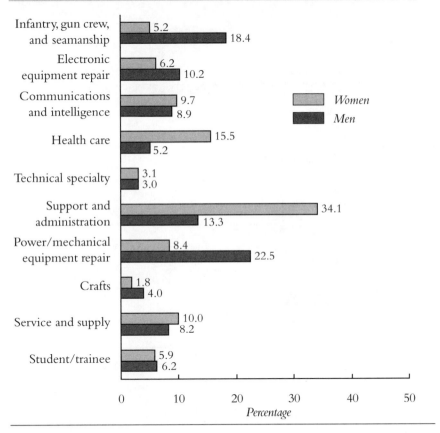

[1]Does not include the Coast Guard, which, in peacetime, is part of the Department of Transportation.
[2]Percentages may not total 100.0 due to rounding.

Source: U.S. Department of Defense, Defense Manpower Data Center, unpublished data, September 30, 2001.

Figure 7-5 • Occupational Profile of Active-Duty Officers in the Department of Defense Services by Sex, 2001 (percent distributions)[1,2]

The changes in the combat exclusion laws in the early to mid-1990s opened air combat and most sea combat positions to women officers. However, submarine, infantry, armor, most field artillery, and special forces positions remain closed to women. Thus, women in the Navy and Air Force can now enter most of their services' key war-fighting occupations, whereas aviation combat positions are the only war-fighting occupations open to women in the Army and Marine Corps.

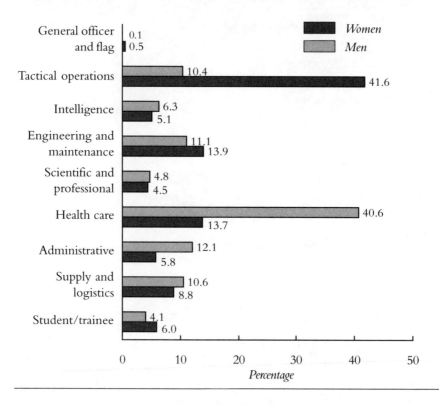

[1]Does not include the Coast Guard, which, in peacetime, is part of the Department of Transportation.

[2]Percentages may not total 100.0 due to rounding.

Source: U.S. Department of Defense, Defense Manpower Data Center, unpublished data, September 30, 2001.

Table 7-4 • Women Graduates of U.S. Service Academies, 1980, 1990, and 2001

Women first graduated from the service academies in 1980, and the percentage of women among graduates of all the academies has generally continued to increase since then.[1] A possible explanation for the acceleration of the increases at the Air Force, Military, and Naval academies between 1990 and 2001 is the repeal of many of the combat exclusion laws that had barred women from war-fighting roles (see Figure 7-5). At these institutions, slots for potential officers who would be prohibited from combat occupations were limited.

Service Academy	Women as a Percentage of Graduates			Number of Women in Class of 2001
	Class of 1980	Class of 1990	Class of 2001	
Air Force	10.9	10.4	17.8	154
Coast Guard	9.2	12.6	25.4	42
Military (West Point)	6.8	9.8	15.9	143
Naval Academy	5.8	9.7	16.6	153

[1]Readers who compare this table with its equivalent in the 2001–2002 edition of *The American Woman* may notice a drop since 1999 in the percentage (although not the number) of women in the Coast Guard Academy's graduating class. This probably does not harbinger a leveling-off in the representation of women at the service academies, since the Coast Guard Academy's classes are so small that the effect of a very small change is magnified.

Sources: Department of Defense, unpublished data provided by U.S. Air Force Academy, U.S. Military Academy, and U.S. Naval Academy, June 1993 and February 2002; and Department of Transportation, unpublished data provided by the Coast Guard Academy, June 1993 and February 2002.

Figure 7-6 • Female and Male Veterans by Age, 2001

The population of veterans in the United States is in the midst of a major shift in age distribution. For many years, a large proportion of male veterans and the overwhelming majority of female veterans were World War II–era veterans, who are (or would be) well over 65 by now. Their predominance has diminished: today, only about 37 percent of male veterans and 13 percent of female veterans are age 65 and over. The great majority of women veterans today are between 25 and 55 years old, and the ratios of females to males among veterans in the age groups under 45 are much larger than among the older veterans.

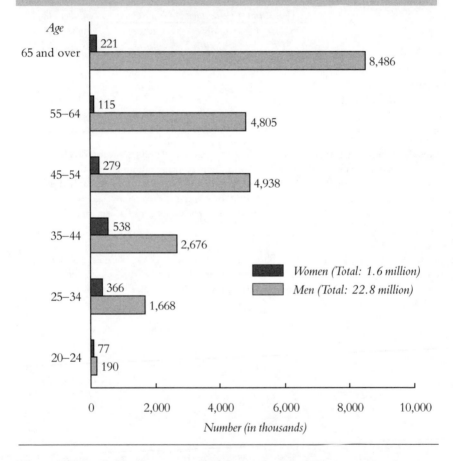

Source: Bureau of Labor Statistics, unpublished data from the 2001 Current Population Survey (annual averages).

Figure 7-7 • Female and Male Veterans by Race, 2001 (percent distributions)[1,2]

Nearly a fifth of female veterans are black, a proportion nearly double that of male veterans (and significantly larger than in the U.S. population as a whole). Asian/Pacific Islanders or Native Americans account for only very small percentages of the veteran population of either sex, although the percentage is a tad larger among the women veterans (3.1 percent versus 2.0 percent). The substantial representation of blacks and other minority women among today's active-duty military women (see Table 7-1) indicates that in the coming years, minority women, especially black women, will account for increasingly large percentages of women veterans (minority representation will increase among male veterans, as well).

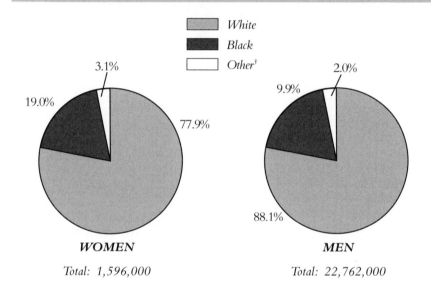

WOMEN

Total: 1,596,000

MEN

Total: 22,762,000

[1]People age 20 years and over.
[2]Current Population Survey data showing female and male veterans by both race and Hispanic origin *or* non-Hispanic origin are not available. This should be borne in mind when comparing the breakdowns of minorities in this figure with the breakdowns in Table 7-1, where Department of Defense data are used. Unlike the Census Bureau, the DOD counts Hispanics as a separate category that does not overlap race.
[3]Includes Asian/Pacific Islanders and Native Americans, not shown separately (data not available).

Source: Bureau of Labor Statistics, unpublished data from the 2001 Current Population Survey (annual averages).

Section 8

ELECTIONS AND OFFICIALS

NEARLY EIGHT MILLION MORE WOMEN than men voted in the presidential election of 2000, the tenth consecutive four-year election in which women outnumbered men at the polls. Women's predominance in the electorate may not be surprising, since women outnumber men in the U.S. population. However, not only are the majority of U.S. voters female, but women are more likely than men to vote.

This fact, added to the sheer size of the female electorate, makes *how* women vote matter to the major parties and their presidential candidates. The findings from exit polls that are presented in this section provide clear evidence that, for years, there has been a gender gap when it comes to voting preferences. Since at least 1980, the typical male voter has been less likely than his female counterpart to vote for Democratic candidates—whether presidential or congressional. However, Democrats have by no means always won on a majority or plurality of women's votes. And even in 2000, when the considerable majority of women voting for Mr. Gore helped give him a majority of the popular vote nationwide, he did not win a majority in the Electoral College.

Women's more-than-equal participation in the electoral process is not reflected in their representation among the elected. Only among elected statewide executive officials (a group that includes, e.g., secretaries of state, treasurers, and governors) has the female percentage reached 25 percent. Findings include:

- In all of the last six presidential elections, a larger percentage of female voters than of male voters voted for the Democratic candidate. Only in the last three, however, did more women cast their votes for the Democratic candidate than for the Republican candidate (see Figure 8-1).

- The gender gap was widest in the presidential elections of 1996 and 2000, when a clear majority of female voters voted for the Democratic candidate. Only a minority of male voters voted Democratic in any of the last six presidential elections (see Figure 8-2).

- It was among college graduates that the difference between women and men in party preference—the gender gap—was consistently widest (see Table 8-2).

- Just as women have been consistently less likely than men to vote for Republican presidential candidates, they have been consistently less likely than men to vote for Republican candidates for the House of Representatives. In none of the election years between 1980 and 2000 did a majority of women *nationwide* vote for Republican congressional candidates (see Figure 8-3).

- Women's representation in Congress, state houses, and city halls has generally increased over the years since 1981, but the pace has been slow (see Table 8-3).

- Eleven women have leadership posts in the second session of the 107th Congress, although only one—House Minority Whip Nancy Pelosi—is in her party's very top leadership. However, the women who chair the Democratic campaign committees have a vital role to play in the future success of their party's candidates (see Table 8-4; see also "Women in the 107th Congress").

- More than twice as many women held federal judgeships in fiscal year (FY) 2000 as in FY 1990. Over that period, women's share of federal judgeships increased significantly at every level and more than doubled at the appellate level. In FY 2000, minority women were fairly well represented among district court judges and magistrates (see Table 8-5).

- In 2001, more than a quarter of the judges on state courts of last resort were women, and all but two states had at least one woman judge at this level. In the courts of last resort of 15 states and the District of Columbia, the chief justices were female (see Table 8-6).

Table 8-1 • Voter Participation in National Elections in Presidential Election Years by Sex, 1964–2000

In 2000, as in every presidential election year since 1980, women not only outnumbered men at the polls but were more likely than men to go to the polls—that is, women's representation among voters was larger than their representation in the U.S. population of voting age.[1]

	People Who Reported Voting as a Percentage of the Entire Voting-Age Population		Number Who Reported Voting (in thousands)	
	Women	*Men*	*Women*	*Men*
1964	67.0	71.9	39,183	37,476
1968	66.0	69.8	40,967	38,016
1972	62.0	64.1	44,869	40,917
1976	58.8	59.6	45,624	41,098
1980	59.4	59.1	49,304	43,782
1984	60.8	59.0	54,499	47,393
1988	58.3	56.4	54,550	47,675
1992	62.3	60.2	60,509	53,311
1996	55.5	52.8	56,066	48,910
2000	56.2	53.1	59,284	51,542

[1]Looking at participation in the 2000 election by U.S. citizens of voting age (as opposed to the entire population of voting age, which includes noncitizens), the Census Bureau found a considerably smaller gender difference: 60.7 percent of the women voted, compared with 58.1 percent of the men.

Source: Census Bureau, *Historical Time Series Tables,* Table 5, <http://www.census.gov/population/www/socdemo/voting.html>.

Figure 8-1 • How People Reported Voting in Presidential Elections by Sex, 1980–2000 (percent distributions)[1,2]

In all of the last six presidential elections, a larger percentage of female voters (F) than of male voters (M) voted for the Democratic candidate. Only in the last three, however, did more women cast their votes for the Democratic candidate than for the Republican candidate.

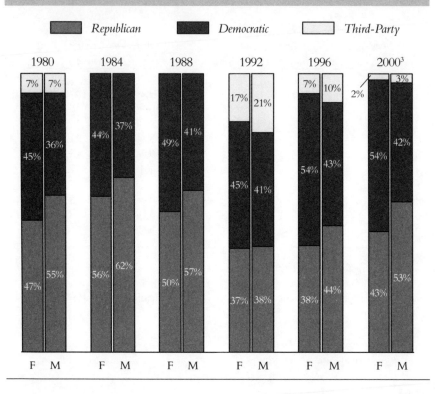

Republican   Democratic   Third-Party

| 1980 | 1984 | 1988 | 1992 | 1996 | 2000[3] |

[1]1980: Reagan (R), Carter (D), Anderson; 1984: Reagan (R), Mondale (D); 1988: Bush (R), Dukakis (D); 1992: Clinton (D), Bush (R), Perot; 1996: Clinton (D), Dole (R), Perot; 2000: Bush (R), Gore (D), Nader.

[2]Percentages may not total 100.0 due to rounding.

[3]Shown here is the breakdown of the popular vote nationwide, which Gore won.

Source: The New York Times Company, "Who Voted: A Portrait of American Politics, 1976–2000," *The New York Times on the Web*, 2001, <http://www.nytimes.com/2000/11/12/politics/12CONN.html>.

Figure 8-2 • People Who Reported Voting for the Democratic Party Candidate in Presidential Elections by Sex, 1980–2000 (in percentages)

The voting gender gap was widest in the presidential elections of 1996 and 2000, when a clear majority of female voters voted for the Democratic candidate.[1] Only a minority of male voters voted Democratic in any of the presidential elections shown here (see also Figure 8-1).

Percentage

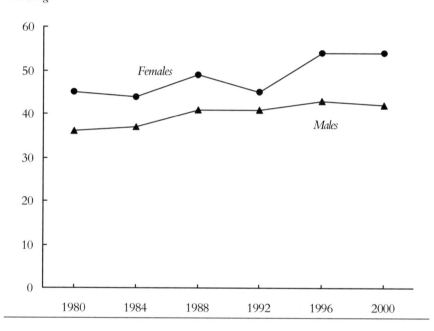

[1]The difference in the likelihood to vote for the Democratic candidate gives the clearest picture over time of the gender gap in these presidential elections. This is because, in 1992 and 1996, the picture was complicated by a third-party candidate who apparently drew more votes from people who would otherwise have voted Republican than from people who would otherwise have voted Democratic.

Source: The New York Times Company, "Who Voted: A Portrait of American Politics, 1976–2000," *The New York Times on the Web*, 2001, <http://www.nytimes.com/2000/11/12/politics/12CONN.html>.

Table 8-2 • People Who Reported Voting Republican (R) or Democratic (D) in Presidential Elections by Educational Attainment and Sex, 1980–2000 (in percentages)[1]

Among voters of all educational levels, a degree of gender difference was evident in most of the presidential elections from 1980 onward. However, it was among college graduates that the difference between women and men in party preference—the gender gap—was consistently widest. (In the election of 2000, college graduates—equally divided by sex—accounted for 42 percent of the voters sampled; non–high school graduates for only four percent.)

	1980		1984		1988		1992		1996		2000	
	R	D	R	D	R	D	R	D	R	D	R	D
Not high school graduates												
Women	41	56	46	52	38	62	27	57	26	63	37	60
Men	51	47	52	47	49	50	38	48	30	56	41	57
High school graduates												
Women	50	44	58	41	50	50	38	43	34	56	45	52
Men	53	42	62	37	50	49	33	43	36	46	55	43
Some college												
Women	52	39	58	41	54	45	39	42	38	53	48	50
Men	59	31	65	33	60	38	37	40	44	42	56	40
College graduates[2]												
Women	42	44	52	47	49	51	36	48	39	53	40	57
Men	59	28	63	36	63	36	42	40	49	41	57	39

[1]The difference in the likelihood to vote for the Democratic candidate gives the clearest picture over time of the gender gap in these presidential elections. This is because, in 1992 and 1996, the picture was complicated by a third-party candidate who apparently drew more votes from people who would otherwise have voted Republican than from people who would otherwise have voted Democratic.

[2]Includes those with postgraduate education.

Source: The New York Times Company, "Who Voted: A Portrait of American Politics, 1976–2000," *The New York Times on the Web*, 2001, <http://www.nytimes.com/2000/11/12/politics/12CONN.html>.

Figure 8-3 • People Who Reported Voting for the Republican Candidate in Elections for the U.S. House of Representatives by Sex, 1980–2000 (in percentages)

Just as women are consistently less likely than men to vote for Republican presidential candidates, they are consistently less likely than men to vote for Republican candidates for the House of Representatives. In fact, in none of the election years shown here did a majority of women *nationwide* vote for Republican congressional candidates. (This is not to say, however, that Republican candidates failed to gain a majority among the women voters in particular congressional districts.)

Percentage

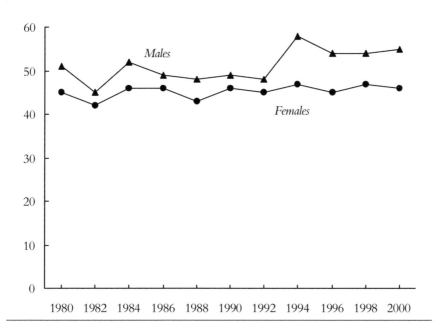

Sources: The New York Times Company, "A Look at Voting Patterns of 115 Demographic Groups in House Races," *The New York Times on the Web*, 1998, <http://www.nytimes.com/library/politics/camp/110998voter3.html>, and unpublished data from Voter News Service 2000 exit poll.

Table 8-3 • Women in Elective Office, Selected Years, 1981–2001

Women's representation in Congress, state houses, and city halls has generally increased since 1981, but the pace has been slow. Of late, it appears to have stalled among statewide executive officials and state legislators and to have faltered among mayors.

Elected Officeholders	Women as a Percentage of All Officeholders											Number of Women
	1981	1983	1985	1987	1989	1991	1993	1995	1997	1999	2001	2001
Members of Congress	4.3	4.5	4.7	4.7	5.8	6.0	10.1	10.7	11.8[1]	12.1	13.6	73
House[2]	4.8	5.1	5.3	5.3	6.7	6.4	10.8	11.0	12.4[1]	12.9	13.8	60
Senate	2.0	2.0	2.0	2.0	2.0	4.0	7.0	9.0	9.0	9.0	13.0	13
Statewide executive officials[3]	10.5	10.5	13.3	13.9	14.3	18.2	22.2	25.9	25.4	27.6	27.4	88
Governors[4]	[5]	[5]	4.0	6.0	6.0	6.0	6.0	2.0	4.0	6.0	10.0	5
State legislators	12.1	13.3	14.8	15.7	17.0	18.3	20.5	20.6	21.6	22.3	22.4	1,666
Mayors of 100 largest cities	[5]	[5]	7.0	11.0	17.0	19.0	19.0	17.0	12.0	16.0	13.0	13

[1]105th Congress. Excludes Susan Molinari, who resigned in mid-1997. Includes four women elected to the House in special elections in 1998.
[2]Excludes nonvoting delegates. As of December 2001, there were two women delegates.
[3]Includes some women filling elective positions by appointment or constitutional succession. Excludes officials elected to executive posts by state legislatures, judges, and elected members of university boards of trustees and boards of education.
[4]As of June of each year.
[5]Data are not available.

Sources: Center for American Women and Politics (CAWP), *Women in the U.S. Congress, 1917–1999,* January 1999, *Statewide Elective Executive Women: 1969–1999,* February 1999, *Women in State Legislatures 1999,* May 1999, *Women in Elective Office 1999,* August 1999, *Statewide Elective Executive Women 1999,* September 1999, and *Women in Elective Office 2001,* December 2001.

Table 8-4 • Women in the Leadership of the U.S. Senate and House of Representatives, 107th Congress, Second Session

Eleven women have leadership posts in the second session of the 107th Congress, although only one is in her party's very top leadership.[1] However, the women who chair the Democratic campaign committees have a vital role to play in the future success of their party's candidates for the House and Senate (see also "Women in the 107th Congress").

Position	Member
Senate Majority (Democratic)	
Secretary, Democratic Conference	Barbara Mikulski (MD)
Chief Deputy for Strategic Outreach	Barbara Boxer (CA)
Chair, Democratic Senate Campaign	
Committee	Patty Murray (WA)
Senate Minority (Republican)	
Vice Chairman, Republican Conference	Kay Bailey Hutchison (TX)
Deputy Minority Whip	Susan Collins (ME)
House Majority (Republican)	
Vice Chair, Republican Conference	Deborah Pryce (OH)
Secretary, Republican Conference	Barbara Cubin (WY)
House Minority (Democratic)	
Minority Whip	Nancy Pelosi (CA)
Assistant to the Minority Leader	Rosa DeLauro (CT)
Deputy Minority Whip	Maxine Waters (CA)
Chair, Democratic Congressional	
Campaign Committee	Nita Lowey (NY)

[1]The very top leadership positions in the House are Speaker, Majority Leader, and Majority Whip, and Minority Leader and Minority Whip. The very top leadership positions in the Senate are Majority Leader and Assistant Majority Leader and Minority Leader and Assistant Minority Leader.

Source: Center for American Women and Politics (CAWP), *Women in Congress: Leadership Roles and Committee Chairs,* February 2002.

Table 8-5 • Women in the Federal Judiciary, Fiscal Years 1990 and 2000[1]

More than twice as many women held federal judgeships in FY 2000 as in FY 1990. Over that period, women's share of federal judgeships increased significantly at every level and more than doubled at the appellate level. In FY 2000, minority women were fairly well represented among district court judges (23 of 125) and magistrates (17 of 109).

	Fiscal Year 1990		*Fiscal Year 2000*		
	Women		*Women*		
	Total Number	*Percentage*	*Total Number*	*Percentage*	*Minority[2] (number)*
Supreme Court	1	11.1	2	22.2	0
Appellate courts[3]	18	11.3	35	24.3	4
District courts[4]	51	9.2	125	17.2	23
Bankruptcy courts	38	12.8	65	19.4	3
Court of Claims	(5)	—	5	26.7	1
U.S. magistrates (full-time)	58	18.8	109	24.6	17

[1]October 1, 1989 through September 30, 1990, and October 1, 1999 through September 30, 2000, respectively.
[2]Data not available for fiscal year 1990.
[3] "Circuit courts" in fiscal year 1990, when category also included the Temporary Emergency Court of Appeals.
[4]For fiscal years 1990 and 2000, included territorial courts and the Court of International Trade. For fiscal year 1990, also included the Court of Claims, the Special Court, Regional Rail Reorganization Act of 1973, and the Judicial Panel on Multidistrict Litigation.
[5]For fiscal year 1990, included in "District courts" category.

Sources: Administrative Office of the United States Courts, *Annual Report on the Judiciary Equal Employment Opportunity Program for the Twelve-Month Period Ended September 30, 1990,* n.d., Table 1, and *The Judiciary Fair Employment Practices Annual Report, October 1, 1999 through September 30, 2000, Conference Edition,* n.d., Table B–1.

Table 8-6 • Women Justices and Judges on State Courts of Last Resort and Intermediate Appellate Courts, 2001[1]

> In 2001, more than a quarter of the judges on state courts of last resort were women, and all but two states had at least one woman judge at this level. On the courts of last resort of 15 states and the District of Columbia, the chief justice was female.

	Women		*States with One or More Women on Court*
	Number	*Percentage*	
Courts of last resort	90	26.5	49[2]
Chief justices[3]	16	31.4	—
Intermediate appellate courts	218	(4)	37[5]
Chief judges	12	(4)	—

[1] "States" include the District of Columbia.
[2] No women served on the courts of last resort of Indiana and South Dakota.
[3] The title is "chief judge" in New York State and the District of Columbia.
[4] Data were not available.
[5] Twelve states have no intermediate appellate courts.

Source: National Center for State Courts, unpublished data, January 31, 2002.

WOMEN IN CONGRESS

THE CONGRESSIONAL CAUCUS FOR WOMEN'S ISSUES AT 25: CHALLENGES AND OPPORTUNITIES*

Cynthia A. Hall

INTRODUCTION

FOUNDED IN 1977, the Congressional Caucus for Women's Issues turns 25 in 2002. Its members, both past and present, have much to celebrate. Over the past quarter-century, the caucus has led a number of successful efforts to achieve economic, educational, and health equity for women. Some of its most significant legislative achievements have come after many years of work, while other smaller, incremental changes also have led to progress in a number of areas.

The caucus's biggest success may well be the continued existence of the organization itself—a bipartisan, diverse group of women members of the House of Representatives reflecting the full political spectrum but joined together in a shared commitment to improving the lives of women and their families. Indeed, concerns have been raised periodically about whether there was a need for a bipartisan caucus; each and every time, the membership agreed that it was important to continue their work together.

Over the past decade, the caucus has undergone significant changes in its organizational and leadership structure, with the loss of its staff and office space on the Hill in 1995 posing its greatest challenge. These changes have occurred against the backdrop of a greatly expanded membership and

---

*The author would like to thank Mary Anne Leary, who provided invaluable editorial assistance, and Jennifer Lockwood-Shabat and Alicia Bond, who read and suggested several helpful changes as this essay was prepared for publication.

a dramatically altered political environment. As a result of these dynamics, the caucus is not the same organization it was 10 years ago.

ORGANIZATIONAL CHANGES OVER THE PAST DECADE

When it was founded in 1977 during the 95th Congress, the caucus's membership included 15 of the 18 women then in the House of Representatives. It was led by cochairs Elizabeth Holtzman (D-NY) and Margaret Heckler (R-MA).

Early caucus priorities included eliminating sex discrimination and expanding employment opportunities for women in the federal workforce. As the caucus grew in the late 1980s and early 1990s under the leadership of cochairs Pat Schroeder (D-CO) and Olympia Snowe (R-ME) (who was elected to the Senate in 1994), its priorities expanded to include women's health, child care, family and medical leave, and violence against women. During the tenure of Representatives Schroeder and Snowe, Congress approved the Family and Medical Leave Act, the Violence Against Women Act, child care legislation, and significant advances in women's health research funding (Women's Policy, Inc. 1997).

The influx of newly elected women in the 103rd Congress (1993–1994) increased the number of women in the House to 47 (48 including a delegate). With 24 new women members, the number of women assigned to congressional committees rose sharply, providing new opportunities for the caucus to expand its influence (Gertzog 1995). Because the caucus was now much larger, it established task forces to better focus the energies of its members. It also became clear that many members were ready for a change in leadership. To address that issue, a new task force was charged with revising the caucus bylaws, which would lead to a reorganization of the caucus leadership (Gertzog 1995; Primmer 1998).

TERM LIMITS FOR COCHAIRS

Representative Maxine Waters (D-CA) chaired the bylaws task force. During task force meetings, she and other members made a compelling case for term limits for the cochairs. This led to the 1994 approval of new bylaws limiting cochairs to one consecutive two-year term and establishing vice chair positions (Gertzog 1995). In 1995, new cochairs were elected for the first time in more than a decade, with Representatives Connie Morella (R-MD) and Nita Lowey (D-NY) elected to lead the caucus during the 104th Congress (1995–1996). Representative Nancy Johnson (R-CT) and Delegate Eleanor Holmes Norton (D-DC) were chosen to serve as vice chairs.

They went on to serve as caucus cochairs in the 105th Congress, thus establishing a fairly consistent pattern for successive Congresses—that of the vice chair using her position as a springboard to the cochair position.

Since the bylaw changes in 1994, the caucus has had eight cochairs, compared with only four in the preceding 18 years. The larger number of women in caucus leadership positions over the past decade has meant broader participation and personal investment in the caucus. At the same time, the frequent leadership changes have made it more difficult to develop and implement the caucus agenda.

RULES CHANGES FOR CAUCUS GROUPS

Representatives Morella and Lowey began their service in the 104th Congress in a very changed and charged atmosphere that would substantially alter the very character of the caucus. In the 1994 election, the Republicans had gained control of the House for the first time in 40 years and were determined to take immediate action to reduce the size and cost of government. On the first day of the 104th Congress, the House approved a rules package that included the elimination of all legislative service organizations (LSOs), the official term used to describe the many caucus organizations. While caucus groups could continue, they had to reorganize as "congressional member organizations" (CMOs), with no separate office space, staff, or membership dues, and no public funding. (The opponents of the LSOs also expressed a desire to reduce funding for House legislative operations. At the same time that the LSOs were eliminated, the House reduced the number of committee staff by one-third.)

The decision to eliminate the LSOs was the culmination of a long-term effort led by then-Representative Pat Roberts (R-KA) (he was elected to the Senate in 1996). The LSO opponents pointed to the expanded number of LSOs, the mismanagement of public funding by some of the organizations, the amount of office space sacrificed to accommodate them, and LSOs' duplication of and encroachment on the functions of committees. Caucus supporters argued—as they had during the years of House debate over LSOs—that the Congressional Caucus for Women's Issues was a model organization and that the effort to eliminate LSOs should be narrowed to curtail the operations of poorly managed groups only. (In fact, the chief proponent of the rule change had noted earlier that if every LSO were managed like the women's caucus, there would be no need for the change.) In addition, because LSOs were supported by dues paid from members' official expenses, no actual cost savings were achieved by their elimination (Primmer 1998).

Nevertheless, the House approved the elimination of the LSOs in early January 1995. The caucus office in the Rayburn House Office Building and its paid staff of five employees were gone by February. The personal office staff of cochairs Morella and Lowey were left to pick up most caucus functions, in addition to their normal congressional workloads.

With support of the cochairs, Lesley Primmer Persily, who had been the caucus's staff director, along with Marjorie Sims, its senior legislative assistant, and Dr. Susan Wood, its deputy director, formed a new nonprofit organization, Women's Policy, Inc. (WPI), to provide legislative analysis and information services on congressional action affecting women and families (Women's Policy, Inc. 1997). The new organization began to publish a weekly news report, *The Source*—similar to the *Update on Women and Family Issues in Congress*, the former caucus report on congressional action affecting women—and to sponsor briefings and other educational events on topics of interest to the caucus membership. WPI filled the information deficit created by the end of the LSOs.

However, in keeping with the new House rules and later Ethics Committee interpretations of those rules, WPI had to remain independent of the caucus. The caucus cochairs and their personal staff were left with the primary responsibility for the development and implementation of the caucus agenda for each Congress. The caucus transition from LSO to CMO was a very difficult one, made more so by the partisan rancor that marked the 104th Congress (1995–1996).

ABORTION AS AN ISSUE

During the caucus's first 15 years, abortion was not considered part of the caucus agenda out of deference to several caucus members who were opposed to abortion. However, in 1992, after most of those members had left Congress, the caucus voted to become a pro-choice caucus (Gertzog 1995).

Abortion issues quickly became a caucus priority, particularly during the contentious years of the 104th Congress, when they dominated both the congressional and the caucus agenda. Representatives Morella and Lowey spent the majority of their tenure leading the caucus membership in active opposition to efforts to limit access to abortion and to eliminate, or add restrictions to, funding for family planning programs. Given the emotional power of the abortion issue and the central role it played in the congressional agenda during the mid-1990s, it united the caucus in a common cause. However, it also prevented some women members of Congress, particularly a number of Republicans, from joining the caucus, either because of their own conflicting views or as a show of solidarity with their colleagues who were opposed to abortion.

When Representatives Johnson and Norton took over as cochairs during the 105th Congress (1997–1998), they decided that the caucus membership would be more inclusive and bipartisan if the issue of abortion were removed from the caucus agenda. As a result, the caucus returned to a position of neutrality on abortion, and its membership grew to include almost every woman member of Congress. That policy continued under the leadership of Representatives Sue Kelly (R-NY) and Carolyn Maloney (D-NY), the caucus cochairs for the 106th Congress (1999–2000). The cochairs for the 107th Congress (2001–2002), Representatives Judy Biggert (R-IL) and Juanita Millender-McDonald (D-CA), lead a caucus that includes all but one woman House member.

CAUCUS LEGISLATIVE ACCOMPLISHMENTS, 1995–2001

THE CAUCUS AGENDA

The regularly changing leadership and growing membership have made it far more difficult for the caucus to put forward an agenda expeditiously at the beginning of each Congress. The incoming cochairs must reorganize and begin anew to draft an agenda, consulting the entire membership, a process that can be quite cumbersome and lengthy.

The cochairs increasingly have asked the "legislative teams" or task forces to develop an agenda and lead the implementation effort for specific issues. Some teams are more active than others, and the caucus cochairs sometimes must step in to pick up the workload for the less active ones. Strong leadership of a specific team has helped position some members for future service as cochair or vice chair by bringing their efforts and commitment to the attention of the full caucus membership.

The process of formulating an agenda also has undergone change. When then-Representatives Schroeder and Snowe chaired the caucus, priorities generally were embraced if a majority of the caucus supported them. In the case of both the child care debate in the late 1980s and 1990 and the eight-year struggle for passage of the Family and Medical Leave Act in 1993, the caucus endorsed specific bills, despite the opposition of some caucus members.

During the 104th Congress, Representatives Morella and Lowey attempted to follow many of the practices of their predecessors. They developed an agenda with input from the members but did not attempt to obtain the consent of every member before moving forward. Because the caucus was a pro-choice caucus at that time, its membership was fairly homogeneous. When members did not agree on an issue, they found common ground and advocated on behalf of those provisions. For example, the caucus of the 104th Congress focused its energies on maintaining the status quo on abortion policy and the Title X family planning program. Led by Representatives Lowey and Morella and ally Jim Greenwood (R-PA), the caucus reversed an effort to eliminate the Title X program.

The caucus also worked successfully to modify several provisions of welfare reform legislation. While caucus members did not all share the same views on welfare reform, they did agree that strong child-support provisions and adequate child care funding must be part of any final agreement.

The caucus also successfully advocated increased spending for women's health research and Violence Against Women Act programs and restored funding for the Women's Educational Equity Act. In addition, the caucus worked to include important provisions for women in the Health Insurance Portability and Accountability Act, health care reform legislation (Clemmitt, Primmer, and Sims 1997).

After the combative 104th Congress, the caucus cochairs for the 105th Congress, Representatives Johnson and Norton, decided to take a new approach to broadening the caucus base and better focusing its legislative efforts. Besides removing the issue of abortion from the caucus agenda, the cochairs developed a "must-pass" agenda, including seven bills that enjoyed the strong support of the caucus membership (Persily 2001).

This streamlined approach was adopted as an alternative to the longtime caucus tradition of introducing omnibus legislative packages on women's health and economic equity. Given the more conservative political climate, a less-sweeping agenda was thought to be a better strategy.

Three of the seven bills on the caucus agenda won approval before the end of the 105th Congress: the inclusion of contraceptive coverage for women participating in the Federal Employee Health Benefits Program; reauthorization of the Mammography Quality Standards Act; and the creation of a commission to encourage more women and minorities to choose careers in science, engineering, and technology (Women's Policy, Inc. 1998; Grundy et al. 1997). The caucus also worked successfully to expand Medicare coverage to include annual mammograms and bone density testing for the diagnosis and prevention of osteoporosis (this measure was part of the Balanced Budget Act of 1997).

While retaining the abortion-neutral policy of the previous Congress, 106th Congress cochairs Kelly and Maloney initially put together an all-inclusive agenda document, making it clear that the listing represented the legislative priorities of the entire membership but that members might disagree with particular proposals within it. However, the caucus ultimately focused on several key pieces of legislation that enjoyed nearly unanimous support among its members. Among the caucus priorities that became law were the following: a bill to allow states to provide Medicaid coverage for the treatment of low-income women who were diagnosed with breast cancer in a Centers for Disease Control and Prevention screening program; the reauthorization of the Violence Against Women Act; a bill to authorize lupus research; legislation to combat international trafficking in women and children; bills to strengthen stalking, sex offender, and date rape laws; and the restoration of funding for the United Nations Population Fund (Women's Policy, Inc. 2000).

The current cochairs, Representatives Biggert and Millender-McDonald, identified the "wellness of women" as a basic theme and asked each legislative team to develop an agenda of a few bills or legislative issues for inclusion in a larger caucus agenda. At the time of this writing, the caucus was circulating the final draft of an agenda among members for approval. While the cochairs were attempting to craft a narrow agenda, they were faced once again with the difficulties inherent in a large organization. Gaining consensus, particularly among a membership representing the entire ideological spectrum, has become an increasing challenge.

Despite the delay in the approval of a final agenda, caucus members were working to expand federal support for preventing mother-to-child HIV/AIDS transmission and to support the permanent authorization of the Department of Justice's Violence Against Women Office as part of the department's reauthorization bill. As part of the appropriations process, caucus members were pushing for additional funding for women's health research and prevention programs and education.

Following the September 11 terrorist attacks, the caucus shifted its focus to issues related to those events and their aftermath. In addition, the caucus was working for passage of several less-controversial bills as the House moved toward an early exit from the first session of the 107th Congress.

THE FUTURE OF THE CAUCUS

With a record membership of 61 women, the caucus has the opportunity to exert a significant influence on the congressional agenda and on the development of policy initiatives moving through the legislative process.

Women House and Senate members hold important positions on powerful committees and within the leadership of both parties. Women in the House chair five subcommittees and hold ranking member positions on 10 subcommittees and one committee. Women in the Senate chair seven subcommittees and hold five subcommittee ranking member positions (Women's Policy, Inc. 2001a, 2001b).

Certainly the impact of having women in these committee positions is evident. In 1990, when the Women's Health Equity Act was introduced, no women served on either the House or Senate Appropriations Committee (Women's Policy, Inc. 1997). As this is written, 10 women serve on the House Appropriations Committee (where five serve on the Labor, Health and Human Services, and Education Subcommittee). Five women serve on the Senate Appropriations Committee (where four are subcommittee chairs and three serve on the Labor, Health and Human Services, and Education Subcommittee) (Women's Policy, Inc. 2001a, 2001b). Over the past decade, federal spending for women's health research has expanded significantly, increasing more than sixfold for breast cancer and more than doubling for osteoporosis (Lockwood-Shabat 2001). While these funding increases were championed by both male and female legislators, the women's advocacy and research communities, and the executive branch, the intervention of the women who served on the appropriations committees certainly ensured that women's health issues were given high priority.

The October 2001 election of Representative Nancy Pelosi (D-CA) to the position of minority whip, the highest leadership position ever held by a woman in Congress, further reflects women's growing power and influence in the legislative branch. Other women are advancing in the party leadership in the House: Representative Deborah Pryce (R-OH) serves as vice chair of the Republican Conference. Representative Barbara Cubin (R-WY) is conference secretary. Representative Rosa DeLauro (D-CT) serves as assistant to the Democratic leader, and Representative Maxine Waters (D-CA) is one of her party's four chief deputy whips. Representative Nita Lowey (D-NY) serves as chair of the Democratic Congressional Campaign Committee.

Women have made similar advances in the Senate. Senator Kay Bailey Hutchison (R-TX) serves as secretary of the Republican Conference, and Senator Barbara Mikulski (D-MD) is secretary of the Democratic Conference. Senator Patty Murray (D-WA) chairs the Democratic Senatorial Campaign Committee, and Senator Barbara Boxer (D-CA) is her party's chief deputy for strategic outreach (Women's Policy, Inc. 2001c).

The expanded presence of women in leadership positions, as well as their representation on all committees and in more influential committee positions, has elevated issues affecting women and families and helped to make many of these issues priorities for the entire Congress. For example, strong bipartisan support led to the passage of the Violence Against Women Act of 1994, its reauthorization in 2000, and its funding during the annual appropriations process. Such issues are now considered part of the mainstream congressional agenda.

The number of women of color elected to Congress has expanded significantly over the past decade and has had an impact on the caucus agenda. Women of color represent almost one-third of the caucus membership. Indeed, the caucus has devoted greater attention to issues affecting women of color in recent years as the number of women of color elected to Congress has grown. For example, legislation introduced by Representative Carrie Meek (D-FL) to authorize research on lupus, a disease disproportionately affecting African American women, was a caucus priority approved in the 106th Congress. Along with addressing health concerns that affect all women, the caucus now is placing a greater focus on the impact of particular diseases on women of color and the factors that may be responsible for poorer treatment outcomes for them.

Given these changing dynamics, the caucus may need to adjust its operations to be more effective. With a much larger membership, it may want to consider ways to streamline the agenda process, particularly during leadership transitions at the beginning of each Congress. The development of a specific policy to address divergent views could be helpful in determining the caucus agenda. For more controversial issues, unanimity within the membership may never be possible. Drawing on its past successes, such as those achieved during the welfare and Medicare reform efforts of the mid- and late 1990s, the caucus may want to identify common ground in major policy debates and concentrate its energies on priority provisions within a larger legislative context.

In pursuit of its goals, the caucus in the past has forged important alliances with the Administration, the House and Senate leadership, male members of Congress, other caucuses, and the women's advocacy community, and should continue to do so. Indeed, the caucus's accomplishments of the past 25 years have been possible only through such combined efforts.

Expanded alliances with women senators also would continue to enhance the strength of the caucus in implementing its priorities. The women senators have shown little interest in forming their own caucus or in joining the House caucus, preferring to work together informally and on an issue-by-issue basis. The caucus may want to make additional efforts to join with the women senators in advocating for specific issues—as in the recent successful effort to obtain Medicaid funding for breast and cervical screening for low-income women and the earlier expansions of Medicare coverage for mammography and bone density testing for osteoporosis. Such a powerful coalition could be highly effective in delineating and implementing a women's issues agenda for consideration in both the House and Senate.

CONCLUSION

As the Congressional Caucus for Women's Issues celebrates its twenty-fifth anniversary, it continues to demonstrate resilience and uniqueness as a bipartisan organization representing a wide range of views. The ongoing challenge is to celebrate its diversity while channeling the tremendous energy and talent of the growing membership into concrete legislative action. Given its many strengths, the caucus can be expected to continue as the effective force for change that it has been over the past quarter-century.

The Congressional Caucus for Women's Issues— 107th Congress

Judy Biggert (R-IL), cochair
Juanita Millender-McDonald
  (D-CA), cochair
Shelley Moore Capito (R-WV),
  vice chair
Louise McIntosh Slaughter
  (D-NY), vice chair

Tammy Baldwin (D-WI)
Shelley Berkley (D-NV)
Mary Bono (R-CA)
Corrine Brown (D-FL)
Lois Capps (D-CA)
Julia Carson (D-IN)
Donna M. Christensen (D-VI)
Eva M. Clayton (D-NC)
Barbara Cubin (R-WY)
Jo Ann Davis (R-VA)
Susan A. Davis (D-CA)
Diana DeGette (D-CO)
Rosa L. DeLauro (D-CT)
Jennifer Dunn (R-WA)
Jo Ann Emerson (R-MO)
Anna G. Eshoo (D-CA)
Kay Granger (R-TX)
Jane Harman (D-CA)
Melissa A. Hart (R-PA)

Darlene Hooley (D-OR)
Sheila Jackson Lee (D-TX)
Eddie Bernice Johnson (D-TX)
Nancy L. Johnson (R-CT)
Stephanie Tubbs Jones (D-OH)
Marcy Kaptur (D-OH)
Sue W. Kelly (R-NY)
Carolyn Cheeks Kilpatrick (D-MI)
Barbara Lee (D-CA)
Zoe Lofgren (D-CA)
Nita M. Lowey (D-NY)
Carolyn B. Maloney (D-NY)
Carolyn McCarthy (D-NY)
Karen McCarthy (D-MO)
Betty McCollum (D-MN)
Cynthia A. McKinney (D-GA)
Carrie P. Meek (D-FL)
Patsy T. Mink (D-HI)
Constance A. Morella (R-MD)
Sue Wilkins Myrick (R-NC)
Grace Napolitano (D-CA)
Eleanor Holmes Norton (D-DC)
Nancy Pelosi (D-CA)
Deborah Pryce (R-OH)
Lynn N. Rivers (D-MI)
Ileana Ros-Lehtinen (R-FL)
Marge Roukema (R-NJ)

Lucille Roybal-Allard (D-CA)
Loretta Sanchez (D-CA)
Janice D. Schakowsky (D-IL)
Louise McIntosh Slaughter (D-NY)
Hilda L. Solis (D-CA)
Ellen O. Tauscher (D-CA)

Karen L. Thurman (D-FL)
Nydia M. Velázquez (D-NY)
Maxine Waters (D-CA)
Diane E. Watson (D-CA)
Lynn C. Woolsey (D-CA)

WOMEN IN THE 107TH CONGRESS*

WHEN DEMOCRATIC REPRESENTATIVE Nancy Pelosi of California was sworn in as minority whip on February 6, 2002, she assumed the second most powerful position in her party's leadership in the House of Representatives.[1]

Women hold other majority and minority party leadership positions in the current (107th) Congress, although none but Representative Pelosi's ranks at the very top (see Table 8-4 in the "Statistical Portrait"; see also "The Congressional Caucus for Women's Issues at 25"). Nevertheless, it is significant that women chair the Democratic Senate Campaign Committee and the Democratic Congressional (House) Campaign Committee. Both committees are charged with finding and encouraging strong Democratic candidates and with raising campaign funds for Democrats who are seeking election or reelection to Congress. Not so long ago it was thought that women could not be effective political fundraisers.

Leadership firsts are welcome evidence that women are at last beginning to break through what seemed to be a congressional "glass ceiling." On the other hand, no woman currently chairs a full committee in either the House or the Senate, and none has done so since the 104th Congress (1995–1996) when then-Representative Jan Meyers of Kansas chaired the Small Business Committee.

Only 209 women (including delegates) have ever served in the United States Congress, and the 75 who sit in the 107th Congress are impressive, individually and collectively. Pioneers and "firsts" abound: Ileana Ros-Lehtinen of Florida is the first Latina (and the only woman of Cuban origin) to be elected to Congress. Heather Wilson of New Mexico is the first and, so far, the only female armed forces veteran in Congress. Tammy Baldwin of Wisconsin is the first openly gay person elected as a nonincumbent.

---

*The editors wish to thank Monica Jacobe for her many contributions to this chapter.

Hillary Rodham Clinton of New York is the first First Lady ever to hold a seat in the federal legislature.

Viewed collectively, in some ways today's women in Congress have much in common with American women in general. Most have been married (although many are no longer married). Most are mothers, many are grandmothers. However, the women in Congress have more education than the average American woman: 93 percent have a bachelor's degree or higher, 32 percent have a graduate degree (or degrees) other than law (one is a physician), and 20 percent have a law degree.

Compared with the men in Congress, women members are much less likely to say that they are lawyers (17 percent of the women versus 42 percent of the men) or that they are in business or banking (19 percent versus 36 percent). But there is little difference in the percentage citing an occupation in education (21 percent of the women versus 20 percent of the men). Fifty-three (71 percent) of the women had already held elective public office when they came to Congress; several others held important posts in their respective political parties.

Fifty-six is the average age of the women in the 107th Congress, which means that many are baby boomers, not incidentally the generation that pushed open the gates to political power for women. Senate women, averaging 55.5 years of age, are somewhat younger than the overall Senate average (60). Women in the House, averaging 56 years of age, are a few years older than the overall House average (54). All said, their age range is narrower than that of their male counterparts, although women in Congress represent at least two generations. First-term Republican Melissa Hart is the youngest at 41; fifth-term Democrat Carrie Meek is the oldest at 76.

Currently there are no minority women in the Senate, but in the House African Americans and people of Hispanic origin are better represented among the women than among the men. Counting the two women delegates, both of whom are African American, 15 (24 percent) of the congresswomen are African American and six (10 percent) are of Hispanic origin. By comparison, six percent of the men in the House are African American and four percent are of Hispanic origin, when the three male delegates are included. (The five delegates who represent U.S. territories and the District of Columbia are not permitted to vote on matters before the full House, although they may vote in committee.) Only one woman in Congress is of Asian heritage; none is Native American.

Democrats predominate among the women in both houses, accounting for 10 of the 13 senators and 44 of the representatives (again counting the two women delegates).

Only 10 states are represented among the 13 women in the Senate, since three states—California, Maine, and Washington—have elected women to both their Senate seats. Seventeen of the women in the House are in California's 52-member House delegation; indeed, no other state approaches California in the representation of women—and minority women—in Congress. Nineteen states have no women in the 107th Congress, and five of these— Alaska, Delaware, Iowa, Mississippi, New Hampshire, and Vermont—have never sent a woman to Congress.

How the 2002 congressional elections will affect this picture is unclear. Two incumbent women are retiring, and several others may face strong challengers. (On the other hand, at least two of the women who are running for Congress for the first time in 2002 appear as of this writing to be shoo-ins.) In the past, the biggest breakthroughs for women have occurred when a large number of congressional seats were open—that is, when the incumbent was not a candidate. Relatively few seats will be open in 2002, so the gender ratio in Congress may change very little in the immediate future. However, in fits and starts, Congress has been slowly becoming less masculine since 1917, when Montana sent Jeannette Rankin to the 65th Congress (before American women in other states even had the right to vote). The pace of change accelerated in the 1990s. In the 101st Congress (1989–1990) there were 31 women (a record number then); now there are 75.

Brief biographies of the women in the 107th Congress follow. For more detailed information about these legislators—including their legislative priorities and their views on key issues—go to http://www.senate.gov or http://www.house.gov and follow the convenient links to the websites of current members. For biographical information on women who have retired—or been retired by the electorate—from Congress, go to http://bioguide.congress.gov, which includes all the women and men who have ever served in either the Senate or the House.

Representative Tammy Baldwin *(Democrat, Second District, Wisconsin)*, who was first elected to Congress in 1998, is the first—and, to date, the only—woman elected to Congress from Wisconsin and the first openly gay person elected to Congress as a non-incumbent. She serves on the Budget and Judiciary Committees. Her first elective office was as a member of the Dane County Board of Supervisors; after four terms, she was elected to the Wisconsin Assembly. Congresswoman Baldwin was born in 1962 and raised in the congressional district she now represents. A graduate of Smith College, she earned her law degree from the University of Wisconsin Law School.

Representative Shelley Berkley *(Democrat, First District, Nevada)*, first elected to the House in 1998, currently serves on three committees: International Relations; Transportation and Infrastructure; and Veterans' Affairs. Before coming to Congress, she served in the Nevada Assembly and worked as a lawyer in the private sector. A graduate of the University of Nevada, Las Vegas, Congresswoman Berkley received her law degree from the University of San Diego. She has two sons and is married to Dr. Larry Lehrner.

Representative Judy Biggert *(Republican, Thirteenth District, Illinois)* was first elected to Congress in 1998. She currently serves on three committees: Science; Financial Services; and Education and the Workforce. She also cochairs the Congressional Caucus for Women's Issues. Before coming to Congress, Representative Biggert served three terms in the Illinois legislature, where she was assistant Republican House leader. In private life she practiced law. Born in Chicago in 1937, she earned a B.A. from Stanford University and a J.D. from Northwestern University. She is married to Rody Biggert and has four children and four grandchildren.

Representative Mary Bono *(Republican, Forty-fourth District, California)* was first elected to Congress in April 1998, in a special election to fill the House seat left vacant by the death of her first husband, Sonny Bono. She currently serves on the House Energy and Commerce Committee. Congresswoman Bono, who was born in Cleveland in 1961, moved to California as a child. She has a B.A. from the University of Southern California. The mother of two children by Sonny Bono, she is now married to Glen Baxley.

Senator Barbara Boxer *(Democrat, California)* was first elected to the Senate in 1992, after 10 years in the House. She chairs the Toxics and Waste Management Subcommittee of the Environment and Public Works Committee and the International Operations Subcommittee of the Foreign Relations Committee. She also sits on the Commerce, Science, and Transportation Committee. Senator Boxer, who was born in Brooklyn, New York, in 1940, has a B.A. from Brooklyn College. Before coming to Congress, she spent six years on the Marin County Board of Supervisors. She is married and the mother of two adult children.

Representative Corrine Brown *(Democrat, Third District, Florida)*, first elected to Congress in 1992, serves on the Transportation and Infrastructure Committee and the Veterans' Affairs Committee. Before coming to Congress, she served for 10 years in the Florida legislature. Congresswoman Brown earned both a B.S. and an M.A. from Florida A&M University as well as an education specialist degree from the University of Florida. She has been on the faculties of Florida Community College of Jacksonville, the University of Florida, and Edward Waters College. She was born in 1946 in Jacksonville, where she still resides. She has one grown daughter.

Senator Maria Cantwell *(Democrat, Washington)* was elected to the Senate in 2000. She sits on four committees: Judiciary; Energy and Natural Resources; Small Business; and Indian Affairs. Senator Cantwell began her political career in 1986 when, at the age of 28, she was first elected to the Washington State legislature. In 1992, she was elected to the U.S. House of Representatives and served one term. Born in Indiana in 1958, Senator Cantwell earned her bachelor's degree at Miami University of Ohio and moved to Washington soon afterward.

Representative Shelley Moore Capito *(Republican, Second District, West Virginia)*, elected in 2000, is the only Republican, and the only woman, to represent her state in the 107th Congress. She serves on three committees: Financial Services; Transportation and Infrastructure; and Small Business. She spent two terms in the West Virginia House of Delegates before coming to Congress. Born in Glen Dale, West Virginia, in 1953, Representative Capito has a B.S. from Duke University and a master's degree in education from the University of Virginia. She and her husband, Charles L. Capito, Jr., have three children.

Representative Lois Capps *(Democrat, Twenty-second District, California)* was first elected to Congress in March 1998, in a special election to fill the House seat left vacant by the death of her husband, Walter Capps. She currently serves on the Energy and Commerce Committee. Born in Wisconsin in 1938, Congresswoman Capps earned a B.S. degree in nursing from Pacific Lutheran University. She also has a master's degree in religion from Yale University and a master's degree in education from the University of California, Santa Barbara. She and the late Walter Capps had three children, of whom two survive. She has three grandchildren.

Senator Jean Carnahan *(Democrat, Missouri)* was appointed to the Senate in 2001 to serve in place of her late husband, Mel Carnahan, who was elected posthumously to the Senate. He had been Missouri's governor. Senator Carnahan must seek reelection in 2002. She sits on five committees: Armed Services; Governmental Affairs; Small Business; Commerce, Science, and Transportation; and the Special Committee on Aging. Before coming to Washington, she spent a number of active years as Missouri's First Lady. Born in Washington, D.C., in 1933, Senator Carnahan had four children with her late husband; one son died in the plane crash in which her husband was killed. She is also the grandmother of two. She holds a B.A. from George Washington University.

Representative Julia Carson *(Democrat, Tenth District, Indiana)* was first elected to Congress in 1996. She is a member of the Financial Services Committee and the Veterans' Affairs Committee. Before coming to Congress, she served in both houses of Indiana's legislature. Born in 1938 in Louisville, Kentucky, Congresswoman Carson attended Indiana University. She has two children and two grandchildren, and resides in Indianapolis.

Delegate Donna M. Christensen *(Democrat, At Large, U.S. Virgin Islands)*, first elected to Congress in 1996, is the first woman delegate to be elected from the U.S. Virgin Islands. She serves on the Small Business Committee and the Resources Committee, and is the ranking Democrat on the latter's Public Lands Subcommittee. Delegate Christensen has an M.D. from George Washington University. Her medical career ranged from private family practice to serving as acting commissioner of the U.S. Virgin Islands Department of Health. Born in New Jersey in 1945, she is married to Chris Christensen and has two daughters and four stepchildren.

Representative Eva M. Clayton *(Democrat, First District, North Carolina)* plans to retire from Congress at the end of this, her fifth, term. The first woman to be elected to Congress from North Carolina, she serves on the Budget Committee and the Agriculture Committee (the only woman currently on the latter) and is the ranking Democrat on its Subcommittee on Department Operations, Oversight, Nutrition, and Forestry. Representative Clayton was born in 1934 in Savannah, Georgia. She holds a B.S from Johnson C. Smith University and an M.S. from North Carolina Central University. Before coming to Congress, she was a member of the Warren County Board of Commissioners. She is married to Theaoseus T. Clayton, Sr. They have four children and five grandchildren.

Senator Hillary Rodham Clinton *(Democrat, New York)* was elected in 2000 to this, her first elected public office. She is the first First Lady ever elected to Congress and the first woman elected to statewide office in New York. She sits on the Budget Committee; the Environment and Public Works Committee; and the Health, Education, Labor and Pension Committee. Born in Chicago, Illinois, in 1947, Senator Clinton is a graduate of Wellesley College and Yale Law School. Her career in the public interest has included serving as chair of the Legal Services Corporation during the Carter Administration and as chair of the Children's Defense Fund (1986–1989). Senator Clinton and her husband, former President Bill Clinton, have one daughter.

Senator Susan M. Collins *(Republican, Maine)* was elected to the Senate in 1996. She serves on four committees: Health, Education, Labor and Pension, where she is the ranking Republican on the Subcommittee on Children and Families; Governmental Affairs, where she is the ranking Republican member on the Subcommittee on Investigations; Armed Services; and the Special Committee on Aging. Senator Collins's career before her election to the Senate included serving as staff director for the Senate Subcommittee on the Oversight of Government Management and as Maine's commissioner of professional and financial regulation. Born in 1952 in Caribou, Maine, Senator Collins is a graduate of St. Lawrence University. She resides in Bangor.

Representative Barbara Cubin *(Republican, At Large, Wyoming)* was first elected to Congress in 1994. She is a member of the Energy and Commerce Committee and the Resources Committee, and chairs the latter's Subcommittee on Energy and Mineral Resources. She also serves on the Republican Policy Committee. Before coming to Congress, Representative Cubin served in both houses of Wyoming's legislature. A graduate of Creighton University, she is married to Frederick Cubin, a physician. They have two children and live in Casper.

Representative Jo Ann Davis *(Republican, First District, Virginia)*, elected in 2000, sits on the Armed Services, Government Reform, and International Relations committees. Before coming to Congress, she spent three years in the Virginia General Assembly and ran her own real estate company. Representative Davis, who was born in 1950 in North Carolina, moved with her family to Virginia at the age of nine. She attended Hampton Roads Business College. She and her husband, Charles Davis, now live with their two sons in Gloucester County.

Representative Susan A. Davis *(Democrat, Forty-ninth District, California)*, elected in 2000, serves on the Armed Services Committee and the Education and the Workforce Committee. Before coming to Congress, she served three terms in the California State Assembly; she had previously served nine years on the San Diego City School Board. Congresswoman Davis, who was born in Massachusetts in 1944, grew up in California and earned her bachelor's degree at the University of California at Berkeley. She also holds a master's degree in social work from the University of North Carolina. She and her husband, Steve, live in San Diego and have two grown sons.

Representative Diana DeGette *(Democrat, First District, Colorado)*, first elected to Congress in 1996, is a member of the Energy and Commerce Committee. Before her election to Congress, she served two terms in the Colorado legislature and worked as a trial attorney. Congresswoman DeGette, who is a graduate of Colorado College and New York University Law School, was born in 1957 in Denver. She and her husband, Lino Lipinsky, live in Denver with their two daughters.

Representative Rosa L. DeLauro *(Democrat, Third District, Connecticut)*, first elected to Congress in 1990, serves on the Appropriations Committee. She is the second highest-ranking woman Democrat in the House, her colleagues having elected her to a second term as assistant to the Democratic leader. Representative DeLauro was born in New Haven in 1943. Her career before Congress included serving as executive assistant to the mayor of New Haven and as chief of staff to U.S. Senator Christopher Dodd (D-CT). She received her B.A. from Marymount University and her master's in international politics from Columbia. She and her husband, Stanley Greenberg, have three grown children.

Representative Jennifer Dunn *(Republican, Eighth District, Washington)*, first elected to Congress in 1992, serves on the Ways and Means Committee. In 1998, she ran (unsuccessfully) for Majority Leader of the House—the first woman in either political party to do so. From 1981 to 1992, she chaired the Washington State Republican Party. Congresswoman Dunn, who was born in 1941 in Bellevue, a suburb of Seattle, holds a B.A. from Stanford University. She is the mother of two grown children.

Representative Jo Ann Emerson *(Republican, Eighth District, Missouri)* was first elected to Congress in 1996 in a combined special and general election to fill the vacancy in the 104th Congress left by the death of her first husband, Bill Emerson, and to a full term in the 105th Congress. She is the first—and, to date, the only—Republican woman to be elected to the House from Missouri. She sits on the Appropriations Committee. Before coming to Congress, Representative Emerson was senior vice president of public affairs for the American Insurance Association and served as deputy director of communications for the Republican National Committee. Born in Washington, DC, in 1950, Congresswoman Emerson is a graduate of Ohio Wesleyan University. Now married to Ron Gladney, she has two daughters and six stepchildren.

Representative Anna G. Eshoo *(Democrat, Fourteenth District, California)* was first elected to the House in 1992. She sits on the Energy and Commerce Committee. Before coming to Congress, she served for 10 years on the San Mateo County (California) Board of Supervisors and worked for 12 years with the Democratic National Committee. Born in New Britain, Connecticut, in 1942, Congresswoman Eshoo has an A.A. from Cañada College in Redwood City, California. She is the mother of two children.

Senator Dianne Feinstein *(Democrat, California)*, first elected to the Senate in 1992 to complete the unexpired term of Pete Wilson (R-CA), was reelected in 1994 and again in 2000. She sits on four committees: Appropriations, where she chairs the Military Construction Subcommittee; Energy and Natural Resources; Rules and Administration; and Judiciary, on which she was the first woman to serve and where she chairs the Technology, Terrorism, and Government Information Subcommittee. Senator Feinstein, who was born in San Francisco in 1933, was Mayor of that city from 1978 to

1988. Before that, she was a member of the San Francisco County Board of Supervisors. She received her B.A. from Stanford University. Married to Richard C. Blum, she has one daughter, three stepdaughters, and three grandchildren.

Representative Kay Granger *(Republican, Twelfth District, Texas)* was first elected to Congress in 1996. She is the first—and, so far, the only—Republican woman to be elected to the House from Texas. She serves on the Budget Committee and the Appropriations Committee. Before coming to Congress, Representative Granger served three terms as Mayor of Fort Worth, following two years on the Fort Worth City Council and seven years on the Zoning Commission. She received her B.S. and an honorary doctorate from Texas Wesleyan University. Born in 1943 and a lifelong resident of Fort Worth, she is the mother of three grown children.

Representative Jane Harman *(Democrat, Thirty-sixth District, California)* was elected to the House in 1992 and served three terms before running unsuccessfully in the California Senate primary in 1998. In 2000, she again ran for a House seat and was elected. She currently serves on the Energy and Commerce Committee. Congresswoman Harman is a lawyer and businesswoman. Her career before Congress included serving as chief counsel on the Senate Subcommittee on Constitutional Rights, as deputy secretary to the Carter Cabinet, and as special counsel to the Department of Defense. Born in 1945 in New York City, she graduated from Smith College and Harvard Law School. She and her husband, Sidney, live in Venice, California, with their two children. She also has two grown children.

Representative Melissa A. Hart *(Republican, Fourth District, Pennsylvania)*, elected in 2000, is the first Republican woman elected to the House from her state. She serves on three committees: Financial Services; Judiciary; and Science. Before coming to Congress, she spent 10 years in the Pennsylvania State Senate, where she chaired the Finance Committee. Born in Pittsburgh in 1962, Representative Hart received her bachelor's degree from Washington and Jefferson College and her law degree from the University of Pittsburgh.

Representative Darlene Hooley *(Democrat, Fifth District, Oregon)* was first elected to the House in 1996. She is a member of the Financial Services Committee and the Budget Committee. Her first experience in elected office was as a member of the West Linn (Oregon) City Council. She went on to serve in the Oregon legislature and, later, on the Clackamas County Board of Commissioners. Representative Hooley, who was born in 1939, received her B.S. from Oregon State University. She has two children and lives in West Linn.

Senator Kay Bailey Hutchison *(Republican, Texas)*, the first woman to represent Texas in the Senate, was first elected to that body in June 1993 to fill the unexpired term of Lloyd Bentsen (D). She sits on four committees: Appropriations, where she is the ranking Republican on the Military Construction Subcommittee; Commerce, Science, and Transportation, where she is the ranking Republican on the Aviation Subcommittee; Veterans' Affairs; and Rules and Administration. Before coming to the Senate, Senator Hutchison was Texas State Treasurer—the first Republican woman to be elected to statewide office in Texas. She also served in the Texas legislature and as vice chair of the National Transportation Safety Board in the Ford Administration. Senator Hutchison is a graduate of the University of Texas at Austin and the University of Texas School of Law. She lives in Dallas with her husband, Ray Hutchison.

Representative Sheila Jackson Lee *(Democrat, Eighteenth District, Texas)*, first elected to the House in 1994, sits on the Science and Judiciary committees and is the ranking Democrat on the latter's Immigration and Claims Subcommittee, the first African American woman in that position. Before coming to Congress, Representative Jackson Lee was a member of the Houston City Council. Previously she had served as an associate municipal court judge. Born in 1951 in Jamaica, New York, she is a graduate of Yale University and the University of Virginia Law School. She is married to Dr. Elwyn C. Lee and has two children.

Representative Eddie Bernice Johnson *(Democrat, Thirtieth District, Texas)* was first elected to the House in 1992. She sits on the Transportation and Infrastructure Committee and the Science Committee, and is the ranking Democrat on the latter's Basic Research Subcommittee. She is currently chair of the Congressional Black Caucus. The first African American woman since 1935 to hold a Texas state elective office, Congresswoman Johnson served in both houses of the Texas legislature before coming to Congress. During the Carter Administration, she was regional director of the U.S. Department of Health, Education, and Welfare. Representative Johnson, a graduate of Texas Christian University, received nursing preparation at Notre Dame. She also earned a master's degree in public administration from Southern Methodist University. Born in 1935 in Waco, Texas, she is the mother of one child and grandmother of three.

Representative Nancy L. Johnson *(Republican, Sixth District, Connecticut)* was first elected to Congress in 1982. She has served on the Ways and Means Committee since 1988, when she became the first Republican woman ever appointed to that committee and the first woman of either party to chair a subcommittee of the Ways and Means Committee. She currently chairs its Subcommittee on Health. Representative Johnson served three terms in the Connecticut State Senate before coming to Congress. A native of Chicago, she received her bachelor's degree from Radcliffe College. She and her husband, Theodore Johnson, have three daughters and several grandchildren.

Representative Stephanie Tubbs Jones *(Democrat, Eleventh District, Ohio)*, first elected to Congress in 1998, serves on the Banking and Financial Services Committee and the Small Business Committee. Before coming to Congress, she served as Cuyahoga County (Ohio) prosecutor and as a judge in both the Common Pleas and Municipal courts. She also worked as an administrator and attorney for the Equal Employment Opportunity Commission. Congresswoman Jones earned her undergraduate and law degrees at Case Western Reserve University. Born in 1949 in Cleveland, where she has lived all her life, she is married to Mervyn Jones; they have one son.

Representative Marcy Kaptur *(Democrat, Ninth District, Ohio)*, first elected to Congress in 1982, is the senior Democratic woman in the House of Representatives. She sits on the Appropriations Committee and is the ranking Democratic member of its Agriculture Subcommittee. Born in 1946 in Toledo, she earned her bachelor's degree from the University of Wisconsin and her master's degree in urban planning from the University of Michigan. She also has an honorary J.D. from the University of Toledo. Before seeking public office, Congresswoman Kaptur was an urban planner. She served as an urban adviser to the Carter Administration and was the first deputy director of the National Cooperative Consumer Bank.

Representative Sue W. Kelly *(Republican, Nineteenth District, New York)*, first elected to the House in 1994, currently serves on three committees: Banking and Financial Services; Transportation and Infrastructure; and Small Business. In the 106th Congress, she was cochair of the Congressional Caucus for Women Issues. Before coming to Congress, Representative Kelly worked as an educator, small business owner, patient advocate, rape crisis counselor, researcher, and community leader. A graduate of Denison University, she has a master's degree in health advocacy from Sarah Lawrence College. Born in 1936 in Lima, Ohio, she is married to Edward Kelly; they have four children and six grandchildren.

Representative Carolyn Cheeks Kilpatrick *(Democrat, Fifteenth District, Michigan)*, first elected to the House in 1996, sits on the Appropriations Committee. She also chairs the Congressional Black Caucus's Political Action Committee—the first woman to hold that position. A teacher by profession, she came to Congress after serving 18 years in the Michigan legislature. Congresswoman Kilpatrick spent her undergraduate years at Ferris State University and Western Michigan University and earned her M.S. in education from the University of Michigan. A native of Detroit, she has a son, a daughter, and four grandsons.

Senator Mary L. Landrieu *(Democrat, Louisiana)* was elected to the Senate in 1996—the first woman ever elected to that body from Louisiana. She is a member of the Committee on Armed Services—the first Democratic woman ever to serve on that committee—and chairs its Emerging Threats and Capabilities Subcommittee. She also serves on the Energy and Natural Resources Committee, the Small Business Committee, and the Appropriations Committee, where she chairs the District of Columbia Subcommittee. Senator Landrieu first won elective office at the age of 23, when she became the youngest woman ever elected to the Louisiana legislature. After two terms in the Louisiana House, she was elected Louisiana State Treasurer. Born in 1955, she is a graduate of Louisiana State University in Baton Rouge. She and her husband, Frank Snellings, have two children.

Representative Barbara Lee *(Democrat, Ninth District, California)* was first elected to Congress in April 1998 to complete the remaining term of Representative Ron Dellums, who retired. She sits on the Banking and Financial Services Committee and the International Relations Committee. Before coming to Congress, she served three terms in the California Assembly and one term in the California Senate. She had worked previously as chief of staff for her predecessor, Congressman Dellums. Born in 1946 in El Paso, Texas, Congresswoman Lee moved with her family to California as a teenager. A graduate of Mills College, she also has a master's degree in social welfare from the University of California at Berkeley.

Senator Blanche L. Lincoln *(Democrat, Arkansas)*, elected to the Senate in 1998, is the youngest woman ever elected to that body and only the second woman to win a Senate seat from Arkansas. She had earlier served two terms in the House (1993–1996). She currently sits on the Energy and Natural Resources Committee, the Special Committee on Aging, and the Agriculture Committee, where she chairs the Subcommittee on Production and Price Competitiveness. Senator Lincoln, who was born in 1960 in Helena, Arkansas, received her bachelor's degree from Randolph-Macon Woman's College. She is married to Dr. Steve Lincoln; they have twin boys.

Representative Zoe Lofgren *(Democrat, Sixteenth District, California)* was first elected to the House in 1994. She sits on four committees: Judiciary; Science; Standards of Official Conduct; and the Joint Economic Committee. Before her election to Congress, she served on the Santa Clara (California) County Board of Supervisors and worked as an attorney. Congresswoman Lofgren is a graduate of Stanford University. After college she worked on the Watergate hearings with then-Congressman Don Edwards (D) (whom she later succeeded in Congress). She later received a law degree from the University of Santa Clara. Born in Palo Alto, California, in 1947, she is married to John Marshall Collins and has two children.

Representative Nita M. Lowey *(Democrat, Eighteenth District, New York)* was first elected to the House in 1988. She is a member of the Appropriations Committee, where she is the ranking Democrat on the Foreign Operations and Export Financing Subcommittee. Before her election to Congress, Representative Lowey served New York State as Assistant Secretary of State. Born in 1937 in Bronx, New York, she graduated from Mount Holyoke College. She is married to Stephen Lowey and has three grown children and six grandchildren.

Representative Carolyn B. Maloney *(Democrat, Fourteenth District, New York)* was first elected to Congress in 1992. She is a member of three committees: Banking and Financial Services, where she is the ranking Democrat on the Domestic Monetary Policy, Technology, and Economic Growth Subcommittee; Government Reform and Oversight, where she is the ranking Democrat on the Subcommittee on the Census; and the Joint Economic Committee. During the 106th Congress, she was cochair of the Congressional Caucus on Women's Issues. Before coming to Congress, Representative Maloney served for 10 years on the New York City Council. She was born in 1948 in Greensboro, North Carolina, and is a graduate of Greensboro College. She and her husband, Clifton Maloney, have two daughters.

Representative Carolyn McCarthy *(Democrat, Fourth District, New York)* was first elected to the House in 1996. She sits on the Education and the Workforce Committee and the Budget Committee. A lifelong resident of Mineola, New York, she became politically active after her husband was killed and her son—their only child—was gravely injured by a man wielding an assault weapon on a Long Island Rail Road commuter train in 1993. Representative McCarthy, who was born in 1944, is a graduate of Glen Cove Nursing School. She has two grandchildren.

Representative Karen McCarthy *(Democrat, Fifth District, Missouri)* was first elected to Congress in 1994. She serves on the Energy and Commerce Committee. Before her election to Congress, she was in the Missouri legislature, where she chaired the Ways and Means Committee. Representative McCarthy was born in Massachusetts in 1947. She received a B.A. and an M.B.A. from the University of Kansas and an M.A. from the University of Missouri at Kansas City.

Representative Betty McCollum *(Democrat, Fourth District, Minnesota)*, who was elected in 2000, serves on the Committee on Education and the Workforce and the Committee on Resources. She began her career in elected public office in 1986 as a member of the North St. Paul City Council. She subsequently served eight years in the Minnesota legislature. Born in Minneapolis in 1954, Representative McCollum earned a bachelor of science degree from the College of St. Catherine. She and her husband, Douglas, have two grown children.

Representative Cynthia A. McKinney *(Democrat, Fourth District, Georgia)*, first elected to the House in 1992, is the first African American woman to be elected to Congress from Georgia and is currently the only woman to represent Georgia in Congress. She sits on the National Security Committee and the International Relations Committee. Before her election to Congress, she served two terms in the Georgia legislature. Born in 1955 in Atlanta, Congresswoman McKinney is a graduate of the University of Southern California and is currently a doctoral candidate in international relations at Tufts University. She has one child.

Representative Carrie P. Meek *(Democrat, Seventeenth District, Florida)*, first elected to the House in 1992, is the first African American elected to Congress from Florida since Reconstruction. She is a member of the Appropriations Committee. She came to Congress following a dozen years in the Florida legislature, where she served in both chambers. Born in 1926 in Tallahassee, Representative Meek is a graduate of Florida A&M University and holds an M.S. in public health from the University of Michigan. She has also received five honorary doctorates from Florida colleges and universities. She has three children.

Senator Barbara Mikulski *(Democrat, Maryland)* was first elected to the Senate in 1986, after five terms in the House. At that time, she was the first and only Democratic woman elected to a Senate seat that had not previously been held by the woman's husband as well as the first and only Democratic woman to have served in both the Houses of Congress. She serves on three committees: Appropriations, where she chairs the Subcommittee on Veterans' Affairs, Housing and Urban Development, and Independent Agencies; Health, Education, Labor, and Pensions, where she chairs the Subcommittee on Aging; and the Select Committee on Intelligence. Born in Baltimore in 1936, Senator Mikulski earned her B.A. from Mount Saint Agnes College and her M.S.W. from the University of Maryland. She began her career in public service as a social worker and entered politics with her election to the Baltimore City Council.

Representative Juanita Millender-McDonald *(Democrat, Thirty-seventh District, California)* entered Congress in 1996, after winning a special election to fill an open seat. She sits on the Transportation and Infrastructure Committee and the Small Business Committee, where she is the ranking Democrat on the Empowerment Subcommittee. She is currently cochair of the Congressional Caucus for Women's Issues. Before coming to Congress, she served in the California legislature and, earlier, on the Carson (California) City Council. With a B.S. from the University of Redlands and a master's degree in educational administration from California State at Los Angeles, Representative Millender-McDonald is now working toward a doctorate in public administration from the University of Southern California. Born in 1938 in Birmingham, Alabama, she lives in Carson with her husband, James McDonald, Jr. They have five adult children and five grandchildren.

Representative Patsy T. Mink *(Democrat, Second District, Hawaii)* was first elected to Congress in 1964 and served six terms. In 1976, she made a bid for the U.S. Senate but lost in the primary. She returned to the House in 1990, having been elected to complete the unexpired term of Daniel Akaka (D), who had been appointed to the Senate. Congresswoman Mink is a member of the Government Reform Committee and of the Education and the Workforce Committee, where she is the ranking Democrat on the Subcommittee on 21st Century Competitiveness. Born in Paia, Hawaii, in 1927, she earned her B.A. at the University of Hawaii and her law degree at the University of Chicago. Before coming to Congress, she served in Hawaii's House and later in its Senate. She and her husband, John Francis Mink, have one daughter.

Representative Constance A. Morella *(Republican, Eighth District, Maryland)* was first elected to the House in 1986. She sits on the Science Committee, where she chairs the Subcommittee on Technology, and the Government Reform Committee, where she chairs the District of Columbia Subcommittee. She also cochairs the Caucus on Older Americans. Before coming to Congress, she served for eight years in the Maryland House of Delegates. Born in Massachusetts in 1931, Representative Morella received her A.B. from Boston University and her M.A. from American University. Before entering politics, she was a professor of English. She and her husband, Tony Morella, have raised nine children, six of whom are her late sister's children.

Senator Patty Murray *(Democrat, Washington)*, first elected to the Senate in 1992, chairs the Transportation Subcommittee of the Appropriations Committee. She also sits on the Budget Committee; the Veterans' Affairs Committee; and the Health, Education, Labor, and Pensions Committee. Before coming to the U.S. Senate, she served in the Washington State Senate. Senator Murray, who was born in 1950, is a native of Seattle. She earned her B.A. from Washington State University. She is married to Rob Murray; they have two grown children.

Representative Sue Wilkins Myrick *(Republican, Ninth District, North Carolina)* was first elected to the House in 1994. She is a member of the Rules Committee, which is an "exclusive" committee—that is, a member of that committee may not serve on any other major House committee. Before coming to Congress, she served as Mayor of Charlotte, North Carolina, after a term on the City Council. Born in 1941 in Ohio, Representative Myrick attended Heidelberg College. She is married and has five children.

Representative Grace F. Napolitano *(Democrat, Thirty-fourth District, California)* was first elected to Congress in 1998. She serves on the Small Business Committee, the Resources Committee, and the International Relations Committee. She began her political career in 1986 with her election to the Norwalk (California) City Council. She was the first Latina ever elected to that body. She subsequently spent two terms as Norwalk's Mayor and then was elected to the California Assembly, where she served three terms. Congresswoman Napolitano and her husband, Frank Napolitano, have five grown children and 13 grandchildren.

Representative Anne M. Northup *(Republican, Third District, Kentucky)* was first elected to the House in 1996. She is a member of the Appropriations Committee and is cochair of the Reading Caucus. Before her election to Congress, she served nine years in the Kentucky House of Representatives. Born in 1948, Congresswoman Northup earned her B.A. from St. Mary's College. She and her husband, Robert Wood Northup, have six children.

Delegate Eleanor Holmes Norton *(Democrat, At Large, District of Columbia)* was first elected to Congress in 1990 and is the first woman elected to represent the District. She serves on the Government Reform and Oversight Committee and on the Transportation and Infrastructure Committee. A professor of law at Georgetown University before her election to Congress, she also served as chair of the Equal Employment Opportunity Commission during the Carter Administration. Congresswoman Norton, who was born in 1937 in the District of Columbia, is a graduate of Antioch College and holds both an M.A. in American Studies and a law degree from Yale University. She has two children.

Representative Nancy Pelosi *(Democrat, Eighth District, California)* was first elected to Congress in 1987. In October 2001, her Democratic colleagues elected her minority whip, the second most powerful position in her party's leadership in the House and a position never before held by a woman. (She took the office in February 2002.) Congresswoman Pelosi sits on the Appropriations Committee and the Select Committee on Intelligence and is the ranking Democratic member on the latter. Before coming to Congress, she served as state chair of the California Democratic Party. Born in 1940 in Baltimore, Maryland, she earned her B.A. from Trinity College in Washington, DC. She and her husband, Paul, have five children.

Representative Deborah Pryce *(Republican, Fifteenth District, Ohio)*, first elected to the House in 1992, is a member of the Rules Committee, where she chairs the Legislative and Budget Process Subcommittee. She is cochair of the House Cancer Caucus, in honor of her daughter, Caroline, who died in childhood of nerve cancer. Before her election to Congress, Representative Pryce served as a judge on the Franklin County (Ohio) Municipal Court. Born in 1952 in Warren, Ohio, she is a graduate of Ohio State University and has a law degree from Capital University in Columbus. She has one surviving child.

Representative Lynn N. Rivers *(Democrat, Thirteenth District, Michigan)* was first elected to the House in 1994. She sits on the Education and the Workforce Committee and the Science Committee. She began her public service as a member of the Ann Arbor school board, of which she was president for three years. Before her election to Congress, she served one term in the Michigan legislature. Born in 1956 in Au Gres, Michigan, Congresswoman Rivers has a B.A. from the University of Michigan and a J.D. from Wayne State University. She has two daughters and lives in Ann Arbor.

Representative Ileana Ros-Lehtinen *(Republican, Eighteenth District, Florida)*, first elected to the House in a special election in 1989, made history as the first Hispanic woman to be elected to Congress. She is a member of the Government Reform and Oversight Committee and the International Relations Committee, and chairs the latter's Subcommittee on International Operations and Human Rights. Before coming to Congress, she served in both houses of the Florida legislature. Congresswoman Ros-Lehtinen, who was born in Havana, Cuba, in 1952, earned both a bachelor's degree and a master's degree from Florida International University. She is married to Dexter Lehtinen and has two daughters.

Representative Marge Roukema *(Republican, Fifth District, New Jersey)* sits on the Banking and Financial Services Committee, where she chairs the Subcommittee on Housing and Community Opportunity. First elected to the House in 1980, she has announced her intention to retire from Congress when her current term ends in January 2003. Born in 1929 in West Orange, New Jersey, Congresswoman Roukema holds a B.A. from Montclair State College. A secondary school teacher by profession, she first held public office as a member of the Ridgewood (New Jersey) Board of Education. She and her husband, Richard W. Roukema, live in Ridgewood. They have three children.

Representative Lucille Roybal-Allard *(Democrat, Thirty-third District, California)*, first elected to the House in 1992, is the first Mexican American woman to be elected to Congress. In the 106th Congress, she became the first woman to be elected chair of the Congressional Hispanic Caucus as well as the first Latina ever to be appointed to the House Appropriations Committee, on which she still serves. Before coming to Congress, she served in the California Assembly for six years. Representative Roybal-Allard was born in Los Angeles in 1941 and received her B.S. from California State University at Los Angeles. She is married to Edward T. Allard III and has two grown children.

Representative Loretta Sanchez *(Democrat, Forty-sixth District, California)* was first elected to the House in 1996. She is a member of the Armed Services Committee and the Committee on Education and the Workforce. Before her election to Congress, she was a businesswoman in Santa Ana, California, specializing in assisting public agencies with financial matters. Representative Sanchez earned her bachelor's degree at Chapman University and her M.B.A. in finance at American University. Born in Anaheim, California, in 1960, she is married to Stephen Brixey. They live in Anaheim.

Representative Janice D. Schakowsky *(Democrat, Ninth District, Illinois)* was first elected to the House in 1998. She serves on the Banking and Financial Services Committee and the Government Reform and Oversight Committee, where she is the ranking member on the Subcommittee on Government Efficiency, Financial Management and Intergovernmental Relations. Before her election to Congress, she served for eight years in the Illinois General Assembly. Born in Chicago in 1944, Congresswoman Schakowsky is a graduate of the University of Illinois. She lives in Evanston with her husband, Robert Creamer, and has three children, including one stepdaughter, and two granddaughters.

Representative Louise McIntosh Slaughter *(Democrat, Twenty-eighth District, New York)* was first elected to the House in 1986. She is a member of the Rules Committee. Before running successfully for Congress, she was a member of the Monroe County (New York) legislature and, later, of the New York State Assembly. Born in Harlan County, Kentucky, in 1929, Congresswoman Slaughter received both her B.S. and an M.S. in public health from the University of Kentucky. She is married to Robert Slaughter and has three grown daughters and six grandchildren.

Senator Olympia J. Snowe *(Republican, Maine)* was elected to the Senate in 1994 after eight terms in the House. She is the ranking Republican member on two subcommittees: the Health Care Subcommittee of the Finance Committee and the Oceans, Atmospheres, and Fisheries Subcommittee of the Commerce, Science, and Transportation Committee. She also sits on the Small Business and Budget committees. She began her political career in 1973, when she was elected to the Maine legislature to fill the seat made vacant by the death of her first husband. Born in Augusta, Maine, in 1947, Senator Snowe received her B.A. from the University of Maine. She is now married to John R. McKernan, Jr.

Representative Hilda L. Solis *(Democrat, Thirty-first District, California)*, who was elected in 2000, serves on the Education and the Workforce Committee and the Resources Committee. Before her election to Congress, Representative Solis served in both houses of the California legislature and was the first Latina to be elected to the California Senate. A graduate of California Polytechnic University, Pomona, she also has a master's degree in public administration from the University of Southern California. She had previously served in the Carter Administration. She and her husband, Sam, live in El Monte.

Senator Debbie Stabenow *(Democrat, Michigan)* was elected to the Senate in 2000—the first woman elected to the Senate from Michigan. She sits on four committees: Budget; Banking, Housing, and Urban Affairs; Agriculture, Nutrition, and Forestry; and the Special Committee on Aging. She spent 15 years in the Michigan state legislature before being elected to the U.S. House, where she served two terms before running for the Senate. Born in Michigan in 1950, Senator Stabenow received her bachelor's and master's degrees from Michigan State University. She is the mother of two children and lives in Lansing.

Representative Ellen O. Tauscher *(Democrat, Tenth District, California)* was first elected to the House in 1996. She currently sits on the Transportation and Infrastructure Committee and the Armed Services Committee. Before her election to Congress, she cochaired Senator Dianne Feinstein's 1992 and 1994 Senate campaigns. She also spent 14 years on Wall Street and was one of the first women to hold a seat on the floor of the New York Stock Exchange. Born in Newark, New Jersey, in 1951, Congresswoman Tauscher received her B.S. from Seton Hall University. She lives in Alamo, California, with her daughter.

Representative Karen L. Thurman *(Democrat, Fifth District, Florida)* was first elected to the House in 1992. She sits on the Ways and Means Committee. Before her election to Congress, Representative Thurman served on the Dunnellon (Florida) City Council and as that city's mayor. She also served for 10 years in the Florida Senate. Born in Rapid City, South Dakota, in 1951, Representative Thurman is a graduate of the University of Florida. She is married to John Thurman; they have two children.

Representative Nydia M. Velázquez *(Democrat, Twelfth District, New York)*, first elected to Congress in 1992, is the first Puerto Rican woman to be elected to the House. She is the ranking Democratic member of the Small Business Committee and also sits on the Banking and Financial Services Committee. Before coming to Congress, she worked as a liaison between the Puerto Rican government and the Puerto Rican community in New York. She also served on the New York City Council—the first Latina elected to that body. Born in Puerto Rico in 1953, Representative Velázquez has a B.A. from the University of Puerto Rico and an M.S. in political science from New York University.

Representative Maxine Waters *(Democrat, Thirty-fifth District, California)* was first elected to the House in 1990. She serves on the Judiciary Committee and on the Banking and Financial Services Committee, where she is the ranking Democrat on the Financial Institutions and Consumer Credit Subcommittee. As one of four Democratic chief deputy whips, she is part of her party's leadership. Before coming to Congress, she served for 14 years in the California Assembly and was the first woman in the state's history to be elected chair of the Assembly's Democratic Caucus. Born in St. Louis, Missouri, in 1938, Congresswoman Waters holds a B.A. from California State University at Los Angeles. She is married to Sidney Williams and has two children and two grandchildren.

Representative Diane E. Watson *(Democrat, Thirty-second District, California)* won her seat in June 2001 in a special election to complete the unexpired term of the late Julian Dixon. She sits on the International Relations and Government Reform committees. She served for 20 years in the California State Senate before President Clinton appointed her U.S. Ambassador to Micronesia, a position she held for the three years before her election to Congress. Born in Los Angeles in 1933, Representative Watson has a B.A. from the University of California at Los Angeles, a master's degree from California State University at Los Angeles, and a Ph.D. from Claremont Graduate University.

Representative Heather Wilson *(Republican, First District, New Mexico)* was first elected to the House in mid-1998 in a special election. She is the first woman veteran ever elected to Congress and the first woman in a half-century to represent New Mexico in Congress. She serves on the Commerce Committee and the Armed Services Committee. A graduate of the U.S. Air Force Academy, she won a Rhodes Scholarship to Oxford University (England), from which she received her master's and doctoral degrees. Congresswoman Wilson served as an Air Force officer until 1989 and was subsequently on the National Security Council staff at the White House. Before coming to Congress, she was secretary of the New Mexico Department of Children, Youth, and Families. Born in Albuquerque in 1960, she is married to Jay Hone. They have three children.

Representative Lynn C. Woolsey *(Democrat, Sixth District, California)* was first elected to the House in 1992. She is the first former welfare mother elected to Congress. She sits on the Committee on Education and the Workforce and on the Science Committee, where she is the ranking Democrat on the Energy Subcommittee. Before her election to Congress, she was a member of the Petaluma (California) City Council for eight years. She was also that city's Vice Mayor. Born in Seattle, Washington, in 1937, Congresswoman Woolsey is a graduate of the University of San Francisco. She has four grown children and one grandchild.

NOTES

1. The information in the paragraphs introducing the congressional biographies was largely compiled or derived from the members' biographies or from these sources: *Congress at Your Fingertips: 107th Congress, 1st Session 2001*, 2001; *Congressional Quarterly*'s website; *Women in Congress: Leadership Roles and Committee Chairs, 2002*, 2002, and *Women in the United States Congress 1917–2001*, 2001. Please see the references for the full citations.

References

THE AMERICAN WOMAN 2003–2004: DAUGHTERS OF A REVOLUTION—YOUNG WOMEN TODAY

CHAPTER ONE: YOUNG WOMEN: WHERE THEY STAND

Bianchi, Suzanne M., and Lynne M. Casper. "American Families." *Population Bulletin* 55, no. 4 (December 2000).

Bumpass, Larry L., James A. Sweet, and Andrew Cherlin. "The Role of Cohabitation in Declining Rates of Marriage." *Journal of Marriage and the Family* 53, no. 4 (1991): 913–927.

Census Bureau. "Census 2000 Summary File 1," <http://www.census.gov/main/www/cen2000.html>, 2001a.

———. Current Population Reports, Series P20–537. *America's Families and Living Arrangements: March 2000* (PPL-143). Washington, DC: U.S. Government Printing Office, 2001b.

———. Current Population Reports, Series P20–514. *Fertility of American Women: June 2000* (PPL-153). Washington, DC: U.S. Government Printing Office, 2001c.

———. Current Population Reports, Series P23–165. "Maternity Leave Arrangements: 1961–85." *Work and Family Patterns of American Women.* Washington, DC: U.S. Government Printing Office, 1990.

———. Current Population Reports, Series P25–917. *Preliminary Estimates of the Population of the United States, by Age, Sex, and Race: 1970 to 1981.* Washington, DC: U.S. Government Printing Office, 1982.

———. Results from the June 2000 Current Population Survey, telephone conversation with Amara Bachu, August 21, 2001d.

King, Rosalind Berkowitz. "Time Spent in Parenthood Status Among Adults in the United States." *Demography* 36, no. 3 (August 1999): 377–385.

Martin, Teresa Castro, and Larry L. Bumpass. "Recent Trends in Marital Disruption." *Demography* 26, no. 1 (February 1989): 37–51.

National Center for Health Statistics. "First Marriage Dissolution, Divorce, and Remarriage: United States." *Advance Data*, no. 323 (May 31, 2001a).

———. *National Vital Statistics Report* 49, no. 5 (July 24, 2001b).

Riche, Martha Farnsworth. "America's Diversity and Growth: Signposts for the 21st Century." *Population Bulletin* 55, no. 2 (June 2000).

Special tabulations of the March 1975 and March 2000 Current Population Surveys, prepared by Deirdre Gaquin for the Women's Research and Education Institute (WREI), 2001.

United Nations. *The World's Women 2000: Trends and Statistics.* New York: United Nations, 2000.

CHAPTER TWO: YOUNG WOMEN, EDUCATION, AND EMPLOYMENT

Bureau of Labor Statistics. "Characteristics of and Preference for Alternative Work Arrangements, 1999." *Monthly Labor Review* 124, no. 3 (March 2001a): 28–49.
———. "Contingent and Alternative Work Arrangements, Defined." *Monthly Labor Review* 119, no. 10 (October 1996a): 3–9.
———. *Current Population Survey: Design and Methodology* (Technical Paper 63). Washington, DC: Bureau of Labor Statistics, 2000.
———. Current Population Survey, 2000. Unpublished data, Washington, DC.
———. Current Population Survey, February 2001. Unpublished data, Washington, DC.
———. Current Population Survey, March 1976. Unpublished data, Washington, DC.
———. Current Population Survey, March 2000. Unpublished data, Washington, DC.
———. Current Population Survey, May 1975. Unpublished data, Washington, DC.
———. Current Population Survey, May 1997. Unpublished data, Washington, DC.
———. Current Population Survey, May 2001. Unpublished data, Washington, DC.
———. *Employment and Earnings* 22, no. 1 through *Employment and Earnings* 48, no. 1. Washington, DC: U.S. Government Printing Office, January 1976–January 2001.
———. "Flexible Work Schedules: What Are We Trading Off to Get Them?" *Monthly Labor Review* 124, no. 3 (March 2001b): 50–67.
———. *Highlights of Women's Earnings in 2000* (Report 952). Washington, DC: U.S. Government Printing Office, 2001c.
———. "Into Contingent and Alternative Work Employment: By Choice?" *Monthly Labor Review* 119, no. 10 (October 1996b): 55–74.
———. *Labor Force Statistics Derived from the Current Population Survey, 1948–57.* Washington, DC: U.S. Government Printing Office, 1988.
———. *Profile of the Working Poor, 1999* (Report 947). Washington, DC: U.S. Government Printing Office, 2001d.
Census Bureau. Current Population Reports, Series P20–537. *America's Families and Living Arrangements: March 2000* (PPL-143). Washington, DC: U.S. Government Printing Office, 2001a.
———. Current Population Reports, Series P60–210. *Poverty in the United States: 1999.* Washington, DC: U.S. Government Printing Office, 2000.
———. *Statistical Abstract of the United States: 2000.* Washington, DC: U.S. Government Printing Office, 2001b.
Jorgensen, Helene J. *When Good Jobs Go Bad.* Washington, DC: 2030 Center, 1999.
Kletzer, Lori G., and Robert W. Fairlie. "The Long Term Costs of Job Displacement for Young Adult Workers." Unpublished manuscript. Department of Economics, University of California at Santa Cruz, 2001.

CHAPTER THREE: BABY BOOM TO GENERATION X: PROGRESS IN YOUNG WOMEN'S HEALTH

Alan Guttmacher Institute (AGI). *Facts in Brief: Abortion.* New York: AGI, 2000a.

————. *Fulfilling the Promise: Public Policy and U.S. Family Planning Clinics.* New York: AGI, 2000b.

————. *Issues in Brief: Revisiting Public Funding of Abortion for Poor Women.* New York: AGI, 2000c.

Alexander, Linda L., Joan R. Cates, Nancy Herndon, and Jennifer M. Ratcliffe. *Sexually Transmitted Diseases in America: How Many and at What Cost?* Menlo Park, CA: Henry J. Kaiser Family Foundation and American Social Health Association, December 1998.

Almeida, Ruth A., Lisa C. Dubay, and Grace Ko. "Access to Care and Use of Health Services by Low Income Women." *Health Care Financing Review* 22, no. 4 (Summer 2001): 27–47.

American Psychiatric Association (APA). *Diagnostic and Statistical Manual of Mental Disorders: DSM-IV.* 4th ed. Washington, DC: APA, 1994.

————. *Mental Health Parity—Its Time Has Come.* Washington, DC: APA, 1999.

————. *State of the States: Parity Laws.* Washington, DC: APA, 2001.

Bazelon Center for Mental Health Law. *Mental Health Policy: Campaign 2000 Briefing Paper.* Washington, DC: Bazelon Center for Mental Health Law, 2000.

Bernstein, Amy B. *Insurance Status and Use of Health Services by Pregnant Women.* White Plains, NY: March of Dimes, 1999.

Blazer, Dan G., Ronald C. Kessler, Katherine A. McGonagle, and Marvin S. Schartz. "The Prevalence and Distribution of Major Depression in a National Community Sample: The National Comorbidity Survey." *American Journal of Psychiatry* 151 (July 1994): 979–986.

Butler, R. "Osteoporosis: Prevention and Treatment." *Practitioner* 243 (1999): 176–188.

Census Bureau. *Historical Time Series—Marital Status.* <http://www.census.gov/population/socdemo/hh-fam/tabMS-2.txt>, 2001a.

————. *Maternity Leave and Employment Patterns: 1961–1995.* Washington, DC: Census Bureau, 2001b.

Centers for Disease Control and Prevention. *AIDS Weekly Surveillance Report.* Atlanta, GA: Public Health Service, December 29, 1986.

————. *HIV/AIDS Surveillance Report, Year-End Edition* 11, no. 2. Atlanta, GA: Public Health Service, December 1999.

————. *Tracking the Hidden Epidemics: Trends in STDs in the United States 2000.* Atlanta, GA: Public Health Service, 2000.

————. *Sexually Transmitted Disease Surveillance, 2000.* Atlanta, GA: Public Health Service, September 2001.

Collins, James W., Jr., and Anne G. Butler. "Racial Differences in Prevalence of Small-for-Dates Infants Among College Educated Women." *Epidemiology* 8, no. 3 (May 1997): 315–317.

Collins, Karen Scott, Cathy Schoen, Susan Joseph, Lisa Duchon, Elisabeth Simantov, and Michele Yellowitz. *Health Concerns Across a Woman's Lifespan: The Commonwealth Fund 1998 Survey of Women's Health.* New York: Louis Harris and Associated, Inc., under commission by The Commonwealth Fund, 1999.

Employee Benefit Research Institute (EBRI). "Sources of Health Insurance and Characteristics of the Uninsured." *EBRI Issue Brief* 204. Washington, DC: EBRI, December 1998.

————. "Sources of Health Insurance and Characteristics of the Uninsured." *EBRI Issue Brief* 217. Washington, DC: EBRI, January 2000.

————. "Sources of Health Insurance and Characteristics of the Uninsured." *EBRI Issue Brief* 240. Washington, DC: EBRI, December 2001.

————. "Trends in Health Insurance Coverage." *EBRI Issue Brief* 185. Washington, DC: EBRI, May 1997.

Eng, Thomas R., and William T. Butler, eds. *The Hidden Epidemic: Confronting Sexually Transmitted Diseases.* Washington, DC: The Institute of Medicine, National Academy Press, 1997.

Gold, Rachel Benson. "The Need for and Cost of Mandating Private Insurance Coverage of Contraception." *The Guttmacher Report on Public Policy* 1, no. 4. New York: Alan Guttmacher Institute, August 1998.

Gonen, Julianna S. "Medicaid Managed Care: The Challenge of Providing Care to Low-Income Women." *Insights* no. 6. Washington, DC: Jacobs Institute of Women's Health, January 1998.

Halmi, Kathryn A. "Eating Disorders." In *Women and Health*, edited by M. Goldman and M. Hatch. San Diego: Academic Press, 2000.

Halmi, K. A., R. C. Casper, E. D. Eckert, S. C. Goldberg, and J. M. Davis. "Comorbidity of Psychiatric Diagnoses in Anorexia Nervosa." *Archives of General Psychiatry* 48 (1991): 712–718.

Health Policy Tracking Service. "State Mandated Benefits: Direct Access to Ob/ Gyns" and "Patients' Rights: Direct Access to Providers (excluding Ob/Gyns)." Prepared for the Henry J. Kaiser Family Foundation's State Health Facts *Online*. <www.statehealthfacts.kff.org>, 2001.

Heck, Katherine E., Kenneth C. Schoendorf, Stephanie J. Ventura, and John L. Kiely. "Delayed Childbearing by Educational Level in the United States, 1969–1994." *Maternal and Child Health Journal* 1, no. 2 (1997): 81–88.

Henry J. Kaiser Family Foundation. "Medicaid's Role for Women Factsheet," November 2001a.

———. "Survey of Women's Health." Unpublished estimates, 2001b.

———. Unpublished estimates based on Urban Institute analyses of the March 2001 Current Population Survey, Census Bureau, 2001c.

Henshaw, Stanley K. "Unintended Pregnancy in the United States." *Family Planning Perspectives* 30 (1998): 24–29, 46.

Institute of Medicine. *Preventing Low Birthweight.* Washington, DC: National Academy Press, 1985.

Itani, Zena, and Jennifer Kates. *Women and HIV: Key Facts.* Menlo Park, CA: Henry J. Kaiser Family Foundation, May 2001.

Kendler, Kenneth S., C. MacLean, Michael C. Neale, Ronald C. Kessler, A. C. Heath, and L. J. Eaves. "The Genetic Epidemiology of Bulimia Nervosa." *American Journal of Psychiatry* 148 (1991): 1627–1637.

Kessler, Ronald C. "Sex Differences in DSM II-R Psychiatric Disorders in the United States: Results From the National Comorbidity Survey." *Journal of the American Medical Women's Association* 53 (1998): 148–157.

Kiely, John L., Michael D. Kogan, and C. Blackmore. "Prenatal Care Surveillance." *From Data to Action: CDC's Public Health Surveillance for Women, Infants, and Children.* Atlanta, GA: Centers for Disease Control and Prevention, 1995.

Laumann, Edward O., John H. Gagnon, Robert T. Michael, and Stuart Michaels. *The Social Organization of Sexuality: Sexual Practices in the United States.* Chicago: University of Chicago Press, 1994.

Levitt, Larry, Jon R. Gabel, Erin Holve, Jain Wang, Heidi H. Whitmore, Jeremy D. Pickreign, Kelley Dhont, Samantha Hawkins, and Philip Kletke. *The Kaiser Family Foundation and Health Research and Education Trust Employer Health Benefits 2001 Annual Survey.* Menlo Park, CA: Henry J. Kaiser Family Foundation and Health Research and Educational Trust, 2001.

Levitt, Larry, Janet Lundy, and Srija Srinivasan. *Trends and Indicators in the Changing Health Care Marketplace: Chartbook.* Menlo Park, CA: Henry J. Kaiser Family Foundation, 1998.

Looker, Anne C., Peter R. Dallman, Margaret D. Carroll, Elaine W. Gunter, and Clifford L. Johnson. "Prevalence of Iron Deficiency in the United States." *Journal of the American Medical Association* 277 (1997): 973–976.

Lucas, Alexander R., C. M. Beard, W. M. O'Fallon, and L. T. Kurland. "50 Year Trends in the Incidence of Anorexia Nervosa in Rochester, Minn.: A Population Based Study." *American Journal of Psychiatry* 148 (1991): 917–922.

Mann, Cindy, Julie Hudman, Alina Salganicoff, and Amanda Folsom. "Five Years Later: Poor Women's Health Care Coverage After Welfare Reform." *Journal of the American Medical Women's Association* 57, no. 1 (Winter 2002): 16–22.

Misra, Dawn, ed. *The Women's Health Data Book: A Profile of Women's Health in the United States.* 3rd ed. Washington, DC: Jacobs Institute of Women's Health and Henry J. Kaiser Family Foundation, 2001.

Mitka, Mike. "A Quarter Century of Health Maintenance." *Journal of the American Medical Association* 280, no. 24 (1998): 2059–2060.

Must, Aviva, Jennifer Spadano, Eugenie H. Coakley, Alison E. Field, Graham Colditz, and William H. Dietz. "The Disease Burden Associated with Overweight and Obesity." *Journal of the American Medical Association* 282 (1999): 1523–1529.

National Center for Health Statistics. *Health, United States, 1978.* Hyattsville, MD: Public Health Service, 1978.

———. *Health, United States, 2000.* Hyattsville, MD: Public Health Service, 2000a.

———. *Health, United States, 2001.* Hyattsville, MD: Public Health Service, 2001a.

———. *Morbidity and Mortality Weekly Report* 34, no. 14 (April 12, 1985).

———. *National Vital Statistics Reports* 47, no. 28 (December 13, 1999).

———. *National Vital Statistics Reports* 48, no. 3 (March 28, 2000b).

———. *National Vital Statistics Reports* 49, no. 4 (June 6, 2001b).

———. *National Vital Statistics Reports* 49, no. 8 (September 21, 2001c).

———. *National Vital Statistics Reports* 49, no. 11 (October 12, 2001d).

———. *Vital and Health Statistics* Series 23, no. 19 (May 1997).

———. *Vital and Health Statistics* Series 21, no. 56 (January 2000c).

———. <http://www.cdc.gov/nchs/nhanes.htm>, 2001e.

———. <http://www.cdc.gov/nchs/about/major/nsfg/nsfgback.htm>, 2001f.

National Comorbidity Survey Program. <http://www.hcp.med.harvard.edu/ncs/>, 2001.

National Committee on Quality Assurance. *The State of Managed Care Quality 2000.* Washington, DC: National Committee on Quality Assurance, 2000.

National Eating Disorders Association. <http://www.edap.org>, 2001.

National Governors Association. *Maternal and Child Health (MCH) Update: States Have Expanded Eligibility and Increased Access to Health Care for Pregnant Women and Children.* Washington, DC: National Governors Association, February 22, 2001.

National Institute of Mental Health. *Women Hold Up Half the Sky.* Bethesda, MD: National Institutes of Health, 2001.

National Institute on Drug Abuse. *National Household Survey On Drug Abuse, 1979* [Computer file]. ICPSR version. Ann Arbor, MI: Inter-university Consortium for Political and Social Research [distributor], 1997.

National Research Council, National Institutes of Health, Food and Nutrition Board NRC. *Recommended Dietary Allowances. Subcommittee on the Tenth Edition of the RDAs.* 10th ed. Washington, DC: National Academy Press, 1989.

Picker Institute. *From the Patient's Perspective: Quality of Abortion Care.* Menlo Park, CA: Henry J. Kaiser Family Foundation, 1999.

Pollitz, Karen, Richard Sorian, and Kathy Thomas. *How Accessible is Individual Insurance for Consumers in Less-Than-Perfect Health?* Menlo Park, CA: Henry J. Kaiser Family Foundation, 2001.

RESOLVE: The National Infertility Association. *Advocacy Update.* Somerville, MA. <http://www.resolve.org/advocacy/update/update0109.shtml>, September 2001.

Rowland, Diane, Alina Salganicoff, and Patricia Seliger Keenan. "The Key to the Door: Medicaid's Role in Improving Health Care for Women and Children." *Annual Review of Public Health* 20 (1999): 403–426.

Salganicoff, Alina, and Roberta Wyn. "Access to Care for Low Income Women: The Impact of Medicaid." *Journal of Health Care for the Poor and Underserved* 10, no. 4 (1999): 453–467.

Salganicoff, Alina, Roberta Wyn, and Beatriz Solis. "Medicaid Managed Care and Low-Income Women: Implications for Access and Satisfaction." *Women's Health Issues* 8, no. 6 (1998): 339–349.

Schur, Claudia L., and Jacob Feldman. *Running in Place: How Job Characteristics, Immigrant Status, and Family Structure Keep Hispanics Uninsured.* New York: The Commonwealth Fund, May 2001.

Schwalberg, Renee, Beth Zimmerman, Larissa Mohamadi, Mary Giffen, and Sheryl Anderson Mathis. *Medicaid Coverage of Family Planning Services: Results of a National Survey.* Health Systems Research, Inc., prepared for the Henry J. Kaiser Family Foundation. Menlo Park, CA: Henry J. Kaiser Family Foundation, 2001.

Substance Abuse and Mental Health Services Administration (SAMSHA). *National Household Survey on Drug Abuse Population Estimates, 1998.* Rockville, MD: U.S. Department of Health and Human Services, 1999.

U.S. Congress. House Committee on Energy and Commerce. Subcommittee on Health and the Environment. *Medicaid Source Book: Background Data and Analysis, 1993 Update.* Report prepared by the Congressional Research Service. 103rd Cong., 1st sess., 1993.

U.S. Department of Agriculture. *Data Tables: Results from USDA's 1994–96 Continuing Survey of Food Intakes by Individuals and 1994–96 Diet and Health Knowledge Survey.* <http://www.barc.usda.gov/bhnrc/foodsurvey/pdf/Csfii3yr.pdf>, 1997.

U.S. Department of Health and Human Services. *Physical Activity and Health: A Report of the Surgeon General.* Washington, DC: Centers for Disease Control and Prevention, National Center for Chronic Disease Prevention and Health Promotion, The President's Council on Physical Fitness and Sports, 1996.

———. *Mental Health: A Report of the Surgeon General.* Rockville, MD: Substance Abuse and Mental Health Services Administration, Center for Mental Health Services, National Institutes of Health, National Institute of Mental Health, 1999.

———. *Women and Smoking: A Report of the Surgeon General.* Atlanta, GA: Centers for Disease Control and Prevention, National Center for Chronic Disease Prevention and Health Promotion, Office on Smoking and Health, 2001.

U.S. Library of Congress. THOMAS. <http://thomas.loc.gov/>, 2001.

Vohr, B. R., A. Dusick, J. Steichen, L. L. Wright, J. Verter, and L. Mele. "Neuro-Developmental and Functional Outcome of Extremely Low Birth Weight (ELBW) Infants." *Pediatric Research* 43, no. 4, Supplement 2 (April 1998): 233A.

Wald, Nicholas J., and Carol Brower. "Folic Acid and the Prevention of Neural Tube Defects." *British Medical Journal* 310 (1995): 1019–1020.

Walters, E. E., and Kenneth S. Kendler. "Anorexia Nervosa and Anorexic-Like Syndromes in a Population-Based Female Twin Sample." *American Journal of Psychiatry* 152 (1995): 64–71.

Wyn, Roberta, Karen Scott Collins, and E. Richard Brown. "Women and Managed Care: Satisfaction with Provider Choice, Access to Care, Plan Costs and Coverage." *Journal of the American Medical Women's Association* 52, no. 2 (Spring 1997): 60–64.

Wyn, Roberta, Beatriz Solis, Victoria D. Ojeda, and Nadereh Pourat. *Falling Through the Cracks: Health Insurance Coverage of Low-Income Women.* Menlo Park, CA: Henry J. Kaiser Family Foundation, 2001.

CHAPTER FOUR: INTEGRATING WORK AND LIFE:
YOUNG WOMEN FORGE NEW SOLUTIONS

Albelda, Randy. "Welfare-to-Work, Farewell to Families? U.S. Welfare Reform and Work/Family Debate." *Feminist Economics* 7, no.1 (2001): 119–135.

Bailyn, Lotte, Robert Drago, and Thomas A. Kochan. *Integrating Work and Family Life: A Holistic Approach.* A Report of the Sloan Work-Family Network, 2001.

Bailyn, Lotte, Joyce Fletcher, and Deborah Kolb. "Unexpected Connections: Considering Employees' Personal Lives Can Revitalize Your Business." *Sloan Management Review* 38, no. 4 (1997): 11–19.

Bureau of Labor Statistics. "Marriage, Children, and Women's Employment: What Do We Know?" *Monthly Labor Review* 122, no. 12 (December 1999): 22–31.

Census Bureau. Current Population Reports, Series P20–514. *Fertility of American Women: June 2000* (PPL-153). Washington, DC: U.S. Government Printing Office, 2001.

DeGroot, Jessica, and Joyce Fine. *A Guide to Shared Care.* Philadelphia: ThirdPath Institute, 2001.

Drago, Bob, and Amy Varner. *Fertility and Work in the United States: A Policy Perspective.* A Report to the National Institute of Population and Social Security Research, Japan, 2001.

Friedman, Stewart D., Perry Christensen, and Jessica DeGroot. "Work and Life: The End of the Zero-Sum Game." *Harvard Business Review* (November–December 1998): 119–129.

Garey, Anita Ilta. *Weaving Work and Motherhood.* Philadelphia: Temple University Press, 1999.

Hochschild, Arlie Russel. *The Second Shift.* New York: Avon Books, 1990.

Radcliffe Public Policy Center. *Life's Work: Generational Attitudes toward Work and Life Integration.* Cambridge, MA: Radcliffe Public Policy Center, n.d.

Williams, Joan. *Unbending Gender.* New York: Oxford University Press, 2000.

CHAPTER FIVE: THE ECONOMICS OF YOUNG WOMEN TODAY

BCA Research. *The Bank Credit Analyst* 52, no. 11 (May 2001): 21–33.

Blau, Francine D., Marianne A. Ferber, and Anne E. Winkler. *The Economics of Women, Men, and Work.* Upper Saddle River, NJ: Prentice Hall, 1998.

Bureau of Labor Statistics. 1998–1999 Cross-Tabulated Tables from the Consumer Expenditure Survey. <http://www.bls.gov/cex/csxcross.htm>, 2000a.

———. *Consumer Expenditures in 1999* (Report 949). Washington, DC: Bureau of Labor Statistics, 2001a.

———. *Highlights of Women's Earnings in 2000* (Report 952). Washington, DC: U.S. Government Printing Office, 2001b.

———. "Spending Patterns by Age." *Issues in Labor Stats* summary 00–16 (August 2000b): 1–2.

Census Bureau. Current Population Reports, Series P20–537. *America's Families and Living Arrangements: March 2000* (PPL-143). Washington, DC: U.S. Government Printing Office, 2001a.

———. Current Population Reports, Series P23–196. *Changes in Median Household Income: 1969 to 1996.* Washington, DC: U.S. Government Printing Office, 1998.

———. Current Population Reports, Series P60–204. *The Changing Shape of the Nation's Income Distribution.* Washington, DC: U.S. Government Printing Office, 2000a.

———. Current Population Reports, Series P20–536. *Educational Attainment in the United States: March 2000 (Update)* (PPL-140). Washington, DC: U.S. Government Printing Office, 2000b.

———. Current Population Reports, Series P60–213. *Money Income in the United States: 2000.* Washington, DC: U.S. Government Printing Office, 2001b.

———. Current Population Reports, Series P60–214. *Poverty in the United States: 2000.* Washington, DC: U.S. Government Printing Office, 2001c.

———. *Historical Income Tables.* <http://www.census.gov/hhes/income/histinc/>, 2001d.

———. *Historical Poverty Tables.* <http://www.census.gov/hhes/income/histinc/histpovtb.html>, 2001e.

———. Housing Vacancy Survey. *Annual Statistics 2000.* <http://www.census.gov/hhes/www/housing/hvs/annual00/ann00t15.html>, 2001f.

Center on Budget and Policy Priorities (CBPP). *A Hand Up: How State Earned Income Tax Credits Help Working Families Escape Poverty in 2000—An Overview.* Washington, DC: CBPP, November 2, 2000a.

———. *Poverty Trends for Families Headed by Single Working Mothers: 1993 to 1999.* Washington, DC: CBPP, 2001.

———. *State Income Tax Burdens on Low Income Families in 1999.* Washington, DC: CBPP, 2000b.

Economic Policy Foundation. "The Living Wage Movement: Gaining Momentum." Economic Policy Foundation News Release (July 25, 2001a).

———. "Women Breaking Through Male-Dominated Fields" Economic Policy Foundation News Release (April 3, 2001b).

Employee Benefit Research Institute (EBRI). "The Impact of Workers' Earnings Profiles on Individual Account Accumulation." *EBRI Notes* 21, no. 10. Washington, DC: EBRI, October 2000a.

———. "Women and Pensions: A Decade of Progress?" *EBRI Issue Brief* 227. Washington, DC: EBRI, November 2000b.

Nellie Mae. *Life After Debt: Results of the National Student Loan Survey.* Braintree, MA: Nellie Mae, 1998.

OppenheimerFunds, Inc. *Gen X Retirement Study.* New York: OppenheimerFunds, Inc., 2001.

Special tabulations of the 1998 Federal Reserve's Survey of Consumer Finance, conducted by Mark Calabria and Darryl Getter for the Women's Research and Education Institute (WREI), 2001.

Wisconsin Policy Research Institute. *Economic Lessons for Welfare Mothers* 14, no. 1 (February 2001): 1–34.

CHAPTER SIX: TAKING IT FROM HERE:
POLICIES FOR THE TWENTY-FIRST CENTURY

Bureau of Labor Statistics. *Employment and Earnings* 48, no. 1. Washington, DC: U.S. Government Printing Office, January 2001.

Economic Policy Institute (EPI). "The Impact of the Minimum Wage: Policy Lifts Wages, Maintains Floor for Low-Wage Labor Market." *EPI Briefing Paper.* Washington, DC: EPI, June 2000.

Heymann, Jody, Renée Boynton-Jarrett, Patricia Carter, James T. Bond, and Ellen Galinsky. *Work-Family Issues and Low-Income Families,* prepared for the Ford Foundation, January 2002.

Matosantos, Ana J., and Melissa C. Chiu. *Opportunities Lost: The State of Public Sector Affirmative Action in Post Proposition 209 California*. San Francisco: Chinese for Affirmative Action and Equal Rights Advocates, 1998.

National Council of Women's Organizations (NCWO). *Women Speak on Affirmative Action*. Washington, DC: NCWO, 2000.

Pérez, Sonia M., and Eric Rodriguez. *Untapped Potential: A Look at Hispanic Women in the U.S.* Washington, DC: National Council of La Raza, February 1996.

Social Security Administration (SSA). *Income of the Population 55 or Older, 2000*. Washington, DC: SSA, February 2002.

———. *Social Security Bulletin, Annual Statistical Supplement, 2001*. Washington, DC: SSA, 2001, <http://www.ssa.gov/policy/>.

AMERICAN WOMEN TODAY: A STATISTICAL PORTRAIT

SECTION 1: DEMOGRAPHICS

Census Bureau. Current Population Reports, Series P20–537. *America's Families and Living Arrangements: March 2000* (PPL-143). Washington, DC: U.S. Government Printing Office, 2001.

———. Current Population Reports. *The Asian and Pacific Islander Population in the United States: March 2000 (Update)* (PPL-146). Washington, DC: U.S. Government Printing Office, 2001.

———. Current Population Reports. *The Black Population in the United States: March 2000* (PPL-142). Washington, DC: U.S. Government Printing Office, 2001.

———. Current Population Reports, Series P20–534. *The Foreign-Born Population in the United States: March 2000* (PPL-135). Washington, DC: U.S. Government Printing Office, 2001.

———. Current Population Reports, Series P20–535. *The Hispanic Population in the United States: March 2000* (PPL-136). Washington, DC: U.S. Government Printing Office, 2001.

———. Current Population Survey, March 1975. Unpublished data, Washington, DC.

———. Current Population Survey, March 1980. Unpublished data, Washington, DC.

———. *Historical Income Tables*. <http://www.census.gov/hhes/income/histinc/>.

———. *Population Projections of the United States by Age, Sex, Race, Hispanic Origin, and Nativity: 1999 to 2100*. Washington, DC: U.S. Government Printing Office, 2000.

———. *Statistical Abstract of the United States: 1980*. Washington, DC: U.S. Government Printing Office, 1980.

———. *Statistical Abstract of the United States: 2000*. Washington, DC: U.S. Government Printing Office, 2000.

National Center for Health Statistics. *Health, United States, 2000*. Hyattsville, MD: Public Health Service, 2000.

———. *National Vital Statistics Report* 48, no. 19 (February 22, 2001).

———. *National Vital Statistics Report* 49, no. 1 (April 17, 2001).

SECTION 2: EDUCATION

Census Bureau. Current Population Reports, Series P20–536. *Educational Attainment in the United States: March 2000 (Update)* (PPL-140). Washington, DC: U.S. Government Printing Office, 2000.

————. Current Population Reports, Series P20–534. *The Foreign-Born Population in the United States: March 2000* (PPL-135). Washington, DC: U.S. Government Printing Office, 2001.

————. *Statistical Abstract of the United States: 2000.* Washington, DC: U.S. Government Printing Office, 2000.

National Center for Education Statistics. *Digest of Education Statistics, 1982.* Washington, DC: U.S. Government Printing Office, 1982.

————. *Digest of Education Statistics, 2000.* Washington, DC: U.S. Government Printing Office, 2001.

U.S. Department of Education, Office of Civil Rights. *Data on Earned Degrees Conferred by Institutions of Higher Education by Race, Ethnicity, and Sex, Academic Year 1978–1979.* Washington, DC: U.S. Government Printing Office, 1981.

SECTION 3: HEALTH

Census Bureau. Current Population Reports, Series P70–73. *Americans with Disabilities: 1997.* Washington, DC: U.S. Government Printing Office, 2001.

Centers for Disease Control and Prevention. *Abortion Surveillance—United States, 1997* 49, no. SS-11 (December 8, 2000).

————. *HIV/AIDS Surveillance Report* 7, no. 2 (1995).

————. *HIV/AIDS Surveillance Report* 12, no. 2 (2001).

————. *Sexually Transmitted Disease Surveillance, 1995.* Atlanta, GA: Public Health Service, 1996.

————. *Sexually Transmitted Disease Surveillance, 2000.* Atlanta, GA: Public Health Service, 2001.

National Cancer Institute. *SEER Cancer Statistics Review, 1973–1998.* Bethesda, MD: National Cancer Institute, 2001.

National Center for Health Statistics. *Health, United States, 2001.* Hyattsville, MD: Public Health Service, 2001.

————. *Vital and Health Statistics* 21, no. 56 (January 2000).

SECTION 4: EMPLOYMENT

Bureau of Labor Statistics, Current Population Survey, March 1980, March 1982, March 1984, March 1986, March 1988, March 1990, March 1992, March 1994, March 1996, and March 1998. Unpublished data, Washington, DC.

————. Current Population Survey. Unpublished labor force statistics, <http://data.bls.gov/cgi-bin/surveymost?bls>.

————. Current Population Survey. Unpublished table, "Average weekly hours at work in all industries and in nonagricultural industries by sex, annual averages 1948–2001." Washington, DC.

————. Current Population Survey, March 1990. Unpublished table, "Number of own children under 18 years, by type of family, labor force status of parents, and family income." Washington, DC.

————. Current Population Survey, March 1990. Unpublished table, "Presence and age of own children of civilian women 16 years and over, by employment status and marital status." Washington, DC.

————. Current Population Survey, 2000. Unpublished table, "Employed and experienced unemployed persons by detailed occupation, sex, race, and Hispanic origin, Annual Average 2000." Washington, DC.

————. Current Population Survey, 2000. Unpublished table, "Employed persons by class of worker and sex, 2000 Annual Average." Washington, DC.

———. Current Population Survey, 2000. Unpublished table, "Employed persons by occupation, class of worker, sex, race, and Hispanic origin, Annual Average 2000." Washington, DC.

———. Current Population Survey, 2000. Unpublished table, "Employment status of persons by veteran status, age, race, Hispanic origin, and sex, Annual Average 2000." Washington, DC.

———. Current Population Survey, March 2000. Unpublished table, "Number of own children under 18 years, by type of family, labor force status of parents, and family income." Washington, DC.

———. Current Population Survey, March 2000. Unpublished table, "Presence and age of own children of civilian women 16 years and over, by employment status and marital status." Washington, DC.

———. Current Population Survey, February 2001. Unpublished table, "Employed persons other than unpaid family workers, by alternative work status, occupation, sex, and age, February 2001." Washington, DC.

———. *Employment and Earnings* 33, no. 1. Washington, DC: U.S. Government Printing Office, January 1986.

———. *Employment and Earnings* 38, no. 1. Washington, DC: U.S. Government Printing Office, January 1991.

———. *Employment and Earnings* 40, no. 1. Washington, DC: U.S. Government Printing Office, January 1993.

———. *Employment and Earnings* 43, no. 1. Washington, DC: U.S. Government Printing Office, January 1996.

———. *Employment and Earnings* 44, no. 1. Washington, DC: U.S. Government Printing Office, January 1997.

———. *Employment and Earnings* 46, no. 1. Washington, DC: U.S. Government Printing Office, January 1999.

———. *Employment and Earnings* 48, no. 1. Washington, DC: U.S. Government Printing Office, January 2001.

———. *Handbook of Labor Statistics.* Washington, DC: U.S. Government Printing Office, 1989.

———. "Labor Force Projections to 2010: Steady Growth and Changing Composition." *Monthly Labor Review* 124, no. 11 (November 2001): 22–38.

———. *Labor Force Statistics Derived from the Current Population Survey, 1948–87.* Washington, DC: U.S. Government Printing Office, 1988.

Census Bureau. Current Population Reports. *The Asian and Pacific Islander Population in the United States: March 2000 (Update)* (PPL-146). Washington, DC: U.S. Government Printing Office, 2001.

———. Current Population Reports, Series P60–180. *Money Income of Households, Families, and Persons in the United States: 1991.* Washington, DC: U.S. Government Printing Office, 1992.

———. Current Population Reports, Series P70–70. *Who's Minding the Kids? Child Care Arrangements: Fall 1995.* Washington, DC: U.S. Government Printing Office, 2000.

———. Current Population Survey, March 2001. <http://ferret.bls.census.gov/macro/032001/perinc/>.

SECTION 5: EARNINGS AND BENEFITS

Bureau of Labor Statistics. Current Population Survey, 2000. Unpublished data, Washington, DC.

———. Current Population Surveys, May 1975 through May 1978. Unpublished data, Washington, DC.

————. *Employment and Earnings* 33, no. 1. Washington, DC: U.S. Government Printing Office, January 1986.

————. *Employment and Earnings* 38, no. 1. Washington, DC: U.S. Government Printing Office, January 1991.

————. *Employment and Earnings* 40, no. 1. Washington, DC: U.S. Government Printing Office, January 1993.

————. *Employment and Earnings* 42, no. 1. Washington, DC: U.S. Government Printing Office, January 1995.

————. *Employment and Earnings* 43, no. 1. Washington, DC: U.S. Government Printing Office, January 1996.

————. *Employment and Earnings* 44, no. 1. Washington, DC: U.S. Government Printing Office, January 1997.

————. *Employment and Earnings* 46, no. 1. Washington, DC: U.S. Government Printing Office, January 1999.

————. *Employment and Earnings* 48, no. 1. Washington, DC: U.S. Government Printing Office, January 2001.

————. "Family and Medical Leave: Evidence from the 2000 Surveys." *Monthly Labor Review* 124, no. 9 (September 2001): 17–23.

————. *Handbook of Labor Statistics*. Washington, DC: U.S. Government Printing Office, 1989.

Census Bureau. Current Population Survey, March 1996. <http://ferret.bls.census. gov/macro/031996/pov/24_000.htm>.

————. Current Population Survey, March 2001. <http://ferret.bls.census.gov/macro/032001/noncash/nc7_000.htm>.

————. Current Population Survey, March 2001. <http://ferret.bls.census.gov/macro/032001/noncash/nc8_000.htm>.

————. Current Population Survey, March 2001. <http://ferret.bls.census.gov/macro/032001/pov/new24_000.htm>.

————. *Health Insurance Historical Tables*. <http://www.census.gov/hhes/hlthins/historic/index.html>.

————. *Historical Income Tables*. <http://www.census.gov/hhes/income/histinc/>.

SECTION 6: ECONOMIC SECURITY

Census Bureau. Current Population Reports, Series P23–190. *65+ in the United States*. Washington, DC: U.S. Government Printing Office, 1996.

————. Current Population Reports, Series P60–188. *Income, Poverty, and Valuation of Noncash Benefits: 1993*. Washington, DC: U.S. Government Printing Office, 1995.

————. Current Population Reports, Series P60–189. *Income, Poverty, and Valuation of Noncash Benefits: 1994*. Washington, DC: U.S. Government Printing Office, 1996.

————. Current Population Reports, Series P60–175. *Poverty in the United States: 1990*. Washington, DC: U.S. Government Printing Office, 1991.

————. Current Population Reports, Series P60–181. *Poverty in the United States: 1991*. Washington, DC: U.S. Government Printing Office, 1992.

————. Current Population Reports, Series P60–194. *Poverty in the United States: 1995*. Washington, DC: U.S. Government Printing Office, 1996.

————. Current Population Reports, Series P60–198. *Poverty in the United States: 1996*. Washington, DC: U.S. Government Printing Office, 1997.

————. Current Population Reports, Series P60–201. *Poverty in the United States: 1997*. Washington, DC: U.S. Government Printing Office, 1998.

———. Current Population Reports, Series P60–207. *Poverty in the United States: 1998.* Washington, DC: U.S. Government Printing Office, 1999.

———. Current Population Reports, Series P60–210. *Poverty in the United States: 1999.* Washington, DC: U.S. Government Printing Office, 2000.

———. Current Population Reports, Series P60–214. *Poverty in the United States: 2000.* Washington, DC: U.S. Government Printing Office, 2001.

———. Current Population Survey, March 1996. <http://ferret.bls.census.gov/macro/031996/perinc/11_000.htm>.

———. Current Population Survey, March 2001. <http://ferret.bls.census.gov/macro/032001/perinc/new08_000.htm>.

———. *Historical Income Tables.* <http://www.census.gov/hhes/income/histinc/>.

———. *Historical Poverty Tables.* <http://www.census.gov/hhes/poverty/histpov/hstpov4.html>.

Census Bureau and Department of Housing and Urban Development. *American Housing Survey for the United States in 1999.* Washington, DC: U.S. Government Printing Office, 2000.

Social Security Administration (SSA). *Social Security Bulletin, Annual Statistical Supplement, 2001 (Draft).* Washington, DC: SSA, 2001, <http://www.ssa.gov/policy/>.

SECTION 7: WOMEN IN THE MILITARY

Bureau of Labor Statistics. Current Population Survey, 2001. Unpublished table, "Employment status of persons by veteran status, age, race, Hispanic origin, and sex, Annual Average 2001." Washington, DC.

U.S. Department of Defense. Defense Manpower Data Center. Unpublished data, Arlington, VA, August 1997.

———. Defense Manpower Data Center. Unpublished data, Arlington, VA, May 31, 1999.

———. Defense Manpower Data Center. Unpublished data, Arlington, VA, March 30, 2000.

———. Defense Manpower Data Center. Unpublished data, Arlington, VA, September 30, 2001.

———. Office of the Assistant Secretary of Defense for Public Affairs. Public Affairs News Release no. 449–94, July 29, 1994.

———. Office of the Chief of Naval Operations. Arlington, VA, 1999.

———. Unpublished data provided by U.S. Air Force Academy, U.S. Military Academy, and U.S. Naval Academy, June 1993.

———. Unpublished data provided by U.S. Air Force Academy, U.S. Military Academy, and U.S. Naval Academy, February 2002.

U.S. Department of Transportation. Unpublished data provided by the Coast Guard Academy, New London, CT, June 1993.

———. Unpublished data provided by the Coast Guard Academy, New London, CT, February 2002.

SECTION 8: ELECTIONS AND OFFICIALS

Administrative Office of the United States Courts. *Annual Report on the Judiciary Equal Employment Opportunity Program for the Twelve-Month Period Ended September 30, 1990.* Washington, DC, n.d.

———. *The Judiciary Fair Employment Practices Annual Report, October 1, 1999 through September 30, 2000.* Conference Edition. Washington, DC, n.d.

Census Bureau. *Historical Time Series Tables.* <http://www.census.gov/population/www/socdemo/voting.html>.

Center for American Women and Politics (CAWP). *Statewide Elective Executive Women: 1969–1999.* New Brunswick, NJ: CAWP, National Information Branch on Women in Public Office, Eagleton Institute of Politics, Rutgers University, February 1999.

———. *Statewide Elective Executive Women 1999.* New Brunswick, NJ: CAWP, National Information Branch on Women in Public Office, Eagleton Institute of Politics, Rutgers University, September 1999.

———. *Women in Congress: Leadership Roles and Committee Chairs.* New Brunswick, NJ: CAWP, National Information Branch on Women in Public Office, Eagleton Institute of Politics, Rutgers University, February 2002.

———. *Women in Elective Office 1999.* New Brunswick, NJ: CAWP, National Information Branch on Women in Public Office, Eagleton Institute of Politics, Rutgers University, August 1999.

———. *Women in Elective Office 2001.* New Brunswick, NJ: CAWP, National Information Branch on Women in Public Office, Eagleton Institute of Politics, Rutgers University, December 2001.

———. *Women in the State Legislatures 1999.* New Brunswick, NJ: CAWP, National Information Branch on Women in Public Office, Eagleton Institute of Politics, Rutgers University, May 1999.

———. *Women in the U.S. Congress 1917–1999.* New Brunswick, NJ: CAWP, National Information Branch on Women in Public Office, Eagleton Institute of Politics, Rutgers University, January 1999.

National Center for State Courts. Unpublished data, January 31, 2002.

The New York Times Company. "A Look at Voting Patterns of 115 Demographic Groups in House Races." *The New York Times on the Web,* 1998. <http://www.nytimes.com/library/politics/camp/110998voter3.html>.

———. "Who Voted: A Portrait of American Politics, 1976–2000." *The New York Times on the Web,* 2001. <http://www.nytimes.com/2000/11/12/politics/12CONN.html>.

Voter News Service. Unpublished data from the 2000 exit poll.

THE CONGRESSIONAL CAUCUS FOR WOMEN'S ISSUES AT 25:
CHALLENGES AND OPPORTUNITIES

Clemmitt, Marcia, Lesley Primmer, and Marjorie Sims. *The Record: Gains and Losses for Women and Families in the 104th Congress.* Washington, DC: Women's Policy, Inc. (WPI), 1997.

Gertzog, Irwin N. *Congressional Women.* Westport, CT: Praeger Publishers, 1995.

Grundy, Catherine, Jennifer Lockwood, Lesley Primmer, Marjorie Sims, and Sally Tyler. *Women's Health Legislation in the 105th Congress.* Washington, DC: Women's Policy, Inc., 1997.

Lockwood-Shabat, Jennifer. *Women's Health Legislation in the 106th Congress.* Washington, DC: Women's Policy Inc., 2001.

Persily, Lesley Primmer. "The Congressional Caucus for Women's Issues: Achievements in the 105th Congress." In *The American Woman 2001–2002: Getting to the Top,* edited by Cynthia B. Costello and Anne J. Stone. New York: W. W. Norton & Company, 2001.

Primmer, Lesley. "The Congressional Caucus for Women's Issues: Twenty Years of Bipartisan Advocacy." In *The American Woman 1999–2000: A Century of Change—*

What's Next? edited by Cynthia B. Costello, Shari Miles, and Anne J. Stone. New York: W. W. Norton & Company, 1998.

Women's Policy, Inc. (WPI). *The 106th Congress At-A-Glance.* Washington, DC: WPI, 2000.

———. *Committee Assignments of the Women Members of the House in the 107th Congress.* Washington, DC: WPI, 2001a.

———. *Committee Assignments of the Women Members of the Senate in the 107th Congress.* Washington, DC: WPI, 2001b.

———. *Quarterly Update on Women's Issues in Congress.* Washington, DC: WPI, November 13, 1998.

———. *Quarterly Update on Women's Issues in Congress.* Washington, DC: WPI, July 6, 2001c.

———. *Women's Policy, Inc. Salutes the Congressional Caucus for Women's Issues, 1977–1997.* Washington, DC: WPI, 1997.

WOMEN IN THE 107TH CONGRESS

Amer, Mildred L. *Women in the United States Congress 1917–2001.* CRS Report 30–261 GOV. Washington, DC: Congressional Research Service, 2001.

Center for American Women and Politics (CAWP). *Women in Congress: Leadership Roles and Committee Chairs, 2002.* New Brunswick, NJ: CAWP, National Information Branch on Women in Public Office, Eagleton Institute of Politics, Rutgers University, 2002.

Congress at Your Fingertips: 107th Congress, 1st Session 2001 (standard version). Merrifield, VA: Capitol Advantage Publishing, 2001.

Congressional Quarterly Inc. "Members' Occupations: 107th Congress." *CQ.com on Congress,* 2001, <http://oncongress.cq.com/characteristics/>.

NOTES ON THE CONTRIBUTORS

Jessica DeGroot is president and founder of the ThirdPath Institute, a nonprofit organization that teaches people how to redesign work to create more time for life outside of work, with an emphasis on sharing in the care of children. Ms. DeGroot has been involved with work and family issues for nearly 20 years and is the coauthor of *A Guide to Shared Care*. She received her M.B.A. from the Wharton School of Business, after which she continued as a member of the executive team responsible for organizing the Wharton Work/Life Roundtables, publishing the *Wharton Work/Life Resource Guide*, and reporting on the findings from the Roundtables for the *Harvard Business Review*.

Marisa L. DiNatale and **Stephanie Boraas** are economists in the Office of Employment and Unemployment Statistics at the Bureau of Labor Statistics in Washington, DC. Marisa DiNatale graduated magna cum laude from Boston University with a B.A. in international relations. Stephanie Boraas holds a B.A. with high honors in economics from the College of William and Mary. Both are pursuing master's degrees in economics at John's Hopkins University.

Joyce Fine works in private practice as a clinical psychologist and as communications director of the ThirdPath Institute. She helps to convert ThirdPath presentations and ideas into written form and leads institute workshops. She is the coauthor, with Jessica DeGroot, of *A Guide to Shared Care*. A trained psychologist, Dr. Fine also has a background in journalism and publishing. She has practiced adult and child psychotherapy, made presentations on psychological testing and children's clinical issues, and provided consultation to schools. She received her M.A. in school and clinical psychology and her Ph.D. in clinical psychology from the Derner Institute of Advanced Psychological Studies at Adelphi University.

Liberty Greene is a research associate in public health information and partnerships at the Henry J. Kaiser Family Foundation. Survey research projects she has managed or worked on include: teens' attitudes about and knowledge of sexual health; communication between parents and children about violence, sex, HIV/AIDS, and discrimination; attitudes of women's health care providers about reproductive health; and public health knowledge and behaviors concerning HIV/AIDS. Prior to that, she was a research assistant at the Joint Program in Survey Methodology at the University of Maryland, conducting statistical analysis and assisting in questionnaire design. She also worked on an epidemiological study of breast cancer at the University of Wisconsin's Comprehensive Cancer Center. Ms. Green received a B.A. in sociology from the University of Wisconsin and an M.S. in survey methodology from the University of Maryland.

Cynthia A. Hall is the president of Women's Policy, Inc. (WPI). She joined WPI in 1999, after 18 years on Capitol Hill working for four members of Congress. From 1987 to 1998, she served as legislative director to Congresswoman Connie Morella (R-MD). She was the staff liaison to the Congressional Caucus for Women's Issues during the 104th Congress, when Congresswoman Morella served as cochair. Ms. Hall received her B.A. in political science from Colgate University.

Lani Luciano is an editor for Kaisernetwork, a news and information website of the Henry J. Kaiser Family Foundation. She was previously a staff writer at *Money* magazine and a commentator on public radio's *Marketplace*. Her work also has appeared in *Barron's* and *Business and Health* and on CNN and Oxygen, among other print and electronic media. She received her B.A. from the College of New Rochelle.

Martha Farnsworth Riche served as director of the U.S. Bureau of the Census from October 1994 until January 1998. Through Farnsworth Riche Associates, she lectures, writes, and consults extensively on demographic changes and their effects on policies, programs, and products. Dr. Riche began her career as an economist with the U.S. Bureau of Labor Statistics. In 1978, she was a founding editor of *American Demographics*, the nation's first magazine devoted to interpreting demographic and economic data for corporate and public executives. In 1991, she became director of policy studies for the Population Reference Bureau. She holds both a B.A. and an M.A. from the University of Michigan and a Ph.D. from Georgetown University.

Alina Salganicoff is vice president and director of women's health policy at the Henry J. Kaiser Family Foundation, where she focuses on health care coverage and access for women. Before joining the foundation, she was associate director of the staff of the Kaiser Commission on Medicaid and the Uninsured, specializing in coverage and access issues facing low-income women and children, Medicaid managed care, and state health reform. Dr. Salganicoff has written numerous book chapters, journal articles, and reports on health care access and financing for low-income women and children. She received an undergraduate degree from Pennsylvania State University and a Ph.D. in health policy from the Johns Hopkins University School of Hygiene and Public Health.

Barbara Wentworth is on the staff of the Women's Health Policy and Health Care Marketplace programs of the Henry J. Kaiser Family Foundation. In addition to researching and writing on women's health policy issues, she manages the foundation's State Health Facts Online website, which displays over 230 indicators of health information for 50 states. Before joining the foundation, Ms. Wentworth worked for Congressman Henry A. Waxman (D-CA) on the staff of the House Government Reform Committee, focusing on such issues as prescription drugs, tobacco, and nursing homes, and on the committee's campaign finance investigation. She received a B.A. from Dartmouth College in 1997.

About the Women's Research and Education Institute (WREI)

Susan Scanlan, *president*
Anne J. Stone, *senior research associate*
Lory Manning, *director, Center for Women in Uniform*
Vanessa R. Wight, *research associate*
Marjorie Lightman, *senior fellow*
Bernice Sandler, *senior fellow*
Anne Kuh, *accounting associate*
Monica Jacobe, *design associate*

The Women's Research and Education Institute (WREI), established in 1977, is an independent nonprofit organization in Washington, DC. WREI gathers, synthesizes, and analyzes policy-relevant information on issues that concern or affect women, and serves as a resource for federal and state policymakers, advocates for women, scholars, the media, and the interested public.

WREI's projects include:

- *The American Woman*, a series of books, published biennially, about the status of women. This volume is the ninth in the series.
- Congressional Fellowships on Women and Public Policy. WREI places talented graduate students from all academic fields on the staffs of U.S. senators and representatives. WREI fellows enhance the research capacity of congressional offices, especially with respect to the implications of federal policy for women. Established in 1980, the WREI fellowship program has given more than 200 women hands-on experience in the federal legislative process.
- Women in Uniform. Since 1989, WREI has monitored the status of women in the U.S. armed forces, gathering and disseminating research findings and data about military women and the issues that concern them, and publishing *Women in the Military: Where They Stand*, now in its third edition. Over time, the project's focus has widened to include women in uniformed civilian services, such as firefighting and policing, as well as the role of women in peacekeeping operations. WREI holds a biennial conference that includes all these women in uniform.
- Hire A Vet, She's a Good Investment. This project aims to improve civilian career opportunities for women leaving the armed forces, both by making

employers aware that women veterans represent a pool of skilled and committed workers and by helping employers find women veterans with the right skills and experience for the job.

- Women's Health. Women's health and policies to improve it have been a focus of WREI's work for a quarter-century. Among recent health reports are *Improving the Health of Midlife Women: Policy Options for the 21st Century* (2001); *The Health of Mid-Life Women in the States* (1998), and *Women's Health Insurance Costs and Experiences* (1994).

- More information about WREI projects and publications can be found on our website at http://www.wrei.org.

ABOUT THE EDITORS

Cynthia B. Costello is a senior research and editorial consultant for the Women's Research and Education Institute (WREI), where she has served as senior editor for the last five editions of *The American Woman*, including this edition. Dr. Costello's previous positions include director of research at WREI, director of research at the American Sociological Association, director of employment policy at Families USA Foundation, and director of the Committee on Women's Employment at the National Academy of Sciences. She is the author of *We're Worth It! Women and Collective Action in the Insurance Workplace* and a number of policy reports on employment, health care, and income security issues. She holds a B.A. in sociology from the University of California and both an M.S. and a Ph.D. in sociology from the University of Wisconsin. Dr. Costello lives in Bethesda, Maryland, with her husband, Peter Caulkins, and their son, Michael.

Anne J. Stone is senior research associate at WREI, where she has authored or coauthored policy analyses on various subjects, including women's employment and the economic situation of older women. She has worked on every edition of *The American Woman* and coedited the fourth, fifth, seventh, eighth, and ninth editions. Ms. Stone lives in Washington, DC, with her husband, Herbert Stone. They have two grown daughters and two granddaughters.

Vanessa R. Wight is a research associate at WREI, where she works on women's employment, economic security, and health issues. She worked on the previous (eighth) edition of *The American Woman* and is coeditor of this edition in the series. In addition, Ms. Wight contributes to WREI's Women in the Military and Hire-A-Vet projects and coauthored the third edition of *Women in the Military: Where They Stand* as well as *Women Veterans' Employment*. Ms. Wight holds a bachelor's degree in anthropology and religious studies from the University of Rochester and a master's degree in anthropology from the George Washington University. She is currently pursuing a Ph.D. in sociology at the University of Maryland. Ms. Wight lives in Kensington, Maryland with her husband, Nicholas Curabba.

INDEX